ADVANCE PRAISE FOR

Masonry Heaters

"In *Masonry Heaters*, a rich and wonderful book, Ken Matesz sweeps away the ashes of our ignorance about the right relationship to fire. He argues—with quiet and crystal-clear clarity—that masonry heaters are the most intelligent, gentle, efficient, environmentally friendly and sustainable, beautiful, and healthy form of heating humans have ever known. There is more knowledge and truth about masonry heaters between these two covers than has ever before been published in English."

—ALBIE BARDEN, Maine Wood Heat Company

"This book is a joy! Ken Matesz guides us on a clear path through the woods to getting an heirloom masonry heater, and offers invaluable information on why we should want to traverse it. Readers will learn about much more than just masonry heaters along the journey, however, including how their house works (or *should* work), and how to have their own radiating energy source at its center—including exactly what it takes to get their masonry heater designed, built, and burning. Not to mention some wonderful stories about the people who have made masonry heaters a part of their lives! May the sun shine on this book."

—TIMOTHY SEATON, President, The Alliance
of Masonry Heater and Oven Professionals

"This book should be on the required reading list for anyone wanting to become a heater mason, or for anyone planning to install and heat with a masonry heater. Matesz has captured the true beauty and user-friendliness of these exquisite heaters, and, with ease, helps guide readers through the process of designing a beautiful, and functional 'piece of the sun' for their homes. I highly recommend the book, as well as masonry heaters."

—TOM STROUD, founding member and former president
of The Masonry Heater Association

"A wonderful book! Well thought out, well grounded in nature, and delightful to read. When I visited a house built around a masonry heater, it was a "just right" experience, and one I have never forgotten. This book is a great introduction from a man who obviously knows and loves the subject."

—DEBRA LYNN DADD, author of *Home Safe Home*

"When I travel in the northern states of the U.S.—particularly New England, where most people depend on heating with oil—I fear for those millions of folks for whom depleting, climate-changing fossil fuels are all that stand between winter comfort, on the one hand, and death by freezing, on the other. *Masonry Heaters* explores one of the most promising alternatives, and its message needs to get out far and wide, and fast."

—Richard Heinberg, Senior Fellow, Post Carbon Institute, and author of *The Party's Over: Oil, War and the Fate of Industrial Societies*

"Masonry heaters provide a quiet comfort that must be experienced to be believed. In this book, Ken Matesz shares his love of masonry heaters and artfully explains how they work, how to use them to provide efficient and comfortable heat throughout the day, and what it takes to install one in your home. This is a truly delightful book."

—David Bainbridge, coauthor of *The Straw Bale House* and coauthor of *Passive Solar Architecture*

"*Masonry Heaters* is informational across the board, and shares common, advantageous characteristics with passive solar design. Both methods of heating rely on heat transfer by radiation rather than convection, which gives a more natural feeling while reducing drafts and noise; both utilize thermal mass, which gives greater thermal stability; and both can allow independence from energy shocks and price fluctuations. I highly recommend this book for people—in any field—who are interested in learning about the design, construction, and use of this superior system of heating."

—Ken Haggard, coauthor of *Passive Solar Architecture*

MASONRY
HEATERS

Photo courtesy of Tulikivi Corporation.

MASONRY
HEATERS

Designing, Building, and Living
with a Piece of the Sun

KEN MATESZ

CHELSEA GREEN PUBLISHING
WHITE RIVER JUNCTION, VERMONT

Project Manager: Patricia Stone
Developmental Editor: Cannon Labrie
Copy Editor: Laura Jorstad
Proofreader: Eric Raetz
Indexer: Shana Milkie
Designer: Peter Holm, Sterling Hill Productions

Printed in the United States of America
First printing August, 2010
10 9 8 7 6 5 4 3 2 1   10 11 12 13 14

Our Commitment to Green Publishing

Chelsea Green sees publishing as a tool for cultural change and ecological stewardship. We strive to align our book manufacturing practices with our editorial mission and to reduce the impact of our business enterprise in the environment. We print our books and catalogs on chlorine-free recycled paper, using vegetable-based inks whenever possible. This book may cost slightly more because we use recycled paper, and we hope you'll agree that it's worth it. Chelsea Green is a member of the Green Press Initiative (www.greenpressinitiative. org), a nonprofit coalition of publishers, manufacturers, and authors working to protect the world's endangered forests and conserve natural resources. *Masonry Heaters* was printed on Somerset Matte, a 10-percent postconsumer recycled paper supplied by QuadGraphics.

Library of Congress Cataloging-in-Publication Data
Matesz, Ken, 1964–
  Masonry heaters : designing, building, and living with a piece of the
sun / Ken Matesz.
      p. cm.
  Includes bibliographical references and index.
  ISBN 978-1-60358-213-1
  1. Stoves, Masonry. 2. Dwellings--Heating and ventilation. I. Title.

TH7436.M37M38 2010
697'.22--dc22

                                                2010019837

Chelsea Green Publishing Company
Post Office Box 428
White River Junction, VT 05001
(802) 295-6300

www.chelseagreen.com

To my parents, John and Ruth,
who taught me the value of work done well.

CONTENTS

This masonry heater has an oven (the upper, arched door). The heater is finished in finely detailed stucco. The customer wanted a relatively conventional fireplace look blended with a five-sided corner-heater design. Three sides are visible here while the two back sides fit squarely in the corner.

FOREWORD

My brother, Howie, and I became Boy Scouts in the late 1950's. Aside from mastering every imaginable knot on our side-by-side steel bedposts, scouting for us was all about camping, and central to the camping experience was Fire. We learned how to find dry wood and tinder in all weather conditions and how to build safe campfires. Early in our scouting journey, we entered a fire-starting competition using flint and steel. We studied the literature, found our flint and steel, and cooked old shreds of cotton sheets in a metal Band-Aid can in our mom's oven until the cotton was bone-dry and black. When the fire-starting competition was held indoors at the wooden-balconied junior high school gym, one of us struck the steel against the flint. The other caught the live spark in a nest of black cloth, carefully folded the cloth over the spark and swung the cloth in circles high and low like a windmill until, in only seconds, we had fire in our hands and won the contest. We did not realize at the time that we had also caught the fire in our hearts.

Years later, I was pushed by an invisible hand and urged by a silent but very clear voice to take on the mission of bringing an enduring masonry heater tradition to North America. Creating the spark of interest in masonry heaters, teaching others how to build them, fanning the knowledge of masonry heaters, and bringing them into their proper place as the Heart of the Home—this has been my life's work. Many people know intuitively when they see and experience a masonry heater for the first time functioning in a home that there is something truly unique, even extraordinary, about these huge, gentle, warming souls. Over a career of more than thirty-five years building and studying masonry heaters, bakeovens, and cookstoves, some of the logic, physics, and goodness of masonry heaters have been gifted to me and to others who build them. During that same period of time, I have been gradually invited to explore even deeper mysteries of fire and its healing power. Recently, I began to study,

in more earnest, some of the ancient fire-gifting stories indigenous to Europe and the world.

In the classic children's tale of Cinderella, the lost glass slipper, left on the steps at the stroke of midnight at the great ball, is carried by the Prince throughout the land, while he looks for the beautiful maiden who wore it to his ball. The slipper only fits one foot, the perfect dusty foot of the maid of the hearth, Cinderella. We all love the magic of the story, the justice and the union of the two partners, and even the forgiveness of the stepmother and her daughters. It is the timeless story of the return to right relationship and harmony in matters of the heart, which is where the fire lives and serves.

Many years ago, I read that there was an ancient fire-carrying tradition in Maine that involved large clamshells lined with blue marine clay and a spiral of some kind of tinder fungus wound like a fuse that could be carried as a living spark all day. This winter, reading a wonderful book by Kerry Hardy called *Notes on a Lost Flute: a Field Guide to the Wabanaki*, I learned that the shells could be carried in a woodchuck pelt slipped over a belt thong or sash with the woodchuck's own cleaned skull the counterbalance weight to the clay-lined shells with their tinder fungus fuse. A gifted woodsman and teacher friend, Ray Reitze, said that he knew the tradition well and that the Wabanaki had used thonged conch shells similarly lined with the clay and tinder fungus fuse and carried the shells in a pack basket in their day-long canoe trips. Ray said that the tinder fungus was the black Chaga fungus that grows on the birch tree. He also pointed out that while the tinder fungus could hold the fire, his Micmac native elder "grandfather" had taught him that the spindle for the bow drill to make fire should be made of spruce, which was the wood chosen to carry the fire within itself.

While in New Zealand, teaching a masonry heater workshop this winter, I learned that the Maori culture had a story about the grandmother fire volcano hiding the fire in three trees during the struggle to create right relationship between humans and fire and water. All three of these trees are the chosen and known trees for making fire with friction by the native people.

Among the ancient Huichol people (who call themselves *Wixáritira*) of Mexico, there flourishes and is shared a remarkable tradition of meeting Grandfather Fire (Tatawari) himself in a way that the heart is opened and the fears and the mind are put at ease, where community grows, and the sacred relationship to all that is, is remembered and restored and kept alive.

In Ken Matesz's rich and wonderful new book, *Masonry Heaters*, Ken sweeps away the ashes of our ignorance about right relationship to fire. Ken guides us and explains with crystal-clear and gentle clarity how masonry heaters are the most intelligent, most efficient, most environmentally sound and sustainable, most beautiful, and most healthful form of heating that humans have ever known. There is more knowledge about masonry heaters between these two covers than has ever been published before in English.

In 2010, as oil gushes up from the ocean floor off the coast of Louisiana and as our earth warms as we continue to use precious resources is if there were no tomorrow, this book makes it clear that we will only have a chance at enjoying tomorrow if we learn how to embrace and hold dear in our lives what really matters. Masonry heaters, which hold a fire, a little piece of the sun, with honor and care, really matter. They show us a gentle, sustainable, intelligent way to live in and heat our homes.

Catch the spark of masonry heaters in your minds and hearts and hands as you read this book and find ways to blow that spark gently into life. Dream, plan, and carefully build and share this warmth with others.

ALBIE BARDEN
July 6, 2010

What Is a Masonry Heater?

"What is a masonry heater?" If I had a dollar for every time I have been asked that question, I would not need to build masonry heaters for a living anymore; I could do it just for the challenge. I have found that, over time, my personal answer has changed, much as you would change your description of a friend the more intimate the relationship becomes. Early in my understanding, a masonry heater was "a high-efficiency fireplace of European origin that stores the heat from a hot, fast fire in thousands of pounds of solid masonry for slow release as radiant heat over the next twelve to twenty-four hours." There is nothing blatantly false or wrong about this definition, of course, and I still use this information in any longer conversation I have about masonry heaters. Now, however, I define a masonry heater as "a piece of the sun—the warm center of the home's universe."

You will hear masonry heaters called masonry stoves, heat-storage fireplaces, *kachelofens, kakelugns, kemence, grubkas, grundofens, putz-grundofens,* Russian fireplaces, Finnish fireplaces, Swedish stoves, contra-flow fireplaces, radiant fireplaces, mass-storage fireplaces, and more. They're all masonry heaters, and they all work on the same principles. They all create a place to go to feel warm, to bask in the sun.

For whatever reason, it took me years of building masonry heaters to realize that the typical home today has no inviting place of luxurious warmth. The thermometer in a home might read 70°F, but people in that home still may have cold hands or feet, or may simply feel cold. What's worse, there is no place in that house for a person to go to finally feel warm. With a piece of the sun—a masonry heater—in the middle of a home, there is no need to feel cold because there is a place to go. There's always a place to soak up the sun.

When I was a teenager, my dad experimented with solar water heating. I became interested in solar heating as well and thought that passive solar heating was the way to go when it came to heating houses. No one owns the sun or the energy it sends our way every day. It's free energy. It's natural energy. Passive solar heating *is* great, but it still has a drawback: There's no accounting for long weeks without blue skies in a long winter. That's what makes masonry heaters even better. Masonry heaters are passive solar energy under human control. With this simple technology, you get to decide when the sun shines in your house. And who doesn't want that happening every day and all day long?

It is fascinating to watch the evolution of ideas concerning energy conservation and green, sustainable energy. You have to wonder at the complicated strategies people will undertake to "solve" the dilemma of becoming energy self-sufficient as a society. So many people have become accustomed to centralized sources of power, such as the gas company, electric company, or of course oil company, that they believe the way to freedom from foreign oil and energy is to create massive infrastructure for a green replacement for fossil fuels. It's as if we've discovered that being dependent on foreign nations for energy is a not-so-good idea, but making sure that people are dependent on corporations for energy is a great one.

Thus we have massive studies and corporate development of ways to turn food crops into energy crops. And even more to the point is the environmental buzzword for renewable solid fuels: biomass. *Biomass,* of course, is the educated person's term for what common people have used for fuel since time immemorial—wood, plants, and animal wastes. Whole industries are popping up "creating" the next fuel on which people can become dependent. It's not technologically advanced just to burn wood cut from the

FIGURE 1. Who wouldn't want the sun shining in their home every day? This brick, stucco, and soapstone heater gently separates a living room from a dining room. The brick chimney is in the right foreground; the soapstone-topped benches contain flues that make these warm seats. The stucco mass behind the chimney contains more flues for heat storage. Photo courtesy of New England Hearth and Soapstone.

trees in the back 40; instead, we must have some large company first turn the wood into wood pellets before we burn that wood in stoves.

Ironically, just 150 years ago the average North American citizen *was* energy self-sufficient. At that time, a family knew it had to supply its winter's fuel, which was primarily wood (though coal was becoming more common). This wasn't something people thought much about. They just did it. If they didn't secure their winter's fuel, they would be cold. It was as simple as that. Today we act like being energy self-sufficient is a pipe dream. Certainly politicians and large corporations would love for the average person to believe

that being energy self-sufficient is nearly impossible. Otherwise, what would we need them for?

Advances in design and function now allow the creation of state-of-the-art wood-fired masonry heaters that approach the energy efficiency of modern gas furnaces and boilers. In 1850, home insulation was nonexistent, and people heated their homes using open fireplaces or very basic metal stoves. Imagine the quantities of fuel required in an attempt to heat an uninsulated home with a 20 or 30 percent efficient stove or fireplace! Now, with today's best masonry heaters at high efficiency and homes well insulated, heating with wood could be a breeze, except for one thing.

FIGURE 2. Heating with a masonry heater can be green, sustainable, enjoyable, and health-supporting. This tall, narrow soapstone masonry heater takes up little floor space, but has enough surface area to produce a considerable amount of heat. Photo courtesy of Tulikivi Corporation.

The missing piece of the puzzle is home size. The average home size in the United States in the 1950s, for example, was less than 1,000 square feet. Now it is more like 2,500 square feet. I personally grew up quite comfortably in an 1,100-square-foot home with a family of four. My wife grew up in a house smaller than that with a family of nine.

I am not suggesting that everyone must have a 1,000-square-foot home. I am pointing out, however, that most average families *could* be quite comfortable in homes of 1,500 square feet *and* it would be easy to be energy self-sufficient with a little passive solar design and a high-quality masonry heater. With good insulation; modern, high-quality windows; and a modest-sized home, a family can today be energy self-sufficient (for heating purposes) with little exertion. It's entirely

conceivable that such a home could be heated with less than two cords of wood annually at a 2009 (in Ohio) cost of less than $400 (or for free with some extra effort).

It all comes down to personal priorities, of course. If someone doesn't mind being dependent on some distant land or corporation; if someone doesn't mind being subjected to the ups and downs of energy markets; if someone doesn't mind the politics and military conflicts that arise around energy; if someone doesn't mind having a heating system that is useless if a winter storm cuts power; if someone doesn't mind having cold feet and nowhere in the house to get warm; if someone can ignore the many benefits of masonry heaters, then a modest home and masonry heater are of little value. But for someone who really craves being free from dependence and likes the idea of getting energy free from the earth and sun, this may all sound very enticing.

This is not to say it's impossible to have a larger house and heat it with a masonry heater. It just means the quantity of fuel that's needed increases. The more fuel needed, the more work is required and the less attractive the wood heating option becomes. The harder it is to be energy self-sufficient, the fewer people will do it. In this way, planning and building a very large house is like asking for an excuse to be dependent on others for fuel. It's a self-defeating behavior, like buying a full carton of cigarettes and all the while saying it's time to quit smoking. Large houses, like gasoline-powered automobiles, are designed for using fossil fuel energy. As I said, it's all about priorities.

This book is about returning to our roots and understanding why doing so is not a bad idea when we can apply some refined knowledge to the problem. Wood heating can be "green." It is "sustainable." It can also be simple and enjoyable, even health-supporting, with a masonry heater. People today in North America can be energy-independent with the simple technologies that have existed for centuries, but have been refined by modern research and development. It's not nearly as hard as politicians and corporations make it sound; it merely requires resetting priorities and acquiring a little bit of knowledge.

I find that people are already returning to their roots but don't quite realize it. New homes today boast granite or soapstone counters and wood floors and trim. People are remembering that these materials are real. They are the standard that manufactured products can never quite duplicate. Real stone and real wood have made a comeback. Not everyone has yet gotten back to "real" when it comes to fire, however. I frequently get calls from people saying, "Well, we built the house with a gas fireplace, but it hardly gives off any heat, and it's boring." What they're trying to say is it isn't real. It's a gas fire pretending to do what wood does for the soul, the eyes, the heart, and the skin. Real fire and real heat will also make a comeback, I predict.

Masonry heaters are here to stay. There is no better way to burn wood. There is no easier way to heat with wood. There is no more comfortable heat than what comes from a masonry heater—a piece of the sun. What is a masonry heater? It's a solution to restoring health, well-being, self-sufficiency, sustainability, and reality. It's a grassroots solution to our energy dilemma. It was Mahatma Gandhi who said, "Be the change you

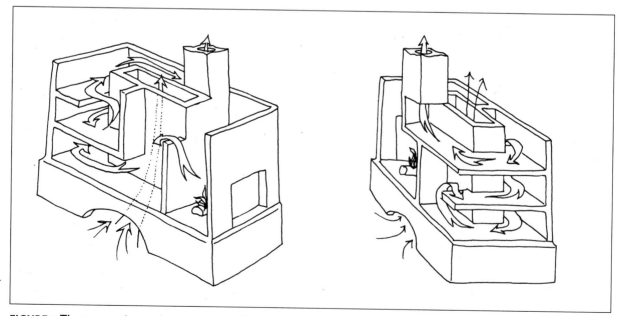

FIGURE 3. The inner workings of a squat Austrian heater. From David Lyle, *The Book of Masonry Stoves*, p. 119.

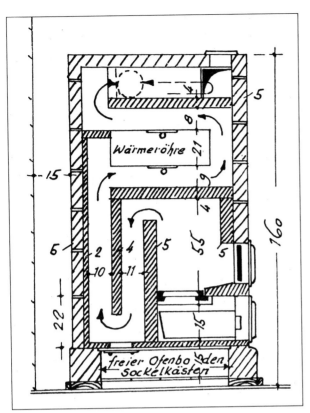

FIGURE 4. A German or Austrian design that is more upright. From David Lyle, *The Book of Masonry Stoves*, p. 178.

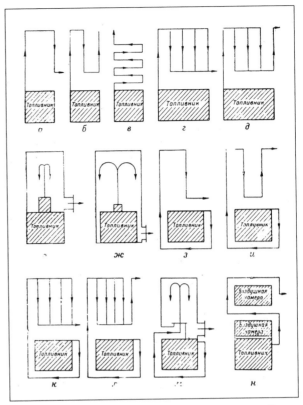

FIGURE 5. A Russian drawing of some of the many different ways that the flues can be configured in a masonry heater. From David Lyle, *The Book of Masonry Stoves*, p. 97.

want to see in the world." If you want to see energy self-sufficiency in North America, start by harnessing the sun via a masonry heater in your home.

So, you might still be asking, just what is a masonry heater? A masonry heater, of course, can be defined in much more technical terms than just "a piece of the sun." In fact, industry-wide consensus, as developed through ASTM International, calls a masonry heater

> a vented heating system of predominantly masonry construction having a mass of at least 800 kg (1760 lbs), excluding the chimney and masonry heater base. In particular, a masonry heater is designed specifically to capture and store a substantial portion of the heat energy from a solid fuel fire in the mass of the masonry heater through internal heat exchange flue channels, enable a charge of

solid fuel mixed with an adequate amount of air to burn rapidly and more completely at high temperatures in order to reduce emission of unburned hydrocarbons, and be constructed of sufficient mass and surface area such that under normal operating conditions, the external surface temperature of the masonry heater (except in the region immediately surrounding the fuel loading door(s)), does not exceed 110°C (230°F).[1]

In short (and practically speaking, for North America), a masonry heater is a wood-burning heat-storage fireplace. Unlike conventional open fireplaces, however, such a heater saves the bulk of the heat produced by the wood fire and stores it in mass for long-term release rather than letting the heat (and room air) go up the chimney. As ASTM International's

FIGURE 6. A masonry heater isn't always just a big, rectangular box. In this photo, it's a challenge to know where the heater begins and ends. Curved faces, tile mixed with stucco, and wooden sitting areas make this heater a one-of-a-kind. Photo courtesy of Biofire, Inc.

technical definition has it, the heat is saved and stored by virtue of heat exchange taking place in various flue channels. These flues are largely responsible for the shape of the masonry heater.

Over the millennia, masonry heaters have taken many different forms in the cold regions of Europe and Asia. While a fireplace is a fireplace is a fireplace, that is, a firebox that vents up a chimney above the firebox—thus, a Rumford fireplace and a walk-in fireplace are still just fireplaces—a Swedish masonry heater may be vastly different in appearance and construction than an Austrian one; the design and shape of a peasant's masonry heater in Hungary will be different from the prince's heater in Russia, and so on.

In this way it is impossible to point to one masonry heater and say that it is the archetypal masonry heater. One masonry heater in Austria may have flues like the ones seen in figure 3—making a heater that is squat and low. Someone in that region, seeing the design of a masonry heater for the first time, may afterward say, "Oh yeah, now I know what a masonry heater looks like inside." Then that person may travel into Germany and see one with flues like in figure 4. Now it starts getting confusing: "You mean a masonry heater isn't just one of those squat things I saw in Austria, but it can be tall like this too?" Of course, yes is the answer.

I like the drawing of flue patterns from Russia shown in figure 5 because it starts to chart the possibilities. Some designs have the flue gases go straight up first, and then go back down. Some have the exhaust go under the firebox before going up. Some have the final exit from the heater up high; others, down low. Yet even with a dozen or so options shown on one page, only the surface has been scratched in terms of the opportunities available. This book is inspired by the remaining infinite possibilities.

So, if you have seen a masonry heater in Canada or the United States before, and it looked like a big box (or, as a friend of mine put it, like a refrigerator), carefully turn page by page through this text as we investigate a little further. You might discover that, although you may not have room in your house, your house plans, or your room addition for a big box, you do have the need for a masonry heater.

Photo courtesy of Warmstone Fireplaces and Designs with Dale Hisler.

PART ONE

Redefining the Hearth

In our modern era, the hearth has slipped away from the central role it played in the lives of families since humans first learned to control fire thousands of years ago. A lot of people never even see a real fire on a regular basis. Out of sight and out of mind it may be, but it is not out of vogue. In fact, in many ways, fire is more important to life today than it ever has been. Modern life would come to a standstill instantly without fire.

Something this central to our existence is something you could call one of the fundamentals of life. If it is a fundamental—a basic necessity—then it must be pretty special. If it is elemental to life, then maybe it actually belongs in the middle of life, in the middle of a home. There are some pretty profound reasons why a functional hearth really does belong in the middle of the home, and that is the primary focus of this first part of the book.

Chapter 1 focuses on the fundamental nature of fire and energy. Masonry heaters are broadly introduced as are new ways of looking at comfort and efficiency. Fire is the ultimate tool, and masonry heaters are expert at using it. The desire for heirloom quality in a home—timelessness in both function and appearance—meshes well with what masonry heaters have to offer in regard to the fundamentals described.

Chapter 2 takes a turn toward history. Remarkably, though masonry heaters have not yet become mainstream in North America, people in the United States and Canada are subtly and regularly exposed to the concept—though many never realize it until just the right moment. Also included is a concise summary of how masonry heater awareness has grown in the United States and Canada over the last thirty years.

Chapters 3 and 4 look at a full range of benefits derived from a masonry heater, many of which cannot be duplicated by heating a home in any other way. Masonry heaters are a source of radiant heat, and that has a meaning few people really understand. Though the sun is a radiant heater for the earth, people seem to have lost the ability to discriminate between radiant heat and other common heating methods.

FIGURE 1.1. A masonry heater is a piece of functional art. Here stone and stucco are combined on the facade, and there is a heated sitting area. Notice how the left side of the tall element is sculpted to artfully miss the structural ceiling beam. The little black squares are ash cleanout doors and give a clue as to where exhaust and heat travel in a masonry heater. Designed and built by Stovemaster; photo courtesy of Alex Chernov.

CHAPTER ONE

The Hearth Is the Reason for the House

Home Is Where the Heart(h) Is

Brrriiinggg! A stunning ring from the electric alarm clock ends a night of blissful sleep. A man hobbles half dazed into the bathroom, switching on the light, turning on the hot water to take a shower, shave, comb his hair. The day's only begun and already he has used one contraption after another. Tools. He eats his breakfast; forks, knives, spoons, mugs, and dishes help accomplish the meal consumption. More tools.

Humans have spent thousands of years developing tools from the simple to the complex. The knife, a tool used four thousand years ago, gets daily use in the home today cutting the morning pastry, while e-mails are downloaded on the PC, a tool unique to the twentieth and twenty-first centuries. People have distanced themselves by light-years from all other animals by their tools. It is true that other animals use tools. But only humankind uses tools to make other tools, and those tools to make yet more tools.

Arguably the single most significant tool humanity has makes all the others possible: You could not use a butter knife or a PC today without the blessings of the gods of fire. From fire comes molten metal and turning turbines. With fire there is travel from the garage to the office, little explosions turning the wheels of cars, the wheels themselves disks of once molten rubber and steel. One way or another, indirectly or not, today's homes are all heated with fire. Fire is the ultimate tool.

For early indigenous cultures, life itself unfolded around the fire because that is where food was prepared and from where light and warmth emanated. There is significance to the very term *around the fire*. For it presumes that the fire is in the center, or heart of the activity. During the day, the members of the tribe may have scattered. Some would go hunting or collecting food; others were herding animals or collecting, yes, firewood. But as the daylight waned and evening chill set in, life continued around the beating heart of the fire. As long as the fire burned brightly, life continued and culture grew. It is around the fire that crafts continued, stories were told, discussions were held, decisions were made, dancers twirled, children played, and food was eaten.

Early on, someone realized that every time it rained, the family or tribal fire was extinguished. So fires then were built under an overhanging rock or inside a cave. Eventually, it made sense to build a structure around the fire that would not only house it, but shelter the people, too. Thus began the process of building homes, from the need to protect the fire that cooked the food, warmed the bodies, and fueled the imagination. Our ancestors knew instinctively that this amazing force in their lives was central and that if it was protected, cherished, and nurtured, it would always be a force for a more fulfilling life. The hearth was born.

Today's modern life, when you think of it, still happens "around" a fire in the sense that nothing we do could happen the way it does without fire. And yet you could walk up to a dozen different folks today and ask them when they last sat and enjoyed a simple wood fire and be surprised to find that it hasn't happened in months, maybe years. If you took these same people hostage one day and placed them in front of a fire for one evening, they would be mesmerized. There is something essential or primal about a blazing fire.

Until the twentieth century, humans always had a real wood fire in their lives—"always" being most of the last fifteen thousand years. Perhaps having a blazing, crackling flame within our view provides some essential nutrient, just as we need the sun on our skin to manufacture vitamin D. This certainly would help

FIGURE 1.2. With a masonry heater complex like this, much of life can still happen around the fire. This soapstone creation features two wood-fired ovens and a cooktop, so a family can do all its cooking and heating from this one central, integrated mass. Notice how the main firebox faces one area, yet the cooktop is firmly part of the kitchen. Photo courtesy of Tulikivi Corporation.

explain why a fire is such a magnet for almost anyone. In *A Pattern Language,* Christopher Alexander writes, "The need for fire is almost as fundamental as the need for water. Fire is an emotional touchstone, comparable to trees, other people, a house, the sky."[1]

The need for fire, then, is not so much bodily as spiritual in nature. It serves the home with its utilitarian heating and cooking while acting as a springboard for the imagination and the emotions, too. Just as a child lies on the ground watching the clouds change shapes, watching a fire entrances us and stimulates our

thoughts and dreams. It is an energy that grounds us and makes us feel safe.

Webster's defines *hearth* as "the floor of a fireplace." This book, however, will be redefining the hearth as the heart and soul of a house. Anyone can build a box with a roof on it, protected from the elements. Until that structure houses a fire of some kind, it is not a place in which anyone really wants to live permanently. People need to be able to eat delicious foods; we need to feel warmth when the weather outside turns bitter; and—perhaps more importantly than you might think—we need a hearth that encourages us to ponder, to imagine, and to dream. The television can't do this, nor can video games. Even human interaction and conversation don't provide that same impetus to think as is stimulated when a single individual watches firewood burn.

It is fair to ask, "If there are such emotional ties to fire and it is so significant to life, why don't more people have a fire to view every day?" There are many possible answers to this. Few could disagree, however, that some of the answer lies in perceptions of comfort and the modern romance with technology. *Comfort* is another term we must evaluate in order to place the hearth in perspective.

Redefining Comfort

Americans have a romance with time and temperature. They wear watches on their wrists and browse the Weather Channel for the day's highs and lows. Sure, it's not just the temperature in which they are interested. They also want to track the weather itself. Temperature, however, is the baseline. If at least the temperature forecast is known, we know how to dress as we make our way through the day. If it's 20°F, the parka and mittens are in order; 90° and out come the swim trunks. Then there are those unpredictable spring days that might bring a total reversal in temperatures. But if it's 65° and sunny, coats are left on their hangers.

Fortunately, technologically advanced heating systems control the indoor environment almost totally. You can be sure that when you wake in the morning, it's 70°F. It's not just that temperature in the bedroom. It's also 70° in the kitchen; 70° in the dining room, living room, bathroom, and family room. The environment has been set on automatic, perpetually piloting everyone into a particular climate that is always moderately warm.

Sensitive electronic thermostats constantly monitor the indoor temperature. A change of 2°F triggers the heating system. Programmable thermostats save energy by allowing lower temperatures while you're asleep or away, but guaranteeing the house is warmer by the time you're home or awake. There are even electronic

FIGURE 1.3. Stucco and stone combine in this large heater. Notice how the chimney is separated from the heater itself by a wood-storage area. The heater and chimney are tied together above the wood-storage alcove with a long curved stone. Fire, stone, and wood are basic natural elements and have a strong effect on human beings—sometimes at an unconscious level. Photo courtesy of Temp-Cast Enviroheat.

controls for humidity. Now hardly a finger is lifted to be "comfortable."

Well, there is more to life than this kind of uniform thermal comfort (which is discussed in greater detail in chapters 3 and 4). People also gauge comfort by the level of effort per unit of time. It seems that for many people, reduced effort equals greater comfort. This is the reason for many of the gadgets we have. Time- and labor-saving devices abound. Such are the results of both the industrial/technological age and the information age. It is amazing that the average modern individual now travels farther from home each day just to go to work than many people of a couple hundred years ago traveled in a year. There are machines to open cans, machines to wash cars, and even machines for brushing teeth. The list goes on and on.

Presumably, the time- and labor-saving devices free more time for people to enjoy other aspects of their lives. Instead of washing the car by hand, there is more time to play with the kids. Instead of chopping all those vegetables with a knife, the food processor does it, and there is more time to enjoy the meal, or make more courses, or go outside and plant some flowers. Likewise with the modern central heating system: Since the furnace takes care of the heating, there is no need to gather, split, and stack firewood. There's presumably more time to do other things or nothing at all.

There are some fundamental principles in physics known as the first and second laws of thermodynamics. Many have heard the first law stated something like, "Energy is neither created nor destroyed, only converted from one form to another." However, it is often forgotten that the second law continues by saying that when energy is converted from one form to another, the new form of energy is less usable, or functional, or available.

Another way of expressing the second law is that heat always travels from the warmer area to the colder. For example, when a piece of paper is burned, for a moment there is a lot of heat (energy). After that brief fire, the temperature spike quickly disappears and what is left are a few ashes and a room that feels no warmer. The blast of momentary heat has been swallowed by the immense pool of cooler air in the room. The potential energy that was in the paper has not been destroyed, but it would be impossible to extract that equivalent energy from those ashes and the infinitely small changes made to the molecules of air in the room and use it for any future purpose.

The second law is also known as the law of entropy, or the measure of the total amount of energy that is no longer readily available to perform any task once the initial task is completed. It can be simply stated that

FIGURE 1.4. Masonry heaters work like the sun, radiating heat from a central source. Here is a very simple heater in colored stucco. All its corners, including those on the lower shelf and the mantel supports, have rounded or bullnosed edges. This detail matches the rounded corners the builder used on all plastered corners in the house, such as in the beam overhead.

this is a measure of the quality of the remaining energy. Entropy is a law that affects many aspects of life, including, specifically, energy expended in simple daily affairs.

That electric toothbrush is a good example. If you brush your teeth with it day after day for several years, you might say, "Hey, look at all the (muscular) energy I saved. My teeth are white and clean and it's no effort at all for me to brush my teeth." You directly experience the lack of effort (manual energy) used to brush your teeth. What you don't notice is any of the following: reduced hand and finger dexterity and strength, dependence on a gadget to do what otherwise requires some skill, use of batteries (stored energy) that eventually run out of energy and must populate a landfill (or hazardous waste facility). The chosen method of brushing teeth (with a machine) replaced an effective one (properly brushing your teeth with an ordinary toothbrush) that had greater entropy.

Using efforts wisely will produce better quality results. The entropy principle still is at work, but the rate is greatly reduced. Many unintended and often unseen consequences of higher entropy are eliminated. Entropy is always working like an impartial juror: It takes the information it is given and gives back exactly what is due.

The peculiar thing about this entropy idea is that it is possible to reduce, or even minimize, entropy. In other words, you can find a use of energy such that when the task is finished, the energy that has been converted has largely been turned into a form that continues to be available for use. This "entropy reduction" is, in fact, the main idea behind the push to recycle newspapers, containers, cardboard, glass, aluminum, and steel. By taking tons of plastic bottles, say, and melting them down and making new bottles, we make use again of a significant portion of the energy that was used to make the originals. The energy to mine or drill for raw material, perhaps some transportation, and some processing steps have already been done once and make the recycled items full of "embodied energy" that is used to make the new. It's easy to see that if those same old plastic bottles were just thrown into a landfill, all that embodied energy is just wasted.

To reduce the entropy, the effort put into heating a home, is to get a maximum return on the investment in energy. When it comes to effective and efficient heating, we can take our cues from nature because we live in a world heated, literally, by one central heating unit: the sun. It's easy to forget this fact on a blustery day in northern Minnesota, for example, when temperatures drop to well below zero. At times like that it appears that the sun does a miserable job of heating. In reality, extremes of weather are directly due to the sheer power of the sun.

The sun is a purely radiant heating "device." It does not heat the air directly. Checking the local air-temperature reading gives no real clue as to how well the sun performs its constant task. This becomes obvious when watching a weather report showing widely varying temperatures across the United States, even at similar latitudes. Air temperature is only affected indirectly by the sun.

What the sun does is something magical that is fully experienced on a perfectly clear, windless day. From 93 million miles away, you feel a most pleasant warmth on your back, or face, or whatever the sun shines upon. This is true whether the air temperature is hot or cold. This is the sun doing its thing at its best: radiating heat to warm some "thing." A "thing" is *anything* that has any significant mass. Air is not included in this group of things. But one item that is definitely included is our planet. The sun spends its days (and humans' nights) sending low-level infrared radiant heat to the earth.

It is this constant, gentle, persistent heat warming this earth and the things on it, sometimes at different rates because of clouds, smoke, smog, and foliage, that sets the stage for the weather. Acres and acres of freshly plowed rich ground soak up heat quickly, warming the air that passes over it. That air rises quickly, pulling more air behind it. Warm air here meets cold air there, and soon there is all kinds of weather. It might be warm and breezy in Iowa while it rains heavily in New York. Weather of all kinds, which results from the movement of warm and cold air, is proof positive that the sun is doing its job of warming the earth; that the sun is still shining.

We should take note of what the sun is teaching. It is the constant warming of the earth itself, not the air on it, that makes this planet habitable. This is the sun using the lowest rate of entropy possible to keep us all alive. Life's existence depends on the sun putting out energy to make things happen. All the joys and unpredictability of the seasons are a testament to the sun's energy.

Those modern, technologically marvelous forced-air heating systems, by contrast, are a fine example of maximizing entropy. Air has almost no capacity to store heat, and at the same time it is like a fluid. Like water, it can (and does) find the smallest possible leaks in the house envelope. Heating air and trying to retain warm air requires a vast amount of energy. That energy, converted to warm air in a home, becomes virtually inconvertible to any usable form. The air is warmed once, slowly disappears through any available crack or crevice, then vanishes into the vastness of the earth's atmosphere. It is interesting that people have imitated one of the sun's effects (warm air), rather than the sun itself, in order to satisfy a craving for steady state warmth—which is only one definition of *comfort*.

For purposes of the discussion of fire and (more specifically) masonry heaters, it is important to redefine comfort within the context of energy and entropy. No longer should people think of comfort as a steady-state condition of unchanging temperature and a world where people put forth less and less effort. Really, this is not comfort at all. True comfort is a state of feeling well, of being well. *Webster's* defines *comfort* as "a state of, or thing that provides, ease and quiet enjoyment." This is not to be confused with "an easy life in which minimum effort is made." A "state of ease and quiet enjoyment" is something that is accomplished by doing things first. It's not possible to appreciate ease unless challenges have been met. It is understood today that true well-being is derived from a life that balances effort with relaxation or ease.

In a sense, real comfort is the backbone of this whole book. And it all starts with the fire. The fire is the reason we can come in from the cold. Almost every house has a fire in it right now. (At least this

FIGURE 1.5. A masonry heater can be made to fit any given space. This soapstone heater's asymmetry follows the line of the stairs. Notice the two wood-storage areas in the stuccoed heater supports. Sometimes these openings in the base allow even the bottom of a masonry heater to become a radiating surface. Photo courtesy of New England Hearth and Soapstone.

is true for almost any house in a climate zone that experiences four seasons.) But usually it's a little blue flame flickering inside a metal box hidden in a closet or cellar. How about bringing back the bright, leaping yellow flames of real wood burning in a real fireplace? How about bringing back the fire that sparks the imagination and draws people together around it? How about bringing back a central hearth that brings forth light, warmth, and good food all from the same renewable fuel?

The hearth is the reason for the house. That has not changed. People have merely forgotten everything a fire does. They can once again take the hearth seriously, however. When a house is planned, you can start with the hearth and watch what blossoms around it. When a house is built, it is to protect the fire that will ensure the well-being of the family within. Some would have us believe that a fireplace of any kind is an unnecessary luxury. But it is truly one of the few necessities of a house. Take away the central vacuum or the

COMBUSTION EFFICIENCY

Combustion efficiency is a whole other matter from heating efficiency. Combustion efficiency compares how much of the fuel was burned with how much was available to be burned. For most combustion appliances, this number is very close to 100 percent. This is pretty straightforward to understand. Natural gas, for example, is enormously flammable. Exposing it to a spark or flame in the presence of oxygen will result in all the fuel being burned. There exist only a few conditions that would prevent the fuel from being completely consumed. In the case of wood, when it is burned in an environment of high heat and good air supply, it, too, will burn with combustion efficiencies approaching 100 percent. Wood-burning equipment—think fireplaces and woodstoves—that starves wood of air and/or attempts to burn it at relatively low temperatures will do a poorer job in this category.

wall-mounted flat-screen TV. Remove the furniture, intercoms, cabinets, counters, and electrical outlets. Skip the indoor plumbing. Discard all these things but keep a warm, central hearth and a family gathered around it will still feel like the house is a home. They will still be able to experience real comfort, a true sense of well-being.

Energy Intelligence or Energy Efficiency?

Those who are planning a home, room addition, or remodeling project are faced with more than just the issue of comfort. They are also faced with the simple question of what type of heating system will be used in the space. Will they have a conventional furnace? Will they have to add capacity to an existing appliance? What is the best way to take care of heating a given space? Invariably, the discussion at some point turns to the question of energy efficiency.

In the twenty-first century, it is easy to believe we are reaching the ceiling, the epitome, of energy-efficient design when it comes to our machinery and appliances. This furnace is 80 percent efficient. Wait, though, *this* one is 90 percent efficient! Ninety percent efficient! That means we could only hope to improve it by a measly 10 percentage points of efficiency. Knowing that nothing is perfect, there is no 100 percent efficient furnace; so this 90 percent efficient furnace is about as close to perfect as humans can ever get. Right?

To gain some perspective on this near-perfect heating appliance, it's helpful to take a look at just what we mean when we say that a fireplace, furnace, stove, or other heating appliance is X percent efficient.

Shedding light on the efficiency requires looking again at the laws of thermodynamics. I previously mentioned the first law of thermodynamics: "Energy is neither created nor destroyed, only converted from one form to another." In most heating appliances, chemical energy bound in the fuel is converted to heat energy. The efficiency rating that you hear quoted for heating appliances is called the first-law efficiency of that appliance. The percentage signifies the amount of heat extracted by the appliance compared with the amount of heat it's possible for that appliance to extract. In other words, there is a certain amount of heat energy available in a given quantity of natural gas, wood, propane, or other fuel. If only 10 percent of the heat available is lost and 90 percent of it is delivered into the home, the appliance is 90 percent efficient. This is called first-law efficiency because it is only describing the process of extracting heat energy from the chemical energy bound in the fuel. The procedure of burning the fuel liberates the heat energy latent in the chemistry of the fuel. No energy is created from the reaction; energy is just converted from chemical energy to heat energy. The efficiency measure tells how well the appliance did at getting that energy from the fuel into the home as heat.

The fascinating thing about first-law efficiency is that it is very misleading when viewed from a larger perspective. Suppose, for example, that I use a propane furnace. Suppose further that I phone a new company to deliver propane, and they use an army tank fueled by propane to haul a trailer to deliver the propane. Army tanks average about 0.5 mile per gallon. If the delivery-man makes a special trip to deliver only my propane with no other stops and drives 25 miles to my house, he uses 100 gallons of propane to fill my 350-gallon propane tank (50 gallons to get here and 50 to get back). If I factored this extra 100 gallons of fuel into the equation of how much fuel it takes to heat my home, the efficiency would suddenly drop severely. In this case, just using my 90 percent efficient furnace to burn 350 gallons of propane means the heat from all but 35 of those gallons was used to heat my home (.90 × 350 = 315). If I now have to consider that 450 gallons of propane were actually used in the process of getting my fuel, then in terms of calculating the efficiency of heating my home, 450 gallons were consumed—but I only received the heat of 315 gallons. Now my first-law efficiency looks very different. Suddenly the efficiency is only 70 percent.

Obviously, no company delivers propane with an army tank, and the odds of a delivery truck making just one stop on a route are slim. The point, however, is that the first-law efficiency measurement is only a small fraction of the whole picture. An extensive analysis of what is required to get fuel into a home tells a more accurate tale of how first-law energy-efficient the process really is. How much energy was used to find the fuel? How much energy is used to extract the fuel? How much energy is used to process the fuel? How much energy is used to clean, restore, or preserve the environment after the extraction of the fuel is complete? How much energy is used to deliver the fuel and maintain the delivery infrastructure? These same questions can be asked regardless of the chosen fuel and regardless of the efficiency of the end-use appliance.

All these energy costs related to getting the energy source to the home add up to what is called the *embodied energy* of the propane itself. Embodied energy is all the energy expended to produce, transport, and otherwise process a given item to get it to its final use destination. Computing the grand total is a monumental task, though not impossible. You'd have to consider the energy used for the initial exploration for the fuel

FIGURE 1.6. Tile trim decorates this stucco heater in the center of a home. Notice there is no visible fire or loading door facing the room. In Europe in the old days, heaters like this were sometimes fired by servants through a fuel-loading door in a back hallway or the kitchen. With a heater like this, the attraction is in the design and color as well as the gentle heat, rather than the fire itself. Photo courtesy of Biofire, Inc.

(which is usually found with or extracted from petroleum or natural gas) all the way to the point at which it is delivered to the homeowner.

You can do the same examination with any fuel, such as wood for masonry heaters. When embodied energy is considered, the "efficiency" of using fossil fuels like propane or natural gas becomes questionable. Most people who burn wood get their supply from within a short distance of their homes. Many homeowners have a few acres of woods themselves, while others get their wood from neighbors. At the very least, most people heating with wood get that wood somewhere from within their metropolitan area, township, or county.

As a simple example, you might order your wood supply from a tree service that works in nearby city. The tree service was employed by someone to remove a tree or trees from a parcel of land. They were not hired to produce fuel. Thus, the energy expended to

FIGURE 1.7. Brick and stucco are finely interwoven in this central heating mass. Note how the off-center door is counterbalanced by the brick-outlined niche in the upper right of the heater. The date of construction is permanently etched into a brick in the left corner. Photo courtesy of Envirotech Masonry Heaters.

drive trucks to the site, cut the tree down, and load it into trucks to be hauled away would have been expended even if the wood was not destined to become a commodity for sale. In this sense, the firewood that becomes available from this transaction is a *by-product*—essentially waste—of the business transaction.

The waste product, wood from the job of removing a tree, has a destination. The destination is the home of the person who has a masonry heater. You could therefore count the energy needed to get the tree from the initial jobsite to the masonry heater homesite as the first embodied energy of the firewood. This might involve the burning of 2 or 3 gallons of gasoline or diesel fuel in the truck that transports the tree and dumps it on the ground at the destination.

At this point you, the masonry heater owner, take over the process. You may use a chain saw to cut the logs into firebox lengths. This process might use a gallon or so of gasoline and oil per cord of wood. In addition, you may employ a gasoline-powered wood splitter and use an additional gallon of gasoline per cord of wood to split the firewood. In most cases, the rest of the embodied energy in firewood consists of human energy expended to move the wood with carts or wheelbarrows, stack the wood under cover, and eventually move the wood into the house for consumption in the masonry heater.

Clearly, the embodied energy in firewood is quite low. If the wood is cut on the lot of the place where it will be burned, the total fossil fuel use might be a couple of gallons of gasoline per cord of wood. If an outside service is used, an additional few gallons of gasoline and some more individual human effort may be involved. An important side note to this, however, is that firewood is (relatively speaking) easily processed without the use of *any* fossil fuels—in fact, for most of human history the world ran on a wood economy. Until the twentieth century, heating, cooking, and the operation of heavy machinery often depended on the burning of wood rather than fossil fuels. It is not easily imagined how we could ever drill for, extract, process, and transport fossil fuels without the fossil fuels themselves (except, of course, by going back to wood energy and steam locomotion).

A similar analysis of, for example, propane as a heating fuel can be done. Propane is essentially a by-product of gasoline and natural gas production in the same sense that firewood could be a by-product of the work of a tree service. (There are, however, significant amounts of propane that are made from crude oil. This process, since it intentionally works to create propane rather than separate it from a higher-quality fuel, would have to include the embodied energy of that particular refining process.) However, propane is not simply "skimmed" from the gasoline or natural gas. Rather, propane itself is only a fraction of a total of petroleum gases that are separated from either gasoline or natural gas.

Once the raw petroleum gases have been separated from the principal fuels, energy-intensive refining is still needed to secure the propane itself, which is typically only about 5 percent of the total petroleum gas mixture. Once this refining has been done, the gas is pressurized (which liquefies it) and put into tanker trucks for transportation and distribution to various propane vendors. The propane vendors then transport the propane, using smaller trucks, to individual homeowners.

Many propane users are familiar with a wintertime routine that includes several refillings of the propane tank throughout the heating season. This one operation of repeated truck deliveries could use the same amount of gasoline as is needed to deliver, cut, and split firewood. The added energy expenditures to refine, process, and initially distribute the propane, therefore, give propane a higher embodied energy figure.

This, however, does not end the considerations. Although knowing the energy efficiency of appliances like furnaces is valuable, at some point we must also face entropy again. Earlier, I summarized the second law as a measure of the total amount of energy that is no longer readily available to perform any task once the initial task is completed. This is just another way of restating the heat-related definition of entropy that says that heat always travels from a warm area to a cooler area; it never goes from cooler to warmer without an additional input of energy. Now it's time to refine this even more and simply state that entropy is the tendency toward disorder.

To understand how the entropy law gets reduced to this formulation, it's helpful to think about heat again. If a container of hot air is opened in the middle of a 70°F room, eventually the air in the container will cool completely. It obeys the second law and releases its heat into the living environment. In greater detail, what was an organized quantity of fast-moving (warm) air molecules melds with a roomful of slower-moving (cooler) air molecules. In other words, a highly organized set of molecules with greater energy became lost in a sea of air molecules of less energy. Order represents energy stored and able to be used. Disorder represents energy dispersed and no longer able to be used.

A vase sitting on a table represents stored energy. If the table is removed from under it, the vase will fall. That stored energy becomes heat released as the vase shatters on the floor; the fracturing and breaking release little bursts of heat from friction. A lesser amount of the energy is also released as sound waves in the air. Will that vase ever have the same potential energy again? Only if someone reassembles it (expends energy). Anyone who maintains a household knows that order in each room requires energy expended to put everything where it belongs. If the energy is not

FIGURE 1.8. Here is a simple stucco heater centrally located in the living space. The open stairway allows the radiant heat to reach all areas of the room. Notice the drying racks above the heater and around the chimney mass. Photo courtesy of Biofire, Inc.

expended, eventually the room comes to disorder as a book gets left here, a drinking glass there, a newspaper on the floor, and a dead plant leaf by the window.

The same issue of disorder versus order must be confronted in regard to obtaining fuel. Currently, fossil fuels are available from various wells or mines throughout the world. In a coal mine, for example, the easiest (most orderly) coal to recover is closest to the initial excavations. As the coal gets used, excavations need to be deeper and more energy is needed to get the coal out of the mine. It's as if you started consuming all the food in the kitchen without replenishing the supply. Eventually, the refrigerator, freezer, and kitchen cupboards would be bare. Next, you have to start walking to the pantry until those shelves are stripped. Now you have to walk down into the basement to the long-term storage freezer. The amount of effort for each meal is incrementally increasing. When all that food is eaten, there is no food in the house, and you will have to expend even more energy to get food from a garden or by walking to the grocery store. If the grocery store stock likewise was not replenished, eventually you might have to go to the next town or county to find food for your next meal. As the easily obtained, highly organized stores are consumed, more and more energy is required to get more food of the same quality. This is the real, hidden cost of fossil fuels. As they are consumed, and since they are never replenished, it will forever get harder, more expensive, and less rewarding to mine or drill for it. It's a certainty that if fossil fuels continue to be exploited at current rates, they will eventually fall out of favor due to enormously rising costs brought about by the increase in entropy—the loss of order as (relatively) convenient supplies are consumed. This will happen regardless of environmental issues such as climate change, pollution, and water quality.

This is what makes wood such an attractive option. Wood will always be renewable as long as trees are replanted and the sun is overhead. With simple management and conscientious use of efficient wood-burning equipment like masonry heaters, people can heat a home and bake the family bread just as easily one hundred years from now as today. The beautiful thing about nature is that it always replenishes trees and plants in a time frame commensurate with human life spans.

The Demise of the Fireplace

As we move forward, there will continue to be other technological solutions for heating homes that rely not on simple science like stored solar energy (either directly or in the form of wood), but on new discoveries. Forays will continue into the use of hydrogen fuel cells. Nuclear energy, both fission and fusion, will remain on the docket. Coal gasification, wind, hydro-electric, the use of sea-wave motion, and a whole host of other alternatives will be researched, refined, tested, and implemented. We cannot even guess what our primary energy sources might be in one hundred years.

What is predictable is that these efforts will mainly be toward finding ways to centralize energy production. When large corporations and government are involved in the process, it is a near certainty that simple, home-based technology based on using stored solar energy, free for everyone to receive, will *not* be the primary emphasis. There is no way to tax (at least not yet) solar gain or trees grown on one's own property. There is no money to be made by energy companies when people fuel their homes using wood. People will continue to be told that centralized energy production is in their best interest.

Centralized energy production seems like a good idea in many ways, and certainly did to millions of people early in the twentieth century. Inexpensive, easily obtained fossil fuels, delivered to the customer's house—first by truck, then by pipeline—made perfect sense. There is a perceived increase in quality of life, as the chore of securing our own fuel is eliminated. We certainly feel prosperous having heat without having to think about it. It only took one hundred years for American citizens to become dependent on someone else to make sure there is heat in the house.

The dependency on fossil fuels has thus nearly killed the traditional, open, wood-burning fireplace. It never was a fantastic heating appliance, and now it is, generally, an energy drain on an otherwise energy-efficient house. Today the fireplace has been almost entirely relegated to the category of superfluous, mood-setting devices. Because fire still pulls at the heartstrings of human beings, fireplaces remain a sought-after amenity to new homes throughout North America. This amenity, however, will slowly disappear from houses everywhere.

Already, generations of people are raised in homes and apartments without any type of fire to view at all. Neither a gas nor wood-fired hearth exists in vast numbers of residences. Newer homes tend more and more to have gas versions. In 2005, according to the Hearth, Patio, and Barbecue Association, gas appliances outsold wood-burning versions by a four-to-one ratio.[2] A look at the hearth industry reveals that when people aren't interested in using a fireplace as a primary heat source, it becomes a novelty item. Designers are freed from the constraints of making an efficient heating appliance. More significantly, they are being freed from the constraints of producing a place to house a bulky, wood fire. Therefore, they are making "fireplaces" that more resemble a flat-screen television set than a

FIGURE 1.9. This masonry heater's crisp, square corners and uniform courses of stone produce clean lines that complement the straight lines of the overhead beams and the lattice-like wooden wall surface. Notice how the same stonework is in the stairway and foyer beyond, successfully blurring the line between where the heater stops and the rest of the space begins. Photo courtesy of Temp-Cast Enviroheat.

fireplace. Indeed, some hang on the wall and come in imaginative shapes and sizes. Many consumers find the fire of a gas appliance to be unsatisfying, however.

Having a place to house a fire in a home, then, is evolving into simply an aesthetic choice. If the fireplace isn't functional *or* it becomes less and less satisfying, it will grace fewer and fewer homes. The traditional fireplace—an open firebox containing a wood fire—will not endure this slow evolution. To be sure, there will always be some people who will insist on having an open, wood-burning fireplace. But the future will be owned by the fireplaces that satisfy either the aesthetic

FIGURE 1.10. (*a*) An heirloom-quality, one-of-a-kind masonry heater can serve generations to come. Here is a custom-designed Tulikivi soapstone model fit cleverly between two living spaces. (*b*) Carved in the dark band is a quote from Goethe: "Whatever you dream you can do, begin it. Boldness has genius, power and magic in it." Photos courtesy of WarmStone Fireplaces and Designs; copyright Mikel Covey Photography.

Fundamentals

It is certainly true that we need a strong foundation on which to build anything. This is true for either a house or a philosophy. If a home's foundation suffers, the home will suffer. If the foundational beliefs of a philosophy are shaky or questionable, it's hard to substantiate the rest. The fundamentals always have to be in place for anything to prosper or thrive.

The fundamentals of a house are relatively few, but they must exist before any amenities are worth considering. After all, what would be the point of investing thousands of dollars in an entertainment system if, say, the roof is subpar, leaks, and will then destroy those electronics? The short list of house fundamentals includes the foundation, framing, insulation, exterior veneer, roofing, windows and doors, floors, and heating system. In essence, the fundamentals of a house are those things that make it a viable, long-term place to live.

Everything else that might go into a house is an amenity. Though modern culture would claim that indoor plumbing and electricity are also fundamentals

demands of consumers or functional heating demands. Those that satisfy both art and function will lead the way. In that sense, then, the open fireplace will continue to die while the masonry heater will survive and thrive as more people become acquainted with it. Masonry heaters are the only wood-burning appliances that blend imagination with superior efficiency and heating ability—not to mention a plethora of other benefits.

As central planners and big energy businesses wrestle with the pains of environmental considerations, increasing worldwide energy demand, decreasing and less easily obtained fossil fuel supplies, rising energy costs, and dozens of other obstacles, individuals should become aware that it is possible to return to something simpler and more basic. You don't have to spend all your free time chopping wood to be more self-sufficient. You don't have to rely on others to supply energy for heating. You can always return to the sound fundamentals.

(and, indeed, local building codes often require them), they are not, in the strict sense, fundamentals. Without a foundation, the home will deteriorate and collapse prematurely. Without framing, there is no way to hold up a roof or siding to keep out weather. Without the roof and siding, there is no longevity to the framing or protection from basic weather. Without the windows and doors, there is no entrance or egress and no light with simultaneous protection from the elements and basic safety. Without floors, you cannot walk around in the home. Without a heating system, winters would be, practically speaking, unlivable. Finally, without insulation, heat cannot be retained.

If you think about quality, durability, and the potential heirloom nature of a home, masonry heaters begin to make sense. Wood has been a reliable fuel forever. The various approaches to home heating developed over the last hundred years represent a blip on the scale of human habitation on earth. We can marvel at electric heat pumps, brag about 90 percent efficient furnaces, or revel in the sensuousness of warm floors. But none of the typical technological heating solutions around today can be considered heirloom-quality and fundamental in nature.

There is no mistaking that coal reserves will diminish, that oil reserves will decline, and that all other fossil fuel sources have limited supplies, especially considering an ever-increasing population. Of what value will warm floors be with no electricity to pump the water; or electricity so expensive that you dare not use it? Of what value is a 90 percent efficient furnace as oil reserves grow in cost, lose availability, and eventually disappear?

Fossil fuels are not fundamentals. They are exotic materials with tremendous energy stores per small unit. Fundamentals are mundane, normal, and relatively easy to find or close at hand. Fundamentals are those things on which we can always depend. Fundamentals likewise can be restored to great quantity even if they are mismanaged and depleted at first. In Ohio, apples and corn are fundamental foods, but mangoes and kiwis are exotic. Water is a fundamental drink, while Gatorade is not. Cotton is a fundamental ingredient for cloth, while polyester is exotic. Wood is a fundamental fuel, while uranium is not.

For a brief time (years, decades, or even centuries), we can base an economy, production, distribution, and life in general on the supply of exotic materials. Such a system is destined to fail, however. Sometimes it is possible to see the end of such a system coming; sometimes it happens very quickly and unexpectedly. Sometimes its end comes with unexpected consequences. What will always be around, however, when the exotics fail, are the fundamentals.

A masonry heater is an heirloom heating system. It is built with materials destined to last centuries. It is built with materials that are common and mundane like clay (bricks), stone, more clay (mortar), and sand, lime, and Portland cement (common mortar). It is built with a design that cannot lose efficiency over centuries. It is built to use fuel that can be regenerated (wood). This combination assures that as long as there's a roof on the home, people to live in it, and trees nearby, there can be heat and comfort. The same can never be said for systems that depend on endless infrastructure and political relationships.

PASSIVE RESISTANCE TO FOSSIL FUELS

In a rural area not far from Ann Arbor, Michigan, sits a home nestled into the earth. From the road, it can barely be seen; it rather blends into its surroundings. A quarter-mile driveway off a dirt road brings you to this special house, built in a special way, and occupied by two special people and their masonry heater.

Joan Paskewitz and Tom Tuer reside here in one of the few passive solar, earth-bermed homes in southwestern Michigan. Joan is a physical therapist at a local hospital, and Tom retired a while back from a career in aerospace engineering. When they talk about their house, however, the two sound like solar architects. Joan says it's crazy that people rarely build with the effects of the sun in mind. "They should pass a law that every house needs to have its long axis facing south," she quips. "Just think how much energy would be saved by doing that one thing!"

Tom and Joan designed their home in the late 1990s and took their plan to an architect to have it drawn after they had it all figured out. The home has an abundance of south-facing glass (triple-pane windows with built-in solar shutters). Joan appreciates the expanses of glass

FIGURE 1.11. Although it looks a lot like a typical house, the Tuer/Paskewitz residence is a functional passive solar and earth-bermed home. Photo by Tom Tuer.

for keeping the home full of lots of light even in the cloudy winter. The main floor is a poured, insulated slab with green tile finish. The first-level north wall is entirely bermed with earth, as are portions of the east and west sides. The ceiling has 12 inches of fiberglass insulation, giving it an insulation value that exceeds R-40. Carefully calculated south-side overhangs invite all the winter sun into the home but exclude the hot summer sun.

The result of the careful planning is that, when the sun shines in the winter, it streams delightfully through the glazing and warms the masonry floor. The floor soaks up that free heat and stores it for slow release over time. The house is comfortably heated by the sun. The whole house is a masonry heater, in that sense. Joan points out one potential problem with passive solar: "We don't get sunshine all that often in the winter in Michigan." Fortunately for them, they also installed a wood-fired masonry heater in 2001, not long after they moved into the house. Theirs is a Finnish contraflow heater with multihued, split granite as the exterior facing. Tom says, "I always wanted a granite fireplace. We enjoy the constant temperature—how it is very slow to cool all that granite." In other words, when the sun isn't shining in the windows, it shines from the masonry heater. When the sun is shining in the windows, they can forgo the use of firewood. It's a perfect symbiotic relationship.

Tom explains, "Unless we've gotten a lot of sun, we always enjoy eating breakfast while enjoying a fire. The evening fire is optional depending on the sunshine we get."

The pair has few disparaging words about the masonry heater. Joan calls it "beautiful" and "functional," and most importantly adds that, "The heat is very nice." She does point out, however, that regularly hauling in wood does, inevitably, mean that some dirt is brought in the house as well. She also notices some ash gets in the

FIGURE 1.12. A granite masonry heater serves as the sunshine when the real sun hides behind clouds at the Tuer/Paskewitz passive solar residence. Stove by Masonry Heater Store, LLC; stonework by Peter Skove; photo by Nancy Matesz.

house from the occasional opening of the firebox door or from cleaning ash out of the ash pit. Tom likes it for its granite, for its comfort, and because he knows it has low emissions.

As to the job of splitting and stacking firewood, Tom says he enjoys it, "both for exercise and for the sense of orderliness and satisfaction that comes from carefully stacking a heap of wood." He stacks the wood on pallets in a simple woodshed with open doorways on both the east and west ends "so I can empty it from one side and fill it from the other." He tries to have all his wood split for a year before feeding it to the masonry heater.

Although the passive solar function of the house and the masonry heater, as a team, are the primary heat source for the house, Joan and Tom also have a geothermal heat pump as a mechanical backup system. They do use one or two zones of this system pretty regularly, but only overnight when the electric rates are lower; one keeps a far distant (from both solar and the masonry heater) bathroom floor warm, and the other keeps a workshop at a reasonable temperature. "Otherwise," says Joan, "I can't remember the last time we used the floor heating during the day at all." She proves it by showing electric bills of less than $80 in January. "And that includes the heat pump, hot-water heating, and the operation of the well pump."

Like many masonry heater owners, Tom and Joan appreciate the heater for its guarantee of security. They recall a winter period when they lost electric power for about twenty-four hours while they had eight guests staying with them. They lit candles for light, and several people slept in the living room near the masonry heater. In an all-electric house like theirs, power outage meant no conventional oven or stove, either. They were still able to feed their friends ham, potatoes, and vegetables cooked in the upper-chamber bakeoven of the masonry heater. Heat, food, and light all came from a real fire and simple, local fuel. There's nothing more secure than that.

A little planning goes a long way. Tom and Joan planned for a house that did not depend on fossil fuels. They chose the path of simple technology and free energy. Their house collects the heat of the sun, and it basks in the dependable heat of a piece of the sun—a masonry heater. Their home is proof that passive solar design and a masonry heater together can make a house solar-heated even in cloudy Michigan.

FIGURE 2.1. A modern-day *kachelofen* with traditional elements graces this Connecticut home. The fluted tiles and cylindrical element with braids and rosettes hark back to another century. Yet this heater boasts a computer-controlled combustion air supply and an efficient internal design facilitated by both a craftsman's experience and computer modeling. Photo courtesy of New England Hearth and Soapstone.

CHAPTER TWO

A Brief History of Fire and Hot Rocks in North America

Though humans probably had little, if any, control over fire half a million years ago, there is little doubt they made use of heat stored in rocks—even if only, like a cat, to take a nap in a warm place. Once control over fire was the norm, storage of heat was a natural result. You can easily imagine a family of cave dwellers becoming ecstatic as they realize the possibilities: They can charge rocks with heat by situating them around the fire, bury the hot rocks just a little below floor level in the sleeping area, and enjoy a heated bed all night long! Perhaps these were the first heated sleeping areas—probably existing a couple of hundred thousand years ago. Similarly, native peoples of many lands have from time immemorial heated rocks, then put them in pots with water, vegetables, and meat, to cook a stew or make a tea when it's impractical to have the pot directly over the fire. Of course, even up to the early twentieth century, people took rocks warmed in a fire or on a stove and used them to warm the ride in a buggy or warm the feet in bed.

I could successfully argue, using scenarios like these, that humans have used masonry heaters for hundreds of thousands of years. It's a little disingenuous, however, to put rocks warmed by the sun or a campfire in the same league as engineered heat-retaining masonry heaters. Much of the delight is the same, but the human thought going into the deliberate planning for the stored heat is, obviously, different.

The Hidden American Experience

I am often asked by new acquaintances what my business is. When I describe masonry heaters, I usually see one of two responses. In the first, the inquiring person's eyes glaze over and he declares that he has never heard of such a heater. Often, however, the inquisitive individual instead gets a dreamy look in her eyes and then says, "Oh, yeah, I remember those tile stoves. We used to see one whenever we went to the art museum!"

When my wife, Nancy, was a child, her elementary school class annually traveled to the Toledo Museum of Art in Toledo, Ohio. As young children will do, they often got tired and rather bored with walking the wide, marble aisles and gazing endlessly at framed artwork. There was always a sense of excitement for the class, however, when they went to what they called the "Swiss Room." There, as the centerpiece, sits a tall, highly ornate tile stove. The museum piece, which is believed to have been created in the late nineteenth century, was designed in the style of Swiss originals from the eighteenth century.

The Toledo tile stove is decorated with scenes from mythology, legend, and the Bible. What really attracted the children, however, was the small, single seat that is part of the stove. One by one, each student would be allowed to climb the two tile steps and sit on the "throne"—which of course would have been the warmest place in the house when the stove was in use. In this way hundreds, if not thousands, of public school students in northwestern Ohio were and are exposed to the concept of masonry heaters, though often the teacher attending may not have an understanding of how such a heater really functions.

Unfortunately, today, at least in that museum, people are no longer permitted to even touch, let alone sit on, the tile stove. Although it is easy to understand the desire to preserve such artwork, it means that observers no longer get a more meaningful understanding of functional art.

Other museums throughout North America also have historic tile stoves, and millions of students have

FIGURE 2.2. The Swiss Room (detail of tile stove), Toledo Museum of Art. This tile masonry heater has been visited by hundreds of schoolchildren over the decades it has been on display. Not long ago, children could climb the steps and sit on the "throne," which would have been the warmest seat in the house. This is a late-nineteenth-century replica of an eighteenth-century original. Photo courtesy of Photography Incorporated, Toledo, Ohio.

FIGURE 2.3. A *kachelofen* similar in style to the one in *The Sound of Music.* Photo courtesy of Vintage Elements, Greenwood, South Carolina.

seen them, though it may not register until they run into someone who actually builds them today. The Adirondack Museum in Blue Mountain Lake, New York, has a tile stove, and the American Swedish Institute in Minneapolis, Minnesota, has several Swedish *kakelugns*. The Metropolitan Museum of Art in New York City has a very ornate stove from Nuremberg in its collection.

But museums are not the only places that masonry heaters are seen by millions of modern US and Canadian citizens. In the film version of one of the best-loved musicals of all time, *The Sound of Music* (1965), the children of the Baron von Trapp (played by Christopher Plummer) settle down on the rug in the parlor to listen to their gentleman father play the guitar and sing with a tile stove in the background against the wall between him and Maria (played by Julie Andrews). More recently (2006), an observant moviegoer could see not one but two beautiful tile stoves in the luxurious home of Crown Prince Leopold (played by Rufus Sewell) in the film *The Illusionist,* set in Vienna, Austria, in 1900.

FIGURE 2.4. One of the *kakelugn* seen in the movie *The Illusionist.* © 2005 Illusionist Distribution, LLC. All Rights Reserved. Photo used by permission of Illusionist Distribution, LLC.

FIGURE 2.5. Heidi teaches Peter to read while Grandfather listens. A tile masonry heater keeps them warm. Illustration by Troy Howell, from the 1945 edition of *Heidi.*

Despite the fact that North America has no centuries-long established tradition of masonry heaters, some children and adults have at least seen them in museums and movies. Perhaps to most Americans such stoves are like a vaguely remembered landmark on a road trip that goes unnoticed until someone points it out later. Often we don't notice otherwise obvious objects if we're not looking for them or are intent on other observations.

Children are often introduced to tile stoves through the story of Heidi, the young Swiss girl who goes to live with her grandfather in the Swiss Alps. *Heidi* was written in 1880 by Johanna Spyri, a Swiss author.

Late in the story, Heidi and her grandfather move down from the mountains into an old, run-down yet once-splendid home in town. The home has been abandoned, and the grandfather takes it upon himself

to patch up what is left and make it habitable for the two of them rather than subject Heidi to the struggle to survive a winter in the mountains. Johanna Spyri writes:

> The four walls were all standing, the dark wood panels showed not a break, and in one corner stood a huge stove, reaching almost to the ceiling, and on the white tiles were big blue pictures. Some showed old castles, with tall trees all round, and underneath a huntsman passing with his dogs. Another picture showed a peaceful lake, under wide-spreading oaks, with a fisherman standing by it and holding his rod far out over the water. There was a seat all round the stove so that one could sit down and study the pictures. This at once took Heidi's fancy. As soon as she came into the room with

FIGURE 2.6. (*a*) An eighteenth-century tile stove that has painted illustrations. (*b*) This close-up of a tile depicts just the kind of scenes Johanna Spyri described in *Heidi*. Project by New England Hearth and Soapstone; photos by Timothy Seaton.

her grandfather, she ran to the stove, sat down on the bench, and began to look at the pictures. But as she moved along on the seat and came behind the stove, something new occupied her whole attention; in the quite large space between the stove and the wall four boards were placed, like a bin for apples. But there were no apples in it; there actually lay Heidi's bed exactly as it had been upon the Alm; a thick bed of hay, with the linen sheet and the bag for a coverlet. Heidi shouted:

"O grandfather, here is my bedroom! Oh, how lovely!"[1]

Heidi's grandfather has provided Heidi with the premium spot to sleep—close to the masonry heater, which, in this case, is a tile stove, the tiles of which have been painstakingly painted with quaint country

scenes. A few paragraphs later Spyri writes that, "Heidi slept soundly in her corner by the stove," as you might imagine. My memory reeled in 2008 when I participated in the reconstruction of an eighteenth-century Swiss tile stove hand-painted with the very types of scenes Johanna Spyri describes. The project stove had pictures in rust red instead of blue. Nevertheless, the story of Heidi came closer to home and it became easier to imagine young children gathering around the stove to study the intricate pictures and soak up the warmth; perhaps children a century ago slept in their straw beds close to this stove as well.

The casual reader of *Heidi* understandably passes over the details of this account. But it is interesting to note that the author of this novel matter-of-factly describes a common architectural feature of her country and how it was used. For example, she states that a "seat ran all round the stove so that one could sit at one's ease" and followed with the confirmation that one would sleep well by the stove. The people of the Old World know how to live with a masonry heater, and North America has been let in on the secret, but heaters have not received much attention.

Less widely known is the nineteenth-century story by English novelist Louise de la Ramée titled "The Nuremberg Stove." The tale is about a poverty-stricken

FIGURE 2.7. A nineteenth-century tile stove with color and shape much like the one illustrated in *Heidi* (1945 edition). Photo courtesy of Vintage Elements, Greenwood, South Carolina.

FIGURE 2.8. In this scene from Ramée's "The Nuremburg Stove," August is heartbroken to hear that his piece of the sun will be taken away. Illustration by F. M. McAnelly.

family. The father, growing desperate, sells the family's tile stove. Everyone is pained, but August, a boy of about ten or eleven, is heartbroken. The story centers on the events that occur as the stove is taken away. The beginning of the story describes the masterpiece:

At the top of the chamber, sending out warmth and color, was a tower of porcelain, surmounted with armed figures and shields and a great golden crown on the summit of all. It was a stove of 1532, the handiwork of the great potter, Augustin Hirschvogel.

The stove, no doubt, had stood in palaces and been made for princes; had warmed the crimson stockings of cardinals and the gold-broidered shoes of archduchesses. It was a right royal thing. Yet, perhaps, it had never been more useful than it was now in this poor, desolate room, sending down heat and comfort to the troop of children tumbled together on a wolfskin at its feet.

Later our protagonist, August, entertains his brothers and sisters with artwork drawn as they sit near the heater:

They were all so happy; what did they care for the snow outside? Their little bodies were warm, and their hearts merry; and August cried, as he looked at the stove shedding its heat on them all: "Oh, dear Hirschvogel, you are almost as great and good as the sun! No, you are greater and better, because he goes

FIGURE 2.9. In Seredy's *The Good Master*, Kate climbs the "beehive" to hide in the rafters. Children and parents alike can be exposed to masonry heaters without even realizing it. Illustration by Kate Seredy.

FIGURE 2.10. The traditional *kemence* from Hungary was often a poor man's heater, fueled with grasses and scrounged sticks. This is the same type of heater described in *The Good Master*. From David Lyle, *The Book of Masonry Stoves*, p. 90.

away all these dark, cold hours; but you—just a bit of wood to feed you—and you make a summer for us all the winter through!"[2]

And so it is. A masonry heater, confirmed ages ago, is a "piece of the sun." An illustration from the book is seen in figure 2.8.

A heater also makes an appearance in Kate Seredy's *The Good Master*. This 1935 book is about a Hungarian farm family and the head of the household (the good master) who deals so well with all the goings-on. We hear mainly about Jancsi, the son, and Kate, Jancsi's cousin from the city who comes to visit. In chapter 2 is the story of the tomboy Kate who mischievously has climbed into the rafters above the family and is subsequently asked how she got up so high and why she will not come down:

> "I climbed on that big white beehive in the corner, but it's hot now, [Mother] made a fire in it," said Kate. She meant the stove. It did look like a beehive, squatting in the corner. There was a bench around it. Jancsi loved to cuddle on the bench, propping up his back against the warm side of the "kemence."

> "Well, now you'll stay there until the 'beehive' cools down. Jancsi! Mother! I forbid you to take her down. She can stay there all night!" said Father.[3]

Once again, we are told of a masonry heater with benches around it that a family, and especially children, lean against to stay warm. It's a "beehive" that will stay warm all night, preventing the mischievous girl from coming down from her perch.

These are three splendid children's stories, set in three different European locations. We hear about the Hungarian *kemence*, a Swiss tile stove, and a German porcelain tile stove. They are vastly different devices, but all keep their young companions warm with gentle heat. The *kemence* was almost always a peasants' stove—a minimal stuccoed "beehive" that was more about function than form. On the other end of the spectrum is the highly ornate porcelain stove depicted in "The Nuremberg Stove," which "no doubt, had stood in palaces and been made for princes,"[4] ornate as it was.

FIGURE 2.11. Here is a modern version of Kate Seredy's "beehive." This custom soapstone heater in Finland sports a heated bench and a carved fish on the mantel. The "beehive" shape contains the firebox and a secondary chamber above a throat. The exhaust travels from the upper part of the dome down into the heated benches and then up into the tall rectangular elements in back before exiting into the chimney flue at center left. Photo courtesy of Tulikivi Corporation.

And then there is Heidi's stove, with quaint pictures of common scenes—somewhere between highly ornate and basically functional. Different countries, different appearance, different construction, but all the heaters give the same reliable heat in the cold regions of the world.

Since virtually every cold northern European country has a strong heater tradition, it's somewhat surprising that masonry heaters have, historically, not been part of the North American scene. The log cabin was a traditional way of building in these same European countries, and this method of construction

FIGURE 2.12. Perhaps this is what Mark Twain thought was "the polished white tomb that stands lofty and heartless in the corner and thinks it is a stove." Photo courtesy of Vintage Elements, Greenwood, South Carolina.

readily took hold in North America as immigrants harvested the vast expanses of both hardwood and softwood forests. Remarkably, a companion construction technique—the masonry heater—never got a foothold, though some were built in scattered locations by now-unknown craftsmen. The sheer amount of forested land, and therefore fuel, mitigated the need for the energy savings that would result from using a masonry heater. And it was easier to haul a metal stove than tons of tile and brick when pioneers spread out across the continent.

On his travels through Europe, Mark Twain experienced and took note of masonry heaters. Interestingly, as a skeptical American, he initially found them to be rather pathetic. In his essay, "An Austrian Health Factory," he writes of his stay in Austria,

> But as a rule I stay in and try to get warm.
>
> And what is there for means, besides heavy clothing and rugs, and the polished white tomb that stands lofty and heartless in the corner and thinks it is a stove? Of all the creations of human insanity this thing is the most forbidding. Whether it is heating the room or isn't, the impression is the same—cold indifference. You can't tell which it is doing without going and putting your hand on it. They burn little handfuls of kindlings in it, no substantial wood, and no coal.

Of course, the "polished white tomb" is a tile stove—a *kachelofen*. Mark Twain obviously had a very poor opinion of the concept as he wrote this essay. It is fascinating that Twain was a quick study, however, and by the time he wrote an essay titled "National Stupidities," he had learned how masonry heaters actually operate, though he still sought improvements:

> Take the German stove, for instance—the huge white porcelain monument that towers toward the ceiling in the corner of the room, solemn, unsympathetic, and suggestive of death and the grave—where can you find it

outside of the German countries? I am sure I have never seen it where German was not the language of the region. Yet it is by long odds the best stove and the most convenient and economical that has yet been invented.

Mark Twain begins by almost repeating his punishing remarks from a year earlier, but quickly segues into praise for the masonry heater, which seems to be found only in the German-speaking countries. The best? Most convenient? Most economical? He continues, possibly referring to himself—the "uninstructed stranger" of not too long ago:

> To the uninstructed stranger it promises nothing; but he will soon find that it is a masterly performer, for all that. It has a little bit of a door which you couldn't get your head into; a door which seems foolishly out of proportion to the rest of the edifice; yet the door is right, for it is not necessary that bulky fuel shall enter it. Small-sized fuel is used, and marvelously little of that. The door opens into a tiny cavern which would not hold more fuel than a baby could fetch in its arms. The process of firing is quick and simple.

He has hit on perhaps the biggest stumbling block for those accustomed to the gaping mouth of an open fireplace: a small door. The door is small, of course, because the fire chamber is small. The fire chamber is small because hardly any wood is used. Because hardly any wood is used, but the heater is always warm, it is very easy to fire. And the result of such little labor? This is what Twain says:

> All day long and until past midnight all parts of the room will be delightfully warm and comfortable, and there will be no headaches and no sense of closeness or oppression. In an American room, whether heated by steam, hot water, or open fires, the neighborhood of the register or the fireplace is warmest; the heat is not equally diffused through the room; but in a German room one is as comfortable in one part of it as in another. Nothing is gained or lost by being near the stove. Its surface is not hot; you can put your hand on it anywhere and not get burnt. Consider these things. *One firing is enough for the day; the cost is next to nothing; the heat produced is the same all day, instead of too hot and too cold by turns; one may absorb himself in his business in peace; he does not need to feel any anxieties or solicitudes about his fire; his whole day is a realized dream of bodily comfort.* [emphasis added]

Here Mark Twain has become the ultimate masonry heater salesman. Who could possibly pass by a heating method that makes his entire day a "realized dream of bodily comfort?" The cost of firing the heater is "next to nothing," and the room is equally comfortable throughout. The unstinting praise he bestows on the *kachelofen* is tempered a bit when he complains that the door is solid and one cannot see the fire, but he recognizes the magic that results from its internal design: "This noble stove is at its very best when its front has a big square opening in it for a visible wood fire. The real heating is done in the hidden regions of the great structure, of course—the open [visible] fire is merely to rejoice your eye and gladden your heart." Incredulous that this is something momentous that is being ignored on the other side of the world, Mr. Twain considers the folly of American stubbornness at not trying this advanced heating option:

> America could adopt this stove, but does America do it? No, she sticks placidly to her own fearful and wonderful inventions in the stove line. She has fifty kinds, and not a rational one in the lot. The American wood stove, of whatsoever breed, is a terror. There can be no tranquility of mind where it is. It requires more attention than a baby. It has to be fed every little while, it has to be watched all the

THE WORLD OF TOMORROW

Betty and Larry Coleman rented a home in Norwalk, Connecticut, from 1973 to 1974. Larry had taken a temporary teaching job in the area, and they had arrived with a baby in tow. They moved into a home that was, at the time, owned by the son of the original homeowners. Those original owners had, in the 1940s, added a couple of rooms and an unusual-looking tile structure, nearly square in footprint; it was perhaps 4 to 5 feet wide and 5 to 6 feet deep. It stood about 6 feet tall. Three of its sides had blue, attractive tile. About 3 feet up the sides of the heater there was attached a masonry platform—large enough and strong enough to serve as a bed for a grown man. The fourth side was seemingly attached to or went through the wall separating the dining/family room from the kitchen. In the kitchen, they found a small firebox door opening into the strange construction.

The original owners had attended the 1939 World's Fair in New York City. The theme of the fair was "The World of Tomorrow." Promoters of this event had imagined it as a celebration of "Man's achievements on a shrinking globe in an expanding universe." There they had seen a magnificent, new (to the United States?) kind of wood-fired heater and decided that they would put one in the room addition they were planning for their home. They commissioned the construction of one in their home. The Colemans' landlord could not say who built the stove or exactly when, though he was certain it was in the 1940s.

The Connecticut home's tile heater, remembers Mr. Coleman, had the tiniest firebox and a very small door. "You couldn't put more than two or three logs in the thing at once," he says today. He remembers well, however, that this small amount of fuel always produced an "amazing amount of heat" from the tile-faced structure, which was presumably about thirty years old when he fired it in 1973. Though both Larry and Betty have held the fond memory of the masonry heater for the past thirty-five years, they believe they have not owned a house since that they felt deserved or could properly be heated by such a fine thing.

time; and for all reward you are roasted half your time and frozen the other half. It warms no part of the room but its own part; it breeds headaches and suffocation, and makes one's skin feel dry and feverish; and when your wood bill comes in you think you have been supporting a volcano . . .

It is certainly strange that useful customs and devices do not spread from country to country with more facility and promptness than they do. You step across the German border almost anywhere, and suddenly the German stove has disappeared.[5]

Today's masonry heaters, as demonstrated by the photos in this book, are certainly far from looking like "solemn, unsympathetic tombs." More often than not, they do have glass doors for fire viewing to "rejoice your eye and gladden your heart." In other words, the modern masonry heater would splendidly fulfill the wishes of a man like Mark Twain. Few who run across them in modern times can come up with any reason why masonry heaters are not the quintessential wood-burning device.

There is no doubt that Americans are exposed to masonry heaters. Some see them on television or the movies, but have no idea what they are. Thousands have seen them in museums, art shows, or antiques stores. Compared with European citizens, relatively few have actually lived with and fully experienced masonry heaters, but masonry heaters have existed in the United States and Canada probably as long as immigrants have come from Europe. It has only been in the last forty years, however, that any meaningful market for masonry heaters has been nurtured in North America.

Masonry Heaters in North America

The development of a masonry heater tradition in North America is a short history, but it involves many people. This text does not claim to be a complete history, and this section is merely a brief outline of how some large ideas grew from a few small seeds. There are scores of unnamed artisans who have tirelessly worked in their respective parts of North America to create the conditions for a masonry heater renaissance. Someday their stories will also be told.

Our story begins in the 1970s and early 1980s during the resurgence of the use of wood heat during the "energy crisis." The Middle East oil embargo led to shortages and gas lines in the United States. In inflation-adjusted dollars, gasoline in 1981 reached a high of over $3 per gallon. Heating oil, of course, followed suit. Multitudes looked for alternative solutions, including solar energy and a return to wood for fuel. Though, as we've seen, most of human history was powered by wood, that fuel was replaced slowly by fossil fuels in the twentieth century. When fossil fuel prices skyrocketed, wood became the cheap alternative that offered energy independence to millions.

In the early 1980s the back-to-the-land, energy, and self-sufficiency magazine *Mother Earth News* embarked on a project to build what it called "My Mother's House." Solar energy and earth-sheltering technologies would be used to produce a very-low-energy house built with techniques of relatively low cost. In part 7 of the multi-installment magazine project, the staff in the North Carolina "eco-village" described the construction of a "so-called Russian fireplace."

Their masonry heater was a single-skin, five-flue design by Basilio Lepuschenko, a carpenter from Maine and immigrant from Belarus. In the mid-1970s he had built a masonry heater for his father-in-law using his memories from the old country as his blueprint. The stoves he designed were narrow but long and tall, usually with either three or five vertical flues above the long, low firebox. Mr. Lepuschenko, now deceased, was one of a mere handful of individuals promoting masonry heaters in the United States during the late

FIGURE 2.13. A brick, single-skin (meaning the inner life and veneer are one-and-the-same, see chapter 8) heater built using Basilio Lepuschenko's plans. The doors, from bottom up, are ash cleanout, fuel-loading door, and soot door. The heater was subsequently stuccoed white. **Photo by Dean Witt.**

1970s wood-energy resurgence. Basilio Lepuschenko had some influence on several key individuals across North America.

Lepuschenko even had a brief business relationship with Albie Barden in Norridgewock, Maine. Barden was a non-mason who felt the hand of Providence on his shoulder, urging him to learn about, teach, and build masonry heaters after reading about them in *New Low-Cost Sources of Energy for the Home.*[6] Albie was already selling woodstoves from his home business, the Maine Wood Heat Company. When he saw a masonry heater in that book he knew he had found his life's work and sought out all the information he could. This research led him to both Basilio and a Finnish carpenter, Sam Jaakola, who had built several heaters. With the information he gathered, he began writing articles about masonry heaters and even obtained a book contract. Though he didn't complete that contract,

THE RIPPLES IN THE MASONRY HEATER POND

I ran headlong into the ripples of Albie Barden's early-1980s efforts to promote masonry heaters in 2005. Linda Murray, living in northern Lower Michigan, called and reported that her Finnish fireplace, built circa 1980, was not functioning correctly after being serviced by a local brick mason. Ms. Murray reported that her brick heater had been the primary heat source for her modest timber-frame house since it was constructed twenty-five years earlier.

She had called the local mason in 2004 because she noticed that (after nearly twenty-five years) some of the firebricks looked like they were deteriorating. She reported that, mainly, the rear, lower firebox wall bricks looked noticeably worn, and there was additional minor deterioration on the lower side walls of the firebox as well. Considering how well the heater had performed for so long and how much she depended on it, she decided to have it serviced and brought back to as close as "like new" condition as possible.

Unfortunately, the mason she finally hired for the job (after getting several estimates) admitted he knew nothing about Finnish fireplaces, but was certain he could restore the heater to pristine condition. The method he chose was to completely remove, via the firebox door, all the firebrick innards of the heater. He proceeded to fill all the heat-exchange pathways (critical for the operation of the heater) with rubble and mortar, and build a conventional firebox designed to simply vent directly into the adjacent chimney. When he was "finished," the masonry heater's new firebox exhausted straight up from the chamber, through a narrow throat, and exited directly into the chimney through the bypass channel. A bypass channel is sometimes used in Finnish heaters to allow exhaust to temporarily bypass the heat-exchange flues of the heater—often to aid in initial start-up when the heater is cold. In this mason's redesign, the bypass was the only path the exhaust could take.

Needless to say, the heater no longer functioned as a heater. Murray was at a loss and explained that she had even shown the local mason the construction plans for the heater—a manual written by Albert Barden III. The mason said he didn't need them "because he had experience building hundreds of fireplaces."

When quizzed, she could not recall the names of the original builders of the masonry heater, but they had done a superlative job constructing a basic, no-frills, red-brick-faced heater that had functioned just as designed for two and a half decades. In order to restore the heater to original function, and to preserve the well-executed brick veneer that showed no signs of cracking or deterioration, I only rebuilt the interior core of the heater. I did this partially through the firebox door opening, and completed the balance by reaching down into (and even climbing into) the heater through the removable slabs at the top of the heater. The local mason ended up paying the resulting bill. He paid a high price for not taking some time to understand what a masonry heater is and how it is built.

he self-published a construction manual years later. At about the same time, articles about Lepuschenko's heaters were spreading across North America, and Basilio was drawing up and selling plans for his designs.

By the time David Lyle's *Book of Masonry Stoves* was published in 1984, though Lyle could list a dozen or so North American sources for tile stoves "of one kind or another," Barden and Lepuschenko were singled out as the starting points for an "increasing number of masons . . . experimenting with brick stoves." Barden's fascination with the "new" old technology drove him overseas to learn more. He traveled to Finland in early 1978. A solid tradition of masonry heaters already existed there. Barden sought to learn and develop professional relationships with those who could help him fulfill his calling.

Back in the States in the spring of 1978, Barden asked Lepuschenko to teach two workshops using

Lepuschenko's designs. The workshops were well attended by masons from both Maine and throughout the United States. Albie Barden's masonry heater workshop career had begun. After reading a book by Heikki Hyytiainen, from Finland, Barden called the author and invited himself and mason Doug Wood on a second trip to Finland; they were hosted by Hyytiainen.

A working relationship blossomed, and Heikki Hyytiainen and Albie Barden eventually collaborated on a book, published in Finland in 1988, titled *Finnish Fireplaces: Heart of the Home*. As Heikki stated in the book, "A profound friendship and cooperation was begun which was the basis for this book and several international workshops and business arrangements between American and Finnish heater groups and firms."[7] Indeed, in those early days, Barden hosted a number of workshops under Heikki's direction that piqued the interest of masons all over North America. Like the concentric ripples from a stone dropped in a pond, the message of masonry heaters spread through the continent.

Not long after Barden returned to Maine from his Finnish fireplace odyssey, a customer contacted a masonry-contracting firm on Vashon Island in Washington State. Partners Tom Stroud, Bruce Dietmeyer, and Richard Ward were asked to build a Russian fireplace. Their response was something along the lines of, "What's a Russian fireplace?" Open to new ideas, however, they looked over the instructions for the fireplace—instructions from Basilio Lepuschenko. (Later, they learned these plans were basically identical to plans available from the University of Moscow.) After careful consideration, they presented an estimate to the client, who found the price too high and rejected it. The seed, however, had been planted.

Around about 1980, Dietmeyer, Ward, and Stroud were approached by a German couple desiring a German tile heater—a *kachelofen*. The partners sold them on the Russian design, which they proceeded to build. The team had produced its first masonry heater. Tom Stroud and his cohorts at the time were also part of an intentional community being built on Vashon Island. The Wesleyan Community was geared toward environmentally sound construction, including passive solar attributes and sustainable materials. They quickly realized that the Russian fireplace was a perfect complement to the community's purpose. It wasn't long before they had another half a dozen or more heaters to their credit.

Meanwhile, in the desert Southwest, Jay Jarpe, a research engineer, was working with a group of individuals led by Robert Proctor, a New Mexico adobe mason. Proctor had received a state grant to build eight *grubkas* in various southwest communities. A *grubka* is yet another type of Russian fireplace. It differed from Lepuschenko's design in that it had its firebox door on one of the long faces of the rectangular heater, rather than on one of the narrow ends.

Proctor's ambitious project was sponsored by the University of New Mexico, and funded through the New Mexico Energy Institute. Each of the eight masonry heaters built was unique and installed at a different elevation. All eight heaters were also fitted with thermocouples to monitor thermal performance and to determine how heat traveled through them. Thermocouples are simply temperature sensors. Such a sensor can be inserted anywhere inside the masonry heater with wires leading to the outside of the heater being attached to a monitor for reading the information sensed by the thermocouple. The construction of these heaters was carefully documented by Mr. Jarpe, who then published a manual in May 1981 titled, "Russian Fireplace: Demonstrations and Workshops."[8]

Dietmeyer, Ward, and Stroud were influenced by the designs that came out of Proctor's projects. They liked the greater versatility of the door location on the long side of the heater and began doing their own experiments with design. Tom Stroud began teaching standing-room only seminars in local libraries—twenty to thirty in a year. The public was enthusiastic, and Dietmeyer, Ward, and Stroud knew something special was happening. Not too far away, Jerry Frisch, another Washington State mason, was likewise running seminars and building heaters, as clients had begun approaching him to build "Russian heaters." Having

FIGURE 2.14. The Envirotech Radiant Fireplace became very popular in the Northwest after its introduction by Dietmeyer, Ward, and Stroud, Inc. This brick heater is well placed between a kitchen and living room. Photo courtesy of Envirotech Masonry Heaters.

been born into a union-mason family, Mr. Frisch quickly grasped the concept and ran with it. He would later show a keen interest in Swedish-style *kakelugns* as well as the Finnish and Russian designs.

With the seeds of a masonry heater culture planted in the southwestern, northwestern, and northeastern parts of the United States, the birth of an entire new industry was imminent. In the East, Barden was busily teaching workshops, predominantly about Finnish fireplaces, in the mid-1980s. He had added cookers (cookstove/ovens) to his repertoire. He likewise was instrumental in bringing a large soapstone masonry heater company, Tulikivi, into the United States. He had also become an importer of quality cast-iron doors and other heater hardware from Finland.

In the Northwest, Tom Stroud and his partners got

the attention of a fifth-generation *kachelofen* builder named Ernst Heuft. Besides being born into a family of heater builders, Heuft went to *kachelofen* school in Stuttgart as a young man. Reluctant at first, he eventually worked with and trained the team for several years. They began building heaters of every shape and size, including two-story behemoths. They built ovens, both domestic and commercial, and masonry cookstoves. Their efforts culminated in their creating a manufactured heater-core kit, the Envirotech Radiant Fireplace (see chapter 8), and a long run of heater building that Stroud estimates resulted in approximately one thousand heaters being built by Dietmeyer, Ward, and Stroud between roughly 1980 and 2000.

By 1990 Barden, on the East Coast, had spoken to dozens of masons at various workshops, and this veritable army of fledgling heater masons was busy spreading the heater gospel in their respective states and municipalities.

In 1988, masonry heaters received exempt status from the US Environmental Protection Agency (EPA). The EPA recognized that masonry heaters are inherently clean burning because they burn wood in a confined firebox with plenty of oxygen and thus have high combustion efficiency. In addition, they recognized that it was not possible to place masonry heaters, which weigh significantly more than the maximum 1,764 pounds, on the typical scales laboratories use to conduct woodstove burn rate and emissions tests.

By 1992, masonry heater proponents, as part of a new ASTM International task group, had secured a new ASTM specification, E-1602. This new specification officially defined masonry heaters and described their attributes in a way that could be understood and accepted by building-code officials around the nation. With EPA recognition as "exempt" and "clean," and with a tool to satisfy building departments, the doors to masonry heater building were wide open by the mid-1990s. Since then, thousands of masonry heaters have been built in North America, and heater masons are growing in both knowledge and number wherever heat for homes is required.

The Fireplace of the Future?

As this book goes to press, the EPA is again reviewing and updating its New Source Product Standards (NSPS). This time, it appears that masonry heaters will not be set aside as simply "exempt." The EPA has been charged to regulate any appliance that burns wood, and masonry heaters are also in their sights. However, masonry heaters have a firm history of high efficiencies and tested cleanliness both in North America and around the world. It may be that masonry heaters will set the standard for all other wood-burning devices.

Whatever may happen, it can now be said that there is, indeed, a masonry heater tradition in North America. Each year more and more heaters are built. Each year more and more masons learn the trade. Those deeply involved in the business of masonry heaters—especially those who have been around them since Basilio Lepuschenko first built a heater for his father-in-law back in the 1970s—can see the volume of interest nearing the point at which it may result in exponential growth. When critical mass hits, it may be seen in short order how American ingenuity can propel a very good thing to historical greatness. At one time in America, each loaf of bread made was assembled, kneaded, and baked by the hands of individual bakers. Now a "bakery" is a manufacturing facility turning out thousands of loaves in a day. This has made bread inexpensive and abundant. The same resourcefulness could make high-efficiency masonry heaters abundant and inexpensive in America. While masonry heaters now are often built by individual artisans, the future may find something different happening. The time to find out is fast approaching.

FIGURE 3.1. This unusual red sandstone masonry heater was designed on the fly, piece by piece. It incorporates 5-inch-thick sandstone slabs for the raised hearth—all cut from the same huge slab of stone. Some of the "scrap" from that (some scraps measured 2 or 3 feet square) formed the upper veneer of the heater below the level of the bakeoven. Other views of this heater can be seen in figures 6.31, 6.36, and 6.43. Heater by Maren Cooke and Ken Matesz; photo by Maren Cooke.

CHAPTER THREE

Thermal Comfort: The Vertical Radiant Advantage

Most people in the United States have never lived in a house that is heated. This may seem a ludicrous claim, but it's nevertheless true. Many are used to saying, "I heat my house with a gas furnace," or "I grew up in a house heated with those old-fashioned radiators." When someone says they live in a house heated with a forced-air furnace but they want to heat their home or room addition with a masonry heater, the truth is that at last they will experience a home that is actually heated.

Masonry heaters are unique heating systems. A masonry heater is, in fact, one of the only ways of heating that actually "heats a house." Many will find this statement a little confusing; they are sure that they have always lived in a warm house. Most heating systems *do not* heat houses. Instead, they provide the occupants with some measure of thermal comfort. Thermal comfort can be achieved independently from houses and heating systems, so it will be helpful to say a bit more about it.

Thermal Comfort

Those who work in the heating or air-conditioning fields must address thermal comfort in every season. Thermal comfort in the summer will relate to how comfortable people feel in the midst of warm or even hot and humid weather conditions. Technically speaking, this topic relates to how people feel in all environments, whether inside or outdoors, in hot summer or frigid winter. Thermal comfort for purposes of this book refers to whether or not people feel comfortable—maybe even warm—in an environment that, without the use of energy, would be quite cool or cold. You don't have to be warm to be comfortable.

What does it mean to feel warm? What does it mean to have thermal comfort? These may seem odd questions at first. Most people might say they know when they are warm and when they are cold; surely they know when they are comfortable. Yet some experience comfort differently than others. Children often parade around outside in shorts and bare feet on days when adults feel chilled. Warmth is relative also. If you've been outside on a cold, snowy day, a room at 55°F seems warm; but if you sit in that room for a while without wearing a coat, you'll likely begin to feel chilly again. This chapter will clarify what it means to be warm rather than just comfortable.

Thermodynamics and Metabolism

Thermal comfort can be defined in a scientific way that tries to measure the perception of warmth. A more objective examination of thermal comfort involves the physics and biology of heat. One branch of physics deals with thermodynamics—the study of changing energy conditions, often in relation to matter in motion. Considering that the human organism is all matter in motion, thermodynamics and human biology are intimately related.

The human body is a heat engine. The metabolism is a heat-producing machine, in fact. The word *metabolism* comes from the Greek *metabol* , meaning "change." Living bodies are all about transformation. Food is eaten and the body efficiently changes the fuel, extracting the energy and nutrients. The body uses these basic materials and the extracted energy to do work, like building or repairing cells and producing the heat it needs to survive. The ability to do physical work comes from that same metabolism.

The human body actually produces excess heat in the process. That heat is dissipated into the environment

FIGURE 3.2. A unique source of thermal comfort: A vertical heater for vertical people. This custom soapstone heater consists of two primary elements. The firebox is contained in the shorter part; the taller part contains most of the flues. The round "disks" are ash cleanout covers, revealing clues as to where various flues are located. Every flue needs a way to be accessed for eventual cleaning. Photo courtesy of New England Hearth and Soapstone.

FIGURE 3.3. This heater features cut stone in an ashlar pattern. One of the two columns rising all the way to the ceiling contains the chimney flue. The other could contain a flue from another appliance or could just balance the appearance. Notice how the vigorous fire fills the whole firebox. Photo courtesy of Temp-Cast Enviroheat.

through evaporation, convection, and radiation. In round numbers, about 25 percent of the excess heat is lost through the evaporation of moisture from the skin. Convection accounts for 15 to 25 percent of the heat loss. (Convection heat loss occurs through exhalation and the action of air movement against the skin.) Radiation—the emission of infrared radiant heat from all body surfaces—then accounts for the remaining 50 to 60 percent. The body is always losing its excess heat in all of these ways.

The key to thermal comfort is tied to this natural

heat dissipation, together with the second law of thermodynamics, which says that heat always moves from warmer areas to colder. This law also says that heat *never* travels the other way—from colder to warmer—without an expenditure of energy. Thus when I set my hot coffee on the table next to me, it always gets cooler and never warmer. Its heat dissipates into the room air and the table below it. Most of that heat is lost to the surrounding air, which rises in temperature by an imperceptible amount because of the heat from the coffee. Some of the heat is transferred to the table below, and I can feel it if I move my cup for a moment. (Someone might argue that ice water set on the table transfers cold to the table—which can be felt when the glass is moved—in apparent violation of this law. The truth is that heat is rapidly moving *from* the table *to* the ice water and thereby greatly reducing the table temperature.)

If I set my fresh, hot coffee in an oven that's 150°F, it will stay hot longer. It will still cool because the coffee started at over 200°. The second law dictates that it has to cool (to release its heat to the slightly cooler surroundings). The warmer surrounding air slows the heat loss. If I put the coffee in the oven at, say, 205°, the coffee would stay unchanged in temperature. Heat loss from the coffee is now zero.

While minimizing heat loss from coffee sounds terrific, humans won't do very well if their excess heat loss is stopped. As heat engines, people need to be able to release excess heat. The normal core temperature of a human is about 98.6°F. The normal skin temperature is 83° to 92°. If the ambient air is also 98.6° (and there is no wind for evaporative cooling), the second law of thermodynamics demands that heat travel from the surroundings, which are hotter, to the skin. Under these conditions (zero heat loss), a person at rest would continue getting warmer and warmer by about 1.8° per hour rather than feeling comfortable. An individual subjected to this heat transfer will eventually suffer from heatstroke and worse.

Instead, it turns out that human beings usually feel comfortable with an ambient temperature around the 70°F mark. Thermal comfort is more likely when temperatures are close to that mark; yet no single temperature is a guarantee of that comfort.

In the final analysis, feeling thermally comfortable is all about heat loss from the body. Thermal comfort isn't about being warm at all. It's more about *feeling too much heat loss or feeling that not enough heat is being lost*. In most heated living spaces people experience some degree of thermal comfort, but they may *feel* either hot or cold. It's possible to go into a home with an indoor temperature of 72°F and *feel* cold. Likewise, it's possible to be in an environment with an average air temperature of 65°F and *feel* hot. Too much heat loss results in feeling cold; not enough heat loss results in

feeling hot. Like Goldilocks's porridge, the balance has to be just right.

Thermoregulation

Fortunately, the human body also has an incredible capacity for adjusting to its environment. This capacity is called thermoregulation. If you feel cold in a house heated to 72°F, it is often because the air around the house is moving. The forced-air furnace blows air, making the curtains dance and your goose bumps grow. You can feel the air move against your hands and cheeks. Meteorologists talk about this phenomenon often in the winter: It's the windchill factor. Moving air at a given temperature feels colder than stationary air at that temperature. Air moving against the skin dramatically increases (convective) heat loss. The increased heat loss triggers the thermoregulatory system to constrict blood vessels in the skin, reducing blood flow to the skin. Blood, one of the primary carriers of heat through the body, can't travel as readily through constricted blood vessels. The body is thus conserving heat—which it needs to do to stay alive. In turn, the reduced blood flow, particularly in the hands and feet, results in the feeling of being cold. Indeed, the surface temperature of the skin under these conditions can get quite low (55° to 65°), even inside an otherwise "warm" house.

Similarly, you can sit near a large window in a "warm" house and feel cold—feel too much heat loss. Often the surface temperature of a window is substantially lower than the other surface temperatures and indoor air temperature. If you observe carefully, you can almost feel heat being sucked from your body toward a cold surface. In this case, you lose an inordinate amount of radiant heat to the window. Like the ice water on the table, the cold window draws heat from all the warmer objects nearby. Again, the skin cools too quickly and the blood vessels constrict. Once again you feel cold as your body acts to prevent excess heat loss.

An additional factor in feeling too much or not enough heat loss is relative humidity. Evaporation of moisture from the skin is another way the body dissipates its heat. In a fashion similar to convective heat exchange, the environment will always seek moisture equilibrium. The laws of physics will not allow something mildly damp to exist against something very dry. Moist skin will quickly lose moisture in dry air. In a room with low humidity of 20 percent, evaporative heat loss from people is much greater than in a room with a relative humidity of 40 percent. This, in fact, is much of what is experienced with summertime air-conditioning. An air conditioner greatly reduces the indoor humidity, and the increased evaporative heat loss from the body makes you feel cooler. In the winter, when the body craves warmth, however, losing moisture too fast triggers the body's heat conservation measures again. Thermoregulation closes the pores of the skin, constricts blood vessels, and reduces blood flow.

The body's ability to adjust to these circumstances is incredible, but not complete. This is, after all, why a protective indoor environment is needed—to compensate for the body's thermoregulation limits. The "just right" conditions actually fit into a relatively narrow range, beyond which the body struggles to compensate. It is that biological struggle against excess heat loss that people are noticing when they say they feel cold. In a setting where heat loss is "just right," no struggle emerges. In the words of John Sieganthaler, in his booklet *Radiant Architecture,* "Thermal comfort is achieved when we are totally unaware of how or where our bodies are losing heat."[1]

With an understanding of what it means to have thermal comfort, it's possible to begin to see why some people claim to have warm houses, but still may not have thermal comfort. Thermal comfort—feeling warm—is not just a matter of setting a thermostat to a certain temperature. In the same way that experiencing life means more than just inhaling and exhaling, feeling warm means more than just living in a house kept at a certain temperature.

What Heats the House?

I have never heard someone ask, "How can I make sure my family never suffers excess heat loss from their bodies?" Yet the previous section showed that this really is the question that needs to be asked if we want thermal comfort. "Heating a house," as we normally understand it, is not really about heating a house at all; it's about thermal comfort for the people inside the house. Narrowing the focus to determine how to achieve thermal comfort requires understanding what heating options there are and discovering how those options approach the goal of thermal comfort. What method of heating is being used? Does it provide thermal comfort? If not, why not?

In general, most people have a heating system that reduces *most* excess heat loss from *most* occupants. In general, designers of heating systems expect that if a heating system provides a degree of comfort to 85 percent of the people who experience it, it is adequate. There is something amiss when it becomes acceptable that 15 percent of the people in a house may be uncomfortable. Would anyone want 15 percent of their housemates hungry? Ill? Unhappy? If not, why would anyone be content with 15 percent of the people in their homes being unable to have thermal comfort?

Another way of saying this is that in a family of seven, it's acceptable for one of them to be uncomfortable. That's really unfortunate for the seventh individual. Often it's an older person whose thermoregulatory system is not quite what it once was. Everyone is different, though, and sometimes it's a very healthy, robust individual who simply doesn't have a good experience in a climate that others find adequate. Sometimes it's not the members of the household at all. Instead it's a guest who prods his wife to take him home early because he can't feel comfortable in the house he visits.

Another version of this same issue is when one or two people are uncomfortably warm when the others are happy. This is the classic dilemma in which perhaps the wife is adjusting the thermostat higher only to have the husband, feeling too warm, adjusting it lower. Neither is quite comfortable in the climate the other prefers, and so the battle goes on day after day.

These are the dilemmas faced by all those seeking that "just right" environment. Yet somehow this dilemma is often completely ignored when selecting a way of "feeling warm" in a new or remodeled house.

FIGURE 3.4. This stucco-and-tile masonry heater incorporates wood for the bench surfaces. Corners are gently rounded, giving the otherwise rectilinear elements a soft appearance. The black loading door gives the classic European look and hints at a small firebox. The shape of the tiles is a traditional one as well. Notice how the heater's bench steps down to the left to follow the level change in the room. Photo courtesy of Biofire, Inc.

More often than not, people accept this either–or situation as the only reality, and choose not to address the real problem of how to create thermal comfort for everyone in the home. In the end, most people still choose one of the most common ways of combating excess heat loss, whatever its shortcomings.

Convection Heat

Convection heating is by far the most widely used heating system in the United States today. An estimated 80 percent of homes throughout the country use some form of convection heating system. A convection heating device works predominantly by heating air and

FIGURE 3.5. This brick-faced masonry heater has a massive heated sitting area to the left. The exhaust travels through flues inside the bench directly after leaving the firebox. The curved shape of the bench expands the walkway from the stairs on the left. Figures 4.6 and 5.1 show other views of this heater.

circulating that warm air throughout the building. Such a system usually comprises a furnace, a fan, and ductwork. The furnace heats the air, and the fan blows it through the ductwork to all parts of the house. Thus it is called a forced-air heating system. Such an arrangement may have a furnace that uses electricity or burns natural gas, fuel oil, propane, or wood to heat the air.

Some of these setups are very sophisticated and may also be part of a larger geothermal system for both heating and cooling. Geothermal furnaces make use of the earth's stored heat to reduce the energy needed to heat or cool air. Geothermal heating methods are often thought of as the most energy-efficient systems available.

Other convection heating arrangements are less complex or are slight variations on the furnace/blower/ducts theme. For example, hot-water radiators are also convection heaters. Here a boiler heats water, which is pumped to radiators in the rooms of the house. The hot radiator in the room warms adjacent air, which rises toward the ceiling, pulling cooler air behind it that is also then warmed by the radiator. This establishes a convection current of air constantly circulating through the room. The hottest air rises and moves across the ceiling while the cooler air travels along the floor toward the radiator. Similarly, electric baseboard heaters use electrical resistance to heat metal elements that power the convection current. The common metal

TYPES OF HEAT TRANSFER

Convection: A convection heating device works predominantly to heat air. A baseboard electric heater, for example, has a very small surface area but achieves quite high temperatures on its surface. These high temperatures encourage convection as cool air approaches the hot elements, gets warmed by that heat, then rises toward the ceiling. This moving air pulls behind it yet more cool air that also is warmed by the heater. A cycle has thus begun that sends warm air up and across the room or living area as cool air continues to be pulled behind the buoyant rising mass.

Conduction: A conduction heating device works to warm something by direct contact. For example, a cold teakettle placed on a hot electric burner of a stovetop will be warmed by that direct contact. Conduction is not a practical space-heating method because it requires constant direct contact with the heat source.

Radiation: A radiant heat transfer involves the movement of heat energy across space and does not require air or contact with objects for the transfer to occur. *Infrared electromagnetic radiation* is the more scientific term for radiant heat. The most familiar example is sunshine streaming through the window of a home. Someone stepping into the path of the sunshine immediately feels warmth from it.

woodstove is perhaps one of the simplest convection heaters. Like the hot-water radiator, metal woodstoves rely mainly on very hot surface temperatures to establish convection currents. All of these systems, in one way or another, mainly heat air.

In a house filled with warm air, the house and people are not heated by that warm air. This is important to realize because it reveals the true nature of convection heating methods. Thick quilts, sweaters, hats, gloves, spun fiberglass, walls, and warm air are all just blankets. They all serve as insulation to keep your body heat from escaping too quickly to the cold outdoors. They do not warm the body; they simply keep the body from losing heat too quickly. Since everybody is different, not every *body* will be comfortable with the same level of insulation. This is the crux of the problem with convection heating. It proposes to insulate every person the same way and merely hopes that this will be sufficient. As stated before, however, this doesn't work for 15 percent of occupants.

For those who *are* thermally comfortable in an environment heated this way, it is vital that the warm air be maintained always at the same temperature or very close to it. If the air temperature drops just a few degrees, it's the same as taking a layer of clothes off while outside. Body heat dissipates more quickly, and it doesn't take long to feel cold. The truth is that millions of people in cold regions of America burn copious amounts of nonrenewable fuels to maintain a high-tech blanket of air around themselves, and many of them still aren't comfortable.

Radiant Heat

Less common but gaining in popularity are forms of radiant heating. Many people today equate radiant heat with in-floor heat. Masonry heaters certainly are sources of radiant heat. While the convective heating methods described above strive to do an efficient job of heating air, radiant systems make little attempt to do so. In fact, radiant heat is the only kind of heat energy that can travel through a vacuum. All radiant systems function in a similar fashion for heating. Generally, some means is used to uniformly heat materials, as when warm water is circulated through tubes in a floor. The warmed materials then become a source of radiant heat. Preferably, masonry or other dense materials are employed for this.

Radiant heat is less understood than convection heat. Most likely this is because so few people actually live with a radiant heating system compared with the near monopoly held by convection heating systems. Telling most people that thermal radiation is entirely different from heating air is like telling a fish that it's

FIGURE 3.6. Front view of the heater shown in figures 4.8 and 8.1. This *kachelofen* was designed, built, and photographed by Ernst Kiesling, Canadian Kachelofen.

also possible for other beings to live in air instead of water. There's no experience on which to base a discussion, so most people assume radiant heat acts just like hot air. Radiant heat doesn't behave like hot air. In fact, radiant heat does not need air at all to do its job.

Getting back to physics, radiant heat is infrared electromagnetic radiation. The type of electromagnetic radiation with which people are most familiar is light. When a light switch is flipped, light immediately travels at, well, the speed of light from the lightbulb to areas all over the room. Light and all electromagnetic radiation travels at 186,000 miles per second; and it will travel that fast throughout a room regardless of the temperature of the air. That's why a campfire is so pleasant even on a cold autumn night. Infrared radiant heat travels directly from the fire to people even when the air is frigid. Radiant heat from masonry heaters and radiant floors is only different from light in that it is not visible. Otherwise, it too travels at the speed of light without the aid or need of air. The radiant heat with which most people are familiar is that from the sun. Everyone has felt the radiant heat of the sun on their cheeks, shoulders, or arms.

Despite explanations of the nature of radiant heat, invariably someone asks, "Yes, but the heat still rises, right?" No. Radiant heat does not rise. In fact, heat does not rise in any case. Hot *air* does rise because it is less dense than cooler air. It is always warm air

that rises and pools in cathedral ceilings and goes up chimneys—but radiant heat does not rise. There is no way to make radiant heat "rise" other than pointing the radiating object upward, just as a warm floor radiates heat toward the ceiling or the radiant heat from some vertical object is somehow reflected upward.

Otherwise, infrared radiation travels as rays directly from a warm *object* until it reaches another *object* that, if cooler, absorbs the radiant heat. Radiant heat is absorbed by things of some mass. It is not absorbed by air. In fact, every object that is warmer than the things around it is a radiant heater. The color of things also influences whether (or how much) radiant heat is absorbed. Dark objects will absorb more radiant heat than lighter ones; and shiny metal, like aluminum foil, reflects radiant heat just like a mirror reflects light.

Radiant heat is absorbed by an object if the target object is cooler. The second law of thermodynamics is unyielding. Something warmer than a radiant object will not absorb heat from that object. Just the opposite will happen: The warmer object always lends its heat to the cooler. This property of heat makes radiant heaters somewhat self-regulating. Just as the hot coffee in a 205°F oven loses no heat, a radiant heater naturally slows its heating (conserves energy) as surrounding objects get warmer. Likewise, as the surroundings get cooler, the heat exchange from the radiant source is greater. The temperature difference between objects largely controls how quickly heat is exchanged. When objects are virtually the same temperature, no significant radiant gain occurs by either object.

Another principle of radiant heaters is that the distance from the heat source affects the intensity of the heat. Thinking of light again, when automobile headlights are seen from a great distance on a pitch-dark night, they are seen as two pinpricks of light. But when the automobile is only 20 feet away, the whole

FIGURE 3.7. This massive soapstone heater is meant to resemble a large boulder. The whole veneer consists of large split-faced stones carefully shaped to blend together as if it were one piece. A multisided door makes fire viewing possible from many angles in the living space. Photo courtesy of Tulikivi Corporation.

FIGURE 3.8. This unique brick-and-soapstone heater features a spacious raised hearth. The bench surface, mantel, and shelves are all made of soapstone. The built-in wood storage and shelves provide both visual interest and practical storage. An arched door and matching arch over the niches are an elegant touch. Photo courtesy of New England Hearth and Soapstone.

area in front of the car is brightly lit. Similarly, with infrared radiant heat, the heat is felt more intensely when you're closer to the radiant heat source, but may not be felt at all from a significant distance. When I put my hands close around, but not touching, my hot coffee cup, I feel its radiant heat; however, I cannot sense that heat when I move my hands a couple of feet away, even though the radiant heat is still contacting my hand. The distance has reduced its intensity.

Infrared radiant heat, again like light, also casts "shadows." A light shining on the front of a solid object casts a shadow behind it. Similarly, an object facing a radiant heat source can have a heatless shadow behind it. Thus if someone puts a hand between mine and the coffee cup, I will no longer feel the radiant heat from the cup. My hand is in the thermal shadow of the intervening hand. When planning to heat with a radiant source, designers and homeowners need to be aware that everything in the house can cast such a heatless shadow. Walls, furniture, rugs, ceilings, and people all have an effect on how well the radiant heat

is felt throughout a house. The most effective design for radiant heat provides the maximum exposure to the radiant source and creates the fewest shadows.

In-Floor Heating

In-floor heating often has flexible, very strong tubing run in a serpentine pattern and embedded in concrete under the finished floor of a room, area, or whole house. Sometimes even the concrete is omitted and the tubing is simply placed under a wood or tile floor directly. A pump circulates hot water from a boiler to this maze of tubing. In this way it is very similar to the hot-water convection heating system mentioned above. This same job of heating the floor is also sometimes done with electrical resistance. In this case, a length of heat-generating electrical wire is embedded in the floor.

Proponents of in-floor heating primarily like to call their systems "radiant floors." In-floor heat does indeed emit radiant heat. (Remember, any object warmer than surrounding objects is a radiant heater.) There are some important reasons why a radiant floor should not be considered a radiant heating system, however.

First, a warm floor simply isn't warm enough to be felt and appreciated as radiant heat. Most radiant floors are maintained at 80° to 85°F. Human skin temperature averages 83° to 92°. People are simply warmer than warm floors. While writing this, I happened upon an advertisement for "radiant" floors in a home magazine. I found it fascinating that the ad used a picture of two adults lying on the floor. Now, I've seen a lot of kids lying on, sitting on, and playing on the floor, but it's unusual for adults to lie on the floor. Of course, this advertisement is right on the money: If someone with such a floor wants to truly enjoy the benefits of this heat on his whole body, the best option is to lie on the floor because the floor is simply not warm enough to truly provide radiant heat to people.

Second, a warm floor, with its large surface area, will necessarily expose a lot of air to its warm surface, thereby heating more via convection. According to John Sieganthaler, "A typical 'radiant' floor system gives off 50% to 70% of its heat as thermal radiation."[2] The quotes around "radiant" are his, apparently in acknowledgment that such a floor is only marginally a true radiant panel. B. F. Raber and F. W. Hutchinson, in their book *Panel Heating and Cooling Analysis,* address this question specifically: When discussing the definition of *radiant panels,* the authors clearly state that "[This] definition is very loose, for it does not distinguish between floor heating panels, which dissipate the greater part of their energy by convection,"[3] and vertical panels that have a greater proportion of their heat dissipation by infrared radiation.

Next, even if a "radiant" floor were a lot warmer, it would still not be experienced as a warm presence like the sun. The horizontal surface of the floor is sending most of its radiant heat vertically. (Infrared rays primarily, though not entirely, depart an object perpendicular to the radiating surface.) Thus, most of the radiant heat from a warm floor bypasses vertical objects like walls and human beings. It is very low-intensity radiant heat that parallels vertical things on its way to the ceiling. You can imagine what the infrared rays "see" of people and things standing on the floor. If the floor were made of glass and someone in the basement looked straight up into the room above, that person would see mainly the soles of feet and just a small cross section of hands, and maybe hips and chins. Also seen would be the undersides of furniture, which, although close to the floor, never get warm enough to become radiating bodies themselves.

Anytime warm floors are discussed, we must consider heating by conduction. Conduction of heat directly to people is a major factor when you opt to have heated floors. To many, the feel of warm floors on the feet is the primary reason for selecting "radiant" floors. The direct contact with the floor, the conducted heat (when the feet are actually cooler than the floor), is what feels good.

These aspects of warm floors show that warm floors really are, mainly, warm floors and not radiant heating devices. Approximately half of such a floor's heat energy is used to heat the air, just like other convection systems. Their primary comfort is achieved by conduction to people's feet, while the remaining radiant aspect is too weak to really be noticed.

FIGURE 3.9. A unique brick and tile-faced heater built according to the system of free gas movement (see chapter 8). The heater incorporates storage and/or work space above the firebox as well as a built-in wood-storage area. On the left side is the door for the integral baking oven. See the other side of this beautiful heater in figure 3.10. Heater designed and built by Stovemaster; photo courtesy of Alex Chernov.

Masonry Heaters

A masonry heater is a true radiant heating system. Except for doors and sometimes chimney dampers, the whole construction is of masonry. The operating principle is simple: The heat from a wood fire is absorbed by the large mass of masonry construction. Often this is augmented by a maze of flues running between the firebox (where the wood burns) and the chimney (through which the remaining warm exhaust exits the house). The various flues direct hot exhaust gases from the fire against as much masonry as possible. This mass becomes warm and radiates that stored heat to the environment.

Most operating masonry heaters will have surface temperatures ranging from 120° to 200°F most of the time. Of course, the surface temperature will vary with the quantity and quality of the fuel that is burned as well as the exact material of which the heater is made. It will also depend on how often the masonry heater has been used. For example, a masonry heater being used in the fall in a home in central Kentucky may only get fired once every two days. In this case, the surface temperatures might stay quite low. But in a home in northern Michigan in January, the heater may get fired as much as twice in one day, and surface temperatures may average 140° to 175°. There are actually many factors that will affect both how the masonry heater is used and how high its surface temperatures will be. (These factors will be addressed in greater detail in chapter 8.) The major point is that under most conditions of heating, the masonry heater will have much higher surface temperatures than other "radiant" heating systems such as warm floors.

The Vertical Radiant Heat Advantage

Most of us have experienced an early-autumn day when the sky is clear and blue and the sun is high in the sky. The temperature is 65°F and there is no wind. On such a day we feel the sun at its best. The warmth penetrates the skin. With eyes closed, we can feel the sun first on one shoulder, then the back, then the other shoulder. It's a luxurious, deeply felt, deeply memorable experience. To be standing in the sun on such a day is to feel the warmth of a masonry heater.

A masonry heater is usually a vertical structure. Most range in height from about 3 feet to around 7 feet. Human beings are vertical beasts. Except when sleeping, covered by sheets and quilts, people stand and sit vertically. Like the masonry heaters, most people are 3 to 7 feet tall. It's a perfect match. Human beings radiate heat. Masonry heaters radiate heat more intensely than people do. The result is that people near masonry heaters feel the warmth the same way they feel the sun. The heat from the sun and from a masonry heater is genuine heat, instead of insulation against the loss of heat.

FIGURE 3.10. This is the backside of the heater shown in figure 3.9. The bakeoven door is on the right, and heated seating on the far left. Notice how the tile pattern is echoed in the floor. It's a lifetime, heirloom heater. Heater designed and built by Stovemaster; photo courtesy of Alex Chernov.

Once you really have an understanding of radiant heat, it's easy to see why it is more desirable than most other options. Really, who could prefer to have blowing lukewarm air when they could have the warm sun on their shoulders? Gentle, radiant heat can be felt as soothing, penetrating heat from a distance. Gentle, radiant heat is felt by people who experience the sun or a masonry heater. A masonry heater heats people from head to toe. The infrared rays from a vertical masonry heater "see" the whole face or profile of an individual. The feet, legs, torso, and head are all "targets" for that radiant heat.

In addition, because the masonry heater is contributing significant heat to walls and furniture from top to bottom, those items are warmer than in a conventionally heated home. Everything in the vicinity of a masonry heater has a higher surface temperature. With higher surface temperatures, heat loss from the body to these objects is reduced. Cold spots in a room are less likely. Even windows, especially those with a low-emissivity (low-e) coating, have warmer temperatures and draw significantly less heat from people sitting near them.

The masonry heater is much warmer than the people and things around it. At just 120°F, it is 50° to 55° warmer than most things around it and at least 35° warmer than people. A masonry heater at full output, with surface temperatures at 150° or more, has an even larger radiant portion. For this reason, a masonry heater is predominantly a radiant heater, giving out 70 to 80 percent of its heat in the form of infrared radiation. This is why people who walk into a room with a warm masonry heater know right away that something special is happening. Some people, upon encountering the heat from a masonry heater, mistakenly, or perhaps innately, look out the window to locate the sun. They know that feeling so distinctly as the radiant warmth that usually comes from the sun.

Masonry heaters heat all things, including walls, floors, furniture, cups, china dolls, dogs, cats, and people. The infrared radiation from a vertical masonry heater warms anything that gets in its way. The result is that every "thing" becomes a battery for heat. Even the items casting heat "shadows" are being thoroughly warmed so that they, too, become radiant heaters. A dividing wall, for example, may get warm and provide radiant heat to the room on the far side of that wall from the masonry heater. At the very least, the much higher surface temperatures will make them more comfortable to be around, lean against, or sit upon and will influence overall air temperature as well.

Masonry heaters address radiant heat in a very practical way. As vertical animals, it makes sense for human beings to live with a vertical radiant heater. The individual in the chair in a room heated by a masonry heater is experiencing full sunlight. The chair, the person, the feet on the stool are all "solar" collectors being hit constantly with radiant heat from a vertical wall that is much warmer than the body and other surface temperatures. The masonry heater permits all people, whether they are sitting on the floor, sitting on a sofa with their legs up, or standing at the kitchen counter, to experience direct radiant heat to all parts of the body.

This vertical radiant advantage is why *everybody* exposed to a masonry heater is truly warmed. A masonry heater isn't just preventing excess heat loss from people, it's actually warming them. Under these conditions, 100 percent of the people present get directly heated, not just the 85 percent target other heating systems achieve. Every person can find a spot that suits their individual warmth requirements. A masonry heater is the only type of heater that truly heats the house, everything, and everyone in it. Each person can experience warmth to the level of his or her need.

On a cold day, someone who comes in the house from a blustery walk in the park may perhaps want to sit as close as possible to something very warm. The masonry heater provides that very warm spot. This person can pull a chair right next to the radiant stones of the heater, or sit on the built-in benches and get the maximum heat benefit. (Masonry heaters can also be enjoyed for direct conducted heat. Often people will lean on, sit against, or lie on a masonry heater just as Heidi did at her home in the Alps and Jancsi did in old Hungary.)

On the other hand, those with high metabolisms, including children and active individuals, may never feel cold. These people may not be interested in sitting right next to the masonry heater. Instead, they will be quite comfortable across the room or even in another room and away from the stove. Another person who has not been outside but whose circulation isn't all that great may find the perfect spot to be just a few feet away from the masonry heater.

Additionally, a person's need for warmth may change over the course of a day. Some may feel chilly when they first get out of bed in the morning, but after their morning coffee may have no trouble staying warm. Someone else may feel warm most of the time but when getting tired at the end of the day feel less warm. Later, the person who got warm on the cozy benches of the heater after a cold walk in the park

moves across the room once recovered from the chill of the outdoor adventure. A masonry heater is the only type of heater that works perfectly for each individual. It automatically, without electronic gadgets or other bells and whistles, provides a comfort level for everyone in the house.

The Ultimate Shadows and the Convective Remnant

Many people, after reading about the way masonry heaters work, ask a very obvious question: "How does one heat the second floor or the bedroom end of the house if the masonry heater is in the main living area?" It is clear that the shadows previously described are still an obstacle to the radiant performance of a masonry heater. When a masonry heater is on the first floor, all the second-floor rooms are shaded from it by the intervening floor. Likewise, in a single-story home, there may be rooms separated by multiple walls from the heater. These are the ultimate shadows for a masonry heater.

There is little hope of feeling direct radiant heat in a room separated from the masonry heater by multiple walls. These rooms are analogous to a forest; the main area in which the masonry heater sits can be thought of as a meadow with bright sunshine. As long as you stay in the sunny meadow, you'll feel the direct warmth of the sun. When you step among the trees, however, the experience of soothing radiant heat is gone.

The important thing to notice is that the absence of the direct radiant heat does not mean that you'll feel cold in the woods. Rather, what is experienced is a similar air temperature but the absence of the radiant warmth. If the air temperature is 70°F in the sunny meadow, it is most likely near 70° under the trees. The air temperature may even be exactly the same in both locations, though usually the temperature is slightly less in the shade.

It is necessary to think about how the areas of

FIGURE 3.12. When there's a masonry heater, there is always a warm place in the house. This heater of soapstone and stucco occupies one end of a large room. The chimney is sandwiched between the heater and the built-in shelves and wood-storage area. It's a picture of simplicity and elegance. Photo courtesy of New England Hearth and Soapstone.

the house are used and how heating energy can be most wisely consumed. In Europe, where heating with masonry heaters is more common, homeowners think critically about how they will be using the home. If the main living areas are adequately warmed by radiant heat, people may not be interested at all in adding significant heat to distant bedrooms. After all, most people, European or not, spend very little time anywhere but in the main living areas during waking hours. When sleeping, they are in a bed with pajamas and quilts over them. Many even prefer cooler conditions for sleeping. It's irrelevant to consider the lack of radiant heat in a room in which you'll be covered with quilts and sleeping. As long as these distant rooms, then, are reasonably warm, there is no reason to expend energy to introduce radiant heat to them.

On the other hand, if a room distant from the primary masonry heater will be used often, the solution may be different. For example, a study or office tucked away for privacy and quiet may be frequently used. In this case, you'd consider installing a small masonry heater in this room. Similarly, in two-story homes, a heater stacked on top of the main-floor heater may be

FIGURE 3.11. Conduction heat from a masonry heater can be enjoyed via seats or benches, and children or pets will always find those spots. This massive granite heater rests dead center in a large home. This heater boasts complete wraparound heated benches and a bakeoven in the chamber above the main firebox. Photo courtesy of Maine Wood Heat Company.

FIGURE 3.13. A masonry heater warms every thing that it "sees." This one sees both the living and dining areas from its central location. The asymmetric shape provides varying levels for placing decorative objects. Tile accents complete the unique look. Under the wood-topped benches are niches for storage of wood or other items. Notice how the chimney becomes part of the asymmetry and decoration. Photo courtesy of Biofire, Inc.

a viable solution. (For more on this option, see chapters 5 and 6.) This way, you can use radiant heat in this oft-visited space when needed, yet you have the option of not firing the heater if the room will not be extensively used over some period.

Earlier, I mentioned that 70 to 80 percent of the heat from a masonry heater is emitted as radiant heat. The remaining 20 to 30 percent does, indeed, come from convection heat. The relatively small surface area, combined with the moderate surface temperature (as compared to woodstoves, for example), of most masonry heaters does not lend itself to a great deal of air heating. This remnant of convection heat, combined with the higher surface temperatures of everything it has heated, is what permits a masonry heater to still influence distant areas of a home that are completely blocked from infrared radiation. The next room over from the heater location, for example, may benefit radiantly just from that uninsulated interior wall's radiant contribution into the room. In other words, a warm wall will become a radiant heat source itself once it has been warmed by the masonry heater.

As the things in the area of the masonry heater become warm, they, and the heater itself, influence air temperature and increase it. This main living area then becomes the warmest area in the house. Our study of physics tells us, however, that this condition is temporary and destined to change. A gentle convection air flow will occur throughout the house as the forces of nature work at equally distributing the warmth everywhere. This is why air temperatures throughout a home heated by a masonry heater are relatively uniform.

It's important to remember that the masonry heater (if fired regularly) is always warm. So this process is ongoing. It is not the case that distant areas are cold, then you fire the masonry heater and things start to warm, then they get cold again later. Since a masonry heater stores and radiates heat for long periods, there is an inherent stability in temperatures everywhere. Unlike a house, with a normal furnace, that gets very cold as soon as the power goes out and the furnace can no longer operate, the masonry heater is always warm and continues to contribute warmth to living spaces long after the fire dies.

Unlike heating systems that *primarily* heat by distribution of warm air, the convection flow created by a masonry heater is so slow and gentle that you never feel it as moving air against your skin. It is merely a secondary remnant of heated air making its way through the home. I must note that this situation assumes a masonry heater designed to heat the whole living space of a house, rooms distant and close. A masonry heater designed to heat just a few rooms will do little to contribute to warming the air in distant areas; additional heating sources will be necessary.

Thermal Comfort Finale

The discussion has thus come full circle. What it really comes down to is that the most common types of

FIGURE 3.14. A heater is a real radiant heat source, like the sun. It actually warms people and the house, not just air. This soapstone heater features split stone and massive smooth stones above the firebox. A multi-sided door enhances fire viewing. Though the upside-down funnel shape gives the impression of smoke going straight from the firebox up the chimney, this is a real masonry heater that redirects the exhaust through flues before it gets to the final exit. **Photo courtesy of Tulikivi Corporation.**

heating systems people choose for their homes, including in-floor heating, are mainly either convection or, well, convection. Convection heat is warm air. Warm air is a thermal blanket. A thermal blanket does not warm anyone; it just reduces heat loss to maintain comfort, much like the blanket under which you sleep at night. Convection heaters are high-technology ways of reducing heat loss.

Conversely, masonry heaters are the choice for a real radiant heat source—like a sun in the middle of a home. They maintain a high enough surface temperature that you can feel heat on your face from across a room. They are much warmer than average body temperature, so the body truly "soaks up" that heat like a solar collector. Masonry heaters provide thermal comfort in the form of real heat gain. And with the masonry heater's vertical orientation, the radiant heat contacts you from head to toe.

A masonry heater's gentle radiant heat works universally. It automatically, without electronic gadgets or thermostats, provides a comfort level for everyone in the house. Closer to it, you feel the heat more intensely; farther away, less dramatically. It is the only truly radiant heater available today that uses wood for fuel.

Though it is clear that masonry heaters have distinct benefits when it comes to providing people with thermal comfort, this is just the beginning of how beneficial this form of heating can be. The health, environmental, and other benefits of masonry heaters are discussed in chapter 4.

ALL IN THE FAMILY

Diamond is a young Labrador/boxer with deep black fur. Like all dogs, Diamond loves a warm spot, and he frequently can be found on the floor right in front of the Ludwig family masonry heater. Often he will sit down and stare at the glass door as if expecting the flames to appear. Like other masonry heater pets, however, he has to wait for the evening when the family enjoys another fire. Diamond is not often alone in appreciating the flames and the warmth of the masonry heater. Dean and Judy Ludwig have seven children. Every one of them loves their heater. Dean puts it simply when he says, "It's like one of the family."

Dean says he first learned a little about masonry heaters about twelve years ago when he and Judy had a timber-frame shop/studio built on their property. The timber-frame artisan suggested they consider a masonry heater, but they didn't really know much about them and opted for an open fireplace and in-floor heat instead. Seven years later they converted a 450-square-foot screened porch into a four-season room. They knew they would have to either add on to the existing forced-air system of the house or find another way to heat the newly enclosed space. This time, they decided to invest in a masonry heater. They purchased a small Tulikivi Soapstone Fireplace. Now, they often wish they had done the same in the studio building.

"You have to realize," Judy points out, "that this new room is almost all windows. We pretty much expected it to be cold in the winter." Dean says, "Not only is this room the most comfortable room in the house, but we cut our heating bill for the whole house!" He explains, "We added about 15 percent onto the size of the house, but we have realized a 20 percent reduction in our heating cost!" Since the fuel for the Tulikivi comes mainly from fallen trees in their 2½ acres of woods, the only cost is their time to gather and split wood. With a family of nine (including three husky teenage boys), that proves to be a fairly painless task.

Judy explains that Owen, the youngest at fourteen, took care of most of the wood preparation himself this year (2009). Dietrich (sixteen) had been mainly taking care of it the previous couple of years. Having committed his time to the wood gathering, Owen also seems to be especially attached to the masonry heater and starts the fires on a regular basis.

Looking at the soapstone heater, though, it becomes clear that everyone in the family is attached. Soapstone from the Tulikivi Corporation is generally a soft, light gray color. Sometimes the same soapstone is used for countertops, for which it is treated with mineral oil that turns the stone charcoal gray or deep green. The Ludwig children embrace the Tulikivi so much that, over the heating season, the Tulikivi turns that dark charcoal color from the oils in their skin. While Judy and Dean talk about the heater, Dietrich and Owen stand against the masonry heater and caress it like they're petting Diamond, rather than soapstone.

All the Ludwig children are homeschooled, with Judy being their principal teacher. Dean is an administrator at a local college. Judy explains, "Everything happens in this room [with the Tulikivi]." She goes on to say that the masonry heater has made a noticeable change in family dynamics. Prior to having the masonry heater, the children would disperse to their bedrooms or some distant corner of the house in the winter. Now, with the Tulikivi in operation seven months of the year, everyone wants to be in the same room with the warm stone and radiant heat. A favorite spot is between the heater and the wall—a space of just about 1 foot. The youngest children, Carl, Kevin, and Grace, fit easily, though Owen also can be found reading books while lying on the floor behind the Tulikivi. Dean complains, "We should have made that space a little bigger. I can't fit back there." Dean nevertheless enjoys soothing his aging joints and muscles with the heat of the fireplace. He points out, "That's something you can't do with forced air."

FIGURE 3.15. The Ludwig family with their masonry heater, which gets so many embraces the soapstone is darkened. A Tulikivi heater installed by Masonry Heater Store.

While Kevin and Carl cannot remember life without a masonry heater, the two oldest, John and Todd, are now off to college. Judy remarks that John, home for Christmas vacation, was heard uttering, "I love this Tulikivi," while he leaned against it. Todd, the oldest, manages to be the only one capable of waging any viable complaint about the Tulikivi when he remarks, "Sometimes if you open the door fast, some ashes get pulled out by the sweep of the door." Dean corrects, "But that *doesn't* happen if you open the damper first!"

The whole family is very glad they chose this way of heating their new room. Judy explains that, as in most renovation projects, their budget dictated many decisions at the time the Tulikivi was added. In hindsight, however, she says, "If I had had any idea how much we would love the Tulikivi, I would have been pressing for heated sitting benches and probably a bigger heater." Dean, an avid baker, suggests that he would probably also want a larger one with a bakeoven option. There's no doubt you've found something good when nine out of nine people in the same family like it and want more of it. And, lest we forget, Diamond loves it, too.

FIGURE 4.1. A small soapstone heater is tucked into a hard-to-use space. Sometimes a home's structural features introduce spaces that aren't very functional. This placement of a masonry heater shows how such an area can become a cozy, warm nook. The sitting areas of this one are not heated internally. The chimney flue is hidden in the wall behind the taller element of the stove. Photo courtesy of Tulikivi Corporation.

CHAPTER FOUR

Benefits of Masonry Heaters

Some people have furnaces so they can feel "warm," but I prefer to build masonry heaters for people who want to be comfortable. Almost any home will have some degree of comfort, because the house has some sort of heating system in it. But in houses full of warm air, surprisingly few people are really comfortable. A lot of these folks even believe they *are* comfortable. In the sense that it is used here, "comfort" is a luxury. Like so many other fine luxuries, a very small minority of people actually have it.

Ironically, the difference with this luxury is not necessarily the price. The difference is mainly in knowledge and awareness. Many very wealthy people can afford total comfort and never get it. Meanwhile I have had clients who had modest budgets but made comfort the priority when they built their homes, and now they get to experience comfort *and* warmth. In almost any construction project, a family could trade a few trendy items or a few hundred square feet of living space for real comfort. But often they don't know any better; they plod on and accept warm air alone as good enough.

Total comfort is the real benefit of masonry heaters. Engineer types are drawn to masonry heaters because of the cool ways they function. Interior design types are drawn to the remarkable versatility of their appearance. Self-sufficiency types like the energy independence of wood burning. But once it's in the house and the engineer, designer, and survivor get a masonry heater fired and warm, what they'll talk about most is the comfort.

Total Comfort

If we accept that virtually any home heating system in use today offers some level of thermal comfort, what is missing from this idea of "total comfort"? What is

this luxury that so few obtain? Haven't market forces, the laws of supply and demand, gotten us maximum comfort for the minimum price? After all, a typical forced-air heating system today is relatively inexpensive. If it's the lowest-price way to provide thermal comfort, what more could we ask?

The old axiom is, "You get what you pay for." Chapter 3 illustrated that a radiant masonry heater performs differently from all of the most common ways of heating. Amazingly, the fact that radiant heat warms people and things directly is only the beginning of the comfort benefits. This simple truth creates advantages for the whole living environment and the whole human organism. Improved overall health and well-being, outstanding safety, and a range of environmental benefits stem from the simple idea that masonry heaters heat people, not air.

A typical modern heating system is controlled by an electronic thermostat. The thermostat operates in a very narrow range of temperatures. For example, a thermostat set at 70°F may activate the furnace when the temperature falls to 69° and allow it to operate until the temperature reaches 71°. As discussed in chapter 3, thermal comfort relies on not noticing any excess heat loss. The tightly controlled furnace assures that temperatures always hover around the "ideal" temperature the homeowner has chosen to curb excess heat loss. A wider temperature range can confuse the human body: One moment the temperature is low enough that thermoregulation measures begin to conserve body heat; the next moment it's warm enough that the body can relax again. Thermostats are designed to prevent this fluctuation from happening. When air temperature is the only aspect under consideration, strict control is necessary to maintain minimum thermal comfort.

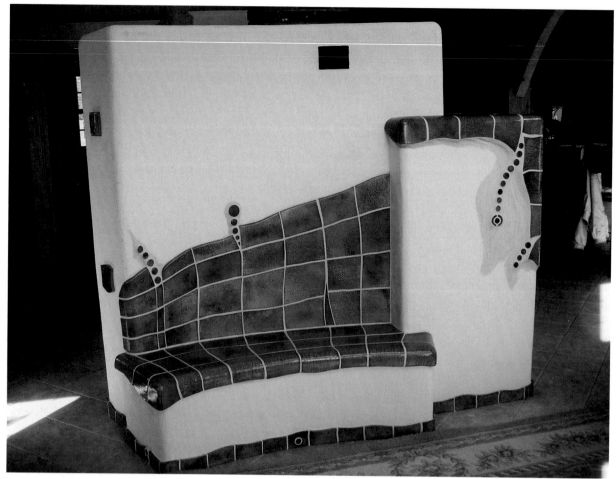

FIGURE 4.2. This heater was built using handmade tiles and stucco. Notice how the sitting area, which is heated, and the taller element have a gentle curve. Masonry heaters can have very organic shapes. Every surface visible here is a heating element. See the firebox side of this heater in figure 6.12. A *kachelofen* designed, built, and photographed by Ernst Kiesling, Canadian Kachelofen.

Real comfort, however, requires so much more than a minutely controlled air temperature. In fact, minutely controlled air temperatures are unnecessary when all the factors of comfort are addressed properly. Humidity, air movement, and surface temperatures are the basic considerations for thermal comfort in the built living environment. On top of these, add the biological needs of easy breathing, unrestricted blood circulation, and freedom from illness. Additionally, there are psychological benefits from safety, quiet, and energy independence. Finally, the environmental benefits of heating with masonry heaters provide the comfort of knowing that our earth is better preserved, that its resources are being used more wisely.

Thermal Comfort in the Built Environment

If you have wet laundry, how do you get it dried? Usually, you put it into an automatic clothes dryer. The clothes dryer is a suitable demonstration of the effect of conventional convection heat on the indoor thermal comfort environment. Wet clothes can represent the natural, somewhat humid indoor air of a house. The warm, dry air of the machine is exactly the same as the warm, dry air that comes from a forced-air furnace or any other convection heater. If a dryer can transform soaking wet clothes to dry ones in a matter of minutes, what happens to the indoor air of a home heated with warm air?

Conventional furnaces and heaters dry the air

in the home, reducing humidity. When humidity is lower, higher air temperatures are required for thermal comfort. This is because dry air accelerates evaporation of moisture from human skin, and increased evaporation makes people feel cooler. That is, after all, why people sit in front of fans on hot summer days: to increase evaporation and feel cooler. Ironically, many modern furnaces are equipped with humidifiers to help restore a more natural humidity level and thereby improve comfort. So a homeowner first pays to have a furnace dry the air, and then pays for the energy to humidify the air.

A masonry heater allows natural humidity levels to reign. Since the masonry heater is not drying the air by circulating warm air, the indoor climate is more naturally comfortable. Ideal relative humidity in a home in the winter is usually between 30 and 45 percent. This level usually prevails if there is nothing operating to dry the air. At these ideal humidity levels, evaporative cooling is held to a minimum, and people feel warmer within a larger range of air temperatures. Many find air temperatures in the 65° to 70°F range to be perfectly acceptable with radiant heat. If an individual is lightly active in this environment, temperatures in the low 60s even feel fine.

Likewise, air movement is the purpose of most heating systems. If warm air was not adequately circulated, the convection heaters could not keep the home air uniformly warm. Being in the presence of moving air, however, is one way the body cools itself. (Remember the fans in the summer.) In the midst of trying to warm us, conventional methods cool us by convective cooling from constant and relatively rapid air movement. (Is there a pattern here? First the air is artificially dried so it then needs to be artificially moistened. Next, warm air, that is meant to keep people warm, is cooling them.) In contrast, the masonry heater creates a calm indoor climate with very little air movement and consequently greater thermal comfort at lower temperatures.

When these conditions of higher relative indoor humidity and calm, almost nonexistent air movement are combined with the naturally higher surface temperatures resulting from infrared radiant heat from the masonry heater, the resulting indoor climate is unsurprisingly enjoyable. Indeed, with cooler air temperatures, the average person comments that the air seems fresher and cleaner. Most people report feeling more energetic instead of drowsy and stuffy. A centrally located masonry heater, a radiant heat source, sets up an indoor climate that mimics the outdoors where the radiant sun gently warms the surface of the earth. This is the environment that has nurtured humankind for thousands of years. It should not be a surprise that it not only feels good, but also has numerous health benefits.

Health Benefits

In the early 1980s, the World Health Organization and others began to recognize patterns of extreme discomfort or illness in workers that dissipated when those suffering left their home or workplace. This was when many first began hearing about sick building syndrome (SBS). This syndrome has been blamed partially on stricter energy-efficiency guidelines that began to be used in the 1970s in an attempt to conserve energy. Homes and businesses that were built "tighter" (less apt to leak warmed air to the outside) created spaces that trapped occupants with toxins that often outgas from composite building materials, carpets, and many other products, not to mention the by-products of human respiration.

Since then, there has been an upsurge in awareness of how to avoid SBS in the United States and around the world. Building "green" or environmentally friendly buildings with the use of more natural materials has been touted as a way to have health-supporting homes. Yet building homes that support good health isn't really all that new. In fact, Helmut Ziehe, founder of the International Institute for Bau-biologie and Ecology, Inc. (IBE), says, "It is as old as the Earth. It's only a new movement in comparison to our industrial way of living."[1]

Bau-biologie is a German term meaning "building biology." More specifically, IBE defines it as the study of "the impact of the built environment on human

FIGURE 4.3. Brick, stucco, and soapstone combine here to create a pleasing rustic look. The soapstone has been oiled, making it almost black. The heater is well placed, radiating into the kitchen behind and to the left as well as into the living room from where the fire is seen. Photo courtesy of New England Hearth and Soapstone.

health, and the application of this knowledge to the construction of natural homes and workplaces; and the holistic interaction of human involvement with the environment and the regenerative sustainability of the environment."[2] Ziehe had already studied *bau-biologie* for years when he brought it to the United States in 1987. It had been founded in Germany after World War II reconstruction efforts produced sick building syndrome there. The German textbook on *bau-biologie* was authored principally by Anton Schneider, under whom Mr. Ziehe studied. Helmut Ziehe received permission to translate the text and brought it with him to found the IBE, an educational organization.

Unlike many of the trendy "green" building concepts that are featured in popular magazines, newspapers, and other media outlets, *bau-biologie* takes an in-depth look at every aspect and angle associated with healthful construction. For example, many builders will consider a composite material "green" as long as it doesn't outgas objectionably. In contrast, when examining individual materials, *bau-biologie* begins asking penetrating questions like:

- From where did the raw materials come?
- How much energy is needed to make this product?
- To what are workers exposed when this product is made?
- How will it affect the environment if it ever becomes waste?
- What impact do the color and texture have on individuals?
- How will this material affect the humidity in the home?
- Will this material benefit the people who encounter it?

When addressing an individual system within a home, *bau-biologie* likewise considers myriad aspects few people think about in selecting a heating method. The first consideration is how to make a health-supporting climate rather than how to cheaply produce heat. More specifically, the goal is to produce a living environment that stimulates rejuvenation; maintains the oxygen supply; improves blood circulation; increases immunity to disease; promotes deep, effortless breathing; maintains healthy ion exchange; promotes adequate transpiration; and produces an overall feeling of vitality.

This goal is not achieved simply by controlling the air temperature in a dwelling. Meeting the goal of a health-supporting environment, at the very least, requires abundant fresh air. The usual intention (with convection heating) of retaining as much warm air as possible is in conflict with the idea of bringing in abundant fresh air. This is not true with radiant heat, since radiant heat does not depend on warm air for its effectiveness.

Gentle radiant heat, like that from the sun or a masonry heater, also improves blood circulation by directly warming the skin. Most people have experienced the flushed skin that results from soaking in a warm bath. Warm skin signals the body to keep blood vessels wide open, encouraging adequate blood flow and natural transpiration. In contrast, the moving air of convection systems triggers the thermoregulation heat-conservation reactions described in chapter 3, closing the pores of the skin and restricting blood flow by constriction of blood vessels.

In addition to optimizing temperature, humidity, air movement, and surface temperatures—the primary aspects of thermal comfort outlined earlier—a health-supporting indoor climate also minimizes temperature stratification, creates and moves as little dust as possible, keeps air fresh, eliminates undesirable odors, provides for optimum ionization, reduces electrostatic charges, does not create electrical and magnetic fields, and keeps noise disturbances to a minimum.

Temperature Stratification

Temperature stratification refers to the variance of temperature that can occur between the floor and the ceiling. Most people know about temperature stratification but simply don't use that term. When folks say all their heat pools at the ceiling and they need a ceiling fan to bring it back down, they are describing a solution to the problem of temperature stratification. With most convection heating systems, the coolest area will be close to the floor and the warmest will be near the ceiling. A thermometer moved incrementally from floor to ceiling would register a slightly warmer temperature each step of the way. In homes with forced-air furnaces and a thermostat set at about 70°F, the temperature at the ceiling may be 80° or more. The temperature at the floor might be 65°, and the target temperature is achieved at wall thermostat level.

A warm, so-called radiant floor creates a different kind of stratification called temperature inversion. This is the situation in which the floor is actually the warmest part of the room while the ceiling is cooler—which is an unnatural environment. Warm floors are generally kept at 80° to 85°F. The ceiling in such a home may be 10, 20, or even 30 degrees cooler.

In stark contrast, a masonry heater creates minimal temperature stratification. Since the vertical surfaces of the masonry heater send infrared radiation evenly throughout a room but do little to heat air, temperatures from floor to ceiling are generally within a few degrees. If the floor is 67°F, the ceiling is not likely more than 70°. In these conditions, the human body experiences a natural balance rather than one extreme at the feet and another at the head. Such conditions encourage even blood distribution through the body while the slightly cooler air encourages deeper breathing. Combined, these effects encourage natural transpiration. Overall, the evenness of the temperatures is like that you experience outdoors with the accompanying feeling of rejuvenation.

Creation and Movement of Dust

Dust is composed of fine particles, often of dead skin cells from people or animals. Plant pollen, fibers from textiles, as well as materials from outdoors can all become dust in a house. It may seem that heating systems don't actually create dust. However, the environmental conditions created by a heating system can strongly influence how much dust is present. In particular, convective systems that dry the air are contributors to dry skin, which can flake off a body much more persistently than in more natural humidity. Drier air will affect cloth and paper similarly.

Dust is readily transported by the moving air of a convection system. Small particles can get pulled right into some of the hottest parts of the heating system. The high temperatures of the heat exchangers of furnaces will super-dry the particles. Simultaneously, blowers break the dust into even smaller particles that can become pervasive irritants. These particles then are distributed to every corner of the house via the ductwork. Similar dust circulation occurs with convection heaters without blowers. These have the advantage of less powerful air circulation but the disadvantage of scorching the dust right inside the room. Metal woodstoves in particular burn dust constantly at extremely high temperatures.

Massive heat-storage systems like masonry heaters and warm floors are far superior in keeping dust creation and movement to a minimum. Their gentler, passive approach to heating minimizes both air dryness and the circulation of dust. Masonry heaters retain the best performance here by virtue of the fact that they do even less air heating than do warm floors. Masonry heaters have no blowers to move air and the particulates it carries. They don't scorch dust particles, because their surface temperatures are too low. Minimizing dust circulation brings relief to those who suffer from allergies; encourages deeper, more effortless breathing; and reduces the transmission of contagious illnesses.

Keeping Air Fresh and Eliminating Undesirable Odors
Because masonry heaters do not scorch dust, they don't contribute to foul smells in a home. Those who have forced-air heating systems recognize the smell of scorched dust. Every fall, when the furnace is first started, you can smell the burned dust that comes from every register in the house. What you may not realize is that this same dust scorching happens for the rest of the heating season; you just become accustomed to the odor and don't notice it again until a significant time has passed without it.

Scorched dust becomes harder and sharper. In addition, it becomes more acidic. This is a constant irritant to the lungs, throat, and nasal passages. Like tiny needles pricking these tender tissues, scorched dust can contribute to many kinds of respiratory ailments and discomfort. The odors and irritants in dusty air are far from fresh and contribute to the feeling that you must "go out and get some fresh air."

In addition, masonry heaters built properly have excellent natural venting (draft) and are operated with closed doors. The doors stay closed until the fire has burned itself out. Therefore, masonry heaters contribute few particles that promote the formation of odors in the home. In my own home, I have had guests exclaim that I couldn't possibly be heating with wood because, they said, it doesn't smell like a chimney in the house. In contrast, open fireplaces (with no doors) and woodstoves (which are dampened to slow, smoky burns) brand a home as "wood-heated" with their continuous contribution of unburned combustion gases into the living space—a little at time every time the firebox is reloaded.

Mold in a home is another health concern. Mold spores in the air are often linked with many kinds of illness, ranging from headaches and allergic reactions to sudden infant death syndrome (SIDS), various cancers, and respiratory problems. Mold growth usually happens in areas where moist air condenses on things with cool surface temperatures. Masonry heaters establish comfort levels by keeping surface temperatures high. Thus condensation of moisture in a home is much less likely. For further discussion about mold, see the section on "Safety and Security Benefits" later in this chapter.

Masonry heaters do virtually nothing to affect the air in a home. Air stays fresh, clean, and cooler in an environment with radiant heat. You get the impression that you're already outside in the fresh air with the sun shining. Heating with natural radiant heat from a masonry heater calls into question the trend to make homes more and more airtight. Since heating air is only secondary with a masonry heater, natural leakages that allow constant refreshment of the indoor air maintain a higher concentration of truly fresh air in the home without the need for mechanical ventilating systems. People are constantly breathing out, exhausting, if you will, the gases and toxins the body needs to eliminate. Ventilation of one kind or another is needed to finally get those wastes out of the living environment so that vital, fresh air from outside can be breathed in. Most

FIGURE 4.4. This enormous soapstone "boulder" masonry heater was designed for the corner of this log home. The massive stones complement the large logs of the walls and ceiling. To the left of the firebox is a bench with wood storage underneath. Once this much soapstone gets warm, it stays warm. Photo courtesy of WarmStone Fireplaces and Designs; copyright JK Lawrence Photography.

FIGURE 4.5. The corners of rooms are usually occupied by furniture. This masonry heater is warm furniture and art at the same time. By building with multiple tiers and sides, a lot of radiating surface fits in a small area and creates visual interest. Notice the small niches repeating the shape of the glazed tiles. The wooden bench surface is comfortable to sit on even when the heater is not in use, while stone or tile surfaces might feel cold at those times. Photo courtesy of Biofire, Inc.

average homes have tiny leaks, primarily around openings like windows, that allow this to happen naturally all day long. As long as these leaks are not a source for uncomfortable drafts, they are a natural source of constant fresh air in a radiantly heated home.

Optimum Ionization

Ionization refers to an atom or molecule either gaining or losing electrons. For purposes of building biology, ionization of the air molecules is of importance to health and well-being. All air molecules carry some kind of charge; it's either a positive or a negative electrical charge. An abundance of negative ions is associated with positive moods, improved performance, increased capacity to work, relief from pain, relief from allergic reactions, improved vitamin metabolism, and even

increased speed of healing or recovery from illness. An environment with excessive positively ionized air (or simply lack of enough negative ions), on the other hand, is associated with poor mood, decreased performance and work capacity, greater susceptibility to illness, headaches and dizziness, and even depression.

Devices or systems with electrical currents tend to positively ionize the air; television sets, computers, electrical appliances, and electrically controlled devices of every kind have this effect. Positive charge is further enhanced by dry air circulated by forced-air and other convection heaters. The problem is compounded by airtight homes with many electronic devices, plastics, and other artificial materials, and the accompanying dry air. These items—nylon carpeting, for example—have a positive charge (inherent in their composition or operation) and draw negative ions out of the air in the home. The drier the air is, the more pronounced is this change to positively ionized air. This is intimately related to static charges, discussed next.

Studies have shown that a room with balanced ionization changes to a very positively charged climate after the room is heated with convection heat. In one study, averaged over five individual tests, a room started with a concentration of 594 positive ions per m³ and 408 negative ions per m³. After warm air circulation, the balance had changed to 296/m³ and 58/m³, respectively. What was a 3/2 ratio became a 5/1 ratio of positive to negative ions.[3]

A similar room heated with a masonry heater increased the level of negative ions because of thermionic emissions—the emission of electrons from hot substances. The ratio started at 5/3 (positive ions per m³/negative ions per m³); after heating with a masonry heater, the ratio became 6/5.

Some of the most natural settings that people find enjoyable—like waterfalls, ocean waves, running streams, and forests—also have higher concentrations of negative ions. Cosmic rays (natural radiation from outside the earth's atmosphere), relative movements of surfaces (friction of water against water or rock), and thermionic emissions are all principal ways that air ionization occurs. This ionization occurs in natural

FIGURE 4.6. A view of a large masonry heater from a balcony. This heater is the sole heat source for a 2,500-square-foot home. The simple brick veneer is complemented by limestone—most of which was part of the paving outside various outbuildings on the property. Other views of this heater are in figures 3.5 and 5.1.

settings without disturbance or modification from human-made interference. Masonry heaters produce an indoor ionization climate that mimics the natural environment.

Fewer Electrostatic Charges

Electrostatic charges, or "static electricity" as the phenomenon is often called, are familiar to most people. Children will delight in rubbing a balloon on their hair or a carpet and then "sticking" the balloon to a wall. Clothes dried in an automatic clothes dryer may come out clinging to one another. The act of rubbing two nonconductive materials together can create substantial static electrical charges; the friction liberates

electrons from one material and transfers them to the other, giving it the (negative) charge. The negatively charged material will then be attracted to other materials, especially those that might have a positive charge. Everyone at some point has gotten a "poke" after walking across a carpeted floor and then touching a metal doorknob. The doorknob acts like a lightning rod that restores electrical equilibrium; it conducts the electrons from the person to the doorknob—an electrical discharge (removal of the charge).

Like the automatic clothes dryer, most homes these days are equipped with a system that circulates dry air and creates the conditions for static charging. Masonry heaters, on the other hand, allow higher or more

FIGURE 4.7. An all-stone masonry heater contrasts attractively with the white walls of a large, open room. The arch-top door is mimicked by the arched top of the heater. Photo courtesy of Temp-Cast Enviroheat.

natural relative humidity. Higher humidity levels mean electrical charges do not build as easily, since water naturally discharges the currents. This frees homeowners from the discomfort and surprise of those frequent electric shocks.

Further, the electrostatic environment influences both the ion balance mentioned in the previous section and the effects of other electric and magnetic fields.

Nonexistent Electrical and Magnetic Fields

Since the 1970s, debate has continued about whether exposure to electrical and magnetic fields created by power lines and home wiring have negative effects on human health. The *bau-biologie* approach is a conservative one: The human body has its own subtle electrical circuitry, and human beings have lived and evolved for thousands of years in an environment largely free from artificially created electrical fields. Only relatively

recently have humans become immersed in an environment of human-made electromagnetic fields (EMFs) such as those produced by household wiring, radio signals, and high-tension power lines. Now people live daily in an environment that, according to Robert O. Becker in his book *The Body Electric: Electromagnetism and the Foundation of Life,* is "a latticework of criss-crossing signals in which there's always the possibility of synergistic effects." He notes that one of the most noticeable effects these fields have on humans is to activate stress responses—essentially indicating that people living in an environment with human-made EMFs never really get to relax. In addition, Becker's investigations show that, "These unfamiliar energies produce changes in nearly every bodily function so far studied."[4] This conclusion is echoed by John H. Gibbons, director of the Office of Technology Assessment for the US Congress, who stated that "under certain circumstances even relatively weak electric and magnetic fields can produce biologic changes."[5]

Masonry heaters work entirely without electricity. They don't have blowers, thermostats, or any other electronic controls. They are, as far as human evolution is concerned, the equivalent of a campfire surrounded by rocks. This is an environment the human body recognizes immediately as without threat. It is an electrically neutral environment in which the whole human body can relax. Heating with a masonry heater reduces dependency on electricity and its accompanying controversies.

Every technological solution to controlling indoor climate requires electricity. Forced-air furnaces require wiring for blowers, thermostats, and electronic ignition. In-floor heating requires thermostats, pumps, and electronic controls as do baseboard hydronic heaters. Even pellet- and corn-burning stoves require electricity for feeding the fuel to the fire. Obviously, electric baseboard heaters and electrical in-floor heating require a vast array of electrical pathways. (These, in fact, are the most suspect as far as internal wiring is concerned. Some of the most controversial health-related problems relate to electrical-resistance heating as used in both in-floor systems and electric blankets. Both of these electrical heat sources make contact with the human body when in use. Just as you feel radiant heat more intensely the closer you are to the source, the effects of electromagnetic field exposure are more profound when your body is closer to the field generator.)

No Noise Disturbances

When I moved into my current home (and before it had a masonry heater), every time the forced-air furnace came on there was a loud, metallic *BANG!* Many of those living in older homes with metal ductwork have experienced similar noises. The air-pressure change as the furnace blower starts sometimes pops metal ductwork sides in or out, making the irritating sound. Likewise, changes in temperature make the metal ducts expand and contract, creating similar pops, pings, and gongs. Newer homes frequently have ductwork made from softer, more flexible materials that don't make as much noise. Nevertheless, furnace start-up and the hum of the machine as blowers run is a frequent background noise.

Similarly, older hydronic systems are notable for their creaks, bangs, and pops as metal piping heats and cools. The expansion of metal materials simply makes itself known this way. Baseboard electric heaters have the same inherent noise contribution. In-floor systems, which now commonly use plastic tubing, are no longer the noisemakers they once were. However, any of these systems that retain a pump, electronic igniter, or blower can introduce annoying sounds into some or many areas of a home.

Masonry heaters, when they are radiating their stored heat, produce no sound at all. There is, of course, the sound of the fire as it burns. Though it is easy for someone to be annoyed by a humming motor or even surprised by an unexpected *ping,* it is most uncommon to hear anyone complain about the sound of a crackling fire. Considering that the fire in a masonry heater is burned at the time of the owners' choosing and only lasts a couple of hours, annoyance at its gentle sparking and crackling is very unlikely. In truth, most people find the sound of a wood fire to be most relaxing and satisfying; perhaps again it is a reminder of the

FIGURE 4.8. The firebox of this heater is to the right and the wood-topped sitting area to the left. All the mass between contains the flues and radiates heat. Notice the hand-painted, handmade tiles. This heater is also seen in figures 3.6 and 8.1. This *kachelofen* was designed, built, and photographed by Ernst Kiesling, Canadian Kachelofen.

way we lived for thousands of years being warmed by an open fire.

Safety and Security Benefits

Fire and Burn Safety

According to a 2010 report from the National Fire Protection Association,[6] more deaths from fires result from central heating systems than fireplaces. Central heating systems, of course, include all manner of natural gas, propane, or oil forced-air furnaces hidden away in basements, cellars, and closets. The same report does say that fireplaces, chimneys, and chimney connectors

FIGURE 4.9. The front or firebox side of this heater has a lot of the traditional fireplace look, but you can also see the bake-oven door to the right, revealing that this is, indeed, something different. Figure 4.10 shows the other side of this masonry heater. Photo courtesy of Envirotech Masonry Heaters.

FIGURE 4.10. Steps, shelves, and different levels add visual interest—and places to put things. The heater's many sides also increase overall surface area for more radiant heat. Photo courtesy of Envirotech Masonry Heaters.

are the leading locations for US home heating fire incidents.

Chimney fires (home heating fires related to chimneys and chimney connectors) are principally due to an accumulation of unburned hydrocarbons that condense and solidify on the inside of a chimney or chimney connector. When a significant amount of this material, called creosote, accumulates and is later subjected to high temperatures, it can ignite. The resulting chimney fire may be limited to the chimney itself or can result in a full house fire. The same NFPA report estimates that creosote was instrumental in 22 percent of all home heating fires from 2003 to 2007.

What the above report doesn't say is that masonry

heaters are even safer than fireplaces and, by extension, safer than typical furnaces. When fired properly they pose almost no threat of fire in chimneys or chimney connectors because of the way they burn.

Creosote is unburned fuel. When dry wood is burned at temperatures exceeding 1,100°F, there is no unburned fuel. Well-designed masonry heaters burn wood at temperatures exceeding 1,100° and thus do not give off exhaust material that will accumulate in chimney connectors or chimneys. In my own home, I once waited five years without having the chimney checked or cleaned. Finally, I decided that I really should have a professional chimney sweep look at it. When he looked up the chimney through an available cleanout opening, he said, "I don't know why you called me, there's nothing in your chimney. Take a look." I took hold of the mirror he used to look up the chimney; sure enough, the light shining down the length of the chimney revealed liners nearly as clean as newly installed ones.

Beside the complete combustion characteristic that makes chimney fires all but impossible, masonry heaters are enormously safe because they are operated with closed firebox doors. Solid doors or doors with glass are closed when the fire is started and are not opened again until the fire is burned to coals. This means that neither sparks nor logs are able to find their way onto a living room rug where they can ignite a house fire. Furthermore, the fire is commonly watched by the owner, which is not true of automatic combustion appliances.

Additionally, the exterior surface of the masonry heater is not hot enough to ignite fabrics, paper, rugs, or wood. Masonry heaters are properly designed to have exterior temperatures well below the 572°F needed to ignite wood. In fact, most masonry heaters will be operating at surface temperatures of less than half that with averages being in the range of 150° (by technical definition, a masonry heater should never have exterior temperatures above 230°)—not high enough to ignite anything in a house. This is in stark contrast with metal woodstoves and common space heaters that run at very high temperatures. Again, the NFPA report says, "The leading factor contributing to ignition for home heating fire deaths (46%) was heating equipment too close to things that can burn, such as upholstered furniture, clothing, mattress, or bedding."[7] Woodstoves operate regularly with surface temperatures above 400° and can operate with temperatures in excess of 600°. These temperatures are high enough to ignite virtually any common household item that might come in contact with it.

From the human standpoint, the surface temperature is important because it determines whether people—particularly children—will get burned. Interestingly, it is difficult to get burned by masonry that is 200°F or less. Although it can feel very hot, you can touch it

and sense its extreme heat and pull your hand away without being burned. Again this is contrasted with a metal stove at 400° or an electric heater with red-hot coils; with these, all it takes is a touch to get a blister. With an average temperature of around 150° or less, masonry heaters are very safe for children. And, in fact, children and pets are attracted to the warmth of masonry and will gladly sit or stand up against a warm masonry heater. Even the metal and glass door parts are of concern only when a fire is burning and for a short time immediately after a fire is out. The main body of a masonry heater can be touched without burning even at its greatest heat output.

Finally, unlike the furnace that ignites its flame many times every day at every hour, the masonry heater is typically only fired once or twice in any day, and at a time of the owner's choosing. The rest of the time—likely twenty hours out of a twenty-four hour day—the heater is providing heat without the need for a flame. People can be home or away, in bed or in another room, but the masonry heater has no live flame that could pose any hazard. Likewise, systems that depend on electricity or red-hot electric heating elements carry with them the possibility of electrical short circuits or even the chance that pets will leave a sock, pillow, or other item against a very hot heating element.

Mold Contamination and Structural Deterioration

Another concern that can arise with forced-air heating systems is mold contamination. Mold is not only a health hazard (see "Keeping Air Fresh and Eliminating Undesirable Odors" earlier in this chapter), but it is a structural hazard when it concerns the wood framing of the typical house.

To understand how mold can be incubated, we can think again about the way an automatic clothes dryer works: Hot air evaporates water from clothes, and the moist air is forced out of the house with a fan-forced vent. (Imagine the moisture that would result if the dryer was vented directly into the house!)

Homes heated with warm air can function much like the clothes dryer. Warm, dry air is evaporating

FIGURE 4.11. A relatively small soapstone masonry heater serving double duty as furniture. The entire backrest is heated. The black soot doors reveal that the backrest interior consists of three horizontal flues one atop the other leading to the chimney at upper left. Niches under the seats and firebox could be for firewood, shoes, or other storage. Photo courtesy of New England Hearth and Soapstone.

moisture from everything, including the skin of the people in the home. The big difference between this and the clothes dryer, however, is that there is no vent sending the moisture out of the house. Each person loses about 600 grams (about 1.25 pounds) of water each day through evaporation. Additional moisture is introduced via bathing, cooking, and people opening doors to go outside or come inside. Where does all that moisture go?

Quite simply, since the water cannot remain in the house (because the warm air dries everything), the warm moist air is forced into the walls of the house through porous materials or via tiny cracks and leaks

in the building envelope. Since the moist air is warmer than all the wall materials, the moisture can condense on or in the wall. This moisture can readily be absorbed by the relatively dry materials within the wall cavities of the house—the space between the inside and outside walls containing wood framing and insulation materials. Moisture in these materials can make them a breeding ground for mold and microbes. This, in turn, can lead to deterioration of wall framing, reduced effectiveness of insulation, and the creation of musty odors in the home.

Since masonry heaters do not excessively heat air, they do not force the moisture out of room air and

FIGURE 4.12. Here's an example of a way to get the gentle radiant heat of a masonry heater into two rooms separated by doors. The firebox of the heater is in one room, but the bulk of the flues and radiating mass is in the next. Notice small niches in the left side of the stucco heater as well as a generous wood-storage area below the firebox. White tiles form a baseboard. A *kachelofen* designed, built, and photographed by Ernst Kiesling, Canadian Kachelofen.

into wall cavities. At the same time, surfaces like walls are warmer with a masonry heater. The warm surface temperatures stabilize the air temperatures as previously described. Surface temperatures and air temperature are virtually the same, so condensation does not occur, and mold, mildew, and the resulting problems are avoided.

Power Loss

Wintertime loss of electric power is one of the most upsetting and possibly dangerous scenarios for most people in North America. In severe weather, such as blizzards and ice storms, roads may be impassable and power lines can be downed all over populated areas. Since most heating systems rely on electricity for operation, loss of power is an immediate problem. In one hour without a furnace, temperatures in a home can drop dramatically. In several hours, the home will have virtually no protection from cold. In some areas, such events occur often in the wintertime and electric power can be off for days or even weeks at a time.

Since masonry heaters require no electricity, their operation is not affected by loss of power. Further, since they store heat for long periods, temporary difficulty getting to a wood pile is not even a hazard. Of course, prudent owners who know a storm is coming will bring wood into the home in advance and be very secure for days of severe weather. Those who invest in a masonry heater with an accompanying wood-fired cookstove and/or oven can function just as well without electric power as they did with it.

Environmental Benefits

Every technology has an impact on the environment. Residential home heating is no exception. Discussions of greenhouse gases, pollution, and land degradation are constant topics in world news. Certainly the list of health and thermal benefits from masonry heaters would be meaningless if masonry heaters were detrimental to the environment. Fortunately, this is far from the case, since masonry heaters score very high marks where they matter most: in the areas of greenhouse gas emissions, particulate and pollutant emissions, and renewable energy.

Greenhouse Gases

Greenhouse gas emissions are a current hot topic, with the subject appearing in everything from presidential debates to TV sitcoms. For all the noise, many people are unaware that "greenhouse gases" have always existed in the earth's atmosphere. Without them, the earth would be uninhabitable—they are responsible for preventing excess loss of heat from the earth. Just as chapter 3 described the thermoregulation controls of human physiology that prevent people from getting too cold, atmospheric collections of various gases are critical to preventing our world from freezing.

The debate, however, concerns the apparent increase of several greenhouse gases due to the fossil and biomass fuel consumption of humans, especially since the onset of the Industrial Revolution in the nineteenth century. Now the primary focus is on one of the several greenhouse gases: carbon dioxide. CO_2 causes approximately 25 percent or less of the greenhouse effect. However, human activity produces large amounts of this gas; an excess of greenhouse gases presumably can produce excess heat retention on earth—global warming.

Residential heating consumes vast amounts of fossil fuels in the United States. Individual home heating and individual transportation (cars) are listed by the US Environmental Protection Agency as top contributors of greenhouse gases. Fossil fuels like oil, natural gas, coal, and propane all have carbon dioxide as principal by-products of combustion. These nonrenewable fuels are, in essence, dense storehouses of carbon. Millions of years were needed to create these vast accumulations of energy. But in the period of a six-month heating season, a single home may consume hundreds of gallons of these fuels to produce heat. These gallons of fuel are forever gone when viewed on the scale of time needed to replace them. The by-product of concern, carbon dioxide, is added to the ecosystem. It's a linear display of entropy that looks something like this:

$$FUEL \rightarrow HEAT \rightarrow CO_2$$

This equation is repeated endlessly in most homes day after day and year after year.

Masonry heaters burn wood at the highest efficiency possible. Most importantly, they achieve near 100 percent clean combustion because of the high temperatures achieved in the combustion chamber. Nevertheless, wood is also a carbon-based fuel, and one of the primary by-products of wood combustion is carbon dioxide, as is the case with all the fossil fuels.

Wood combustion has a distinct advantage, however. Unlike the linear equation of, say, oil (fuel $\rightarrow$ heat $\rightarrow CO_2$), wood is part of a natural cycle that is, in fact, a necessary part of the relationship among trees, humans, and the natural environment. Trees eventually die. When they die and fall, they will, if not used as a resource, rot where they lie. This natural decay will release the same carbon dioxide into the atmosphere that occurs when wood is burned cleanly in a masonry heater.

Assuming there is an attempt to manage forests, as there already is, new and growing trees will replace those that are harvested. All these trees require carbon dioxide for growth. In fact, about half the weight of wood is carbon. Trees consume carbon dioxide in the atmosphere. When a tree falls and rots or is cut down and

FIGURE 4.13. A masonry heater veneered with soapstone bricks. To the left of the firebox is a large wood-storage area under a bench. This heater also features a functional bakeoven. Photo courtesy of Empire Masonry Heaters, Inc.

burned in a masonry heater, the carbon dioxide released is consumed by other growing trees. There is a natural offset of carbon consumption for the carbon liberated by combustion. This is a carbon cycle rather than a linear effect releasing carbon dioxide with no counterbalance:

$$\text{FUEL} \rightarrow \text{HEAT} \rightarrow CO_2 \rightarrow \text{FUEL}$$

Thus, wood as a fuel is considered to be carbon-neutral. Even the Environmental Protection Agency states that if more biomass fuels (fuels made from plant waste including wood products) were used to supplement fossil fuel consumption, greenhouse warming could be brought under control. The EPA's booklet *State Bioenergy Primer* affirms this carbon neutrality in no uncertain terms: "Biomass is generally considered to contribute nearly zero net GHG [greenhouse gas] emissions." A clean-burning masonry heater is an ideal heating tool when you think in terms of environmental costs and benefits.

Pollution and Particulates

The combustion of any carbon-based fuel can be accompanied by significant amounts of pollutants and gases in the exhaust (smoke). The burning of wood, like the burning of its older relatives, coal and oil, is essentially the combustion of hydrocarbons—hydrogen combined with carbon. Products of incomplete combustion of wood (which is most notably found in stoves that are designed to burn wood slowly and at relatively low temperatures like most metal woodstoves) can include large amounts of soot and creosote.

Black soot and brown creosote are different types of unburned hydrocarbons. There are dozens of different hydrocarbon compounds that can form from this incomplete combustion process. These become part of the exhaust and are the visible (smoke) waste from burning solid fuels like wood. They are known technically as particulate matter or simply particulates. Wood also has a significant amount of minerals in its composition. These minerals do not burn and are the visible remnant of wood burning, found in the firebox after the fire goes out—the ashes.

Complete wood combustion (100 percent combustion efficiency) results in very clean exhaust. In practice, however, 100 percent combustion is never quite achieved. Such combustion requires temperatures in excess of 1,100°F throughout the entire burn of fuel. The design of a good masonry heater firebox is such that combustion efficiency is close to perfect, however, with combustion efficiencies of perhaps 95 percent. This minor imperfection in combustion is generally associated with both the beginning and ending phases of the process.

In other words, when a fire is first lit, temperatures are relatively low. A burning match touches paper, burning paper ignites kindling, and, finally, burning kindling ignites the principal fuel load (logs). This start-up process necessarily involves inefficient burns and therefore the release of unburned hydrocarbons. The initial firebox (the materials—bricks, for example) temperature may only be 200°F, and the lit match is only slightly above the ignition temperature of wood—maybe 600°F. It takes some time for temperatures to rise and achieve the point (1,100°F) at which clean combustion occurs. This temperature is achieved relatively quickly in a warm masonry heater; clean combustion will begin in as little as five or six minutes. Similarly, when the main fuel load has burned to coals, temperatures will decrease and incomplete combustion will again occur, though by this time most of the carbon-based material has been vaporized, and the inefficiency will mainly result in a slightly greater release of gases like carbon monoxide (CO).

Every masonry heater is unique. Even identical heaters will get slightly different use. Different types of wood, different quantities of wood, greater or lesser times between firings, and many other factors will determine how long it takes to achieve complete combustion in a masonry heater.

Given that masonry heaters do thus achieve very clean combustion, the primary pollutant from burning wood in a masonry heater is particulates—tiny particles of waste accompanying the gases exhausted from the chimney. The small amount of unburned hydrocarbon compounds released from well-designed masonry heaters is far below that which result from typical metal woodstoves, outdoor wood-fired boilers, and even the amounts generated in today's coal-powered electrical generating plants.

The combined data from testing of different masonry heaters in accredited laboratories over the last twenty years reveals that the amount of particulates from masonry heaters as a class of appliances falls around 2.8 grams per kilogram of fuel. In other words, about one-quarter of 1 percent of the weight of wood fuel is released as particulates into the environment.

To put this into some perspective, Washington State, which has some of the strictest air-quality standards in the United States, requires fireplaces to be cleaner than EPA standards. Washington's standard requires fireplaces to have particulates of less than 7.3 grams per kilogram of fuel. The average masonry heater is therefore producing much less than half of the particulate emissions allowed by Washington's strict standard. More recently, a 2007 test of one masonry heater yielded particulate emissions, averaged over three tests, of only 1.0 gram

FIGURE 4.14. This masonry heater is more a sculpture than just a functional stove. Stucco can be shaped in any way, as the multiple curves reveal. With the pillows on the heated sitting area, this piece of art also serves as furniture. Photo courtesy of Biofire, Inc.

per kilogram; a 2010 heater test found an emission of 0.384 gram per kilogram (see chapter 8).

This level of particulate emissions means masonry heaters release less particulate emissions into our environment than that contributed by heating with electricity or coal, and nearly the same as fuel oil. Only kerosene, propane, and natural gas—all fossil fuels—produce significantly less particulates than wood burning in a masonry heater; yet they are unsustainable fuels emitting carbon dioxide and various acids.

Renewable Fuel

Renewable energy is becoming more and more a mainstream idea. Very few people stop to consider the meaning of renewable fuel, however. Instead, we hear that wind power or solar power are renewable energy sources while oil and natural gas are nonrenewable resources. A moment of reflection will put this into better perspective.

Renew means, according to *Webster's New World Dictionary,* "to put in a fresh supply of" or "to make new or fresh again." Talking about renewable energy, then, means talking about having fresh or new supplies of energy. Truthfully, *all* energy sources used today, whether wind, solar, oil, gas, coal, or wood, need to be lumped together. Either they are all renewable fuels or they are all nonrenewable, depending on the perspective taken.

All energy sources used today exist because of the sun. Without the sun shining on the earth, there would be no wind, no plants, no animals, no decaying plants and animals, and, therefore, no fossils and fossil fuels. The sun, as huge and reliable as it is, will not be around forever. Someday, like all stars, it will die. In this way, all energy sources on Earth are nonrenewable.

On the other hand, if the life expectancy of the sun is about five billion more years, it seems nonsensical for humans, who didn't exist on Earth until less than one million years ago, to gauge renewability or longevity of resources against a time line that eclipses their existence! In this view, *all* energy sources *are* renewable. Oil and natural gas, for example, take from ten to three hundred million years to form. Theoretically, new oil reserves will be refreshed about fifteen times before the sun is extinguished!

The difference is entirely in scale. Sunshine and wind are available virtually every day at some capacity. Coal, oil, and natural gas will take (virtually, in the scale of human life) forever to renew. On top of this is the fact that fossil fuels are available to only those corporations, companies, countries, and other entities that happen to have the technology and real estate to drill or mine for them. It is therefore a fact that those who become dependent on these sources will subject themselves to the limited competition among this very limited number of suppliers.

Sunshine, wind, and wood, however, are plentiful throughout the United States, in varying amounts, wherever heating of homes is needed. Of these, wind is not readily usable for significant space heating, while solar heating is unreliable in long winter periods of cloud cover. Wood, then, is the locally or regionally available resource readily usable for heating homes.

Wood is stored sunshine. A tree can easily grow to a mature size in less than a human lifetime. Further, masonry heaters do not require only the use of hardwoods like oak and maple. Many work just as well (or better) with softwoods like pine, larch, or very fast-growing trees such as poplar. Even fallen twigs and small branches are great fuels for masonry heaters. This versatility inherent in good masonry heater design makes finding suitable, plentiful fuel easy for most homeowners in virtually any region of North America. Wood's performance as a battery, storing the energy of sunshine, is a perfect way to use solar energy without having to wait for a sunny day.

Infrastructure is also an issue with energy sources. Consider the pipelines, tankers, drilling rigs, mining equipment, and fueling stations along with the roadways needed to get natural gas or oil to a home for furnace use. With wood as the resource, however, you can often obtain your fuel by taking a walk through the forest and picking up fallen sticks or branches, then cutting them with a saw or ax. If you don't have your own woods, roads are all you need to get to someone who does. (For more information about obtaining wood for masonry heaters, see chapter 10, "Fuel to Burn.")

Benefits of Simplicity

Ostensibly, people appreciate technologically advanced automatic heating systems at least partially because of how easy and convenient they are to use. People need to feel warm, and common furnaces help them to do so without them having to do any more than write a check each month for the fuel cost and maybe an occasional repair. However, it's not hard to envision a future when prices of fuel may become enormously high and access to the fuel infrastructure may become very difficult—a time when the convenience of automation might be outweighed by the price.

Masonry heaters allow us to balance a very high level of convenience with much better individual control and choice of fuel cost. Most people who think about heating with wood have visions of endless hours cutting, splitting, and stacking firewood. Then they think about needing someone to constantly stoke a fire and clean up the mess of many armloads of wood brought into the home each day. This is all ameliorated with masonry heaters.

Masonry heaters often use only a fraction of the wood of common woodstoves. A family of four can stack a winter's supply of wood for a 2,000-square-foot home in one weekend. The real convenience, however, is the way a masonry heater is used.

A typical masonry heater owner enjoys burning a wood fire in the evening. He or she will bring an armload of wood to the heater, stack it in the firebox, and set it on fire. This whole process will occupy less than fifteen minutes. Then the fire is simply enjoyed, usually through glass doors, for about two hours. There is no need to poke and prod the fire and no need to add more wood. When the fire dies to coals, most owners will open the doors and rake the coals together for quicker consumption. Finally, the coals and all will burn to ash, and the air-supply vents to the fire and chimney dampers, if any, will be closed.

This is the total work and effort required to obtain heat for the next twelve to twenty-four hours. Depending on the design of the heater, the size and insulation of the house, the outdoor temperatures, and the comfort level of the occupants, this process may be repeated as often as once every twelve hours or as seldom as once every couple of days. (Masonry heaters can also be designed to be fired more frequently, but few people opt for this.) Many homeowners already choose to enjoy an evening fire. Since the effort put into lighting a fire in a fireplace is virtually the same as in a masonry heater, you can gain complete control of heating a home with what amounts to no extra work. The advantage, of course, is that with the masonry heater, you get all the benefits listed in this chapter.

Even the task of starting a daily fire is easy. Unlike a regular fireplace that is usually cold, a masonry heater in normal use is always warm. Starting a fire in a fireplace that is already warm is very simple. Opening the door or chimney damper immediately begins a chimney draft that makes a match touched to paper and kindling quickly burst into flames. There is no battle to first try to get wood burning so that there is some warmth to

FIGURE 4.15. Here is a soapstone heater that combines different shapes and textures in its radiant appeal. Notice the split stone "bricks" on either side and the decorative grating on the firebox door. Where's the chimney? It's in the wall behind. Photo courtesy of Tulikivi Corporation.

establish chimney draft. This same instantaneous draft assures that there is very little, if any, smoke spillage into the room. The air in homes that use masonry heaters smells clean and fresh. Homes with masonry heaters do not smell like soot and smoke.

There is, of course, maintenance required. Because wood burning always has ash as a waste component, the ash will need to be removed periodically. This is a job that will usually be done about once per week and generally takes just fifteen minutes or so. Inner parts of the heater are also vacuumed or swept, usually once per year. And finally, door glass, if used, will need to be cleaned occasionally. This job is largely one of wiping the ash off with a damp cloth. Sometimes there are more stubborn soot stains, but they are easily removed. (See chapter 12 for more details about such maintenance.)

There is no method of burning wood that is simpler. Masonry heaters are so easy to use that they can be called the lazy man's woodstove. No one needs to tend a fire constantly. No one needs to be home by a certain time to make sure the fire doesn't die (and thereby let the house get cold). No one is a slave to the fire.

Total Value

The many benefits of masonry heaters have been covered in this chapter and the previous ones. These benefits to individual owners or owners-to-be are attractive. Together they point to one mighty conclusion: Masonry heaters are valuable assets. The value of a masonry heater can be verified by concisely considering some basic aspects of value: durability, serviceability, dependability, and quality.

Durability
As a built object, a masonry heater is nearly indestructible when made right. It has no moving parts other than hinges or slides on doors, and maybe a sliding or rotating chimney damper. There are no electronic parts to fail or become obsolete. There are no motors to be rebuilt or replaced. It is a mass of masonry, attractively assembled in an indoor setting. When properly built in an *exterior* setting, masonry structures can last centuries. How long will an *indoor* masonry structure endure? It is safe to say it is virtually of limitless life span. Bugs won't consume it, mold can't diminish it, and fire won't consume it.

When it *is* used as designed, it may have a shorter life, but this shorter life is measured in centuries rather than years or decades. As I mentioned in chapter 2, I recently helped rebuild an eighteenth-century masonry heater that was moved to the United States from Europe, a testament to the longevity of these fireplaces.

Serviceability
A properly designed and built masonry heater, when used regularly and to its potential, will degrade over time. It is essential that it be built to use the most durable techniques and materials for long-term,

high-temperature use (see part 3). When such techniques and materials are used, a masonry heater can go decades with little need for attention. It will one day need repair or service. Perhaps once in a decade or two, the firebox, where the most intense heat is encountered, might need repairs. If properly designed, the firebox can be satisfactorily repaired by a knowledgeable person in less than a day.

After a human lifetime of use, the inner life (core) of the heater may suffer from cracking or deterioration caused by decades of expansion and contraction. Again, a well-designed heater can be completely overhauled in a manner analogous to restoring a classic car. The heater can be disassembled, discarding damaged interior parts, and rebuilt to be like new again.

Dependability
Perhaps one of the most outstanding features of a masonry heater is that, coupled with its virtually limitless life span, it has virtually unlimited dependability as well. Given the simple maintenance and upkeep required, a good masonry heater will always work, and it will work just as well after twenty years as it does the first day it is used. It will still burn cleanly, and it will still heat efficiently. It won't, over time, somehow require more fuel to achieve its results, like a car with a worn engine.

For this reason, every good masonry heater is an heirloom fireplace. It can be passed on to generations to come, and each of those generations can depend on it to function perfectly. As long as there are humans and trees, a masonry heater built today will be a useful, practical device. If the day comes when there are no trees, it is likely humans will have met their end anyway, and masonry heaters will no longer be needed. No other reasonable heating method used today offers this sort of ageless dependability.

Quality
Assuming that a masonry heater is designed and built by a reputable and knowledgeable heater mason, the measures of quality are vast. You can start with the perceived quality of all-masonry construction (durability

FIGURE 4.16. A very large soapstone-and-stucco heater complex. Notice the multiple levels and asymmetry. To the far right can be seen, at middle, a shelf that sits under a bakeoven door. As with many masonry heaters, the chimney is not visible at all. There is another view of this heater in figure 6.39. Photo courtesy of New England Hearth and Soapstone.

and beauty), and proceed to outline the improved quality of life linked with the high quality of heat: improved health and vitality, improved comfort, improved energy independence, ease of use and maintenance, enjoyment of fire, and improved security.

If you were shopping for a high-quality car, you likely wouldn't search for the least expensive car and simply ask whether a particular automobile actually travels from point A to point B as a means of measuring quality; it's a given that any car will have a price that reflects its performance and quality features. It's assumed that every car, whether high-quality or not, at least performs the most basic function for which it was made (getting from one place to another). Simple functionality is not the measure of quality in an automobile. Regarding

home heating, you should likewise look at the qualities it can offer. The cheapest means of keeping folks from feeling too much heat loss is not a measure of quality. Once it is understood that home heating systems permanently and definitely affect health, comfort, safety, and the health of the planet, it becomes important to seek a higher-quality heating system.

Cost

No one considers a masonry heater without at some point asking the inevitable question, "How much does it cost?" Many ask this question first, without having first learned about the remarkable benefits of masonry

FIGURE 4.17. This massive red-brick masonry heater has granite accents. The room is yet to be finished, but the towering chimney will be entirely visible when the cathedral ceiling is done. Notice that this heater has two bakeovens, one above the main firebox and one to the left. Photo courtesy of Maine Wood Heat Company.

heaters. Readers who flipped to this section, wondering if they should invest in this book, are urged to leaf through this whole chapter first. Many people have paid large sums of money to have a custom fireplace that does not perform at all like a masonry heater. Once the value is understood, the cost, as Mark Twain said, "is next to nothing."

Masonry heaters are an investment, rather than a purchase. Simple purchases are made for items that will be used, perhaps used until they are no longer functional or useful, then replaced with another purchase. The purchase of a masonry heater is an investment in something that will not only still be around after decades, but it will most likely be worth more than its original purchase price.

Historically, fireplaces in homes are a selling point—even when they are simple fireplaces that do little, if any, heating. A home with a fireplace will be considered more valuable than a home without one. Homes with permanent, beautiful masonry heater installations should enjoy higher values over time, particularly should the security of heating with fossil fuels from distant lands become more precarious. Masonry heaters are still new enough to the United States market that no reliable data exists to support this, other than the historical attractiveness of wood-burning fireplaces in general.

The actual cost of a masonry heater is variable. Because masonry heaters can be built with so many different materials and in so many different configurations and sizes, pinning down a price is difficult. In essence, you could conceivably scrounge or salvage materials, learn the technology, and build a heater for little more than the price of various mortars and perhaps hardware like doors—as little as a few thousand dollars. This would be an unusual case, though, and most homeowners will likely want to hire a knowledgeable, trained individual or company to install such a fireplace.

With regard to the cost, it is reasonable to say that a masonry heater will cost about the same amount as a car. This necessarily leads to the question, "What kind of car?" That, specifically, is the point. At the time of this writing, you can still buy a car for under $10,000. Likewise, you can spend $100,000, and a vehicle can be purchased for virtually any price between those two amounts.

A compact, no-frills stucco masonry heater that heats just a few rooms will be one price, while an intricately designed heater using antique tiles and incorporating an oven, cooktop, heated benches, and other features will cost much more. Soapstone costs more than bricks, and tiles cost more than stucco, and so on. There is certainly no way to claim that even a single heater of set design will cost a given amount no matter where it goes. Building-site access, site conditions, foundation requirements, local material prices, and varying labor rates all will influence the cost of a given heater. It can simply be expected that a good masonry heater will cost about the same as an automobile. In comparison with other heating systems, it will likely be less expensive or competitive with higher-end systems like geothermal or in-floor systems, yet it retains the advantages and durability that no other system can match.

Conclusion

Masonry heaters use no complex moving parts, no fancy electronics, and are not dependent on power grids. They use fuel that can be grown in a generation. They strip automation from the heating equation in favor of human action and intelligence. They sit peaceably in a home, drawing the attention only of those who wish to admire their beauty, kindle a fire, or bask in their radiant aura. They don't stir dust or dry the indoor air. Masonry heaters are easy to maintain and easy to use. They last a long, long time and hold value just like the heat they retain.

Masonry heaters store heat. That's simple enough. But thinking about what that means turns that simple phrase into a profound insight. Fuel can only be used once. Heat is a fleeting energy derived once from fuel that can be used only once. Consuming nonrenewable fuels for heat, in light of this, seems preposterous, like accelerating while approaching the end of a dead-end street. Storing heat derived from renewable energy sources, however, is the ultimate degree of conservation. It's a way of saying, *Let's carefully use what we have now while we allow nature to replenish our supply.* Heat storage is the beginning and end of the story of masonry heaters. From the simple statement *Masonry heaters store heat* comes the renewable energy benefit of this technology.

FIGURE 4.18. One distinct advantage of stucco is the ability to make virtually any shape look good. Here an organic, rounded shape is decorated with just a few tiles and purposefully imperfectly round arched niches. Notice a sitting area built off the right side of the heater. Photo courtesy of Biofire, Inc.

Then there is the profoundly human aspect of using a central radiant hearth. Masonry heaters actually benefit human health and vitality while offering comfort and security. The unique warmth is a magnet for family and friends. Its circle of comfort draws people together. Families sit together near a masonry heater to read, talk, knit, draw, laugh, sing, and simply be together. It helps us remember that we are not alone—that others feel the cold, too, and need to be warmed. Masonry heaters are the only method of heating today that approaches the goal of total comfort.

Photo courtesy of Temp-Cast Enviroheat.

PART TWO

Designing a Piece of the Sun

The various benefits of masonry heaters, as described in part 1, can only be experienced, of course, when the heater is used. Before the masonry heater can be used, it must be built. Before it can be built, it needs to be designed. Before it can be designed, you need to determine how large it needs to be and where it is going to fit into the floor plan of your house. You also must choose among a range of additional features that all deserve consideration. A masonry heater is a highly specialized, carefully crafted heating appliance. The following three chapters will give you a detailed account of many of the considerations required for getting the maximum return on the investment in an heirloom heating appliance.

These chapters and, indeed, this entire book, are not a replacement for an experienced, educated, and responsible masonry heater professional. They will, however, help the future masonry heater owner make many important decisions. These pages are meant to give you all the tools you need to understand what the whole project entails and what you can expect to have to decide as the project unfolds.

This is not to say that you couldn't use the information in this book and subsequently assume a do-it-yourself project. Individuals with masonry experience, in particular, will feel highly qualified to tackle such a venture. My own experience has been, however, that surprisingly small misunderstandings or assumptions sometimes lead to expensive, nearly irreversible (read: expensive) defects that can significantly diminish the functional qualities of an installation. For ambitious masons, I hope that this book, and this part in particular, will stimulate a desire for professional development. For interested homeowners, I hope the material presented here will stimulate the asking of the right questions of someone who may be hired to build a masonry heater. If you, having read this material, know more about the subjects than the builder, a red flag is waving.

Chapter 6 discusses the design itself—including material options, shapes, sizes, material properties, and more. Chapter 7 tells how to determine what size of masonry heater you'll need for a given living space. There are so many options to consider once you start exploring all the possible features. Before specifics like precise design, materials, and even size are considered, it's wise to explore exactly where a masonry heater should reside as a permanent, lifelong friend and companion of your family. The options are discussed in chapter 5.

FIGURE 5.1. A centrally located brick masonry heater. This one boasts a large heated bench to the left, a "white" bakeoven to the right, and limestone accents. Notice the keystone above the door and the inlaid stone partway up the chimney. Figures 3.5 and 4.6 show other views of this heater.

CHAPTER FIVE

Location

Imagine a Lamborghini sports car, say, a Lamborghini Gallardo Spyder, a sleek, glistening, beautifully engineered automobile. It has a 502-horsepower, turbocharged engine capable of taking this vehicle from 0 to 60 miles per hour in 3.8 seconds. The top speed is 195 mph. It has Pirelli tires, alloy rims, front and rear independent suspension, and a six-speed manual transmission. Of course, it's also a metallic Rosso Leto Red convertible and has black leather racing bucket seats. Everything about it says high performance, speed, power, agility, and control.

Now suppose it's a Saturday afternoon; a clear, sunny day. The car is clean, waxed, polished. It just had a tune-up and oil change. The tank is full of gas. What better thing to do with this unbelievable sports car than to . . . lock it up in the garage, right? What possibly could be better than leaving it alone in the dark, cool garage and going to sip lemonade on the back porch?

Those who are die-hard environmentalists are nodding their heads: "Yes, better to leave that gas-hog, carbon-emitting, high-tech polluter where it can do no more harm." (After all, it does only get 9 miles per gallon in the city.) But those who have driven sports cars, those who have a need for speed, those who have fond memories of their first car, first race, or just an open road with no one around, are saying, "You nutcase, take that thing out for a spin. It doesn't belong in a dark, dank garage on a day like this!"

Put It in the Basement?

Those encountering the masonry heater concept for the first time are prone to thinking that the perfect location for the heater is in the basement. The tons of mass, combined with the erroneous belief that "heat rises," leads to the inference that this heavy-duty heat-producing thing should be down below. From that location, neophytes reason, the constant heat output will then heat the entire upstairs living space simply because the heat rises.

A masonry heater is a central heating system. Like a conventional forced-air furnace, it burns its fuel in a small (compared with most open fireplaces) firebox,

FIGURE 5.2. This masonry heater was built in a basement because it was remodeled and became a primary living space. The red-brick heater features a limestone mantel as well as limestone-capped heated wing benches on either side. The bricks in the center square above the mantel are slightly inset. The owner plans to one day put handmade tiles here.

and all the heat produced is distributed from that location to surrounding areas of the space. The fact that most masonry heaters well exceed a ton in weight and are heat-producing appliances makes it reasonable, to many people, to assume that its best location is the basement.

In reality, it is just as ridiculous to hide a masonry heater in a basement as it is to park that Lamborghini in the garage on a perfect day for driving. Neither can be enjoyed fully if hidden away; both achieve their potential when they are used as intended.

Chapter 3 addressed the common misconception that heat rises and described the unusual radiant heat qualities of a masonry heater. Once you begin to grasp the concept of gentle, radiant heat, it becomes clear that the basement is only a good place for a masonry heater if the basement is primary living space. For some situations, the basement *is* a good location for a masonry heater. The best thing to say about location is simply that a masonry heater should be in the area of a home in which people spend the most waking time.

Primary Living Space

The house I grew up in with my brother, mother, and father was, by today's standards, small. The finished living space comprised all of 1,100 square feet. Roughly half of that space was devoted to three small bedrooms, a hallway, and one and a half baths. The remainder was a kitchen with eating area and a living room. In the winter months, if we weren't in bed for the night, we spent most of our time in the living room or kitchen. Period. The living and kitchen areas were the primary living space.

Today my family and I live in a house more than twice the size of my parents' house. It has roughly 2,400 square feet of living space including four bedrooms, two and a half baths, a recreation room, a formal dining room, a laundry/mud room, a living room, and a kitchen with eating area. Where does my family spend most of its time? Well, even with all the room we have,

the primary living space is still the living room and the kitchen; it's an area that has no more living space than the primary living space of my childhood home.

Anyone considering a masonry heater needs to think clearly about what is or will be (or what you *want* to be) the primary living space. It pays to reflect on how the living space in your current home is used. It's a good bet that, if you're building a new home, its similar spaces will be used in similar ways for similar lengths of time. An addition to, or remodeling of, an existing home likewise may not substantially change the way primary space is used. What I'll designate as *primary living space* is the default location where the various members of the home are most likely to be found during waking hours.

This analysis is critical when contemplating a masonry heater. The reason is that a masonry heater is more akin to a dear friend and companion—who also happens to be generally popular—than it is to a fireplace. A dear friend and companion is someone with whom a lot of time is spent. Good friends want to be together, to be close to each other. A popular individual attracts people. Everyone wants a chance to be around him or her. A masonry heater's gentle warmth is likewise a people magnet.

This concept of the heater as central differs from that used by most architects and designers who specify a fireplace for the home. Often, to these individuals, a fireplace is neither a functional heating appliance nor a crowd-pleasing personality to the degree I'm emphasizing here. To be sure, designers appreciate the ambience of a fire and recognize that a fire does attract people. The difference is crucial, however.

A fire is mesmerizing to watch, and a fireplace can be built and decorated to be an attractive ornament. A fire that is not meant to contribute significantly to heating a space is a delight to watch, but is relatively valueless as a warm companion. A conventional fireplace funnels most of the heat it produces, along with heated room air, up the chimney. The common fireplace, then, is a decorative amenity; indeed, many new, modern fireplace designs look more like framed pictures than they

FIGURE 5.3. A masonry heater is best placed centrally in the main living area of the home. This bluestone heater serves as a room divider between the eat-in kitchen, the living room, and a hall leading to other parts of the house. The view is from the balcony and shows the entire 18-foot-tall chimney. The heater itself is six-sided with the chimney coming off one of the triangular sides. Another view of this heater is in the photo at the beginning of part 4.

do actual fireplaces. This is the reason that architects so commonly place a fireplace against a wall as a focal point, rather than placing it within the heart of the living space as a gathering point.

Primary living space is best outfitted with a masonry heater when you realize that the main attraction of a masonry heater is not the fire itself, but the steady warmth that radiates from the mass. The fire itself can also be enjoyed in any masonry heater with glass doors, but, like an attractive person's appearance, it is only the spark that ignites an evening of conversation. A masonry heater is not a wallflower; it is an appliance with a depth of commitment to your comfort

and well-being. The heater's discourse is its unbending intent to make its company comfortable. Like an attractive person with an intelligent mind and a good sense of humor, a masonry heater is something you long to be around.

The Center of Attention and a Gathering Point

While conventional fireplaces are often the focus of attention, a properly installed masonry heater becomes the *center* of attention. This is not in the sense that those around it can only focus on it and what it's doing. Those who live with a masonry heater or find themselves near one don't usually spend all their time admiring its appearance or its performance. It is, rather, the center of *instinctual* attention. Like sunshine when you're cold, or food when you're hungry, or light when it's dark outside, people automatically gravitate toward the area in which the heater exists. The masonry heater is the gathering point, rather than the focal point.

You can observe this instinctual activity around a campfire on a summer evening. Very seldom does anyone walk away from the campfire to mingle with others. Everyone gathers, instinctively, around the fire to talk. If comfortable chairs were set up in a circle, facing one another, some distance from the fire, you'd see the people taking the chairs and moving them *around* the fire. If the chairs were hard to move, they'd stand around the fire or sit on the ground—but given the choice, they wouldn't likely stay away from that fire.

This same behavior persists around a masonry heater. It is therefore important, once the primary living space is defined, to imagine what the best spot is for this kind of gathering, whether it's a small gathering of just the immediate family or a larger gathering of friends and family. Plan the space for the expected use. If you entertain on a regular basis, your solution will be different than for a home where only

FIGURE 5.4. The masonry heater is a gathering point. This one has a see-through firebox and sports a fully functional "black" bakeoven. This heater can be seen in better detail in figures 3.1, 6.31, and 6.36. Heater by Maren Cooke and Ken Matesz; photo by Maren Cooke.

the immediate family will be around. The space for entertaining needs to be larger and more open, while a small family may simply gather in a modest dining area or family room.

The aspect of entertaining and, particularly, cooking figure into the location decision as well if you hope to incorporate a baking oven or masonry cookstove into the mass. There is an obvious disconnect in having a fireplace with a baking oven located a room away from the kitchen. It may seem obvious to most people to have an oven facing the kitchen or, at the very least, a dining area. This does not stop people from forgetting this detail when making initial plans. The oven is functional, of course, wherever it is located in the house. It is far better, however, to have it in a room in which food is either prepared or eaten.

More than One Primary Living Space?

It is possible to have more than one area in the home that gets a lot of daytime use. For example, someone who works at home may have an office or den. Other popular rooms are recreation rooms, theater rooms, sewing rooms, or other specialty rooms in which one or more people go often, usually for specific kinds of activities. Although it's true that these spaces get regular use, they don't quite fit the classification of primary living space as it's used here. Primary living space is still the overriding, default location in a home where you're most likely, at any given time, to find the majority of the family members.

Offices and special rooms are just that: special areas. When designing a new home (or expanding an

FIGURE 5.5. Here is an heirloom-quality soapstone heater perfectly located for enjoyment and heating of the living space. Large split or rock-faced soapstone blocks create a gently tapered heater body rising from lightly supported, cantilevered wing benches. Its location between the living room and kitchen, near the stairs, and also visible from the foyer give it a commanding position. Photo courtesy of WarmStone Fireplaces and Designs; photo copyright JK Lawrence Photography.

existing home), consider the merits of creating these special areas separately from the primary living areas. If they must be separated, perhaps they also deserve their own, small masonry heater to bring radiant comfort there as well. Another option is to locate these areas as appendages immediately accessible to the primary living space. After all, if you're going to be home all day, won't you want to be near the most comfortable area?

The best option is simply to think carefully before creating a special-use space. For example, you may believe the home office must be a separate, private space so you can concentrate and get work done without interruption from other people and activities. But if it's more likely that you'll be the only one home during the day, who is there to distract you? Will a

home theater or entertainment room really improve life substantially over a great room that is well equipped for movies and games? All these are individual, subjective choices that need to be measured against costs, reasonableness, and long-term life in a home. An expensive entertainment room for the kids might sound terrific, until you consider that the kids might be moving out of the home in four or five years.

This book assumes, above all else, that if you're interested in masonry heaters, you're likewise interested in amenities that result in permanent improvements in the comfort, pleasure, and utility of a home. Heirloom basics like high-quality framing and insulation, coupled with heirloom artifacts like high-quality windows, floors, cupboards, counters, and masonry heaters will generally benefit a family and future generations regardless of changes in availability of nonrenewable resources, trends, or technology. This will be the case whether there are two people living in the home or a family of ten. The same can't necessarily be said for amenities purchased for a single use or benefit like theater or entertainment rooms or high-tech heating and air-conditioning equipment. As mentioned earlier, it's the fundamentals that count.

The simple fact is that a masonry heater can have a much more powerful pull on people than you realize at first. If you appreciate its features and benefits and plan ways to maximize enjoyment of those benefits, you won't be disappointed. Easily the single most important step to maximum enjoyment is locating the masonry heater in the most favorable gathering area of the primary living space.

The Chimney Rules

Once you've established the primary living space, it's time to figure out the exact location for the masonry heater. Given that many modern homes have quite large spaces and that rooms have (often) four walls, there are still many locations in which the masonry heater could serve its purpose as the gathering point. The fact that a masonry heater needs a chimney will help to further refine this location.

Often, people who see a masonry heater for the first time, either in person or in pictures, suppose that the appliance actually needs no chimney. In many installations, the chimney isn't visible because it's in a chase hidden in a wall behind, to the side of, or some distance away from the firebox. The truth, of course, is that any solid-fueled heating appliance needs a chimney. Some people will inquire whether the masonry heater can just be "direct-vented" out its back to the outside, like some gas appliances. The simple answer is no.

A masonry heater works entirely (well, almost) by virtue of a chimney. Without a properly operating chimney, the masonry heater won't function properly. How do you know if the chimney is operating correctly? Quite simply, a chimney is working correctly if the exhaust of the appliance *always* goes up the chimney under normal operating and living conditions. A chimney that works sometimes or only under certain conditions is not a chimney that operates correctly. For example, if a chimney works only if the wind comes from a certain direction, it's a dysfunctional chimney. As with most things, it is possible to "make" a dysfunctional chimney work. It's much better to plan to have a fully functional chimney, however.

The Physics of Chimneys

With a basic understanding of the physical laws behind good chimney performance, it becomes easy to envision the best site for a chimney. Knowing this location will help you decide where, in the primary living space, to put the masonry heater.

Webster's New World Dictionary defines *chimney* as "the passage or structure through which smoke escapes from a fire, often extending above the roof." This definition can be improved by saying that the chimney is a structure through which exhaust from a fire is directed vertically out of a house. The term *vertically* is necessary to clarify the fact that horizontal structures that connect a masonry heater or other appliance to a chimney are, indeed, *connectors,* but not chimneys themselves. Gently angled portions of chimneys are still vertical, in the sense that they serve only to modify the location of the vertical chimney slightly, and do little to restrict the overall vertical movement of exhaust.

In order to understand good chimney function, it is necessary to revisit the common statement that "heat rises." As discussed in chapter 3, heat itself does not rise. It is more accurate to say that hot or warm air rises. In a properly operating chimney, then, warm exhaust goes up the chimney and out of the house; the appliance works properly and no dusty, objectionable, potentially harmful gases enter the living space. It's time to examine more closely the statement that warm air rises.

Does Warm Air Always Go Up a Chimney?

Few people, save physicists and engineers, ever ponder this question. Most of us simply accept that warm air rises, just as we accept that objects fall to the ground when dropped. Anyone, however, contemplating the use of a wood-burning masonry heater should be fully aware of the complete answer to this question, because it will lead to an understanding of how to place a masonry heater so that it attains maximum performance and provides maximum enjoyment for decades to come.

Some will quickly answer the question, saying that of course warm air (exhaust) will always rise up a chimney because it is *lighter* than cooler air. Warm air is more buoyant than cold. When air gets warmed, it expands—its molecules spread out—making it lighter (less dense) than cooler air; so indeed warm air does rise. Many fireplace users nevertheless have been frustrated and aggravated over exhaust (smoke) that did *not* go up the chimney, but rather came into the home, stained the front of the fireplace, or much worse. If the chimney is wide open and the exhaust of the fire is warmer than room air, why isn't it rising up the chimney?

You may recall the second law of thermodynamics (see chapters 1 and 3), which stated that heat always travels from the warmer area to the cooler area and not the other way around (without an energy input). In a similar fashion, air (or any other fluid, liquid, or gas) will always travel from an area of higher *pressure* to an area of lower pressure. This additional understanding combining "hot air being lighter" and "air under higher pressure moving to an area of lower pressure" is crucial. If all we need to know is that hot air is lighter, then there would be no satisfactory answer as to why many common fireplaces, which are just fireboxes with open chimneys above them, frequently spill smoke into the house. The lighter warm air should readily just go up the chimney provided. Obviously, there's more to this than meets the eye.

Think about watering plants in the garden. If you use a common hose nozzle—the kind that can spray

FIGURE 5.6. Like many masonry heaters, this one appears to have no chimney because the chimney is built into the wall. It uses terra-cotta tiles to contrast with stucco, as well as niches and decorative shapes for great appeal. Notice that the black loading door does not have glass. Since a masonry heater is used only for part of the year in most locations, many folks don't want to look into an empty firebox during those warm seasons. Others would never give up the option of seeing the fire. Photo courtesy of Biofire, Inc.

a stream or fan or various other patterns—and when you're done spraying, you shut the nozzle and go to the spigot on the house and turn off the water supply, the hose will be pressurized. With the water supply off, you could again pick up the hose and open the nozzle. For a brief time, water will be forced out of the hose, though the water spigot is off. The water in the hose had been under higher pressure than the surrounding environment.

Or think of the painful experience of getting a flat tire on a bike, car, or mower, and hearing the air, once under contained pressure in the tire, whistling out of the puncture until the air pressure inside the tire matches the air pressure surrounding it.

These common occurrences are demonstrations of the general idea behind chimney performance as well. Exhaust from an appliance will go up the chimney and out of the house *only* if the easiest way for air under higher pressure to leave the house is up the chimney. It matters not how expensive the chimney was, how big or small its diameter, whether it's brick, clay tile, refractory, or metal. The only real factor is whether the chimney was designed to be the best place in the house for pressurized air to escape. In simpler terms, the chimney needs to be the best leak in the house envelope, the conditioned living space.

Stack Effect

Think *smokestack*. Since it is known that hot air typically rises out of a chimney (a "stack"), *stack effect* is the name given to this phenomenon. It can be defined more accurately as "the difference in pressure created by the difference between the air temperature in a container compared with the air temperature outside that container." This definition recognizes that both temperature *and* pressure play a role in a properly operating chimney. Stack effect isn't present only in chimneys, however. Stack effect relates to *any* container.

A house, like a chimney, is a container of air and it, too, is a sort of chimney. After all, in the winter, it (hopefully) contains air that is warmer than outside air. Just as in a true chimney, the warm air in a house will want to rise. Since most homes are not airtight plastic bags, they generally have tiny leaks through which outside air can enter, and inside (warm) air can leave. In general, outside air will leak into the home in a lower level and warm air will leak out of the house at an upper level. The house is thus performing the same way a chimney does, funneling warmer air out its "top."

The Pressure Is On

This condition of air entering low and exiting high gives a clue to the general air pressure conditions existing in the home. If air is entering the house on the first floor, the air *pressure* there has to be negative or lower than the outdoor atmospheric pressure. If the warm air is being forced out of the leaks on the second floor, for example, then the second-floor area must be under positive pressure (higher pressure than the atmospheric, outdoor air pressure). This is known, again, because air always moves from an area of higher pressure to an area of lower. Air at atmospheric pressure rushes to the area where the pressure is low, and air at a pressure higher than atmospheric rushes toward the outside of the house, where the pressure is lower. The air-temperature difference is creating the different pressure regions.

Somewhere between the negative pressure area and the positive pressure area is an elevation where the pressure is neither positive nor negative. This is called the *neutral pressure plane* or *neutral pressure zone*. At the neutral pressure plane, the air pressure is the same as outdoor atmospheric pressure. Here air will neither be drawn in nor expelled from the house. Below the neutral pressure plane is the volume of the house with pressures lower than atmospheric (negative pressure), and above it is the volume of the house with positive pressure.

The location of the neutral pressure zone varies from house to house, but in most modern, reasonably well-built homes, the neutral pressure plane is somewhat above the vertical midpoint of the heated envelope of the house. In a common two-story house, for example, built over a crawl space, the neutral pressure plane is likely to be at or above the actual floor level of the second story. Likewise, a home with a full basement and two full floors will likely have the neutral pressure plane above the midline of the first main floor above the basement.

Connecting Air Pressure with Chimney Function

Since both the entire home and the chimney of an operating masonry heater are subject to the stack effect, think of the chimney as being a chimney inside a chimney. Both the house and its chimney are systems

FIGURE 5.7. By properly locating a chimney, you can make sure the smoke always goes up and a white stuccoed heater always stays white. This granite-trimmed heater has an upper-chamber "black" bakeoven. Through the arched bakeoven door glass, you can see the fountain of flame that has just come through the throat from the main firebox below. Notice wood storage to the left and the masonry chimney transitioning to stainless steel on the right. Photo courtesy of Maine Wood Heat Company.

that contain air at higher pressure that wants to escape to an area of lower pressure. Both are systems containing air that is warmer than the air outside them. The chimney in operation contains exhaust that is warmer than the air in the house, while the house confines air that is warmer than outside. Stack effect operates in both structures, and *it's the pressure conditions that determine which system is the better chimney*. In other words, if the pressure driving warm air to the upper parts of the house is stronger than the pressure attempting to drive exhaust up the chimney, the exhaust will come out of the masonry heater and into the house rather than going up the chimney.

As noted above, the neutral pressure plane of a typical house is above its vertical middle plane. The primary living space of most homes tends to be on the first level, and the masonry heater is usually in the primary living space. The masonry heater, then, is usually in the part of the house below the neutral pressure plane, in the area with a pressure *lower than* outside atmospheric pressure (negative pressure). This is the part of the house that wants to draw air into the house from outside. If the pressure created in the chimney is not greater than this negative pressure, the negative pressure will pull air (and masonry heater exhaust) into the living space through the chimney—which functions then as a direct connection to outdoor atmospheric pressure.

In good design, the reverse happens: The temperature difference that wants to drive the flow of exhaust up the chimney (called the draft) is reliably stronger than the house stack effect. In this case, the chimney and appliance work properly; all the exhaust goes up the chimney every time the heater is used.

The Chimney Rules

Of course, the effect everyone wants is for the smoke to go up the chimney and not into the room. A masonry heater is a lifetime, maybe even a multi-lifetime fireplace. It stands to reason, then, that wisdom would have every masonry heater equipped with a chimney that will reliably send its exhaust up the chimney and nowhere else. Since most masonry heaters are likely to be installed below the neutral pressure plane of the house, every attempt should be made to install a chimney that will always overcome the negative pressure inherent to that location. Fortunately, the rules for making this happen are few and simple. Anyone who has a masonry heater installed and follows these rules will be blessed with maximum performance of the appliance:

1. Plan for the chimney to be located within the heated confines of the home.

The basis for this rule is simple: If the chimney (and the air in it) is already at room temperature, it is ready at all times to become the best place for exhaust to leave the house. The chimney, in essence, is the best "leak" in the house envelope, just waiting for the masonry heater door or chimney damper to be opened, at which point immediate draft will begin because of stack effect.

A chimney outside the heated space, on the other hand, will, in the winter, contain cold air. This air is colder than room air and, depending on changing weather conditions and mass-storage factors, could also be colder than ambient outdoor temperatures. This is nearly a surefire way to make the house a better chimney than the chimney itself. The house, operating under natural stack effect, will pull masonry heater exhaust into the house. The heat of the fire simply will

FIGURE 5.8. The chimney here is completely inside the house and exits the room very close to the ridgeline. This white stucco heater utilizes the system of free gas movement described in chapter 8 and features heated seating and wood storage as well as a "white" bakeoven. Designed and built by Stovemaster; photo courtesy of Alex Chernov.

CHIMNEYS THAT CAUSE PROBLEMS

The chimney rules tend to keep the chimney in locations where it will exit the roof of the house relatively close to the ridge—the highest point of the roof. Another very good reason *not* to have the chimney close to the lowest point of the roof is that it can become a more likely place to generate roof leaks. A chimney comes through a hole in the roof. Though good roofing and flashing practices will usually prevent leaks around a chimney, when a chimney is downstream from most of the precipitation (and anything else) that falls on the roof, it is much more likely to accumulate dirt or catch tree branches and other debris that can degrade the watertightness over time. A hole (chimney location) at the highest part of the roof will be subject to much less wear and much less water—an additional precaution against eventual leaks.

not easily overcome the stack effect, the draft, of the house itself.

2. Ensure that the chimney passes through the tallest heated part of the house.

Stack effect is powered by the differences in temperatures and the resulting differences in pressures. The height of the stack (either the house itself or the chimney) also influences the pressure. A taller house will have higher positive air pressure in the uppermost floor than a shorter house. Similarly, a taller chimney will have better draft. As long as the chimney serving a masonry heater is passing through heated space (as per Rule 1 above) all the way through the tallest, heated area of the house, it will continue to have superior stack effect and provide the best venting. It has superior draft because it is as warm as, yet taller than, the tallest heated part of the house; the positive pressures in it are always higher than those in the house.

It should be noted that this rule automatically

FIGURE 5.9. An example of a chimney offset from a heater to a desired location for travel through the rest of the house and through the roof. Heater by New England Hearth and Soapstone.

discourages having chimneys anywhere along the eave wall of a room with a sloped cathedral ceiling. The chimney does not have to be right at the apex of such a room, but it should be very close. This rule also discourages the placement of the chimney in a one-story addition to a two-story house. Additionally, following this rule keeps chimneys, particularly large masonry chimneys, from being located at the low points of a roof where they will collect more leaves and snow, and be washed by more rain. In other words, they're less subject to causing roof leaks or maintenance problems as time passes.

3. Avoid the use of powerful exhaust devices.

Kitchen stove exhausts, bathroom exhaust fans, and even furnaces with assisted draft fans venting to the outside can sometimes be powerful enough to depressurize the house. Although natural stack effect of the house will be overcome by a chimney that follows the first two rules, an exhaust fan is another story.

Bear in mind that the actual air pressure that achieves positive draft—the pressure driving exhaust up the chimney—is still very weak. Think of how slowly a hot-air balloon rises into the sky; it doesn't represent a lot of power. An electric fan, on the other hand, may move many cubic feet of air per minute, far surpassing the modest air pressures of the drafting chimney. Such a device can easily pull air (and exhaust) down the chimney as the air pressures try in vain to neutralize the negative pressures created.

In the construction phase of a house, it's possible to install a make-up air device that automatically compensates for the air being drawn out by the exhaust fan when it's activated. In existing homes where this automatic feature has not been installed, be aware that such appliances can reverse the flow of exhaust in a chimney. Simply refraining from using these high-volume fans during the limited time that a masonry heater is fired will assure that reversed drafts do not happen.

4. Follow the advice of the masonry heater professional or manufacturer regarding chimney height.

Most masonry heater professionals will encourage minimum chimney heights for the heaters they install. As a general rule, they should suggest a chimney at least 15 feet tall, and many heater professionals want to see no less than 20 feet. A common, single-story home that is 24 feet wide and has an 8-foot ceiling and shallow roof pitch will have a ridge height of at least 12 feet. Since most construction codes pertaining to chimneys will require the chimney to be 2 to 3 feet above the ridge, even a masonry heater in this house could have 15 feet of total height. The greater the height, the more pressure that is developed in the chimney and, thus, the better the draft.

Of lesser importance, but frequently mentioned by stove and fireplace professionals, is a general warning not to install offsets in the chimney. Offsets are slightly angled portions of chimney that are used to meet the location from which the chimney exits the ceiling or roof. Building codes (see chapter 9) and/or manufacturer's instructions (for factory-made chimneys) may limit the angle and total distance of these offsets. Because offsets interrupt the rapid vertical movement of exhaust up a chimney, they can tip the balance toward possible reverse flow of exhaust under some conditions. If the four rules above are followed, then gradual, short offsets are rarely an issue for masonry heaters. It is wise, however, to consult with a professional to see if there's any reason offsets cannot be used in a given project. Masonry heater designers should factor offsets into the design of the heater to be built because any offset will change the dynamics and speed of draft, if only a little.

Sometimes the above-mentioned offsets are used to relocate a chimney either before or as it goes through a second-floor space. Obviously, the prime location of the heater and chimney on the first floor or main level of the home often necessitates that the chimney travel through the second-floor space, if the home has one. In new construction, the location of the chimney must be taken into account when designing the home's second floor. This will be just as important as the main-level design, in order to assure that the chimney can be properly built without interfering with the space directly above the masonry heater. This is one of the chief reasons why a masonry heater professional should be involved *during* the design process. There are many possibilities that the professional will be ready to suggest for any such dilemmas. In advance of hiring a professional, read the section "Multistory Retrofits" later in this chapter regarding chimney and heater placement.

The rules for chimney placement go a long way toward determining the best location for a masonry heater. With the location already narrowed to the primary living space, the chimney's functional requirements should begin to articulate a zone in that space that would assure good chimney performance. Now it's time to get really specific. A masonry heater is just as permanent as the home itself, if not more so. The final decisions will shape how spaces are used for decades to come.

Functional Requirements of Radiant Heat

As I pointed out previously, radiant heat is electromagnetic radiation. In other words, it behaves just like light in every way, except that it is not visible to the human eye. If you turn on a light in a closet, then shut the door, anyone outside the closet will not get to experience the light from the bulb. Similarly, if a heater is confined to a small space bounded by walls, you won't get to experience its radiant heat outside those four walls. As discussed in chapter 3, the walls of a house are the ultimate shadow makers for a masonry heater's gentle radiance.

If your intention in having a masonry heater is only to heat a single room, then this limitation is not a hindrance at all. In fact, the well-defined space will enhance the comfort you experience there. Assuming the heater is properly sized to that space, it will gently heat everyone and everything in that room. It will *not,* as many would conclude, overheat that space and make it uncomfortably stuffy and unbearable—unless the masonry heater was not properly used or was improperly designed for the space. See chapters 7 and 8 for more on proper design.

In the primary living space, which might include a kitchen, living area, dining area, and more, the uniqueness of radiant heat requires some consideration. There are two overriding qualities of a masonry heater to keep constantly in mind. First, as described earlier, it is a gathering point. Second, it heats living space primarily with radiant heat that travels over distance to things and people. If you put one of these qualities too far out of mind, the other will dominate the way the heater is used and enjoyed.

For example, one of my clients decided, against my advice, to locate his heater in a corner formed by an L-shaped staircase. Although this location is still in the primary living space (which includes the kitchen, dining area, and living room), it is removed from the living room and on the edge of the kitchen. The owner is generally happy with the performance of the masonry heater to heat the primary living space; however, when he has guests in the winter, they gravitate and stay close

FIGURE 5.10. Though this masonry heater is central to the primary living space, a wall separates it from the dining area. Making the bench to the right heated would have ameliorated this. Instead, it is mainly sitting area with storage below. Notice a lot of provision for firewood and the use of soapstone tiles to carry the color of the heater into its accessories. Photo courtesy of Tulikivi Corporation.

to the heater rather than straying into the living room. Although his living room is large and set up to accommodate many, his guests remain on the fringe of both kitchen and living room.

Other clients have placed the masonry heater in the center of a living room area, but have separated it from the other frequent-use areas by walls or staircases. Thus the heater is perfect as the gathering point, but does much less to contribute gentle radiant heat to other parts of the primary living area. Most people who are investing in this degree of comfort will want

to experience it over all of the primary living space and locate the heater in the best gathering place of the primary living area.

The Central Hearth in the Open Floor Plan

Following the "chimney rules" and paying attention to the actual function of the heater serve to put the hearth—the place for a fire—in its rightful location. There is no more appropriate place for a masonry heater than the center of activity and enjoyment of a home. The sacred fire has always been the thing around which human life unfolds. The natural benefits of the heater are begging to be maximized by such a location. The requirements for good chimney operation likewise serve to force the issue, dictating that the masonry heater be somewhere close to the center of the home. Getting the maximum function from a chimney and combining it with the maximum comfort possibilities presented by the radiant heat—a gathering point and radiant comfort throughout the primary living space—demands that a masonry heater be located centrally.

Put simply, the single most effective way to get the maximum enjoyment from a masonry heater is to have it centrally located in the main living area of the home with no walls present to impede its waves of heat. In a central location, the exhaust is virtually guaranteed always to go up the chimney, people can easily gather around, and radiant heat can readily find its way into every corner of every part of the primary living space.

The primary living space is not private space to which people go to seek solitude. It is always the hub of activity. Walls, thus, are unnecessary obstructions, not only to the gentle radiant heat, but also to including everyone. Without walls, someone cooking in the kitchen can still effectively communicate with someone in the living room. A smile, a gesture, a fire, and comfortable heat all combine and mix in a pleasant, unrestricted way. Without walls, furniture placement, area-specific functions, and the masonry heater itself define spaces. Without walls, guests and family members alike can easily mingle, explore, and find a personal spot while still being involved in the festivities.

Timber-frame homes, log homes, geodesic domes, and houses utilizing free-span trusses all encourage open floor plans. Even conventionally framed homes, with careful design, can certainly be built to provide optimum conditions for a gathering area and radiant heat. An open, unrestricted floor plan surrounding the masonry heater will forever allow residents to fully enjoy everything the heater has to offer.

FIGURE 5.11. This finely sculpted stucco heater has no walls around it to hinder its heating ability. A simple but curved wooden bench follows the contours of the heater, and delicate tile accents add just a little color. Every curved surface here will radiate heat like the sun. Photo courtesy of Biofire, Inc.

Locations in a Retrofit or Closed Floor Plan

Although there is no change to the parameters you'd use to find a good masonry heater location in an existing house, there are additional challenges that can threaten the viability of such a project. Obviously, this is less true if the masonry heater will be part of a substantial remodeling project in which even structural changes to the home may take place. In a renovation in which walls might be removed and the floor plan completely redone, locating a masonry heater requires no more considerations than already mentioned. Those who are adding a heater without other major changes, however, will have more to think about.

For many older homes with fireplaces, it seems like using the existing fireplace location—an existing chimney—is a sensible, no-brainer option for the masonry heater. Unfortunately, so many such homes have the existing fireplace *through* an outside wall. Some will even have a double-whammy violation of the "chimney rules"—the existing chimney is not only outside the warm envelope of the house but also in a single-story addition to an otherwise two-story house. This scenario is a virtual guarantee of poor chimney performance and therefore poor masonry heater performance.

It is possible to reline an existing chimney that is otherwise an outdoor, cold chimney. If the outdoor location is the only problem (the only violation of the chimney rules), relining the old chimney with an insulated liner *may* lead to satisfactory results. It is still questionable, however, and is worth careful consideration before moving ahead with plans for a lifelong, heirloom masonry heater installation. The input of a professional masonry heater designer is invaluable under these conditions. Again, consider the functional requirements of masonry heat as described earlier, as well as the practicality of the location as a gathering point.

Such compromised scenarios are often no-win situations; you may be better off instead abandoning fireplaces and chimneys that so flagrantly violate the most basic rules for good performance. Think of that wall where an old ineffective fireplace was sited as an opportunity to add furniture once you close the fireplace permanently. It is worthwhile to then do a careful analysis of the primary living space near the centerline of the house and completely within the heated regions of the house. A better location exists somewhere in that living space.

Single-Story Retrofits

In most single-story homes, a retrofit is not all that challenging. The masonry heater will likely displace or change current furniture arrangements. The existing floor plan also may not be "open" at all. It goes without saying that a retrofit into an existing home with a desire for minimal remodeling will rarely result in the ideal masonry heater situation. The fact is that most homes in the United States were not and are not designed around a functional central hearth. Compromise will have to be made, but most of the same considerations apply. Good chimney function and a location in the most-used area of the home will still provide great enjoyment.

The "closed" floor plan—where every room is distinctly separated by walls from every other room—necessarily decreases the degree to which radiant heat can be enjoyed throughout the home. This doesn't mean a masonry heater must be rejected, but it may alter the strategy you use to heat the living space. Radiant heat simply does not penetrate walls (though it *can* warm them through and through). Especially in smaller houses, or houses in which the primary living space really is just one room, the closed floor plan can actually magnify the enjoyment of the masonry heater in that space. As always, it's critical to "know thyself" and plan the heater for the way your family lives. Sizing a heater to the space is discussed in detail in chapter 7.

Since there is no upper floor, chimney placement isn't much of an issue; it will not affect other living spaces of the house. In fact, once a suitable location is determined, the only challenging aspect in a single-story home is the support structure for the masonry heater. See chapter 9 for more on this topic.

Multistory Retrofits

As in a single-story existing home, the support structure and the proper placement of the heater in the space needs careful thought. The multistory home, however, has the additional complication of one or more floors of living space above the location of the masonry heater, unless, of course, you're going to place the heater itself on the uppermost floor. (In this case, support structure through living space *below* the heater will need a lot of planning.)

FIGURE 5.12. The chimney of this soapstone heater goes through to the second floor. Careful planning keeps it out of the way upstairs. This one-of-a-kind soapstone creation is shown in figure 1.10 as well. Photo courtesy of WarmStone Fireplaces and Designs; photo copyright Mikel Covey Photography.

The first step is to locate one or more reasonable sites for the heater and chimney. You can temporarily mark the floor with a potential chimney location. The eventual chimney size is of little consequence at first; right now you're just determining a center point. Then take careful measurements from reliable reference objects. Exterior walls are best as references as long as the walls remain in the same plane all the way through the other upper stories (this is not the case in some designs with cantilevered second floors).

For example, if the proposed chimney center point on the main level is 12 feet from the south wall and 15 feet from the west wall, you can go to the next floor level and make the same measurements to locate where the chimney would be. (Be sure you take those measurements with the measuring tape perpendicular to the reference wall.) If additional obstacles exist upstairs, like interior walls, the thickness of that wall must be taken into account as the measuring proceeds. Most interior walls of conventional homes are 4½ inches thick. Thus, you may measure 10 feet within a bedroom, add 4½ inches for the thickness of the interior wall, then measure another 1 foot and 7½ inches outside that wall to get the full 12-foot measurement.

This type of measurement will reveal where the chimney would pass through the second floor given the chosen location below. If the location falls squarely in the middle of a hallway, for example, it's obviously unsound. If it falls in a closet, the corner of a room, or reasonably close to one of these relatively out-of-the-way locations, a good solution to chimney placement may be at hand. It's important to note here that masonry heaters, in general, are very versatile in how they can connect to a chimney. If the proposed chimney location downstairs would bring the chimney center point reasonably close to a usable space upstairs, it could very well be that a minor movement of the chimney or the masonry heater or both will bring the chimney squarely through a place that does not adversely affect living space on the upper floor.

It is understood here that as you're making these initial investigations, you may not really know how big the chimney for the masonry heater needs to be. You also may not know whether it will even be a metal flue of some kind or a masonry chimney. In most cases, a masonry chimney will be the type that will take up the most total space. Even some of the largest masonry heaters commonly used in homes require no more than an 8-by-12-inch clay-lined masonry chimney that has outside measurements approaching 17 by 21 inches. You can use this size as a guide for estimating how the chimney will fit through the second-floor space. If the center-point measurement, for example, was 8 inches from one wall and 10 inches from the other (at the corner of a bedroom, perhaps), a slight adjustment in actual placement could have the flue fitting right into that corner of the room.

If you're uncomfortable with doing this sort of initial study, consult with a masonry heater professional, who will be more confident about what can be done, what size chimney might be used, and other details about a potential installation. I've outlined the procedure here to help you discover for yourself the viability of the project, perhaps before you hire a professional for a more complete analysis. Some people will, however, insist there is no way to make a masonry heater and chimney work inside their homes. They may be surprised to find that an experienced eye can sometimes find a good location that satisfies most design parameters and runs right through the center of the house. I once retrofitted a large masonry chimney into the middle of an existing home, finding a path that successfully traveled through two additional floors of living space. I did this without altering wall locations or taking the chimney right through the middle of prime activity space.

Location Redux

Like a high-performance sports car, a masonry heater is not meant to be hidden away in a closet, basement, or other rarely visited space. By identifying the primary living space, you likewise identify the best general area to locate this high-performance heating appliance. By further following the best rules for maximum chimney performance, you assure that a masonry heater performs at its best and never asphyxiates residents when being fired. The same "chimney rules" further define how to locate the masonry heater in the primary living space. Similarly, understanding the role of the heater as a gathering point or center of attention, as well as its vast heating potential, refines the search for the best final location.

Retrofits are an even greater challenge because all the usual considerations should be followed, yet you must also compensate for existing conditions that probably aren't ideal for masonry heaters. Nevertheless, retrofits are common and can be successful if you take care to find a good location.

In the final analysis, the best site for a masonry heater is almost always as a central hearth around which activity will flourish. Whenever possible, this central location also offers open space around it so that soothing, placid radiant heat can be experienced throughout the primary living space.

FIGURE 6.1. This heater features granite and marble stones laid as a mosaic, creating artwork within the artwork. Stucco sculpts a swirl around the chimney as it rises to the ceiling. A simple black door reinforces that the beauty here is the stove, regardless of whether a fire is burning. Photo courtesy of Stuart Davies.

CHAPTER SIX

Design Options

Given what we have learned so far, it is clear that masonry heaters are not, in the common use of the term, fireplaces. Masonry heaters need to be classified differently. The word *fireplace* conjures definite stereotypical visions and expectations. For most of us in the United States, for example, it immediately triggers a picture of a fire burning in a large rectangular opening—often around 3 feet wide and a couple of feet high—with some kind of mantel above. It also conjures thoughts about *unpleasant* features, most of which don't exist with a properly designed masonry heater: Slow, smoldering fires, frequent adding of more wood, the smell of unburned wood, and soot and ash in the house all coalesce around visions of a "fireplace."

A masonry heater will never be a fireplace, if the above is an accurate depiction of one. For purposes of discussion, the term *traditional fireplace* refers to this old idea of an open firebox with a large opening and characteristic surrounds and mantel. A traditional fireplace is nothing but a large firebox with a flue opening directly above it. By definition, a masonry heater is not a traditional fireplace.

In reality, there are very few similarities between masonry heaters and traditional fireplaces. One similarity is that both have a hearth—literally, the place on which to build a fire—and firebox as a container for the fire. Second, both (traditionally) are built with masonry materials of some kind, like bricks, stone, and mortar. In today's world, even that is becoming rarer; common fireplaces are now built with the traditional fireplace look but a metal firebox and a surround of common building materials like wood framing and drywall. To say they are virtually the same is like saying a violinist and an orchestra are virtually the same thing because they both play music. The violinist may be very talented and play beautiful solos, but she will never be able to accomplish, on her own, what the entire orchestra does together. Traditional fireplaces and masonry heaters each contain a fire, but only the masonry heater offers a symphony of features and benefits in addition to the solo enjoyment of a fire.

Meeting Expectations

When people in North America decide they want a fireplace in their home, they generally have in mind the traditional fireplace. This is merely because this is what they have always seen. It may be what they have experienced throughout childhood and with friends and neighbors. Historical buildings have the traditional fireplace, and the traditional fireplace appears in texts documenting the settling of America. The concept of a masonry heater has simply never crossed their paths.

Until you take the time to learn about it, a masonry heater seems like an inadequate fireplace. Why would anyone want a masonry heater? It doesn't have the feature that we most expect from a fireplace—a big, open firebox for fire viewing. It's bulky and takes up floor space. It is nothing like what you're accustomed to.

It's time to forge new expectations. Rather than expecting a particular appearance, you should be expecting versatility and performance. Today automobiles, for example, come in every shape, size, and category. Few would relish the thought of a horse-drawn carriage to get them to the afternoon meeting forty miles away. People have realized the freedom of transportation offered by autos. They can likewise experience the freedom of fire and warmth divorced from an outdated, inefficient traditional fireplace design.

FIGURE 6.2. A brick, Finnish-style masonry heater often has the standard fireplace look that many homeowners desire. Notice the deep brick raised hearth and the ornate brickwork and arch around a square door, giving the appearance of a larger opening. Photo courtesy of Maine Wood Heat Company.

There are, in fact, some masonry heaters that roughly mimic what typical North American citizens picture to be a "fireplace." Most notable is the Finnish-style contraflow masonry heater. Although it still does not have the large open firebox of a traditional fireplace, it does have a (usually) symmetrical design that people can recognize as fireplace-ish. Frequently these heaters will have mantels centered above the loading door and will be faced in common brick or natural stone. If such a heater is built as part of and through a wall separating two spaces, it can further the conventional fireplace look. These recognizable aspects can bridge the chasm between traditional fireplaces and masonry heaters for those who just cannot let go of the fireplace idea and expect a certain "fireplace" look.

New Possibilities

If you can give up your expectations for what a place for fire must be, masonry heaters are absolutely the most exciting hearth products in existence. In a very real sense, if your mind can imagine a heater design, and it doesn't defy the laws of physics, it can be built as a masonry heater; it can be a truly unique place for fire that will always be warm. Masonry heaters can be

FIGURE 6.3. The symmetry of a mass of stone with a centered firebox against a great room wall looks much like a traditional fireplace. Well-executed stonework here tapers to a chimney that exits right through the ridge. Notice the massive stone used as a mantel. Photo courtesy of Temp-Cast Enviroheat.

FIGURE 6.4. A simple asymmetrical heater design. Here the smooth, honed soapstone of the lower part of the heater segues artfully into split-faced stone at the top. Wood storage offset to the left completes the resistance to symmetry. Photo courtesy of Tulikivi Corporation.

and have been round, square, oblong, cylindrical, free-form, short, tall, multitiered, domed, arched, asymmetrical, and more. For example, many traditional Swedish *kakelugns* are tall cylinders, while Austrians and Germans have often embraced *kachelofens* with no symmetry at all. The fact that stucco can smoothly cover any shaped surface means a free-flowing organic form can be used.

A Place to Start

Design starts with the three major design aspects of a masonry heater. (There is a fourth aspect—the support structure—but we won't consider it right now, because it is dictated in large measure by the design of the mass above.) These three major design aspects are the firebox, the flues (often called heat-exchange channels), and the chimney. Of these, the firebox and flues, together, truly are the masonry heater, while the chimney is an optional element in the overall design. By this I don't mean that you can exclude a chimney; every masonry heater needs to be connected to a chimney. Rather, not all masonry heaters need to incorporate the chimney into the overall appearance. Sometimes the chimney will be a visible, commanding design aspect as it towers through a home and exits a cathedral ceiling. Other times it will be completely hidden from view. The

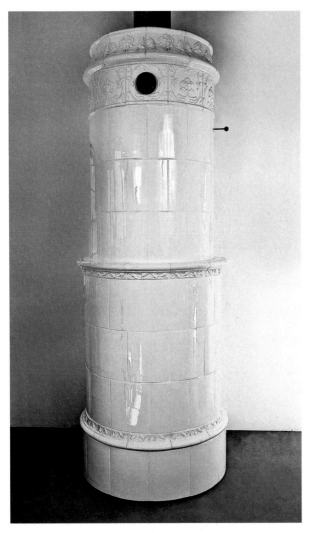

FIGURE 6.5. The tall cylindrical style of a traditional *kakelugn*. Note the intricate braids and textures cast into the tile, especially at the top. Photo courtesy of New England Hearth and Soapstone.

FIGURE 6.6. Free-form shapes can be made with the use of stucco. Delicate splashes of color dot this heater, which almost looks like ice cream in a cone. Niches and continuous changes in size add yet more interest. Photo courtesy of Biofire, Inc.

masonry heater itself consists of the firebox and whatever mass contains the flues, which are the primary aesthetic aspects of the heater. They are connected to the oft-invisible chimney.

While the chimney itself may not be a major design element, it is the crucial starting point for the rest of the design. In many cases, the chimney is, indeed, completely hidden in walls and chases until it reaches the attic and/or roof to finally exit the house. Yet it is vitally necessary and needs to be located properly in the home for proper functioning, as described in chapter 5. Once located, the

chimney is the first parameter of design around which to work. One way or another, the design has to get exhaust from the firebox, through the flues, to the chimney.

Chimney High, Chimney Low; Chimney Here, Chimney There

Though the chimney itself is entirely vertical, with a masonry heater there is no definite starting point for it. The chimney starting point, the place at which the masonry heater connects to the chimney, is highly variable. A masonry heater can attach to the chimney high—perhaps close to the 8-foot ceiling of a conventional home—or it can connect low. Many heaters will have an exit to a chimney close to floor level. Every location in between these alternatives is possible as well. The place at which the heater is attached to the chimney will be determined by the rest of the design at the same time that the rest of the design is partially dependent on the physical (floor plan) location of the chimney.

Many will be confused by the attention placed on chimney location. It is difficult for those new to masonry heaters to let go of the idea that the chimney

FIGURE 6.8. You might think the heater pictured here has no chimney, because the flue has been artfully hidden in the wall behind. This is one of Tulikivi's newest, more modern designs featuring a new firebox design (see chapter 8) and soot doors hidden inside the ash drawer access area below the firebox. This makes for clean, unbroken lines. Photo courtesy of Tulikivi Corporation.

and the "fireplace" are the same thing. The traditional fireplace is, really, just a chimney with a large space at its base in which to build a fire. The chimney for a masonry heater is just a chimney—just the escape hatch for exhaust. It no longer dictates the location of the firebox as it does in a traditional fireplace. The chimney can be somewhere above the firebox, next to the firebox, behind the firebox, or many feet away

FIGURE 6.7. Here the massive chimney structure is a commanding aspect of the interior architecture. This enormous structure will all be visible in this large space with high ceilings. The brick is complemented by massive granite beams and trim pieces. The beams span from one column to the next above the heater. One of the columns contains the actual chimney flue. Photo courtesy of Maine Wood Heat Company.

from the firebox. Presumably, the chimney has been located using the chimney rules from chapter 5. If so, the chimney has a set location. The remaining design must always work toward linking to that fixed location. The beauty and versatility of masonry heaters is that there is nearly an infinite range of ways to get from the firebox location to the chimney. It is therefore clear that the masonry heater is the most versatile wood-burning appliance ever conceived.

A single masonry heater requires a single chimney structure—and usually a smaller structure, in cross section, than is required for an open fireplace. (The chimney size in open fireplaces is dictated by the size of the firebox opening, which is usually quite large.) In a home with tall cathedral ceilings, a single-flue chimney can have a skyscraper look to it because it is

FIGURE 6.9. This chimney attaches to the masonry heater at its top. The chimney for the heater is partially supported by the unheated "leg" to the left of the heater. The stucco has horizontal inset lines to break up the large, flat surface. This photo reinforces that stucco, like tile, offers unending color choices. Photo courtesy of Envirotech Masonry Heaters.

very tall, but very small. Those who want an exposed chimney structure, for aesthetic reasons, may want to consider if there is a way to incorporate another flue into the structure. Exhaust from a gas water heater, a backup furnace, or even a vent for a range hood can be directed into a second or third flue in one chimney structure. You can also consider the possibility that one day you may want to add another masonry heater (in a basement living space or an upper level), and simply supply a flue for this future addition at the outset. The additional flue(s) will give the chimney width and breadth to accompany its height, thereby decreasing its potentially spindly appearance.

If the installation does not involve exposing the chimney at such heights, it can be more readily incorporated into the design of the masonry heater and may even be difficult to identify, at first glance, as a chimney. How well it blends with the rest of the heater will in large part be determined by the rest of the design and layout of the house. Some may not want the chimney to blend at all into the mass, preferring that it be clearly what it is. Others will opt for giving the masonry heater a furniture quality; the masonry heater becomes an aesthetic piece that would be unachievable with an obvious chimney.

The Source of Power—The Firebox

Most homes are connected to "the grid"—short for the power grid—the infrastructure that enables the distribution of electricity and other energy services to residences. In such a scenario, the home (or, more specifically, those living in the home) is the end user of the energy that comes to the home. If natural gas is piped in, it isn't expended until some appliance in the home is ignited and burns the gas. If electricity is wired to the home, it is not consumed until lights are illuminated, motors are activated, or appliances are switched on. Everyone knows, however, that the power was not generated at the home.

Somewhere, many miles away perhaps, there is a power-generating station. For example, a coal-burning power plant burns the fuel and transforms the heat energy to electricity. The electricity is then transmitted through the wires and substations to the residence. In the home, the electricity is used. Most people are therefore, though perhaps unconsciously until now, familiar with the concept of generating energy in one place and using it elsewhere. It is no leap to understand that the source of the power is only the source, not the end.

In the masonry heater, the power source, the "generating plant," is the firebox. The electricity-generating plant uses coal, or maybe uranium; the masonry heater uses wood. The hot gases, then, are the vehicle through which heat gets to the rest of the masonry heater via the flues. The flues are like the wires in "the grid." They

FIGURE 6.10. The chimney flue can connect to many masonry heaters near floor level. Here it connects at the lower left side.

FIGURE 6.11. The firebox is integral with the mass of this heater built using the core kit sold by Envirotech Radiant Fireplaces. Photo courtesy of Envirotech Masonry Heaters.

carry the power (heat) to all parts of the masonry heater the same way wires carry electricity to a neighborhood. The heat itself is conducted through the masonry materials to the living space just as smaller wires conduct electricity to a light socket.

This analogy serves to demonstrate and amplify the fact that the firebox of the masonry heater is the power source, but it does not directly determine the shape of the rest of the mass. The firebox is, however, responsible for supplying approximately half of the heat output of the entire heater. Its size and capacity *do* very directly determine how much mass sits between it and the chimney. (Firebox design is discussed in greater detail in chapter 8.) The firebox can be integral with the rest of the mass, or it can be a separate element of the whole masonry heater design. Masonry heaters that have become standardized, as in the case of many kit-based heaters, often have the firebox integral to the whole mass. These standardized designs, once

again, often appeal to those who are intent on something approaching the traditional fireplace look. Those who have fully grasped the unlimited possibilities of masonry heaters will often, on the other hand, have a firebox standing almost completely independent of the remaining mass; the two are connected only as needed to provide the passage of exhaust into the heat-exchange (flue) elements.

The word *firebox* seems to imply, indeed, a box. Usually we think of boxes as being square or rectangular. The imagination is set free, however, when *firebox* is replaced with *container*. The firebox is, after all, the container of fire. It holds the fire and prevents the wood, coals, embers, and gases from going where they're not supposed to. The freedom of *container* is that everyone knows of containers of all sorts of shapes and sizes. There are round containers like cylinders, spheres, and ovals. There are multisided containers that are octagonal or pentagonal in shape. It is even possible to have a container—a firebox—that is not symmetrical in all respects. And there is, indeed, the ever-practical cube or rectangular box form that most of us expect in our rectilinear surroundings.

There are, of course, various structural and functional requirements that need to be met to have an effective firebox design for a masonry heater. If the goal is to contain the fire and heat, the firebox shape must be conducive to containing, rather than dispersing, the heat and other elements of a fire. As long as the firebox functions as a container, any of the aforementioned shapes are realistic and possible.

As with any project, there are also budgetary considerations. Building a firebox that literally is a box of rectangular shape, using bricks and other materials of rectangular shape, will be more cost-effective than, say, trying to build a cylinder with rectangular materials.

FIGURE 6.12. The firebox for this heater is a stand-alone element with the mass it powers behind it. Handmade tiles and the curves of the mass beyond the firebox are perfect examples of the endless possibilities. Another view of this heater is in figure 4.2. *Kachelofen* designed, built, and photographed by Ernst Kiesling, Canadian Kachelofen.

FIGURE 6.13. A one-of-a-kind masonry heater designed to fit a customer's taste, decor, and living space. This concept has been approved, with slight modifications, by the client and will be constructed of structural tiles for a residence in southern Ohio.

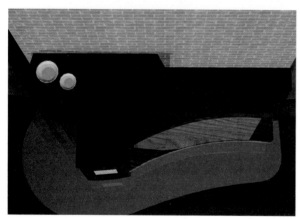

FIGURE 6.14. The plan view shows the unusual shapes possible in masonry heater design.

The effort needed to properly cut and fit virtually every piece to make some odd shapes is substantial. In Europe, where the masonry heater concept has undergone hundreds of years of development and never fallen entirely out of favor, there are specially shaped materials readily available that permit odd-shaped constructions with much less labor intensity. As masonry heaters become more mainstream in North America, no doubt independent manufacturers of specialty parts will fulfill the same purpose here. This will eventually make the unusual shapes more budget-friendly. The results of literally "out of the firebox" thinking can be stunning.

The Mass for Heat Exchange—The Heating Elements

Every part of a masonry heater, including the firebox, is built with dense materials that radiate heat. If the firebox is incorporated into the mass that includes all the flues, then obviously all of it is the primary heating element. Some would therefore argue that "the mass" is the *entire* masonry heater. This is true. For the purposes of discussion, however, the mass of the heat-exchange area will be separated from the firebox precisely to explain how they can be separate design elements.

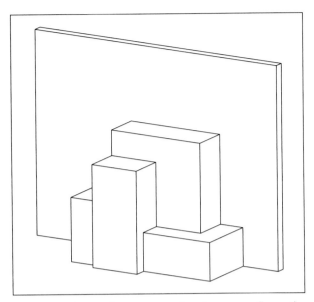

FIGURE 6.15. Imagine laying out a 40-foot-long square flue on the ground, then cutting it into various lengths. The result is numerous "boxes" containing flues. These boxes can then be stacked or recombined to make various different shapes and arrangements. This drawing shows just one of the infinite ways these flues can be combined to make an asymmetric heater design.

FIGURE 6.16. As suggested in figure 6.15, this masonry heater is a combination of "boxes" containing all the flues in an asymmetric design. Add stucco, tile, some wood for a bench, and a niche for wood storage and you have a beautiful masonry heater. Photo courtesy of Biofire, Inc.

Because it's possible to largely separate the three main elements—chimney, firebox, flues—the mass is mainly defined by the body of the heater that contains all the heat-exchange channels (flues). This mass containing the flues is then a primary heating element of the masonry heater, even though the mass that incorporates the firebox also provides about half of the gentle, radiant heat.

The size of the mass required to meet the heating goals of the space will certainly influence the design; this will be discussed more in chapter 7. Here, however, the aim is to describe the freedom and versatility inherent in the masonry heater concept. Freeing the view, for the moment, from constraints and dictates of size allows the exploration of all the possibilities in strictly design terms. The firebox element and the flue element(s) connect to make a whole. One cannot function without the other and still be considered a masonry heater. But in a well-designed masonry heater, the bulk of the available mass will reside in the heat-exchange area.

The flues in even a small masonry heater can be quite long. For example, a firebox with a floor area of just 1.5 square feet may have a total flue length of around 40 linear feet! If you imagine a 40-foot chimney, 8 inches square, turned horizontally, the picture becomes clear. Such a flue could run the full length of many houses. Divided into 3- or 4-foot lengths, this flue has a dozen or so pieces that can be run in various directions. There could be one rectangular box 4 feet long and 5 feet tall containing more than half of those flue pieces, coupled with two or three smaller boxes each containing two or three of those flue lengths, making a sculptured set of boxes connecting the firebox—another box perhaps 2 feet wide and 4 feet tall—to the chimney.

With the basic idea in place, you can get creative. Suppose that single larger element was turned into a rounded shape, the firebox is turned into a cylinder, and the rest becomes curved benches. You might end up with a heater that looks like the one in figure 6.17. Suddenly a heater with the same general size parameters has a completely different appearance while

FIGURE 6.17. Instead of thinking in terms of boxes, curves and cylinders can be used. Photo courtesy of Biofire, Inc.

maintaining the same heating potential. Or you could retain all the original shapes and simply move them around into a different arrangement. Of course, these elements could also simply be redrawn in different sizes and shapes but containing the same length of flues. The possibilities are endless, and this is just one particular size! A larger masonry heater would require *more* flue length and *more* overall volume and/or surface area. There is no exhausting the potential range of options for a given set of size parameters.

Additional Elements

Many people who invest in masonry heaters realize the inherent opportunities. Who would not have an attraction to a warm seat in the dead of a cold winter?

Since the flues of the masonry heater can be part of nearly any shape and size, an obvious choice is to have them form sitting areas—benches, seats, or platforms. A low platform could be large enough to lie on; it could even be an appendage into a bedroom, making it a bed. Since a masonry heater is a gathering point, it's just logical to consider incorporating sitting areas into the mass. Those coming in from the cold will forever appreciate a warm place to sit; without it, they are relegated to standing against the heater.

Seats or benches do not have to be heated. It is also possible to make a bench independent of the flues, yet providing a place to sit and lean back against the warm body of the heater. A wooden bench, though not heated, will feel comfortable, whereas a masonry

FIGURE 6.18. This entire masonry heater is a sitting area made with structural tiles or *kacheln*. The firebox is in the far right of the photo, the box-like short structure facing another part of the room. Photo courtesy of New England Hearth and Soapstone.

bench often feels cool if it's not directly heated by the flues. For this reason, wooden benches are also an attractive option.

Masonry heaters provide gentle warmth to a home using stored solar energy, in the form of firewood, to heat living space. It's a bonus that you can also bake artisanal, brick-oven bread with that same renewable energy. Because a heater is meant to store heat for such long periods of time, creating and using a baking oven is a logical step toward greater energy independence. A masonry heater with bakeoven is an oven that is "always on" in the heating season. Temperatures remain relatively constant for such extended periods that dependable cooking of everything from breakfast porridge to stews to pizzas and bread is possible in a built-in oven. To learn more about baking in a masonry heater bakeoven, see chapter 11; also see the section in this chapter on baking ovens as stand-alone companions to masonry heaters.

If you can have a warm seat, it's not a stretch to have a variety of "seats" for other purposes as well. Small niches or shelves facing an entry can be a warming and drying place for gloves and hats. Shelves or compartments facing the kitchen can keep food warm before a meal or provide a place for proofing bread. A small, secluded alcove could be a place for a pet to sleep. In this same line of reasoning, hooks can be incorporated into the mass for hanging coats. Rods can be situated over the top of the heater or over a platform for drying wet clothes. Small compartments or shelves can

FIGURE 6.19. This brick heater boasts a bakeoven, shelves, nooks, a working surface, and sitting areas. Heater designed and built by Stovemaster; photo courtesy of Alex Chernov.

be created for shoes or boots. A popular compartment in masonry heaters is for firewood storage; it's handy to have an alcove large enough to hold firewood for one or two firebox loads of fuel. The warmth of such a compartment keeps firewood dry and prewarmed for easy fire starting.

The wood-storage compartment can also incorporate a wood waiter, which is a spin-off from the very old idea of a dumbwaiter. Today, however, a wood waiter is operated with electric motors rather than a manual pulley system. It is, essentially, an elevator for the wood supply as seen in figure 6.20. If wood is either kept in

or brought into the house through a basement, you can load a quantity into the wood waiter, which will transport the fuel up to the next floor, reducing both the effort required and the potential mess that sometimes accompanies the transfer of wood from one place to another. The wood waiter can be located right next to the masonry heater, or it can be sited elsewhere if space is an issue. You can even conceal it in a cabinet.

Always bear in mind that additions or appendages to a masonry heater that do not contain internal flues can actually impede heat transfer and radiant heating. For example, a large wood-storage cavity built right next to

FIGURE 6.20. A wood waiter lets motors do the heavy lifting when fuel needs to be on the next floor up. | FIGURE 6.21. A hinged cover over the wood waiter can match the floor so it becomes almost invisible. | FIGURE 6.22. When the waiter must be some distance from the masonry heater, a wheeled cart effortlessly gets wood from one place to the other with no mess. Photos courtesy of W. B. Fowler Industries, Inc.

a radiant wall of the heater will greatly affect how much radiant heat you receive from that wall, just as building a heater against a wall will reduce its radiant effect.

Heater Companions

Most people would enjoy being a companion to a warm, inviting masonry heater, but the type of companion I'm discussing here is a second functioning heater to go with the primary masonry heater. This second masonry heater could be above, below, or on the other side of a wall from the primary heater. It could also be a masonry cookstove, sometimes called a cooker. And it could also be a stand-alone masonry bakeoven, functioning completely separately from the primary heater. All these options are differentiated from the previous amenities by the fact that they are, by themselves, appliances that operate separately, yet complementarily, to the original masonry heater.

A Second Heater?

Those who appreciate the unique radiant heat available from a masonry heater may want to consider a second heater (or more) in their house plans. Sometimes it just makes sense to have more than one masonry heater, especially in a larger, multilevel house or a house with a lot of area spread out on a single level. The floor plan of a given house may not be conducive to or open enough for some important areas to receive the gentle warmth of radiant heat from one masonry heater. A long, narrow home, like some ranch styles, will benefit greatly from radiant masonry heaters in more than one area if you're intent on energy independence and penetrating radiant heat throughout. Two or more smaller heaters arranged strategically in a home provide even greater heating versatility, particularly in parts of the year when only a little heating is needed, like early autumn or late spring.

The idea of a companion heater is that, though it has its own chimney flue, it shares the chimney mass with the primary heater. It could very well be a masonry heater just to the other side of a major dividing wall

of a home. For example, the masonry heater for the primary living space may be against an interior wall separating the great room from a master bedroom suite. A small room heater could be situated in the master bedroom and tied into the same chimney mass that serves the larger heater.

All the aforementioned design considerations apply with adding a second heater. You still need to figure out how to get the exhaust from the firebox to the chimney. The proximity of the two appliances can render some interesting creative opportunities that, again, can incorporate options like heated sitting areas, niches, and additional, stand-alone heating elements. It's entirely possible to have one or more heating elements that have flues from both appliances running through them.

Stacked Heaters

As the name implies, stacked heaters are built one atop the other; the one below supports the one above. This design is a way to get all the benefits of radiant heat on two floors distinctly separate from each other. In a closed-floor-plan two-story house, the second floor (or a first floor above a basement that has well-used living space) will not benefit at all from the radiant heat of a masonry heater, though it will receive convection heat. Building one heater above the other is one way to get radiant heat on both floor levels and still make use of the same chimney structure or chase. The chimney, of course, would have to now contain two separate flues (see chapter 9).

If one heater is literally built on top of another, the bottom heater is the foundation for the upper heater. Be aware that masonry heaters are designed to efficiently store *and* transfer heat from their very hot interiors to the living space. This generally means that the heater walls are not designed to support a lot of weight. In addition, a masonry heater is subject to expansion and contraction as it heats and cools. This is one reason it's generally unwise to make a masonry heater a support structure for other elements of the house.

There are some heater designs, however, particularly those that are built from premanufactured core kits,

FIGURE 6.23. This soapstone heater extends through the ceiling into the second floor. It's one version of a two-story heater. | **FIGURE 6.24.** Here is the second-floor portion of the heater shown in figure 6.23. Having the heater extend into another level of the house provides radiant heat to that upper level. In this case it's a simple seat, though it could have been designed to be larger or taller with more heating capacity. Photo courtesy of New England Hearth and Soapstone.

that are meant to have two individual, disconnected components. The inner life, or core, is distinctly separated from the outer veneer by an air gap or some kind of thermal expansion material. In these designs, the majority of expansion forces are present in the independent inner life. While the outer shell (veneer) does get warm, it isn't subject to as much movement as the core. This type of design is therefore more suitable as the foundation for another heater above.

This is *not* meant to suggest that every such veneer is adequate to serve as a foundation for another structure. If you're contemplating this arrangement, talk with a qualified structural engineer about the possibilities. Every home is different. Ceiling heights are different, seismic requirements are different, materials are different, and loads are different from one project to the next. I simply can't address all of these considerations adequately in this text.

Similar in nature, but having less complexity from the structural engineering standpoint, is the idea of a two-story masonry heater. Since such a structure only needs to support itself, only its particular self-imposed stresses (along with, again, any seismic concerns) need to be taken into consideration in its design. The two-story heater otherwise accomplishes the same goals as the stacked heaters. Having heating mass on two levels of the house assures radiant heat in each. Unlike stacked heaters, a single, tall masonry heater has only one firebox (though it, too, could be designed with more than one). This means that, like any single masonry heater, it needs to be fired only once or twice each day. The firebox would be on the lower level; wood only needs to be supplied at that level. In other words, the two-story heater incorporates flues that travel from the firebox through mass on the first level *and* the second level before emptying into a chimney. You've seen a stretch limo; in essence, a two-story heater is a stretched version of a single-story heater.

In summary, this means that heating with a two-story heater is somewhat simpler than heating with two. The flip side is that the idea of two separate heaters actually lends more versatility in how the living space is heated. Like any other masonry heater, the two-story heater can be custom-designed for the space just as surely as two could be.

Cookstoves (Cookers)

Another stand-alone masonry heater companion is a masonry cookstove. These cookstoves work on the same principle as masonry heaters themselves—with one important difference: The metal (usually cast-iron) cooktop is one of the primary heat-transfer materials. Usually the exhaust of the relatively small firebox load of wood contacts the cooking surfaces first, then continues through the masonry mass. In this way, high surface temperatures are achieved on the cooking surfaces and residual heat not captured there is transferred to the masonry mass of the stove structure. The masonry cookstove, then, is simply a small masonry heater with a specialized function—cooking.

Obtaining complete cooking and heating capabilities with a masonry heater complex provides the potential for nearly complete energy independence for many people. Just a hundred years ago, cooking and heating with wood was commonplace in North America. With the introduction of the heat-retaining capabilities of masonry heaters, doing so today entails far less work than it did in those days. It also involves much more comfortable heat. A cooker with baking oven combined with a masonry heater (also with optional baking chamber) gives owners freedom from fossil fuels for two everyday needs.

A cooker can be built in a variety of ways. A masonry cookstove may primarily be a masonry structure with appropriate accommodation made for a forged-metal oven component, the required firebox, cleanout doors, and, of course, the metal cooktop itself. Alternatively, the entire assembly (save the cooktop), including an oven, could be built entirely with masonry—as is the case with most heaters. Also, an appliance like this may have no oven at all; it may be designed strictly for a cooktop.

A metal oven obtains heat from a combination of the immediate exhaust from an existing fire, and the stored heat in the masonry, though the latter will be most important for long-term cooking over the course of a day. In designs incorporating an all-masonry oven chamber, the oven itself is another firebox. This cooktop-and-oven combination unit then may require two chimney flues; one is for the

FIGURE 6.25. A masonry heater complex. Heater, oven, and attached cookstove make great companions and provide heating and cooking self-sufficiency. Note the wood-storage area and soapstone heated bench tops and trim. Photo courtesy of Maine Wood Heat Company.

FIGURE 6.26. This cookstove features a metal oven. The oven is warmed by the mass of bricks, not by a fire directly in the oven chamber. Photo courtesy of Envirotech Masonry Heaters.

FIGURE 6.27. A cookstove with no baking option. The upper door is for the firebox; the smaller lower one, for ash removal. Photo courtesy of Tulikivi Corporation.

FIGURE 6.28. A cookstove/bakeoven combination in which the oven is a masonry combustion chamber. Photo courtesy of Tulikivi Corporation.

cooktop firebox and the other for firing the oven. It's also possible to have an appliance equipped with an oven and a cooktop using only one flue, though often these designs will require you to choose which firebox to use at any given time; you can't use both at the same time on one chimney flue.

When a cooker appliance is mated with a masonry heater, it can of course be treated the same as you may treat any other second masonry heater joined with the first. A major difference is, of course, that a cooker has additional limitations on its design. The fact that a metal heat-transfer surface is involved reduces the total length of flues that can service the appliance. Metal cooktops quickly absorb heat from a fire, drastically cooling the exhaust immediately. Therefore, there is not as much residual heat remaining that can be routed through long flues. The design must be sure to get the exhaust to the chimney with sufficient heat for good chimney draft. This consideration means that amenities like heated benches, platforms, or other heating elements are greatly restricted for cookstoves, just as they would be for quite small masonry heaters in general.

Baking Ovens

Bakeoven chambers are generally popular options for a masonry heater. However, not everyone will want a baking oven that is always tied to a masonry heater used for heating living space. Once the masonry heater is idled for warmer months, the baking oven becomes of little value. Few will want to fire a masonry heater in warm (or hot) weather just to bake some bread. For many prospective homeowners, in milder climates, this could mean six months of the year in which baking in the brick oven would not be a reasonable option. Those who want to bake throughout the year will want other choices.

There are, of course, masonry bakeovens that double as primary heaters. In other words, these are masonry heaters that have a bakeoven chamber as the primary firebox. Wood burned in the baking chamber produces the heat to warm the mass of the heater for warming the living space. At the same time, the bakeoven chamber is charged with a lot of heat for long-term cooking and baking. (See chapter 11 for photos and more information about these.) This, of course, is no different in effect from having a masonry heater with a primary firebox and accessory bakeoven. Either way, the oven

FIGURE 6.29. The bakeoven, inside the low arched door, is strictly for baking and not for heating. Photo courtesy of Maine Wood Heat Company.

is functional only when you intend to heat your living space with the heater.

A more attractive choice, for those who want the benefits of brick-oven baking all year round, is to have a baking oven that is *only* a cooking appliance and does not aim to heat living space (see figure 6.29). Such an oven retains heat in its massive structure, but is insulated to prevent the heat from migrating out of the mass. In a sense, it is a masonry heater operating in reverse: The wood fire warms all the masonry materials; the stored heat is used to promote long-term, continuous heating of the oven chamber. Every effort is made to limit the amount of heat escaping to the exterior of the structure—into the living space. Using a brick oven like this, you can bake all summer long with wood fuel without unduly warming the inside of the house.

A baking oven is a tremendous addition to a masonry heater. Using stored solar energy in the form of wood, storing it again as heat in a mass of masonry,

then making use of that heat over extended periods for heating and cooking is the ultimate statement of freedom, independence, and wise use of resources. There is no more immediate way of creating security in a home than to provide a way to heat and cook that doesn't require constant fire-tending and uses locally harvested fuel.

Material Options

The versatility of the design of masonry heaters is matched by the types of materials that can be used in their construction. Masonry materials used for the visible, aesthetic look of the heater range from the simple, like plain stucco, through various bricks, colored refractory concrete, any species of stone, and structural tile. In addition, these materials can and have been combined in innumerable ways. Having said this, I should note that all masonry materials are *not* created equal. There are definite advantages and disadvantages to some over others. A masonry heater is a multi-generational, heirloom-quality addition to any home. Consider all the possibilities with ultimate care, for it will be around virtually forever. Drapes get changed twice per year, carpet every ten years. A roof might be replaced in twenty years. A masonry heater? It's meant to be there for a lifetime (or longer).

Thermal Behavior of Veneer Masonry

A masonry heater is an entirely functional heater. Virtually every one of its visible surfaces is meant to aid in the work of heating. Though you will want to choose something aesthetically pleasing, the thermal characteristics and thicknesses of those materials will affect the performance of the heater. The choice of veneer materials, in a very real way, will determine how warm the masonry heater will make you and your space at any given time.

High-quality masonry heaters today consist of mainly two components, the inner life (also called the core) and the veneer. The inner life of the masonry heater (see chapter 8), which includes the firebox and all the flues, must be constructed with high-quality heat-tolerant masonry called refractory bricks, plates, tiles, or concrete. The high combustion temperatures and thermal cycling—being exposed to high heat followed by long periods of gradual cooling followed by intense heat again—necessitate a limited range of high-quality materials. The exterior veneer, however, isn't exposed to the same punishing environment. The veneer is where pleasing appearance must be balanced well with cost, reliable longevity under hot conditions, ease of maintenance, and, as outlined here, thermal performance.

The factors that affect how well a veneer material is suited to the masonry heater project are called its thermal properties. The properties of concern are the material's density, conductivity, specific heat capacity, diffusivity, and emissivity. The thickness of the material is also of concern. See the accompanying table 6.1 for quick reference to the varying capacities of each material discussed below.

Density

Though some would claim this to be a descriptive term for a younger sibling, the density of a type of brick or stone is how much it weighs per unit of volume. Frequently, density is measured in pounds per cubic foot or kilograms per cubic meter. You can get an idea of density by loosely crumpling a sheet of newspaper. The ball of paper might be fairly large. If you further compress the paper between your hands, you can make it quite small. It is still the same sheet of paper; it still weighs the same amount. The density, however, has changed. It has become denser—heavier per unit of volume. If you try to compare a rock to a brick of the same size, it may not be obvious which one is denser. You'd have to take careful measurements of both. In general, a denser masonry material can hold more heat than a less dense material. Since storing heat is something desired in masonry heaters, density is a plus.

Conductivity

Just as some materials are good at conducting electricity, and some people are good at conducting orchestras, thermal conductivity is a measurement of a material's ability to conduct, or transmit, heat. It is often measured in BTUs (British Thermal Units) per foot per hour per degree Fahrenheit (BTU/[ft hr °F]) or in watts per meter per degree Kelvin (W/[m °K]). The higher this number is, the quicker the material transmits heat. The idea of the masonry heater is to get the heat of the fire into the living space over a certain period of time. Those familiar with a cast-iron stove know that heat transfer through metal is almost instantaneous. Indeed, metal conducts heat about as fast as it conducts electricity. This fast conductivity is the reason someone gets burned almost immediately upon touching a hot metal stove. All masonry materials, on the other hand, are many times slower than metal at transferring heat, which is why you don't get burned by masonry that is 200°F.

Specific Heat Capacity

The specific heat capacity is the amount of energy required to raise the temperature of a given amount of material by a certain temperature unit. This necessarily means that a material that requires a lot of energy to increase its temperature by 1° holds its temperature well. Thus, the specific heat capacity of a material is the amount of heat a measured amount of material can hold when its temperature is increased incrementally. In essence, the specific heat is truly the measure of how much heat a substance can hold. This measurement is often given in BTUs per pound per degree Fahrenheit (BTU/[lb °F]) or in kilojoules per kilogram per degree Kelvin (kJ/[kg °K]).

Since, unlike density, this is the actual measure of heat-storage capacity of a material, it plays a very important role in the ability of a masonry heater to store heat for long periods of time. Combine this *with* the density (actually, multiply it *by* the density), and you get a material's actual heat capacity—how much heat it holds per unit volume, called the volumetric heat capacity.

Diffusivity

The verb *diffuse* means "to spread." A glob of peanut butter could be spread with a knife over bread in a certain amount of time. In thermodynamics, diffusivity is the rate of speed at which heat spreads through a material. In a television commercial for paper towels, a towel is placed on top of a puddle of liquid. Rapidly, the liquid spreads into the towel in all directions. This is rapid diffusion of liquid into the pores of the towel. You can think of heat acting the same way in a masonry material. If a given material has a high rate of diffusivity, the heat travels quickly to all its regions, like water in a paper towel. If the material has a low rate of diffusivity, it is like watching the paper towel commercial played in slow motion; the heat diffuses slowly.

Diffusivity is measured, usually, in meters squared per second (m^2/s). This rate is determined by using the previously mentioned thermal properties; diffusivity is equal to the conductivity divided by the material's volumetric heat capacity. Thus, it is a measure of the ratio between how well the product transfers heat and how well it stores heat. Masonry materials, with few exceptions, are good heat-storage mediums. The diffusivity value clarifies further how quickly a given material will get heat into a living space and how evenly warm the body of the heater will be. Those materials that conduct heat more quickly have higher diffusivity and more rapidly lend heat to the surrounding area while still storing enough for the designed heating period.

Diffusivity is an important measure in materials for masonry heaters. Ideally, a masonry heater surface achieves high enough temperatures for quality radiant heat, retains high enough temperatures for the designed period of time, yet is never hot enough to be a touching/safety hazard. High diffusivity among masonry materials indicates a more complete use of the heat generated by each fire, assuming the material is of appropriate thickness. Materials with lower diffusivities will still be good at long-term heat storage, but less effective at the actual job of heating from firing to firing, when compared with the same heater (of the same total mass) built with more diffusive materials.

Emissivity

Most people building or remodeling have heard of low-e windows. The *e* stands for *emissivity*. These windows are designed to prevent heat from radiating out of the house or, in the summer, heat radiating into the home. With masonry heaters, the goal is to have excellent radiant properties, so a masonry heater should be built using high-emissivity materials. Fortunately, most masonry materials are both good absorbers and emitters of heat energy. Alas, there are still measurable differences between materials.

Emissivity is a dimensionless coefficient. It is actually a comparison number between the material in question and a black body. In science terminology, a perfect black body is a perfect absorber and emitter of radiant energy. Such a perfect body emits all energy available to be emitted and absorbs all radiant energy that contacts its surface. This perfect black body is given an emissivity coefficient of 1.

Most solid building materials are relatively good emitters. Masonry materials as a set usually have emissivity coefficients ranging from about 0.85 to 0.95. This means that they have radiant properties 85 to 95 percent as good as a perfect radiant emitter, the black body. Interestingly, cast iron, typically used for metal stoves, is a relatively poor radiant material, having an emissivity coefficient of about 0.24. There are, however, some important differences among masonry options.

Thickness

The thickness of a material also plays an important thermal role in how a masonry heater works. As you can imagine, the thicker a dense material is, the longer it takes to get heat from one side (the inside of the masonry heater) to the other (the outside), where it radiates into the living space. Given a specific amount of heat produced by a fire, a wall that is 4 inches thick will be much slower to get the heat to the living space than will a wall of the same material but only 2 inches thick. A thicker masonry heater wall, then, is more suitable for heat storage than for heat dispersion. A wall that is thinner introduces less heat storage, but gets heat into the living space quicker. A thicker wall

TABLE 6.1. Thermal Properties of Common Masonry Heater Materials

	Density (kg/m³)	Conductivity (W/m °K)	Specific Heat Capacity (kJ/kg °K)	Volumetric Heat Capacity (kJ/m³ °K)	Diffusivity (X 10e-6 m²/sec.)	Emissivity	Thickness (range or value in inches)
Common brick	1,500-1,900	.67-1.0	.84	1,260-1,596	.42-.79	.90	4
Firebrick	2,000	1.0	.88	1,760	.56	.80	1.25-4.5
Granite	2,300-3,000	2.4-3.5	.84	1,932-2,226	.95-1.8	.45	1.25-6
Limestone	2,200	1.5	.84	1,848	.81	.95	3-6
Sandstone	2,150	1.3	.84	1,806	.72	.93	3-6
Soapstone	2,980	6.4	.98	2,920	2.2	.95	1.25-3
Tile (*kacheln*)	2,000	1.3	.85	1,700	.76	.90	1.5-2.5

of a particular material, given consistent application of heat over consistent periods of time, will provide a more steady surface temperature than a thinner wall of the same material. Simultaneously, that more constant temperature will always be lower than would be experienced with a thinner veneer.

As you can see, the various thermal qualities of these dense masonry materials have a synergistic effect on the heater's performance. If a veneer material has very high conductivity, but is not great at storing heat, the surface temperatures will be higher but the heat won't last very long. If the material used has low conductivity and is very thick, the surface temperatures will be much lower and the heat will be retained for a very long time. If that surface temperature is *too* low, the space isn't heated as well as it might have been. Every combination in between is possible. The question becomes, therefore, "Over what time period will the heater be expected to heat and how much heat is required (in the living space) in that time period, before the masonry heater is fired again?" This question is further addressed in chapter 7.

All of this is complicated also by the amount of fuel (and therefore total amount of heat) that is expected to be used at every firing. In a given heater design, a few crumpled newspaper sheets burned in the firebox will never warm all the mass. At the other extreme, if inappropriate materials were used for the design, an appropriate load of cordwood may produce more heat than

the mass can accommodate, resulting in excess losses up the chimney. A good heater design is geared to the space to be heated; it produces the right amount of heat with a specific amount of fuel, resulting in high enough surface temperatures to heat the living space for the time period over which it was designed to heat. Anyone proposing to physically design and build a masonry heater should be familiar with these complex issues and understand the ramifications of these details before proceeding with a project. Homeowners looking to have a heater built don't necessarily need to know all these details. They can, however, use the information in this chapter and the next to screen would-be builders and to understand the basics of why certain materials and methods may or may not be the best choice. Table 6.1, "Thermal Properties of Common Masonry Heater Materials," is an invaluable aid to understanding the physical reasons for choosing among the following materials.

Common Bricks

Common, solid red brick has frequently been seen as a finish material for masonry heaters. It's a material well understood and quickly handled by experienced masons. As masonry materials go, it is fairly inexpensive and readily obtainable, usually at any masonry supply house in almost any area of North America. A skilled mason can offer special coursing styles, special patterns, and various arches using bricks of common size, jumbo size, or even Roman style. Since bricks also are available

FIGURE 6.30. Common brick is an oft-used material for masonry heaters. Photo courtesy of Envirotech Masonry Heaters.

FIGURE 6.31. The chimney (far right) of this sandstone heater was built using long, thin Roman brick. Project by Maren Cooke and Ken Matesz; photo by Maren Cooke.

in varying color ranges, the likelihood is that anyone who generally likes brick can choose an appearance and theme using locally purchased common red brick. As table 6.1 shows, however, common brick rates the lowest of all common masonry materials in its thermal properties. In addition, common bricks are quite thick. At a nominal 4-inch thickness, their performance as a veneer material on a masonry heater is poorer than some other materials when it comes to responsiveness—the ability to get heat into the room quickly.

Another consideration is that brick's rough, porous texture makes cleaning a little more challenging. It cannot be simply wiped with a cloth or dusted with a feather duster—dirt readily "sticks" to the porous, coarse surface.

Stucco

It is a little misleading to list stucco as a different finish because stucco requires a substrate on which

to be applied. Most commonly, stucco is applied over bricks—preferably firebricks. It could also be applied over concrete blocks, though concrete blocks, not being fired-clay materials, are not, in the least, a refractory (heat-resistant) material. Stucco affords a vast number of surface-finish options. There are various textures and colors available. Some stuccos can even be repainted when you repaint a room to change its colors. Stucco can be swirled, brushed, and stippled in myriad ways. Of course, it can also be applied very smoothly for a very refined look as in figure 6.33, or possibly a southwestern look.

Another advantage of stucco is that you're not limited to using bricks in their thickest dimension for the underlying substrate. In fact, a superior heat-transfer and heat-storage combination is obtained by using firebricks, laid as shiners, for the stucco substrate. (Shiners are simply bricks laid on their narrow edge, instead of the typical broad edge.) The firebrick wall

RESPONSIVENESS

Responsiveness refers to how readily the heat output of the masonry heater responds to the heat introduced by burning the firewood. It's much like the way you might refer to a sports car having responsive steering. In a car with good steering response, a small movement of the steering wheel immediately translates to a change in the direction of the car. A responsive heater starts radiating heat relatively rapidly after a fire and can achieve higher surface temperatures.

A masonry heater that is not very responsive takes longer to get warmer, and an increase in wood use sometimes affects the duration of heat storage more than it influences surface temperature and immediate heat output. A masonry heater with too much mass is considered sluggish. A sluggish heater usually has lower surface temperatures overall because the heat is moving so slowly that the exterior cools almost as fast as new heat reaches it.

Though all masonry heaters have some level of responsiveness and some level of heat storage, the ideal masonry heater is very responsive over the time period in which it is meant to heat; it has the right amount of heat storage to assure the heater will be evenly warm until the next firing cycle. In winter, one day may be close to 32°F, and the night might drop to 0°. With a sluggish (slow-response) heater, there is no real way to accommodate such drastic weather changes. With a responsive heater, a change in the amount of fuel used results in more immediate adjustment to the changing outdoor climate (and resulting demand over the short term) for more heat output.

Thicker veneers like common bricks and many natural stones often combine less impressive conductivity and diffusivity with excessive mass. This combination can sometimes make a heater that is very sluggish indeed. In homes that may use more than one masonry heater, one strategy is to use a massive, sluggish heater for primary bulk heating, but have one or more heaters that are more responsive to adjust for relatively rapid changes in heating requirements. If you're going to be using only one masonry heater, you'd be wise to keep responsiveness in mind.

---

has a diffusivity 15 percent improved over the red-brick construction as well as greater volumetric heat capacity. Although stucco itself has figures roughly comparable to red brick, it is not the primary heat-storage and heat-transfer medium, so you benefit directly from a firebrick veneer covered in stucco versus the red-brick veneer.

Another plus to stucco, for those who particularly want to use all-natural, mainly local materials in their project, is that natural clay-based stuccos are available. With this idea, you can literally build a high-output masonry heater that is almost 100 percent clay with no Portland-based mortars—that is, clay bricks, clay mortars, and clay stucco! See chapter 8 for more information about materials used inside the masonry heater.

Stucco shares with brick the characteristic of a relatively coarse surface, especially if it is deeply textured. If the stucco is applied smoothly, it is a little more easily cleaned than a brick heater, since it has few or no mortar joints that can collect dust and dirt.

Natural Stone

Stone remains probably the most sought-after surface material for masonry heaters. Once upon a time, people gathered around an outdoor fire contained by a ring of stones. North American pioneers, without access to manufactured bricks or other masonry products, laid up their open fireplaces with river rocks or stones gathered while clearing land for farming. Stone's long-standing use as a fireplace material over the course of history has already made its mark in the masonry heater world. Fire and rocks are such basic attractions for humans that it is no wonder that more people request stone for their masonry heater than all

FIGURE 6.32. This one heater demonstrates several of the different brick coursing and pattern options that are possible. Photo courtesy of Maine Wood Heat Company.

the other material options combined. Many people even have distant childhood memories of a warm rock in the sun next to a favorite swimming or fishing hole. It seems quite obvious that warmth, fire, stone, and people are meant for one another.

Natural stone can be found in such a vast array of styles, colors, patterns, and textures that virtually any aesthetic taste can be met as well. Random stone, ashlar pattern, dry-stack, and large slabs all have been and can be used for masonry heaters. Granite has hues ranging from pure black, through various blues and greens, and on to white. Marble is likewise available in many shades. There's bluestone, limestone, sandstone, onyx, dolomite, slate, travertine, soapstone, and more. There is little doubt that stone offers immense design appeal. Some stone veneers will be smooth, honed, or polished

for easy cleaning, while others have a very rough texture that requires more effort to maintain.

For all its variety, however, most natural stones pose some limitations to the masonry heater concept. Usually, though not always, stone is one of the most expensive materials to use for construction, even if you have it "for free" on your property. The care, time, and physical effort required to produce excellent stone-work demands that it cost more, on balance, than other options.

A mason laying bricks can work along at a rapid pace, since each piece is relatively uniform, square, and straight. Compare this with, say, a random-pattern stone finish, in which a mason may either spend considerable time just *finding* a stone that fits in a given location, or spend similar time *making* the stone fit that space (or both!). Even though one single stone may take up the same space as six or eight bricks, the eight bricks can be laid in minutes while the single stone may take an hour to find, chisel, and finally set in place. Of course, there are "stonemasons" who pride themselves more on speed than other considerations and can lay stone, "swimming" in mortar, in very short order, for little attempt is made to fit one stone to the next. Those who appreciate this appearance may find a masonry heater laid in stone to be quite economical.

Another consideration with natural stone is its thickness. Stone is, by nature, often very irregular in size and thickness. Often appearance will demand that the overall wall thickness of the project will be determined by the average thickness of the thickest material available. For example, if the material at hand is 3 to 5 inches thick, and a significant amount of it is close to 5 inches thick, then the project will be laid up as a 5-inch-thick veneer. Likewise, stones that are much thinner than 3 inches are more difficult to lay structurally. Therefore, it is very common for stone veneers for masonry heaters to be at least 3 inches thick—and more likely 4 to 6 in total thickness.

As described earlier, a thicker veneer results in greater heat storage but, generally, lower surface temperatures. If surface temperatures are too low, the heater will be incapable of heating the space for which

FIGURE 6.33. A highly refined look achieved with stucco, a versatile material. It's used in a simple, compact design with clipped corners and a small "cupola" on top. Note the small loading door on the left and the abundant wood storage. Photo courtesy of Biofire, Inc.

it was designed. At the very least, if the temperatures are too low, it could mean that the heater could have performed better with another material (or the same one, but not as thick). In general, most stone veneers are too thick, considering the thermal properties of the material, to make a very responsive heater. As table 6.1 shows, there are some important exceptions to this. Thermal performance varies from stone type to stone type.

Though there are considerably more stone types than are discussed here, these are some of the stones most commonly available and used for masonry heaters. You'll find that many of the other stone types are closely related to granite, limestone, or sandstone by category (igneous, sedimentary, or metamorphic) and are therefore similar in performance, if not in cost and workability.

Granite

Granite has made a huge comeback recently as, particularly, a choice material for countertop applications. Its near indestructibility under normal household use as well as its color variety make it highly desirable for counters. In addition, it can be polished to a high luster that highlights its crystalline structure and coloring, giving it a truly exotic appeal.

Granite is, however, one of the hardest stones in common use. It is much harder to work and shape than the softer stones mentioned below. This simply means that labor costs for installing it will be among

FIGURE 6.34. Here is a wonderful example of a finely crafted stone masonry heater. The dark granite heated benches and heater cap contrast with the lighter stone used on the main body of the heater. Photo courtesy of Maine Wood Heat Company.

FIGURE 6.35. An owner-veneered limestone masonry heater. The sandstone slabs used over the heated benches and as the capping stones at the top of the heater are from an old sidewalk.

the highest within a category that is already of a higher cost. In addition, granite itself is an expensive stone. If it's not already available on site, it will be expensive to purchase and ship to the site. Figure 6.34 is a good example of a granite masonry heater.

Limestone

Another very common stone, limestone, like granite, has been used in construction for thousands of years and is still a common feature in masonry work of many kinds. Limestone, owing to its namesake, lime—which readily takes on the tint of oxidized minerals that may have accumulated in it—can range in color as fully as granite. There are white, gray, black, orange, and red stones in this family. Travertine is closely related to limestone because of its carbonate ingredients. In general, limestone is easier to work, because of its softness, than granite and can even be "polished" with good sandpaper. Simple steel chisels that would be ineffective on granite will split limestone easily. Limestone also is easier to quarry and cut than granite or marble and so

tends to be a less costly stone. Some limestone varieties are even too soft for common structural use. Well-known limestone products like Indiana limestone, on the other hand, are excellent structural stones that have been used extensively for building for centuries.

Sandstone

As its name implies, sandstone is a sedimentary rock composed largely of sand particles from various types of rocks and minerals. Like many stones, it is available in many colors ranging from simple whites and tans

FIGURE 6.36. A massive heater incorporating thick free-form slabs of sandstone. The main front bench slab alone weighs nearly 1,200 pounds. This same heater, viewed from the opposite side, is shown in figure 3.1. Project by Maren Cooke and Ken Matesz; photo by Maren Cooke.

FIGURE 6.37. This is a massive split-soapstone-faced masonry heater made with stone from Finland. Notice the carved scene in the stone above the firebox, a small warming compartment with a wooden door, and a large wood-storage niche. Photo courtesy of Tulikivi Corporation.

to deeply striated or colored stones of red, brown, and yellow. Also, like most structural stone types, sandstone has been used for centuries throughout the world for construction projects of every kind. Sandstone is often the material you see in patio floors featuring large flat stones, called flagstones. It is very plentiful and found in great quantities in the United States and abroad, making it a lower-cost stone to buy and use for various projects. Sandstone is also relatively easy to work and shape. Like limestone, common steel chisels and other stone-working tools are effective for shaping sandstone. Figure 6.36 shows a heater built with 5- to 6-inch-thick slabs of sandstone.

Soapstone

There are good materials for masonry heaters, and there is soapstone. The differences in thermal performance among the various materials can seem important, until all of them are compared with soapstone. Add to this fact the information that soapstone is very easy to cut and otherwise modify, polish, and carve and I believe that soapstone is, by far, as close to being the perfect material for masonry heaters as humankind will ever find.

Soapstone is a completely natural stone that is found all over the world. Some deposits are very soft. These are considered the carving grades and are used for all manner of artwork. Other deposits are much harder and yield soapstone that is appropriate for architectural use including construction of walls, floor tiles, and masonry heaters. Some of the harder soapstone comes from Finland and is used for heaters like the one shown in figure 6.37.

Soapstone, also called steatite, is a metamorphic rock formed under heat and pressure from olivine and other mineral components. One of its principal mineral components is talc, which is familiar as talcum powder. It is the talc content, making up more than one-third of soapstone, that gives the stone a "soapy" feel. The talc content also is responsible for making soapstone easy to tool and cut. Soapstone's hardness and strength come primarily from its magnesite content, also more than one-third of its composition.

Soapstone, like granite, has received more attention in recent years as a kitchen countertop material. Long before that, however, it was used as countertop material in chemistry labs all over the world. The reason for this is that soapstone is not damaged by most extreme chemicals. For example, strong acids will not damage soapstone, and only very powerful alkalis will corrode it. In other words, soapstone is not subject to staining and damage from common household foods and chemicals. Unlike granite, soapstone can be easily damaged by sharp, hard objects; at the same time, scratches in soapstone can be easily repaired, which is not true with granite.

Distinct from most other natural stones, the structural varieties of soapstone are not as easily found in a broad spectrum of colors. Though reds and other colors exist, most structural grades of soapstone have a grayish hue, though their underlying colors can range from green to dark blue. All of these, if honed by machine, leave a light gray appearance. Although this color is neutral and complements many other common building materials, including most woods and most other stone types, there are individuals who simply are not drawn to this gray appearance. Others find its soft hues and marble-like veining to be incredibly beautiful.

Whatever the aesthetic preference, soapstone is, like granite, a more expensive stone. The structural

FIGURE 6.38. Soapstone almost always has a gray appearance on masonry heaters, but it often has marble-like graining that gives it great character and enduring beauty. The wing benches here are not heated. Notice cylindrical stones encasing the chimney. This would be difficult to do with most other stones. Tulikivi stove by Masonry Heater Store.

soapstone needed for masonry heaters is not readily available in all locations of North America. Some of it is imported from Canada, Finland, Brazil, India, and even Africa. Because it is not likely to be found just lying about the property, it will have a higher cost than the many more common stones like sandstone, limestone, and even granite. The ease with which it can be worked, however, can decrease the labor cost associated with using it in a masonry heater project. Because of this and its thermal performance, soapstone deserves the attention of anyone considering a masonry heater.

As table 6.1 illustrates, soapstone easily qualifies as the premier material for heat-storage fireplaces. In most cases, a soapstone heater isn't four to six times more expensive than brick or other stone masonry

FIGURE 6.39. Lots of soapstone translates into lots of heat storage. This heater is also seen from another angle in figure 4.16. Photo courtesy of New England Hearth and Soapstone.

heaters, though its thermal performance characteristics can be at least four times more superior; it deserves careful consideration as a veneer material.

Tile

In Germany, Austria, Hungary, and other European countries, the tile stove, or *kachelofen,* has been ubiquitous for centuries. Of course, a *kachelofen,* as mentioned before, is a masonry heater. Figure 6.40 shows a classic tile masonry heater from the old country. In the United States, when the word *tile* is used, it always conjures pictures of the ceramic tiles used on bathroom or kitchen floors, counters, or walls. This is the North

American exposure, usually, to tile. It is no surprise that when tile is mentioned as a masonry heater surface option, people envision going to the flooring outlet to pick out the right material for the job. The reality is that, although floor tiles can be considered for use on masonry heaters, real masonry heater tiles are just like those used on European heaters.

Kacheln (tiles) do share with their floor and counter relatives a basically impervious glazed surface. Tile masonry heaters are among the easiest to keep clean and looking new because they cannot be stained or discolored and have such a smooth surface. Like any tile, *kacheln* are available in a whole rainbow of colors

FIGURE 6.40. This is a fine example of a masonry heater with an exterior made entirely of tiles. Photo courtesy of New England Hearth and Soapstone.

FIGURE 6.41. The backs of heater *kacheln* reveal the *rumpf* that makes these tiles different from the flooring and wall tiles most Americans know. Project by New England Hearth and Soapstone; photo by Ken Matesz.

from earthy tones to pastels to bright, almost fluorescent, shades. The nearly unlimited color range, good thermal performance, and appropriate thickness of masonry heater tiles, as well as the fact that they can be handmade in virtually any shape and size, makes the tiled masonry heater one of the most promising and versatile options.

A masonry heater tile differs significantly from a common floor or wall tile in that it is a much more three-dimensional and structural component. While flat tiles need to be adhered to a flat substrate (usually brick if used in a masonry heater application), a regular *kachel* (stove tile) is designed to be the actual structure of the masonry heater exterior.

In appearance, such a tile, on the finished, glazed exterior, may indeed look like some common tiles. On the back, however, it has an appendage called a *rumpf*. The back (see figure 6.41) looks like a tile that has had a bowl or deep dish attached to it. (Such a tile, though around 2 inches thick, is principally hollow on the backside.) The *rumpf* is necessary to connect neighboring tiles together, which is done with wire clamps made of steel. *Kacheln* are not simply glued to a substrate the way floor tiles are; rather they are set in clay mortar and mechanically fastened to one another. Flat tiles cemented to a substrate may or may not, in the long run, survive the expanding and contracting of the masonry heater. See figure 6.42 for an example of a modern tile heater; another recent tile heater can be seen in figure 2.1.

FIGURE 6.42. A real *kachelofen;* it's a masonry heater built with structural tiles. Photo courtesy of Biofire, Inc.

Pressed Earth or Adobe

Those interested in low-embodied energy, local materials, and sustainable construction methods will be particularly interested in combining a masonry heater's benefits with available, on-site materials like clay and earth. Building with earth is as old as construction itself, and buildings with earthen walls can be found all over the world. Perhaps one of the most commonly known earth-construction materials is the adobe brick. Adobe is little more than clay, sand, and water combined, set in brick forms, and allowed to dry in the sun. Similarly, pressed-earth blocks are often a predominantly clay soil, sand, a little cement, and some water compacted mechanically into a dense brick. All such bricks may have some plant fibers added as reinforcement in a manner similar to adding steel or fibers to concrete for added strength. In essence, adobe and other earth-based construction methods are the precursors of modern brick construction. Bricks, after all, are primarily clay also. A major difference is that common bricks or firebricks are also fired at very high temperatures, while adobe or pressed-earth blocks generally are not subjected to more than natural sunlight.

Theoretically speaking, you could construct a masonry heater entirely from handmade bricks of this nature. Even firebrick, the usual choice for the inner life of the masonry heater, is a fired-clay brick. The idea of using entirely local, on-site earth and simple human energy to make bricks and build a masonry heater could excite many avid environmentally minded builders with enough time to devote to the project.

However, it is vital to understand that there are, indeed, reasons why modern refractory firebricks and common bricks are the norm, and pressed-earth and adobe bricks are not. At least one of those reasons is that firebricks are specifically and carefully designed to withstand the abuses of daily hot fires without deterioration for many, many years. The same cannot be said for hand-pressed or sun-dried earth bricks, which will deteriorate relatively rapidly under the various forces at work in masonry heaters. There is mechanical abuse (from firewood loading), thermal shock (periods of significant cooling followed by rapid heating), and the abrasion and deteriorating effects of the exhausts of wood fires. While it's grand to have visions of minimum environmental impact by using inexpensive, self-made bricks and mortar, you need to consider the immense time loss of building this way only to have to rebuild the structure in the not-so-distant future.

It is therefore more reasonable to consider using handmade bricks only for the exterior veneer. Even here, though, you must be aware that adobe bricks are likely to have even lower thermal performance characteristics than common bricks, which are already low on the scale. The fact that many pressed or hand-formed bricks contain plant fibers and such means that they have lower conductivity, lower mass, and correspondingly low heat-storage capacity, diffusivity, and so forth. Although little actual data exists for adobe bricks' thermal performance, their close relationship to standard bricks means they are not going to perform any better than the manufactured variety, and likely somewhat worse.

What Are the Options?

Masonry heaters are the most versatile wood-burning devices in the world. Because they do not depend on a chimney from the top of a firebox, the arrangement of the design elements is limited only by imagination. Fireboxes, heat-storage mass, and chimneys can be separate elements of virtually any shape. Additional features such as sitting areas, warming nooks, and wood-storage niches can be added to the design. In addition to this amazing flexibility, masonry heaters can be veneered with any masonry material imaginable, from common bricks to handmade tiles to natural stone, each with unique thermal properties. Now that these unique elements have been discussed, it's time to explore how to know what size masonry heater is needed in a given living space.

DESIGNING FUNCTIONAL ARTWORK

For as long as we've contemplated building a house, we've known that we wanted a masonry heater. They are clean, efficient, beautiful, and they utilize modern carbon rather than the fossil carbon used to heat most homes, a key difference for global climate change. As it turns out, we didn't build a new house; we've spent the last six years (and counting) expanding and renovating a house dating from 1950.

Though I grew up in the woods, and value being close to nature, we chose to live in the city where my spouse, Neil, can commute by bicycle (he's an atmospheric chemist on the faculty of Carnegie Mellon University). But we are living more or less in the woods, as we're on the edge of a 600-acre urban forest. I spend most of my time working on the house and on various gardens in our little permaculture oasis, as well as some teaching, consulting, and volunteering on issues of urban sustainability: air quality, land use, and local and urban agriculture. We have two daughters (who usually bike or walk up to the local public school), who have enjoyed being nestled into the woods as we are—and seeing (and sometimes helping) the house come together.

As an artist, it was a joy to design and build the heater and surrounding structural members together with a couple of experts in their respective fields. On the structural design, we collaborated with an architect but also had definite ideas of our own. The architect determined the engineering requirements, but we felt free to alter the materials, layout, and other aspects of the building in a continuous conversation with him.

The main room (shown in figure 6.31) wound up being remarkably reminiscent of the house my parents built from scratch in the woods of the Hudson Valley, with tree-pillars supporting radiating oak beams and a great many windows connecting us with the outdoors. Rather than a heater and support pillars of brick as first envisioned by the architect, we have branching trees rising out of a stone hearth, and a brick chimney beside the stone heater. (One of the beams held up by the trees was longer and wider than structurally necessary, so I set to carving; now we have oak leaves, acorns, Celtic braiding, and a dragon overlooking the living room.) We were able to salvage enough Roman brick from the old exterior wall of the house and a nonfunctional chimney to build the new chimney. The chimney being rectangular, it seemed natural to use a medium like brick, but for the hexagonal heater I felt that more organic forms and natural materials were in order (and we would be unable to match the exterior of the house, as Roman brick is no longer generally available).

The sandstone we chose came from only 50 and 100 miles away. A huge slab of Maryland Red sandstone was cut into sections for the free-form hearth, partly to make the sections supporting the roof structure separate to allow for expansion and contraction. The largest section is a broad, raised, heated hearth. This particular chunk of stone weighed close to 1,200 pounds, so we set it into place using a block and tackle suspended from the stout oak beams above. The natural weathered edge of the sandstone slab goes all around the outside of the wraparound hearth. Since the original slab was larger than the footprint of the hearth, however, Ken [Matesz] and I were able to cut the remaining material so that the first 3½ feet of facing above the benches all came from the same slab—some pieces as large as 2 by 3 feet, others in the form of strips that we placed edge-on beneath the mantels. Above that level, the stone is mostly glacial till from just north of Pittsburgh.

The stone veneer on our heater ranges from 4 to 6 inches thick. Ken built the core and helped me do the stonework up to the mantels. I finished the stonework as time permitted and incorporated ergonomically shaped "backstones" where the chimney meets the hearth. For the rather hefty capstone, we had friends over for a stone-raising party.

FIGURE 6.43. Maren Cooke relaxes on the heated bench of her artistic creation. Project by Maren Cooke and Ken Matesz; photo by Maren Cooke.

A decision made during the core construction phase kept us from burning the heater for several years. Trying to get the most energy possible out of the wood we burn, we had Ken install a hot-water jacket, a stainless-steel pipe passing through the stone facing and the firebrick core wall, where it hugs one side of the firebox before looping back out. If the house had been designed around the masonry heater, we would have made the house more compact; the hot-water tank would be on the second floor, and natural convection would circulate the water. We have no second floor, though, and our household plumbing feeds from the area below the heater. In addition, the necessary pumps, valves, and heat exchangers are fairly complicated and expensive, especially in combination with areas of radiant floor in the basement and future solar thermal panels on the roof. The water jacket remained unconnected and we could not fire the heater without risking damage to the pipe (since there was nothing circulating to keep it cool). In the interim, we went without hot water for almost four months one winter while I tried to eco-optimize the replacement for a dead water heater.

Recently a friend who is an expert on steel helped us devise a workaround by circulating air through the pipe instead of water. Now, instead of a multi-thousand-dollar system in the basement, we have a forty-dollar ventilation fan and some copper fittings. And I have begun thinking about a really nifty heated drying rack . . .

Because the stonework dried under a roof for years and the concrete had so long to cure, we accelerated the initial break-in process somewhat, burning two small fires a day for a week (first just kindling, working up to full loads). Several days went by before the exterior started getting warm. Ken had forewarned us that we would get little heat from the initial small "break-in" fires. It takes some time for heat from a little firewood to initially warm that much mass. The larger fires warmed it nicely. The firebox, after we began using full loads, was soon scoured clean by the heat. The secondary combustion chamber took longer to self-clean and lived up to its name *black oven* for a while. It was slow to heat up, with the massive stone surrounding it, but did a nice job early on roasting some pumpkins for pie—and has baked some fine loaves of bread! Now we can break bread (as well as share lovely fires) with family and friends, without feeling guilty about wood-burning emissions—a notable concern for an air-quality activist and an atmospheric scientist in a region with serious pollution issues.

by Maren Leyla Cooke, Pittsburgh, Pennsylvania

FIGURE 7.1. This is a very straightforward, elegant, and well-placed brick masonry heater. Notice the inset herringbone brick pattern above the mantel. The heater was built all the way to the ceiling, giving the impression of the huge mass continuing on, though the workings of this heater end about 1 foot below the ceiling. Photo courtesy of Envirotech Masonry Heaters.

CHAPTER SEVEN

Heating Requirements of the House

Would anyone bake cookies without knowing how much flour to use? Does a traveler set off on a trip without knowing a destination? Should you buy a house if you don't know the price? You could answer yes to any of these questions; yet most of us would rather have a plan of action. It's sensible to know the recipe before starting to cook. It certainly is wiser to know where you're headed before setting off. It's reasonable to check prices before committing to a sale. It is likewise a good idea to know how much heat is required for a space before having a masonry heater installed.

In most new home construction, a heating, ventilating, and air-conditioning (HVAC) specialist examines the plans for the house and does a careful analysis to determine what size furnace and/or air conditioner is needed for the space. All 2,000-square-foot homes are not created equally. Different roof pitches, different framing sizes or spacing, different kinds and numbers of windows and doors, and different kinds and amounts of insulation all influence how much heat is required for a particular living space. Even a single 200-square-foot room in one house will not require the same heating as the same room in another. One might have wood floors, the other carpet. One might have five windows, the other two. You must look at all the pertinent factors to decide what kind of heater is needed for each living space.

The other side of this coin is that all masonry heaters are not created equally, either. As chapter 6 described, different configurations and materials will perform differently. Even a single design built with differing materials will perform differently. One relatively simple design is based on a traditional Finnish contraflow heater. (You can read more about this in chapter 8.) There are several core kit manufacturers of heaters of this general design. Though one of these kits may be assembled the same way with the same type of refractory materials, the exteriors may be faced very differently by different masons, with different bricks, stones, mortar, and other options. All of these seemingly insignificant differences can make a heater that functions in significantly different ways. Cookie-cutter heaters don't necessarily give cookie-cutter results.

In addition, each homeowner has individual preferences and goals to be achieved with a masonry heater. You may be looking forward to being entirely energy-independent. Not only that, but you may want to enjoy a fire three times per day. Another individual may be looking to simply heat the primary living space through most of the heating season, but may be unconcerned if the heater will not heat the whole space on the coldest days of the year. This person may want to know that this can be achieved by heating the appliance only once per day. Yet another person may be looking at the masonry heater as being only a backup source of heat in emergency situations and may have less concern about how often the heater needs to be fired, so long as it will be a dependable source of emergency heating. Each homeowner needs to be shown a way to achieve his or her heating goals.

This chapter takes as its starting place this basic question: "Over what time period will the heater be expected to heat and how much heat is required (in the living space) in that time period, before the masonry heater is fired again?" This question must be adequately answered *within* the framework of whatever other physical, budgetary, and aesthetic demands you or your site conditions may place on the project. There is no one-size-fits-all answer to every similar project. Something as simple as a chimney that is 10 feet taller can completely change the outcome.

FIGURE 7.2. The heater pictured here is the same type the author sometimes takes to home shows. It's a medium-sized soapstone heater with a bakeoven option. Photo courtesy of Tulikivi Corporation.

Though this type of specificity is sound advice, it does not mean that masonry heater design is so rigid that one heater design can only work in one particular house. In fact, though the preceding statements stem from designing a heater to fit a particular living space, it is also perfectly possible to do things another way: You can, instead, start with a heater design and build a home or living space around it. A given heater, faced with specific materials, will impart specific amounts of heat over a specific period of time. Knowing this, a primary living space, or, indeed, a whole house, can be designed such that it is certain that the proposed heater will fulfill all the needs of heating that space. Similarly, if you have more flexible desires as to how much space must be heated with a masonry heater, you may be able to use one of many different designs to achieve these ends, though it's still worthwhile to understand the ramifications of the choice of a definite heating device. Masonry heaters have built-in versatility, but some of that comes with a price.

The Versatility of Mass

It is common for people seeing masonry heaters for the first time to think of them as overgrown wood-burning stoves. I've owned a portable, lightweight masonry heater to take to home and garden shows for years. Invariably, someone recognizes it as some kind of heating stove that is at least double the size of many typical metal wood-burning stoves. They comment to their companions, "You have to have a really big house for a stove like that!" Their assumption, based on the propensity of metal stoves to overheat because their heat is unfettered by any substantial mass, is that all wood-burning appliances are likewise uncontrolled heat producers. In reality, the actual masonry heater of which they are seeing a replica is designed for literally just the main living area of a common home—perhaps 1,000 square feet of space with 8-foot-high ceilings.

What's more significant is that a masonry heater of this size could be put into a *smaller space,* like a single family room of just 400 or 500 square feet, and still be used effectively and without overheating the space. The reason for this is that it's the warm mass that heats the living space, not the fire itself. The amount of firewood used, or how often a fire is burned, determines how warm the mass gets. The heater that could heat 1,000 square feet, using a load of firewood once per day, may very well heat the smaller space using a firewood load every thirty-six hours or even every two days. Quite simply, more firewood warms the mass more significantly (makes it warmer) so that it can then heat a larger space. Less firewood charges the mass with less heat, which then provides milder heat to the area.

This flexibility does not come without a cost, however. There are at least two hidden costs to the plan of using an oversized masonry heater. First, installing a heater that is larger than necessary for a given space will usually cost more money than a more appropriately sized masonry heater. This is easily foreseen and understood. There is also a risk of greater inefficiency in actual everyday use. The inefficiency may not be quite so obvious—at least not at first. Since such a heater will provide the gentle radiant heat you desire for a space, it may seem just fine. There are telltale signs of inefficiency, however.

A masonry heater is meant to be a clean-burning, efficient way of using firewood. The principal means of achieving efficiency and cleanliness is to burn dry firewood at very high temperatures. The above-mentioned heater, designed for 1,000 square feet of living space, has a firebox and mass created to absorb the heat from enough firewood to warm that mass sufficiently to warm a 1,000-square-foot area. If said heater is going to be used to heat only half that space, it will need much less wood. The result of burning significantly less wood than that for which it was designed is that achieving the high temperatures for clean, efficient combustion is simply not possible in that firebox. A smaller percentage of the available fuel is therefore actually consumed, and more of it escapes out the chimney. More than likely you'll notice that the firebox always has a coating of black soot. Soot will likewise condense on door glass and, very likely,

creosote deposits will occur throughout the flues and in the chimney. Such a scenario introduces greater maintenance issues combined with greater environmental issues because the oversized masonry heater is not operating within an optimum range that promotes clean, efficient combustion.

The versatility of a high-mass heat-storage device like this is, then, a good thing to a point. It is wise to have a heater with some excess capacity so that during long spells of unusually cold weather, the heater can meet the challenge. Likewise, it is good to know that when the weather turns milder, you can fire it less frequently or with less wood and still experience its subtle, radiant heat. As with any engineered device, there are limits within which you should strive to remain. The goal should be to meet maximum heat demand, accommodate minimum demand, and all the while assure clean and efficient combustion. This goal is met by properly sizing either the living space to the proposed heater or by designing or specifying a particular heater for the existing space requirements.

Heating Requirements

The first step in designing a masonry heater is to know how much heat is required for the given space over a particular time period. In terms of a home in a cold climate, the heating requirements of that space are equal to the amount of heat that the building loses over a period of time at a specific target indoor temperature. This heating requirement calculation is often referred to as the heat-loss calculation. Obviously, if a structure never lost any heat that was produced or collected within its confines, it would forever stay at or near the temperatures produced by that heat.

Practically speaking, zero heat loss is impossible. Every building material, including insulation, has some combination of porosity, conductivity, and a degree of leak-proneness. In addition, thick insulation requires thick walls that have typically high labor and material costs. Window and door openings are prone to tiny leaks, while glass itself is a poor insulator. And of course,

WHAT ARE BTUS AND KILOWATTS?

BTU stands for "British Thermal Unit," which is simply the amount of energy required to raise the temperature of 1 pound of water by 1°F. (This definition assumes liquid water and standard atmospheric pressure.) When speaking about masonry heaters, BTUs are used to refer to the *power* produced by the heater. Power is energy (or work) delivered over a period of time. You might say, for example, that a particular masonry heater outputs 10,000 BTUs per hour. In this context, you'll often simply see the measure in "BTUs"; the hour units are presumed.

A kilowatt (kW) is 1,000 watts. Again, a watt is a unit of power. Most people know that a 100-watt lightbulb gives off more light than a 40-watt bulb—the one is more powerful than the other. Similarly, a masonry heater that throws more kWs of heat is a more powerful heater.

Since both units are often used in North America as measures of power, they also relate directly to each other. One kilowatt is equal to 3,412 BTU/hr. One BTU/hr equals about 0.293 watts (.000293 kilowatts). A fairly large masonry heater would output 6 kW, which is then 20,472 BTUs/hr (6 × 3,412 = 20,472).

whole twenty-four-hour period. Likewise, calculating heat loss for the whole house can involve quite cumbersome, large numbers if the time period is long. So, more as a matter of convenience than anything else, heat loss and masonry heater output will be calculated in BTUs per hour or kilowatts, units that are both used regularly in North America.

Much of this chapter, then, will focus on calculating the heating requirements (heat loss) of a simple house. Using these procedures, and with careful math and record keeping, you can discover the basic heating needs of a room, several rooms, or a whole house. Armed with this information, you can, with confidence, be ready to move on to the next step of determining what kind of masonry heater will meet those heating requirements. If done well, these calculations will allow anyone to ascertain whether or not a proposed heater is likely to be adequate for a specific project.

The last section of this chapter will provide parameters by which you can know approximately how much heat will be available from a given masonry heater. Designing a masonry heater can be a very exacting science, and the proper calculation of every aspect of such work is far beyond the scope of this text. Chapter 8 will cover the basic design parameters for a good-quality masonry heater. However, there is basic information you need in order to have a good sense of the limits and capabilities of masonry heaters; these are covered at the end of this chapter.

Basic Heat-Loss Calculations

In order to make this calculation process easy to follow, we'll take a 1,000-square-foot home of rectangular shape as our example. It is 25 feet wide and 40 feet long; its floor plan is shown in figure 7.3. Its walls are 10 feet tall, and it has an insulated attic and crawl space. I've created this design with round numbers and simple dimensions to make following the procedure as easy as possible. At this stage, there's no reason to get bogged down in calculating wall sizes with fractions of a foot or a few extra inches. Learning the process is what is

people go in and out of houses, exposing the indoors to the cold outdoors. Thus, there are two primary ways in which heat is lost from a building. Either it is lost because heat conducts through materials to the outside, or it is lost because of some kind of leak, often called infiltration. There really is no way to completely prevent heat loss from a dwelling from time to time. This continuous winter heat loss is the whole reason for heating.

Masonry heater heat output will be calculated on a per-hour basis. In other words, a given heater produces a certain amount of heat every hour, on average, based on a total daily heat output. Although you could simply calculate a daily total, the hourly average is a more manageable number than that required for the

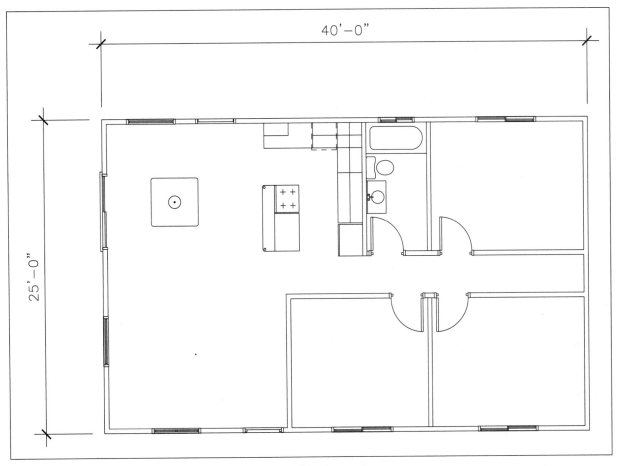

40'–0"

25'–0"

FIGURE 7.3. Floor plan of a sample home for which a heater will be designed.

crucial here. Still, do not be deceived into thinking a larger, more complicated dwelling is enormously more difficult to analyze.

The important point is to carefully move step by step through each procedure regardless of the size or complexity of the house. No matter how complex a house looks, it still has all the same ingredients. Every house has walls, a roof, and a floor. You should plan to tackle a subject house one aspect at a time, just as in the following example. It's always helpful to number the outside walls. This sample has just four. Yours may have six, eight, ten, or more. The number is irrelevant as long as you systematically analyze each wall and can compile that data in an easy-to-read format. In the end, you simply add totals from each wall, each square foot of floor, each square foot of ceiling, and so on to get to a total number that will be the heat loss from the home.

A large home with complicated layout, odd angles, and many turns will take more time, but is, in reality, no more complicated to calculate.

In addition, some people may be planning only to heat one or just a few rooms. If the living areas of the house beyond those rooms are heated with some other source, then interior walls confining the area heated by the masonry heater are not considered areas of heat loss. In other words, if your goal is to have a room heated to around 68°F and the room on the other side of the wall is already 68° or more in temperature, it's not possible to lose heat to that other area. (Remember the second law of thermodynamics from chapter 3.) For example, suppose the plan is to heat a 30-foot-by-30-foot great room with a masonry heater. If two out of the four walls confining that great room are interior walls separating the great room from other rooms heated in some other

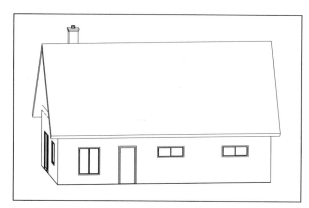

FIGURE 7.4. Our sample home. It would be easy to calculate heat loss if houses didn't have windows and doors.

way, then those two walls represent wall area having zero heat loss. Single rooms abutting other heated areas, then, are even simpler subjects for heat-loss calculations.

First Part: Heat Loss by Conduction

Calculating the amount of heat that is lost from a home would be extremely easy in most houses if it were not for the fact that walls also have openings in them for windows and doors. For the most part, heat loss through the walls themselves is by conduction. As chapter 3 discussed, conduction is the transfer of heat directly through a material rather than heat transferred by convection (air flow) or radiation. When heat loss from a home is due to loss of warm air, it is called infiltration. Essentially, infiltration means leaks. Exterior walls of a home don't generally have significant infiltration (leak) potential unless they have openings cut in them for windows or doors. Because most walls *do* have these openings, it will be necessary to also calculate or estimate losses by infiltration, which will be done as a separate operation later in this chapter.

The easiest method, assuming all walls have the same thickness, materials, and insulation qualities, is to simply add up the total area of all walls first, then use this single number to calculate heat loss. In the process of determining total area, you must subtract both window and door areas from each wall area. Windows and doors have a very different level of heat transmission than solid, insulated walls, and their conductive heat loss must be computed separately. So, at the same

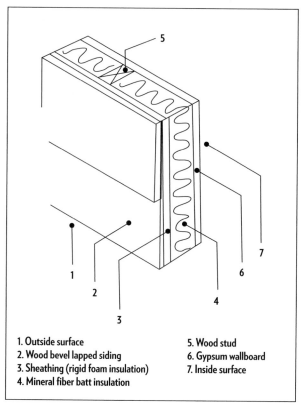

1. Outside surface
2. Wood bevel lapped siding
3. Sheathing (rigid foam insulation)
4. Mineral fiber batt insulation
5. Wood stud
6. Gypsum wallboard
7. Inside surface

FIGURE 7.5. The composition of a conventionally framed wall. Illustration reprinted with permission from ASHRAE.

time that you're computing area, you can begin a list of the windows and doors. As in the wall-area calculations, if all the windows are of the same quality, once a list is made, a total area of window can also be made for one simple window-heat-loss calculation. This same "divide and conquer" classification technique is useful throughout the whole heat-loss calculation procedure.

For those who may perform this analysis on new home plans, it may be that the drawings already incorporate window and door schedules listing quantities, sizes, and qualities (or manufacturer) of all the windows and doors. This makes the job even easier since you now only have to calculate wall areas and refer to the window or door schedule to know how much area to subtract for each opening.

Step 1: Conduction Heat Loss Through Walls
The basic calculation is to find the total area (square feet) of wall surface and the total R-value of the wall.

The R-value is simply the resistance (R) to heat flow through a material or assembly of materials (see appendix B for R-values of common building materials). It is measured in hr-ft²-°F/BTUs. The area (A) is divided by the R-value (R) to obtain a total transmission value of heat through that wall in BTUs/hr-°F.

$$A \div R = BTU/hr\text{-}°F$$

The walls of the sample structure are conventionally framed (see figure 7.5). This means they are built with 2-by-4 studs and the wall cavities are filled with fiberglass insulation. The inside of the walls are covered with ½-inch Sheetrock. The outside is sheathed with ½-inch plywood. Over the sheathing is a ½-inch layer of Styrofoam insulation and wood siding.

The structure has four walls. Walls 1 and 3 are each 40 feet long and 10 feet high (see figures 7.6 and 7.7).

$$40 \text{ ft} \times 10 \text{ ft} = 400 \text{ ft}^2 \times 2 = 800 \text{ ft}^2$$

However, wall 1 has three windows and one door with a total area of 61 ft². Wall 3 has a 21 ft² door and three windows totaling 32 ft². This leaves 686 ft² of real wall surface (total wall area − total window/door area = real wall surface):

$$800 \text{ ft}^2 - 114 \text{ ft}^2 = 686 \text{ ft}^2$$

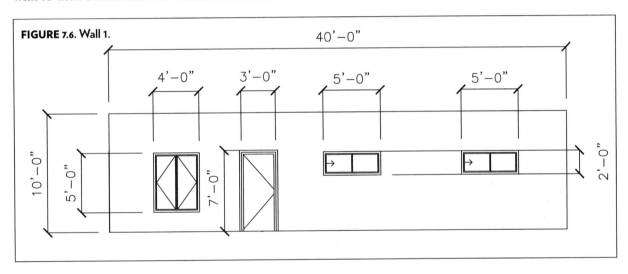

FIGURE 7.6. Wall 1.

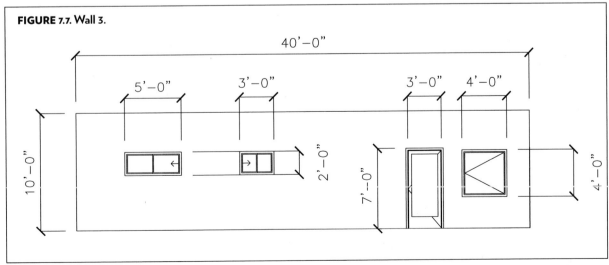

FIGURE 7.7. Wall 3.

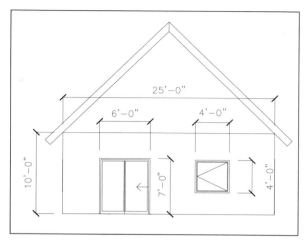

FIGURE 7.8. Walls 2 and 4 are identical in size. Wall 2 has no windows or doors, however.

Walls 2 and 4 are each 25 feet long and 10 feet high (see figure 7.8):

$$25 \text{ ft} \times 10 \text{ ft} = 250 \text{ ft}^2 \times 2 = 500 \text{ ft}^2$$

Wall 2 has no windows or doors but wall 4 has one sliding glass door of 42 ft² and one window of 16 ft². These sides then have a real area of 442 ft²:

$$686 \text{ ft}^2 + 442 \text{ ft}^2 = 1{,}128 \text{ ft}^2$$

Therefore, the total real wall surface area (A) is 1,128 ft².

The R-values for the sample wall are as follows:

½ inch Sheetrock	00.45
3.5 inch fiberglass insulation	12.00
½ inch plywood	00.63
½ inch Styrofoam	02.50
Wood siding	01.02
Total	**16.60**

The total R-value of this wall assembly is the total of all these; (R) = 16.60. The total heat-loss transmission is calculated by dividing real wall surface area by R-value:

$$1{,}128 \text{ ft}^2 \div 16.60 \text{ hr-ft}^2\text{-}°\text{F/BTU} = 67.95 \text{ BTU/hr-}°\text{F}$$

Therefore, the total conduction heat loss through these walls is 67.95 BTU/hr-°F.

Step 2: Conduction Heat Loss Through Windows and Doors

There are three doors; one is a solid-core wood door and the others are glass doors. There are seven windows. In this case, since the two glass doors are the equivalent of large windows, the calculation will be based on nine windows with a total area (A) of 148 square feet. The remaining door is 21 square feet.

The R-value for the windows and glass doors is 3.13 (these are double-pane insulated glass units with a low-e coating as seen in appendix B), resulting in the following calculation of total conduction heat loss:

$$148 \text{ ft}^2/3.13 \text{ hr-ft}^2\text{-}°\text{F/BTU} = 47.28 \text{ BTU/hr-}°\text{F}$$

The R-value for the 1¾-inch-thick solid-core wood door is 3.03, so the equation for conduction heat loss of this door is:

$$21 \text{ ft}^2/3.03 \text{ hr-ft}^2\text{-}°\text{F/BTU} = 6.93 \text{ BTU/hr-}°\text{F}$$

It is significant to notice that the total wall surface, being nearly 1,200 square feet, loses only one and one-quarter as much heat as the windows and doors that only occupy 169 square feet. In other words, even modestly insulated walls like these lose nearly five and one-half times less heat per square foot than do high-quality, low-emissivity wood windows! This is a fantastic argument for only having windows of the highest quality and in as few places as are needed for enjoyment, light, and visibility. One of the easiest and least expensive ways to save energy is to eliminate a window in favor of insulated wall whenever practical. A wall without openings costs less to build, has much less chance of infiltrating air, and eliminates an item subject to breakage, failure of operation, and eventual costly replacement. Certainly you do not wish to have a house with no windows, but a house with appropriate, carefully considered glazing will be both more economical to build and easier to heat.

FIGURE 7.9. This stucco heater with tile trim features a heated "couch." Notice the wood storage under the firebox and specialty picture tiles asymmetrically located. Photo courtesy of Biofire, Inc.

Step 3: Conduction Heat Loss Through the Ceiling
In our sample home, like many homes, the attic is a vented space. Therefore, the calculations for heat loss depend solely on the thickness and type of insulation and the type of ceiling material. Other constructions may have a cathedral ceiling with a construction more closely related to wall construction with inside Sheetrock, insulation, outside sheathing, roofing paper, and the roof itself. Regardless, the overall analysis of the ceiling is, in most cases, simpler than for walls because the ceiling is usually continuous, with no openings like doors and windows. Obviously, skylights and attic accesses should also be considered if they in any way compromise the overall thermal protection offered.

The model home in this sample has a ceiling space measuring 25 feet wide and 40 feet long. It is 1,000 square feet of uninterrupted, insulated ceiling. Its only materials are ½-inch-thick Sheetrock and 12 inches of loose-fill fiberglass insulation. Since the house has a ventilated attic, the space above the insulation, although protected from the deleterious, heat-draining effects of wind, is nevertheless at outdoor temperatures.

The R-values for the component materials are as follows:

½ inch Sheetrock 00.45
12 inches fiberglass insulation ...42.00
Total **42.45**

With a total R-value of 42.45 hr-ft²-°F/BTU, and a total area of 1,000 square feet, the equation for transmitted heat loss of the ceiling system is (A/R):

$$1,000 \text{ ft}^2 \div 42.45 \text{ hr-ft}^2\text{-°F/BTU} = 23.56 \text{ BTU/hr-°F}$$

Step 4: Conduction Heat Loss Through the Floor

The model home in this sample has a floor space the same as the ceiling, measuring 25 feet wide and 40 feet long. Again, it is 1,000 square feet of uninterrupted, insulated floor. Its materials are ¾-inch-thick plywood subfloor, ¾-inch-thick hardwood flooring, and 10 inches of fiberglass batt insulation in the crawl space. Like the ceiling, the crawl space is ventilated. The crawl space is, for all practical purposes, the same as outdoors minus the wind. Therefore it is necessary to calculate the resistance to heat flow through the materials that make up the floor. Again, we refer to appendix B.

The R-values for the component materials are as follows:

¾ inch plywood 00.93
¾ inch hardwood......................00.68
10 inches fiberglass insulation ...35.00
Total **36.61**

With a total R-value of 36.61 hr-ft²-°F/BTU, and

a total area of 1,000 square feet, the calculation for the transmitted heat loss through the floor of this house is:

$$1,000 \text{ ft}^2 \div 36.61 \text{ hr-ft}^2\text{-°F/BTU} = 27.29 \text{ BTU/hr-°F}$$

Step 5: Total Heat Transmission

Now that the entire envelope of the house has been examined, we can determine the total amount of heat loss through all surfaces of the home at any given time by adding all the above totals together, a number representing all the heat being lost at once through the walls, ceiling, doors, windows, and floor. In this case,

$$\text{Walls + Windows + Doors + Ceiling + Floor =}$$
$$67.95 + 47.28 + 6.93 + 23.56 + 27.29 = 173.01 \text{ BTU/hr-°F}$$

If this were the end of the procedure, it would now be known that, in order to maintain *each* 1-degree temperature above outside temperature, you would need to input nearly 175 BTUs per hour to maintain that temperature. More will be said about this later; but now it is necessary to move on to the next means of heat loss—air infiltration.

Second Part: Heat Loss by Infiltration

The "science" of examining heat loss due to infiltration or leakage for a yet-to-be-built home or room addition is only science to a certain extent. It is also a large part conjecture and assumption. When you sit down with a set of blueprints for a home, there really is no certainty at all as to how well sealed the home will be from leakage. In the end, what will determine leakage is how careful the builder is when it comes to critical leakage areas of the home. Even very careful builders are subject to mistakes or oversights. Likewise, an existing home's infiltration level is one of supposition and conjecture. With all siding, insulation, windows, doors, trim, and so forth in place, there is no obvious way to calculate the heat loss by leakage.

It is possible, with an existing structure, to have a reliable test done to determine how "tight" a house is.

FIGURE 7.10. A blower door assembly in place to check the leakiness (infiltration) of a house. Photo by Alexandra Stewart, Portland, OR.

There are businesses and builders who perform what is often called a "blower door test." The blower door is a powerful fan assembly that is temporarily mounted in the frame of an exterior door of a residence (see figure 7.10). The idea is to have the entire house closed in the fashion it would be for winter weather, with the blower door, which seals completely, taking the place of one of the exterior doors. A calibrated blower door test assembly permits the tester to reliably and accurately measure the air pressure differences between the inside and outside of the house as well as the total quantity of air drawn from the house. With the house sealed, the blower is activated and the home is depressurized (because the fan is blowing out from the house). The measuring devices monitor the pressure as it stabilizes back to natural pressure conditions. With the data from this test, how much air leaks into the home in a given period of time can be determined exactly.

The overall goal of either an exacting blower door test or an estimation procedure is to determine how many air changes per hour (ACH) occur through leaks in the envelope of the house. The analysis allows you to picture the entire leakiness of the home as if it were one leak. In other words, the total number of the various cracks and crevices through which air might leak are added together. For example, a study might show that the total leakage in a home is equal to having a perfectly airtight home with a single 3-inch-square hole through one of the exterior walls to the outdoors. Knowing the size of that hole and the infiltration and exfiltration pressures related to stack effect permits the calculation of how much air comes in and leaves the home every hour through that leak. The more times that the volume of air in the home is changed or replaced with fresh air due to leakage, the more heat that is lost because of that leakage. Conversely, a home that is "tighter" and has less air changes per hour (ACH) will be easier to heat.

Fortunately, as discussed at length in chapter 3, since masonry heaters are not designed primarily to heat air, heat loss by infiltration is not as much of a problem. In general, with radiant heat, you're comfortable at lower air temperatures. Given two identical homes, the one maintaining lower air temperatures will have less total heat loss. This is because the temperature difference between outside and inside drives stack effect (see chapter 5). Stack effect is the driving force bringing cold air into the home. Since air heating is not the primary objective with the masonry heater, the extra load from infiltrated colder air is of lesser significance in the primary living space. The difference is subtle, but evident.

There are a number of ways to calculate or estimate the infiltration in a given home. Some give the appearance of being more accurate because they involve minute calculation of the lengths of the supposed cracks around various openings like windows and doors. The cracks—the expected paper-thin (or smaller) spaces that are susceptible to air leakage—are measured and added together to give, again, a total size of the imagined "hole" in the envelope of the home. The calculation is further complicated by the need to

FIGURE 7.11. This massive soapstone masonry heater has split-rock-faced stone accents and a green serpentine arch. Notice the shallow niche above the wraparound mantel and cylindrical stone wrapping the chimney flue. The heater is perfectly placed in the middle of the primary living space. Photo courtesy of Tulikivi Corporation.

examine supposed wind conditions around the building, determine which walls will encounter the most wind and have the most "cracks," as well as, additionally, the actual speed of the wind. I find this calculation tedious at best, and wildly erroneous at worst, since it is based on conjecture anyway. Not all "cracks" are actually leaks, and the wind and weather conditions, as well as local landscaping, can change all the results.

Others may disagree, but a suitable accuracy and dependability can be achieved by other estimating procedures. Most notably, there are now significant records on file of the airtightness of modern homes. Enough contemporary homes have been blower door tested to provide a database of reliable information about the number of ACH that a given structure is likely to have. For example, the ASHRAE Handbook of Fundamentals offers data suggesting that half of all

houses built recently have 0.5 ACH or less and that the vast majority of them have a rate of 1 or less ACH. The more tightly constructed homes have as low as 0.2 ACH, though loosely constructed homes can have a rate ten times that at 2 ACH. Obviously, what is needed is for anyone doing this analysis to know what makes one house have the maximum tightness and another the minimum.

The data referenced above indicate that the majority of homes built by reputable builders who have knowledge of and put into use best practices will have 1 or less ACH. Those who are building a new home can inquire with the builder as to what efforts they will be making to reduce air infiltration. Those who are contemplating a masonry heater in an existing but fairly new home can be relatively confident that theirs is likely this good as well. Those with homes more than

TABLE 7.1 Winter Air Exchange Rates (ACH) as a Function of Airtightness

Class	Outdoor Design Temperature, °F									
	50°	40°	30°	20°	10°	0°	-10°	-20°	-30°	-40°
Tight	0.41	0.43	0.45	0.47	0.49	0.51	0.53	0.55	0.57	0.59
Medium	0.69	0.73	0.77	0.81	0.85	0.89	0.93	0.97	1.00	1.05
Loose	1.11	1.15	1.20	1.23	1.27	1.30	1.35	1.40	1.43	1.47

Note: Values are for 15 mph wind and indoor temperature of 68°F. Table reprinted with permission from ASHRAE.

twenty years old should be less confident and be especially careful in judging the airtightness of the home. A relatively reliable estimate of ACH for most homes can be obtained by using table 7.1.

An important piece of information now needed is the outside design temperature (ODT) at the location of the house being analyzed. The ODT is the minimum temperature usually experienced in the locale where the house is to be built or where it rests if existing. This information is usually available from the local weather service, or see appendix C to find a comparable city close to your building site.

The headings of the ACH table relate to guidelines of how tight the house is or is expected to be using the following information:

- **Tight:** New houses with full vapor retardant, no fireplace, well-fitted windows, weatherstripped doors, one story, and less than 1,500 square feet of floor area fall into this category.
- **Medium:** Medium structures include new, two-story frame houses or one-story houses more than ten years old with average maintenance, a floor area greater than 1,500 square feet, average fit windows and doors, and a fireplace with damper and glass closure.
- **Loose:** Loose structures are poorly constructed residences with poorly fitted windows and doors. Examples include houses more than twenty years old, of average maintenance, having a fireplace without damper or glass closure, or having more

than an average number of vented appliances. Average manufactured homes are in this category.

Armed with this data and understanding, it is now possible to calculate the infiltration rate of our sample home. In this case, the sample is less than 1,500 square feet in floor area. It is also a new, well-built home with high-quality windows and doors. It is noted here that the above guidelines list a home as "tight" if it has no fireplace. Keeping with strict terminology and recognizing that a masonry heater is *not* a fireplace per se, it is possible to still fit this example into the "tight" category.

The concern in the guidelines is that a standard fireplace—an open firebox that exhausts immediately into a chimney above—is simply a large hole in the envelope of the house. This single, oft-chosen amenity is so widely recognized as a heating liability that it helps determine if a home is "tight" or "medium." Owners-to-be should realize that it *is* possible to have a masonry heater built that likewise leaks if the doors are not gasketed and do not close tightly and if the chimney has no 100 percent closure damper (see sidebar and figures 7.12–7.14).

Consult with the builder of the masonry heater to verify how the heater will be built in relation to this concern. Those masonry heaters without tightly closing gasketed doors and/or 100 percent closure dampers can sway the home into the "medium" or, possibly, the "loose" category.

This sample home is located in the Cleveland, Ohio, area. Referring to appendix C, we see that Cleveland experiences a winter season low of 0°F. The chart is compiled with historical weather data, and the

WHAT IS A DAMPER?

A damper, within the context of masonry heaters, is a device used to dampen or reduce the flow of exhaust in a flue. Most often it is installed in a chimney flue—though, theoretically, one could be installed in the flues of the heater to redirect the flow of exhaust for specific purposes. Often a damper is one of two types: Sometimes it is a sliding plate of steel with a handle on the end that you can push in (to close) or pull out (to open). Other types are steel plates that swivel within the flue. You turn the handle 90 degrees one way to open it and the opposite way to close.

Most dampers used with masonry heaters are not "full closure" dampers. In other words, by design, they cannot close the flue 100 percent. Often they only close to about 95 percent. This is a safety measure. If someone inadvertently closes the damper before the fire is actually extinguished in the firebox, the partial opening assures that potentially lethal gases like carbon monoxide will still make their way up the chimney.

FIGURE 7.12. An example of a guillotine damper pulled out to open the flue.

FIGURE 7.13. A round stainless-steel damper in the open position. The damper plate swivels out of the way—controlled by a handle on the shaft to the right.

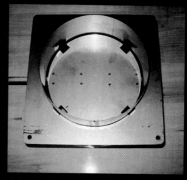

FIGURE 7.14. The damper in the closed position. Slots and a loose fit make this a 95 percent closure damper.

expressed lows indicate that, on average, the geographic region experiences temperatures *above* that temperature 99.6 percent of the year. In other words, on average, the region of Cleveland only experiences temperatures less than 0°F only about 0.4 percent of a calendar year. That represents about thirty-five hours; it is less than two full days. Of course, this is historical, averaged data and does *not* mean that Cleveland never had (or never will have) periods colder than that for an extended period. However, history shows that more than a few days in which it gets colder than 0°F are relatively unlikely.

If the designer uses this data and designs a masonry heater for this low, it is of great certainty that the heater will produce the heat the home needs for more than 99 percent of the year. Should that average low be breached, it is unlikely that the homeowners will experience discomfort unless the temperature falls significantly lower for an extended period of time. Likewise, you could opt to design to a higher seasonal average, for example by choosing an outside design temperature that is only breached 10 percent of the year (about five weeks). In this way, the designed heater would accommodate all but the coldest month of the year. This is a way of designing to save expense on the construction of a heater (because a smaller heater is needed), but recognizing that the masonry heater is necessarily supplemental heat or an emergency backup, not the sole source of heat for the space.

The sample home, then, most closely relates to a home in table 7.1 that has an outdoor design temperature of 0°F and is of "tight" description. The home therefore has an expected infiltration rate, described in air changes per hour, of 0.51. This means the volume of air in the home is changed 0.51 times every hour; the house receives a complete fresh air infusion every two hours.

Finally, with the ACH number in hand, it is possible to calculate the amount of energy required to compensate for infiltrating air and thereby help maintain a chosen target indoor design temperature (IDT). This number is achieved by multiplying the volume of the living space by the ACH and the specific heat of air at standard air pressure. (You will recall that, in chapter 6, specific heat represents the amount of heat that a material—in this case air—can hold.) For this sample dwelling, the equation looks like this:

$$\text{Heat Loss (by infiltration)} = \text{Specific Heat of Air} \times \text{Air Pressure} \times \text{Volume of House} \times \text{ACH}$$

Therefore:

$$\text{Heat Loss} = (.018 \text{BTU/lb-}°\text{F})(.075 \text{lb/ft}^3)(10,000 \text{ft}^3)(.51 \text{ft}^3/\text{hr}) = 91.8 \text{ BTU/hr-}°\text{F}$$

Third Part: Total Heat Loss

Now that a figure for infiltration heat loss and conductive heat loss has been obtained, it is a simple matter to add them together to get a quantity representing total heat loss from the home described:

$$\text{Total Heat Loss} = \text{Infiltration Heat Loss} + \text{Conductive Heat Loss}$$

$$\text{Total Heat Loss} = 91.8 \text{ BTU/hr-}°\text{F} + 173.01 \text{ BTU/hr-}°\text{F} = 264.81 \text{ BTU/hr-}°\text{F}.$$

The total heat loss is expressed in BTUs per hour per degree Fahrenheit. The term *per degree Fahrenheit* refers to the difference between the temperature to be maintained inside the living space and the outside design temperature mentioned in the previous section. The temperature inside, or IDT, is often named in local building codes, commonly at 68°F. Absent such codes or authorities attempting to enforce them, you should relate to experience, bearing in mind that radiant heating is usually quite comfortable even when air temperatures are lower than usual in the vicinity of the heater. As a general rule, it is practical to use the 68°F figure for these calculations. Very few would ever complain if the designed masonry heater warms better than expected, but the reverse is not true.

The house in question, in the Cleveland, Ohio, area, experiences 0°F ODT and has an IDT of 68°F. The difference between the two is 68°F. To find the amount of heat needed per hour in this particular house, then, it is merely a task of multiplying 68°F by the total heat loss (THL):

$$(68°\text{F}) \times (264.81 \text{ BTU/hr-}°\text{F}) = \textbf{18,007.08 BTU/hr.}$$

Fourth Part: Additional Factors

The total heat-loss number purports to express how much heat must be added to the living space every hour by a heating system. However, houses are not desolate spaces devoid of all other inputs. The heating system alone is not the only source of heat in a typical house. Electrical appliances of all kinds also produce heat, as do the people who live in the house. Some modern computer and entertainment systems can generate tremendous amounts of heat, as do refrigerators, freezers, lights, and any other appliances that run automatically. In addition, a given home may have south-facing windows that allow winter sunshine to penetrate and aid in warming the house. All of these additional factors can be considered in the calculation process.

Occupants

The amount of heat produced by human metabolism is surprisingly high and should not be ignored in heating calculations. A homeowner doing these calculations

FIGURE 7.15. Even the television and sound equipment in a home contribute heat. This unusual plastered heater serves as an almost nondescript room divider but still offers heated sitting and sculpted "steps" above the firebox. Photo courtesy of Biofire, Inc.

will know how many people will be living in the home. Likewise, a designer can estimate based on the design of the living space and number of bedrooms. In general it is assumed that a master bedroom will usually have two occupants and each additional bedroom will have one. Since the minimum ODT expressed earlier normally happens at night when everyone in the family is home, it can be assumed that the maximum human heat input is present for these calculations. For purposes of heating calculations, it is assumed that each person will be outputting at least 230 BTU/hour into the living space. In the example here, the two-bedroom home houses three people who contribute a total of **690 BTU/hr.**

Appliances

If you know for sure of specific heat-producing appliances or accessories that will almost always be in the home, you can add the heating contribution of those items. In particular, computers and high-amperage entertainment systems and televisions can contribute a great deal of additional heat. Lights that may be designed to be "always on," like accent lighting, can also be reliable contributors of additional heat. In general, however, it is assumed that daily cooking, laundry, and a running refrigerator will contribute approximately **1,600 BTU/hr.** This is the figure that is used here in the sample home.

Solar Gain

Be careful how you consider solar-heating gains in a home. If the home is specifically designed to collect *and store* solar energy, it definitely needs to be considered. Other homes, however, may receive some solar gain through windows during the day, but may not have enough thermal mass in the home to reliably store any significant portion of that gain. If particular efforts are not being made to store solar gain, it is best to disregard the solar influence. This is true because minimum temperatures typically are experienced long after the solar gain occurred; the coldest temperatures generally occur as daybreak approaches—perhaps twelve to sixteen hours after the last valuable solar input into the home.

This text is insufficient to properly cover all the necessary information regarding solar gain. However, a designer should be cognizant of the fact that glass, particularly south-facing glass, will result in heat gain in a house in winter. In general, even in cold, northern climates, it is possible on sunny days to receive a couple thousand BTUs per square foot of double-paned glass windows. Bear in mind that these windows don't have to be south-facing. Good-quality windows can transmit even reflected sunlight into a home and result in heat gain.

In our sample home, for example, that has 130 square feet of windows, there could be solar gain of as much as (130 ft²) × (1,000 BTU/day-ft²) = 130,000

BTU/day in the month of January—the coldest month in Cleveland. There is always, however, an absorption factor governing how much of that entering heat energy is absorbed by the surfaces in the house. Ceramic tiles and light-painted walls might only absorb 40 percent of that energy. In this case, the total energy absorbed in the whole day is 40 percent of that 130,000 BTUs or 52,000 BTUs. Dividing that total by twenty-four hours in a day, the total heat gained by solar absorption through windows is **2,167 BTU/hr.**

There is much more information needed to fully understand and reliably discover the gains associated with sun through the windows. Each locality has its average monthly amounts of solar gain based on weather conditions. Every house is situated differently in relation to the sun's apparent path through the sky. Different materials and surfaces in the home absorb different percentages of the solar energy that strikes them. All these factors and more influence total gains, or lack thereof, from insolation. This information is available from sources related to passive solar heating, and you should consult those sources for more in-depth study.[1] If you're calculating heat loss for purposes of installing a masonry heater, you may forgo this amount of detail unless, again, your home is purposely being designed as well for solar gain. Rarely is oversizing a masonry heater a liability. As always, a more thorough examination can be achieved by consulting a masonry heater professional with more specific knowledge about how to proceed.

Fifth Part: Grand Total Heating Requirements

Having considered all the forces acting on increasing or decreasing the amount of heat this model home requires, it is a simple matter of addition and subtraction to find the grand total of heating energy it needs per hour. The starting point is the total heat loss calculated earlier:

$$(18,007.08 \text{ BTU/hr}) - 690 \text{ (occupants)} -$$
$$1,600 \text{ (appliances)} - 2,167 \text{ (solar gain)} =$$
$$\text{Grand Total Heat Loss (GTHL)}$$

$$\text{GTHL} = 13550.08 \text{ BTU/hr}$$

This grand total heat loss number represents all the heat that must be generated, on average, every hour of the day in order to heat this sample home in Cleveland, Ohio, on the coldest days of the year. On the days when it is warmer, which was discovered to be 99.6 percent of the year, this much heat does not have to be generated. Again, the calculation could have been done to find the amount of heat needed to accommodate conditions under which only 99.0 percent of the days are warmer. A somewhat smaller masonry heater would be needed and somewhat less wood consumed. I, however, recommend that, if you aspire to use a masonry heater as the sole source of heat in a home, it is always better to have calculated for the worst-case scenario than to find yourself disappointed in an unusual season in which severe weather drops outdoor temperatures well below normal or average for an extended period of time.

A Word of Caution

Some readers may decide that the foregoing example calculation is a strong enough basis for estimating another project. In other words, you could decide that since this example calculated the needs for a 1,000-square-foot home, a house exactly double in size with similar insulation will have simply double the heating requirements. This is an erroneous assumption, especially if the geographic location is different. Remember that winter weather is different from place to place, and different houses are built differently. Even walls of the same thickness may have different kinds of insulation, subtly different material thicknesses or makeup, and so forth. It is always better to know than to guess!

Calculating Heater Size— A Prelude to Chapter 8

Once you're aware of the heating requirements for a given space, it is possible to discover what size masonry heater you need to heat that space. That process starts by simply analyzing the fuel. If a home requires 13,600

BTU/hr, as does the model examined in the previous section, it is clear that you need to know how much fuel needs to be burned to produce that much heat. Then it needs to be clear how often fuel is expected to be burned in the masonry heater. If a heater is going to be fired once every day, it will need a firebox of a different size than a heater that is going to get fired twice, or another heater that is going to get fired three times. Finally, you need a thorough understanding of the materials and technical design parameters for making a good masonry heater.

The Energy Content of Wood

Any typical air-dried wood contains approximately 6,400 BTU per pound. (Air-dried wood generally has a moisture content of 15 to 20 percent.) Continuing with the scenario developed in the previous section, the heater being designed for the 1,000-square-foot home in Cleveland needs to burn enough wood to generate 13,600 BTU per hour. You might jump to the conclusion that this calculation is immediately very simple. Two pounds of wood produce nearly 13,000 BTU, so you need the equivalent of about 2 pounds of wood per hour, or 48 pounds per day. Actually, 50 pounds of wood contains 320,000 BTU, which, divided by 24, is 13,333 BTU per hour—nearly the exact amount apparently needed. However, it's not quite that simple.

Efficiency

A pound of wood burned at near 100 percent combustion efficiency—meaning that every available combustible element in the wood is consumed—will release about 6,400 BTU. Masonry heaters generally do have combustion efficiencies approaching 100 percent. Very little wood is wasted when burned in a masonry heater.

However, there is another kind of efficiency measure that is more relevant to the question of how

FIGURE 7.16. An heirloom heater built with white tiles. Soapstone trim pieces lend some contrast to this clean-lined design. Notice the three protruding tiles above the firebox. These are soot cleanout doors held in place by clay mortar. Photo courtesy of New England Hearth and Soapstone.

FIGURE 7.17. The author with 34 pounds of oak—half the required fuel for heating the sample home in Cleveland on the coldest day of the year. Photo by Aaron Matesz.

much wood you need to burn to heat a specific space: heating efficiency. As mentioned in chapter 1, this is the ratio between how much heat is available from the consumed wood and how much of that heat actually makes it into the living space. This measure is exactly what separates a good masonry heater from a superb one. Virtually all masonry heaters will liberate nearly 6,400 BTU from a pound of wood. Some will only get a little more than half of that heat into the living space, though, while others will get considerably more.

The best masonry heaters will readily achieve heating efficiencies of 80 to 90 percent; the vast majority of the heat liberated by combustion remains in the living space. Medium-grade heaters will be achieving efficiencies in the 70 to 80 percent range. Average

heaters will produce heating efficiency numbers of roughly 55 to 70 percent. You must recognize that 100 percent efficiency is never a possibility with a wood-fired appliance. As discussed in chapter 6, it is chimney draft—the temperature difference between the exhaust of the masonry heater and outdoor temperature—that drives the operation of the appliance. Some heat must be allowed up the chimney or the system cannot operate. Therefore, masonry heaters achieving 80 to 90 percent heating efficiency are astoundingly high-efficiency appliances.

It is not necessarily a poor decision to install a heater that has somewhat lower efficiency. Think about purchasing other relatively durable items—even the house itself. Very often the better designs, products, and workmanship will cost substantially more. In return, the result is something that performs better, lasts longer, and needs less attention over its lifetime. Someone who likes masonry heaters and wants to install one, but is relatively certain that this home is a transition residence—one that they will occupy for several years before moving on to something else—may opt for a more moderate investment in the masonry heater. Likewise, someone who is mainly looking for backup heat or an emergency hedge may not be as concerned about ultimate heating efficiency. Those who are building an heirloom home for the rest of their lives, however, may want to indulge in the masonry heater that will provide several lifetimes of high-efficiency performance. They will want only the best. What separates the best masonry heaters from the average is entirely in the realm of technical design. You will find more in-depth discussion of technical aspects of interior heater design in the next chapter.

How Much Wood . . . Really?

This chapter introduced a proposed project. The heating requirements of that sample home were found to be 13,550.08 BTU per hour on the coldest day of the year in Cleveland. And it is now known that dry, seasoned firewood of virtually any species contains about 6,400 BTU of stored solar energy. Finally, it is realized that even the best masonry heater will not get all of that 6,400 BTU per pound into the living space. Varying efficiency levels will change that.

In the next chapter, this examination will be used to come up with a completed masonry heater design. It will likely have an efficiency rating in the medium range. A masonry heater that achieves about 75 percent efficiency delivers 4,800 BTU of energy from a pound of wood into the home. Therefore this particular heater will require the equivalent of 13,550.08 BTU/hr ÷ 4,800 BTU = 2.82 pounds of wood per hour. In other words, this masonry heater must consume just 68 pounds of wood to heat this home on the coldest day of the year! For more information about quantities of wood, refer to chapter 10. The heating demands of the house have been analyzed and the quantity of wood needed is understood. Now it is time to create a heater that uses that wood and heats that space.

ON THE EDGE OF THE GREAT PLAINS

In northwestern Indiana, in a small town close to Lafayette, home of Purdue University, there lives a family of four that is totally self-sufficient when it comes to heat. Ellen Gundlach, who lectures on statistics at Purdue, and Erich Gundlach, a chemist at a nearby pharmaceutical company, built a modest timber-frame home there. As they were getting ready to build, they sought a way to heat the 2,000-square-foot home using little fossil fuel but great simplicity. They looked at geothermal heat pumps, solar hydronics, and, of course, wood heating. After all their investigation, they decided to use a masonry heater as the primary heat source in the home. Erich says he delights now in "thumbing my nose at fossil fuels! We're very happy with our masonry heater."

Although it was tempting for them to consider some of the newer, high-tech ways of heating, they finally opted for the masonry heater concept at least partially because, says Ellen, "there are no high-tech gadgets to break down. With the masonry heater, it's just stone and wood. There's nothing to fail." Such is the security someone seeks when they plan to live the rest of their lives in a home on the edge of the Great Plains where "it gets quite cold and the wind never stops," according to Erich. His statement about the wind is supported by the fact that, recently, a multi-unit wind farm was built not far away.

Both Ellen and Erich agree that they share one regret when it comes to the masonry heater: They both wish they had had more money so that they could have put in a bigger unit with more heated bench. Their soapstone heater complex includes a Tulikivi TU2200 with heated benches that start on the front of the heater, wrap around the right side, then turn to go behind it before ending at the massive, two-flue masonry chimney. The section of heated bench behind the Tulikivi separates the masonry heater from a soapstone cookstove/bakeoven combination in the kitchen. That heated bench between the cookstove and masonry heater they call the "heat cave."

Ellen explains that it derived its name because it is just big enough for one person (with narrow hips) to sit. There, the lucky one gets heat from below from the bench, from both sides via the cookstove and the masonry heater, and from the back because the lower part of the chimney is warm. Erich says they frequently "fight for bench space," though he concedes that he usually lets the kids, eleven and eight years of age, sit there. "More heated bench would have solved that problem, but our budget at the time just wouldn't permit it." Ellen adds that every member of the family, at one time or another, has fallen asleep on the warm bench.

In addition to their day jobs, Erich and Ellen operate a family farm selling milk, eggs, and meat. They also plant a garden every year from which they get their vegetables. Erich explains that, with the bakeoven available, they have now established a pizza-making tradition on most weekends. Their homemade pizzas are about as homemade as they can get. Erich milks the cow and immediately transforms it into homemade mozzarella cheese; it's a process he says takes about half an hour. Meanwhile, Ellen and the kids gather vegetables from their own garden and chop them. They make pizza sauce from their own tomatoes. When the pizza pies are all assembled, they bake them in the masonry bakeoven. Erich laughs, "I have to admit, I am still guilty of going to the store to buy the flour for the crust! Ellen keeps telling me I need to start growing wheat, too." Obviously, though, with full-time jobs and a farm to run besides, they have their hands full. Other than their pizza tradition and weekend cooking, they say the cookstove gets relatively little use because of their busy schedule and because the primary masonry heater does most of the year's heating.

Erich advises that anyone considering heating with a masonry heater does have to be aware that, unlike modern technological heating solutions, a masonry

FIGURE 7.18. The cookstove/bakeoven unit in the foreground gets occasional use while the main heater, center left—facing the living room—is the primary heat source for this 2,000 square foot home. Tulikivi by Masonry Heater Store. Photo by Erich Gundlach.

heater demands that you start fires every day. He takes it in stride, though. He explains that keeping farm animals means he is already well accustomed to just doing daily tasks like feeding the animals and firing the masonry heater. "Once you start doing it," he says, "it just becomes part of the daily routine and I never really think about it. I just do it." His reward is that he can come in from doing chores and find a warm place to sit.

Since the Gundlach property is not heavily wooded, they frequently purchase firewood for their masonry heater. They do get some from friends cutting down trees or other scrounged sources, but they still purchase some portion of wood in most years. Incredibly, however,

Erich reveals that they heat their home all year on, "at most," 2 full cords of wood. "Even when we buy it all, in our area we can heat our home for a whole season for about $250," he remarks. The cookstove/bakeoven part of the complex isn't even needed for heat much of the season, until it really gets cold. He credits the high efficiency of the masonry heater combined with the excellent insulation offered by his SIP (structural insulated panels) insulation.

Ellen points out that, unlike a fossil fuel system, which requires a lifetime commitment to paying whatever fuel costs occur, the masonry heater cost is almost entirely up front. "We understood that we either pay now for a good-quality system, or we pay a higher total [heating] cost over the rest of our lives." Obviously, they chose the method that gives them more total control over their home heating.

Ellen and Erich suggest that anyone considering a masonry heater should definitely do one thing: "Get heated benches no matter what! And lots of them!" Like so many owners, the family makes a beeline for the masonry heater first thing on winter mornings. They also advise that homeowners really should put in a backup heating system in case they have to leave their home for a long period of time during the heating season. The Gundlachs chose to use inexpensive electric wall heaters for this purpose, but still have not installed them, though they've lived in their house since 2005. They also appreciate having an ash dump from the heater into the basement foundation; it needs cleaning just once every few years. (Erich cleans it out in about half an hour with a Shop-Vac repeatedly emptied—a process he says is much faster and cleaner than shoveling by hand.) The Gundlach family is living proof that masonry heaters provide a simple way to become energy self-sufficient—even on the edge of the blustery Great Plains.

Photo courtesy of New England Hearth and Soapstone.

PART THREE

Building a Piece of the Sun

With careful consideration for locating a piece of the sun in the perfect spot for a lifetime of enjoyment, the design proceeds. Masonry heaters can be virtually any shape, any size, any color, and any texture imaginable. Some masonry materials have obvious advantages, but they all can be used effectively. With the choices made for materials, shape, and location, it is possible to move on to considering the actual construction of the heater.

Masonry heaters have a life of their own, once they are put into service. The life they lead is entirely dependent on how they are built. Most people readily understand the versatility of the veneer—the outside appearance of the heater. But few people have any awareness of the work, design effort, and intricacy that can be part of the inner life, the engine, of the masonry heater. New owners are often bewildered by the quantity and scope of materials as well as the custom crafting necessary on the inside of a masonry heater in order to assure that all the beautiful surfaces outside become radiant delights.

Building a masonry heater is no small undertaking. While common wood-stoves and new metal box fireplaces can be set in place in a day and fired the next, custom-designed masonry heaters can take weeks to construct. Manufactured masonry heaters are also available that reduce this time substantially—even to one or two days in some cases—but the design and appearance choices may be more limited. As always, a prospective owner must consider all the options and make a decision based on exactly what it is that will occupy a prominent place in the house for generations to come. It can be a wholly unique, one-of-a-kind, heirloom heater, or it can be an "out-of-the-box," manufactured heater with only the outer skin customized to the homeowners' wishes. Chapter 8 provides an overview of the knowledge necessary to make these decisions intelligently.

Designers or builders of heaters need to be always refining skills and knowledge and expanding the repertoire of materials and techniques they use in every new project. Such personal development assures that every heater is better than the last and that they can confidently plan a new project to properly fulfill both the desires of the homeowner and the requirements of gentle radiant heating. Within the scope of that knowledge, they must be aware of various code requirements at every level and have a complete grasp of possible ways to support a masonry heater with an adequate foundation structure. Homeowners likewise need to be generally informed about what limitations exist in this regard. These topics are covered in chapter 9.

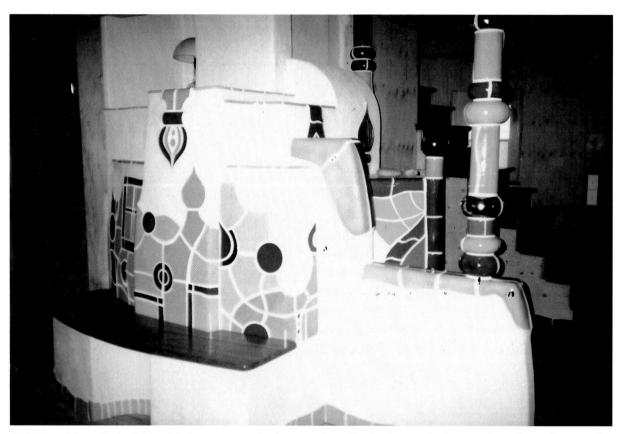

FIGURE 8.1. This is the backside of the heater seen in figures 3.6 and 4.8. The handmade tiles forming the backrest of the wooden seat create a picture of spires similar to the actual ones that exist over the firebox. Combining handmade tiles with handcrafted heaters means an infinite range of possible designs. *Kachelofen* designed, built, and photographed by Ernst Kiesling, Canadian Kachelofen.

CHAPTER EIGHT

The Inner Life—Cores and Flues

The term *inner life* is a perfect description of the internal structure and function of a masonry heater. Many heater builders simply call this the *core* of the heater. A well-designed, high-efficiency masonry heater is, however, a heater mason's attempt to create a living, breathing, heat-producing entity that mimics the very humans it is meant to warm.

The human body has an inner life as well. The inner life of a human consists of all the functional elements contained within the skin of the body. Principally there are three realms in the human body: the metabolic realm, the physical circulation (rhythmic) realm, and the nervous and sense realm. In the biological system, there is no separation between the container—the skin—and the inner life.

A functioning masonry heater does not have the multiple intricacies of a biological system, but it does move and breathe. Like a living being, it takes in fuel and uses it primarily to produce heat. While doing so, it naturally moves; it expands as it gets hotter and contracts as it gets cooler. Like the human skin, the facing material of the masonry heater must be able to move with this breathing motion of the inner life. If the human skin did not move with the in- and out-breaths of the lungs, the body would not function properly; nor would the container survive. Eventually, the skin—the container—would be unable to contain the constant, rhythmic pressure and would rupture. Similarly, the masonry heater skin (finish material) can rupture (crack) if it cannot move with the breath of the heater.

Some heater builders address this problem by separating the inner life from the facing. This is usually done with either an insulation/expansion material or small (less than ½ inch) air space. Yet this seems to defeat the very purpose of the masonry heater, which is to efficiently transfer heat from the inner life to the veneer for release into the living space. High-efficiency windows, for example, use an air space between two panes of glass to increase insulation value. The question we must ask is, "Why would we want to decrease the ability of heat to move from the inside of the heater to the outside surfaces where it needs to be to heat living space?"

Simultaneously, if there is no container actually

FIGURE 8.2. The inner life of this modular heater is wrapped, per manufacturer's instructions, with cardboard. Veneer material is thereby separated from the inner life by a ¼-inch gap. When the unit is used, the cardboard will disintegrate, leaving a ¼-inch air gap. Photo by Wendell Short.

holding the inner life, then it can expand at will and there truly is nothing to contain it. A biological system without an integrated container of skin is not a pretty sight. Likewise, a heater core that is not directly contained by the veneer can degenerate. Sometimes this manifests itself as ever-widening cracks on interior components of the inner life or simply as the gradual opening of joints—a slow, methodical deterioration over time.

This comparison of general philosophy of how to handle the inner life is just one distinction between masonry heaters built with an integrated approach that asks the inner life and veneer to function as one cohesive unit and others built creating a separation between the two. Both types are viable and effective masonry heaters and have their place in the North American market. Just as you can drive to work in a high-performance Ferrari or in a four-door Hyundai, you can heat space with a state-of-the-art custom masonry heater or a basic, mass-produced heater of set design. I find the integrated approach to be more like a Ferrari, though others might disagree. Regardless of which avenue you take, the heater will have an inner life—a core—that needs to be built.

Together with the above two different approaches to building a masonry heater are two totally different approaches to the entire design of the heater. For a heater built with a predesigned inner life, the form of the exterior size and general layout is largely dictated

by the core. In the truly custom approach, the first step is designing the container—the skin. This is what makes masonry heater design truly magical—the possibility of designing virtually any kind of shape, after which the inner life must conform to those parameters. Again, like a living being that can move the body into all manner of shapes—a fetal ball or a spread-eagle stretch—the inner life conforms and follows the shape of the outer layer.

This chapter, then, is divided into three different sections. First is a basic outline of one way to design a heater for a specific space in a particular geographic place with the assumption that it is to be built with the integrated-container/inner-life paradigm. Although this text cannot cover in detail all the aspects of such design, it seeks to enlighten the reader about the possibilities available, the parameters dictating design, and how the design is generally conceived. The actual design and construction require a greater mastery and understanding of all the variables inherent in designing a living, breathing masonry heater for a specific space and to a particular person's preferences.

The first section is augmented at the end by a photo sequence of the construction of a heater built with the integrated-container and inner-life approach. Each step of the construction is described in detail. The project is a simple, small masonry heater in comparison to what is possible, and therefore serves as a gentle introduction into the complexities that can be encountered. Every custom heater is different. The one featured had to meet tight parameters set by the homeowner.

The second part of the chapter explores some of the most basic core kits on the market that can be built with a modicum of masonry heater understanding, yet produce very respectable and predictable performance with good longevity. As will be seen, a set core (inner-life) design purports to produce a one-size-fits-all solution to heating that takes little account of the many variables that influence performance. Yet thousands of people live happily with these heaters as well.

The final part of the chapter briefly outlines other entirely different solutions to heater design and construction—some using core kits again, some that are nearly off-the-shelf, whole heater packages, and another completely different approach to heater design.

Calculating a Heater's Size

In chapter 7, a sample home was calculated to need 13,550.08 BTUs of heat each hour of the day (on the coldest day of the year), and it was found that this amount of heat can be supplied by 68 pounds of wood per day using a heater that is about 75 percent efficient. No matter what house or living space is to be heated, the calculations always start from this position. You must know the amount of heat required for the given space; from this the amount of firewood fuel can be determined. The amount of firewood is then a guide to the size of the firebox. The size, height, and construction of the chimney flue determined by and combined with the geographic location and elevation of the site help determine the minimum and maximum length of flues. The quantity of fuel and the characteristics of the chimney will also relate to the cross-sectional size of the flues within the heating elements of the masonry heater.

The length of flues will then relate to the chimney size, its structure, and the size of the heater itself. Obviously, if the heater is capable of having a minimum of 20 feet of flues, but the size of the mass only accommodates 12 feet of flues, the heater mass is too small, and excessive heat will be sent up the chimney. On the other extreme, if the heater is only capable of having a maximum of 20 feet of flues but there is enough mass to accommodate 30 feet, then not all of the mass can be utilized. The total length and size of flues and their relationship to the amount of mass is one of the principal determinations of the efficiency of the heater. Those heaters that have only average to mid-range efficiency ratings of 55 to 75 percent have too little flue length for the amount of wood to be used, while those with efficiencies approaching 90 percent have optimized the amount and size of flues to the amount of mass available.

A Sample Heater for a Sample House

Building on chapter 7's examination of a particular house, here it will be our task to look at what could be built for that space. Having already determined heat loss/heating requirements and quantity of wood, the next factor to look at is geographic location followed by chimney height and structure.

Geographic Location

The reason geographic location is important is that each area has not only different weather conditions, but also a different elevation above sea level. This may seem irrelevant at first, but it is not. For example, the boiling point of water at higher elevations is lower—roughly 1 degree per 500 feet of altitude change. In other words, water will boil at 212°F at sea level, but at 1,000 feet above sea level, it will boil at 210°. This is because the air pressure is lower as altitude increases, as seen in figure 8.3. Chimney draft is entirely a result of differences in air pressure. And chimney draft is a very weak force. In fact, typical chimney draft pressure is comparable to the pressure a sheet of paper exerts on a table. As geographic location changes, the

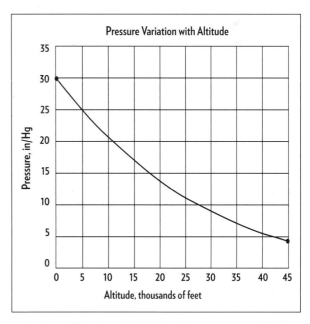

FIGURE 8.3. This chart clearly shows how air pressure declines as altitude increases.

draft will change—as will, correspondingly, the airflow rate to the combustion chamber.

In addition, as altitude increases, the amount of oxygen available for combustion decreases. The design of the heater must account for this to assure that the fire has the necessary amount of oxygen for complete combustion. Insufficient air will lead to inefficient burns and poor performance. Even small changes in elevation must be addressed. For example, Cleveland, Ohio, is at 777 feet above sea level. Cleveland is only about 500 feet lower in elevation than Akron, but the difference in air supply to a masonry heater is measurable.

Akron, Ohio is at 1,210 feet above sea level. Generally speaking, the higher the elevation, the weaker the strength of draft and the slower the flow of combustion air given similar temperature conditions. This combustion air-flow rate is calculated with a factor determined by the elevation figure. In the case of Akron, with an elevation close to zero (geodetically speaking), the factor is just below 1 and the combustion air-flow rate is about 78 ft³/min. At a significantly higher elevation, like 3,100 feet above sea level, this rate would be slower, at 69.6 ft³/min. In other words, the combustion air-flow rate is slowed by 10 percent by changing just the one variable—geographic elevation. Using Cleveland's elevation, the difference is more subtle. The calculated air-flow rate in Cleveland is close to 75.9 ft³/min, a 3 percent change from Akron. The designer of the heater must compensate for any differences and introduce a calculated means of assuring that adequate oxygen will reach the combustion chamber given the slower air-flow rate and weaker draft.

Such is the nature of this type of custom masonry heater design process. When one variable changes, all others must change also, or performance, output, and enjoyment are not kept at a maximum. Having the right heater for a space is more akin to getting a custom-tailored suit than it is to picking one up at a clearance sale. If you just buy a suit off the rack at the store, it may serve the general purpose of clothing, but it doesn't really fit right. A tailor, however, will make sure the waist size is perfect and the pant length, neck

size, shoulder cut, and so forth make you look natural in the clothes. Likewise, a custom-tailored masonry heater fits the surroundings in shape, size, and function.

Chimney Height and Structure

If identical masonry heaters are built in two identical neighboring houses with two different chimney systems, the heaters will not function equally in both houses, even if the chimneys are both located in the same room and have the same height. For example, a stainless-steel, insulated, 8-inch-diameter chimney flue and an 8-by-12 clay-lined flue don't have the same cross-sectional area. They also do not have the same capacity to insulate flue gases or the same frictional effect on gases moving through them. The steel chimney will facilitate more rapid movement of hot gases while the clay will be slower. The goal is to have the appropriate rate of movement such that there is sufficient time for the right amount of heat to be extracted from the exhaust within the masonry heater before it gets to the chimney. Then, once the exhaust does make it to the chimney, it must be sufficiently warm to make it all the way up and out of the chimney flue without cooling to the dew point—the point at which the gases can condense on the surfaces of the chimney flue walls (above 113°F).

The height of the chimney also plays a huge role in the calculation of the heater itself. Given two chimneys of identical construction (for example, 6-inch-diameter, double-wall insulated stainless steel), the one that is taller will have stronger draft pressure. If two identical masonry heaters are put, respectively, in one house that has an 18-foot chimney and another house that has a 30-foot chimney, the one with the taller chimney will likely lose more heat up the chimney. Some masonry heaters are built with chimney dampers that can be used to restrict the draft—an imperfect way to adjust for a heater not really designed for the situation. Similarly, air supplies can sometimes be restricted. Again, such manual "adjustments" amount to guesses as to how to get the best performance as opposed to designing the heater specifically for the on-site conditions, including the actual height and construction of the chimney.

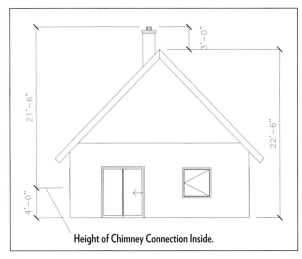

Height of Chimney Connection Inside.

FIGURE 8.4. The height of the chimney must be determined based on the height at which it connects to the masonry heater.

As a rule of thumb, a heater will need a 6-inch-diameter (inside) chimney if its fuel load is about 34 pounds, as in our sample heater. A larger heater that uses around 40 pounds of fuel per load will need a 7-inch-diameter chimney, and larger heaters that use about 45 pounds of fuel will need an 8-inch-diameter flue. In the sample home for which this design is intended, the chimney will be a 6-inch-diameter, double-wall stainless-steel flue. The flue will connect to the masonry heater 4 feet above the floor. The reader will recall that this house has 10-foot-high ceilings. It also has a steep, 12/12 roof pitch, meaning the angle of the roof is 45 degrees. The gable end walls are 25 feet long, so the legs of the 45-degree triangle created by the roof pitch are each 12½ feet long. This means the total height of the house from the floor to the ridge of the roof is 22½ feet. Since the chimney connection occurs 4 feet off the floor, the total height of this chimney (above the connection to the heater) will be 21 feet, 6 inches. (The chimney flue will rise 3 feet above the ridge.)

Firebox Size

The firebox of a masonry heater needs to accommodate both the quantity of fuel to be used and the expanding, hot gases that result from combustion. The fuel load is the principal factor. In the example here, the design is based on having a heater that gets fired,

at maximum, twice per day—once every twelve hours during the coldest weather. It was determined that this would require 68 pounds (30 kilograms) of wood every day or 34 pounds (15 kg) every twelve hours. The firebox needs to be designed to accommodate 34 pounds (15 kg) of wood.

The surface area of the firebox is calculated by multiplying the weight of the wood in kilograms by a constant of 900. (So far I have used only standard units rather than burden the text with reference to both metric and standard. However, these heater calculations originated in Europe, and no current equivalent exists using standard American measurements. So the calculations in this chapter are best done in metric units, though the answers can be readily converted to feet, inches, pounds, and so forth as needed.) In this case, 900 × 15 kg provides a firebox surface area of 13,500 cm² (2,093 in²). This number represents a box—a container—that disregards any openings in the firebox like the door opening or the exit for flue gases. In addition, it is known that the minimum firebox floor area is 100 cm² (15.5 in²) of floor area for every kg (2.2 lb) of fuel used. In this example, it means that the minimum firebox floor size is 1,500 cm² (232.5 in²). Note that, as described in chapter 6, the firebox does not have to be square or rectangular. For this heater, it could be almost any shape as long as it keeps to these size parameters.

The Three T's—Time, Temperature, and Turbulence
The firebox is the power plant for the rest of the masonry heater (and the living space itself). It must be sized properly to achieve the results of clean, complete combustion. If it doesn't happen in the firebox, it isn't going to happen! The three T's of time, temperature, and turbulence are the key to success here.

The firebox must always be neither too large nor too small. If it is too small, the needed firewood may not fit and/or there will not be enough room for the expansion of hot gases. This would cause the gases to rush out of the firebox too quickly—compromising the need for adequate time for the gases to be exposed to the high temperatures needed, though turbulence—the mixing of gases during combustion—may be good.

If it is too large, the firebox gases will move too slowly and it may be difficult to achieve high enough temperatures. Likewise, a large, cavernous firebox, as in the traditional fireplace, provides no conditions of turbulence for the fuel and oxygen to mix thoroughly for complete combustion. In general, a too large firebox provides too much time and not enough temperature and turbulence.

Overall, the goal is to have the combustion gases present in the firebox for one second. That is just the right time. The best temperatures are 1,400° to 1,800°F. *Turbulence* is naturally created by having the right-sized firebox and the right amount of air supplied. The right amount of air is made available through air inlets that open to 10 to 12 cm² (1.5 to 1.9 in²) per kilogram (2.2 pounds) of fuel load. The sample heater, with a fuel load of 15 kg (34 lb) per firing, will need at least 150 cm² (22.5 in²) of air-supply opening. A hole that is 3 inches wide and 8 inches long would be just about right.

Most people are surprised at how much air is really required for clean combustion. These facts make it clear why it is that both traditional open fireplaces and metal woodstoves rarely burn cleanly. The former receives way too much air and has almost no turbulence, while the latter gets damped so tightly that it has way too little air and consequently no turbulence. In both cases, the conditions are not provided for high-temperature, clean combustion.

The Flues

Designing the flues is one of the most challenging parts of the design process. As I mentioned earlier, the shape of the outside of the heater is already designed according to the tastes and desires of the owner-to-be. The designer of the heater must have started such design with a basic understanding of how much heat can be provided to a living space by a given surface area of warm masonry. Now a firebox size is in place. What is left is to fill out the "body" of the heater with flues that occupy all (or as much as possible) of the volume within the designed skin.

The simplest rule for beginning the design of the flues is that the *minimum* length of the flues is expressed as a function of, once again, the weight of a load of fuel wood. (Minimum length = 1.3√weight of wood in kg.) In the case of this example, which uses 15 kg of wood per firing, the minimum length of the flues is just over 5 meters (more than 16 feet) of flue. This is, again, the *minimum* length of heat-exchanging flues that should be used in this heater. Frequently the actual amount of flue used is much longer than the minimum—even by a factor of two! There are many variables that affect this outcome. Not only do these variables affect the length of the flues, but they also affect the overall performance and efficiency of the heater.

Temperature, Speed, Distance, Volume, Friction, and Absorption

The primary factors affecting the heating efficiency of any masonry heater are the temperature and speed of the exhaust, the distance the exhaust must travel, the volume of space provided for the traveling exhaust, the friction of the materials of which the flues are made, and how well the heat from that exhaust is absorbed (conducted) into the masonry mass. Although these are individual characteristics, they work together seamlessly in an efficient masonry heater design. An error in designing for one will influence at least one of the other factors and thus result in lower heating efficiency.

For example, if the hot exhaust travels too fast through the flues of the heater, there isn't adequate time for heat to be absorbed by the mass. It is comparable to driving too fast down a street while looking for a particular address; you could easily miss it. Flue gases traveling too rapidly bypass the absorption capabilities of the flue lining material and can end up leaving town (going up the chimney) before their heat is dissipated. This excess heat goes up the chimney and reduces the heating capability of the masonry heater.

Conversely, if the exhaust is traveling too slowly in relation to how well the masonry materials absorb heat, the exhaust is cooled too thoroughly, too quickly. Just as driving too slowly will mean you can't get everywhere you need to go, exhaust that goes too slowly will cool too soon and not make it through all the flues. Some of the mass just won't get warmed much or enough, *and* there may not be enough heat remaining to drive chimney draft. The latter case leads to condensation within the heater itself or in the chimney flue; it may also result in a heater that belches smoke into the house. The heater in this case may never get warm enough for adequate heating. This same effect is achieved if the flues are too long, too voluminous, or made of materials of friction, thickness, or conductivity adverse to adequate absorption in relation to the amount of heat available. Flues that are inadequately sized in relation to the speed of the gases will not be warmed adequately.

Of course, the speed of the exhaust through the flues is influenced not only by the volume and frictional properties of the flue, but also by direction and change of direction. Warm flue gases going up a vertical flue will travel much faster than the same-temperature gases going *down* a vertical flue. In horizontal runs of flues, a straight run offers greater speed than a run with many turns, especially complete-reversal (180-degree) turns.

All these considerations are further complicated by the design of the heater itself. In odd-shaped, special heaters, there may be areas where it is easy to use a flue of size comparable to a chimney cross section, while other places within the heater may demand height or width restrictions—or even odd shapes. It may be that a certain area must constrict the flue size in order for everything to fit. This can be done, but, as always, it changes the dynamics of the whole system; other flues may have to be increased in size to accommodate the changed parameters in the constricted area.

As you may now understand, there is no simple solution to a custom design. You must seek an elegant solution that permits the inner life to have superb contact with the skin and still provides the correct speed of exhaust for good absorption of heat, all the while assuring that when the gases finally get to the chimney flue, there is just enough heat for the exhaust to make it all the way to the top without hitting the dew point. A truly custom-calculated masonry heater

is a remarkably functional work of art and an engineering and mathematics challenge. Yet its operation is simple and will require no chimney dampers. All it needs in terms of hardware is a good (properly sized) air supply and a tight-closing, gasketed door.

The Design of the Sample Heater

Several textbooks would need to be written to encompass all that the previous outline covers. Indeed, to understand the minute details, an engineering or physics degree is probably a first step. Fortunately for heater builders, there are already individuals who know the engineering behind the workings of a superb masonry heater and are willing to either educate others or sell computer software with necessary spreadsheets and computation programs to help the designer solve the many dilemmas that present themselves even in some of the apparently simplest designs. Some of these resources are found in appendix A.

The Design Process Continues

In chapter 7, we determined the size of heater required for our sample house. Using information from chapters 5 and 6, the homeowners had a pretty good idea as to what options are available for designing and locating a masonry heater. The heater designed for the Cleveland home has a firebox floor area of 1,500 square centimeters, a total firebox surface area of 13,500 cm² (2,093 in²), and specified flue length of no less than 5 meters (more than 16 feet). Its chimney is 21½ feet tall from where it connects to the heater and is a 6-inch-diameter insulated pipe. The chimney will go through the roof near the ridge, following all the chimney rules.

The homeowners were concerned that a masonry heater might take up a lot of floor space in this modest-sized house. With a 1,000-square-foot home, there isn't much space to spare. They were delighted to realize that the masonry heater could be as much furniture as it is heater. The kitchen was designed with a dinette area. With no other dining room, it was clear that the owners would always need a table and chairs in the dining area of the kitchen. Therefore, this heater will

FIGURE 8.5 (left, top). Functional art: a masonry heater that serves as the seating around the kitchen table. | **FIGURE 8.6** (left). Making the heater function as furniture can change the perspective of someone who says, "I have nowhere to put a masonry heater in my house." | **FIGURE 8.7** (above). A view of the firebox element that powers this unusual masonry heater.

consist of a firebox connected to a flue run in a bench that defines the kitchen eating area. It is truly functional heated artwork (see figures 8.5–8.7).

This is real masonry heater designing. The owners-to-be and the masonry heater professional must converse carefully about the desires, needs, lifestyle, and design preferences. Do the clients like symmetry or asymmetry? Even if they think they like symmetry, are they willing to explore asymmetrical options as well? What space limitations exist? What shapes and colors does each person like? Curves? Geometrical shapes? Tall and thin? Fat and squat? Is the heater going in a sleeping area? If so, maybe it can have a sleeping platform. Is it going in a living or great room? Maybe it should have a lot of heated seating.

Always remember that, above all else, a masonry heater is the warmest spot in the house. Most homes have no warm spot, just bland sameness everywhere. A home with a masonry heater has a place that invites people to be warm. No one ever need feel chilly in a home with a masonry heater. The design process must discover where people will want to be to feel that warmth when they need it the most.

This turned out to be easy for the homeowners in this sample case. The house is small and the living, dinette, and kitchen areas are close together. Putting a masonry heater virtually anywhere in those three rooms would provide great radiant warmth through all the main living area. The owners realize, however, that everything they do, they do at the kitchen table. When they pay the monthly bills, they sit at the kitchen table to do so. When the kids work on building a model or doing artwork, they do it at the kitchen table. Ditto for homework. And, of course, where else would the family members eat their meals? They read the morning paper

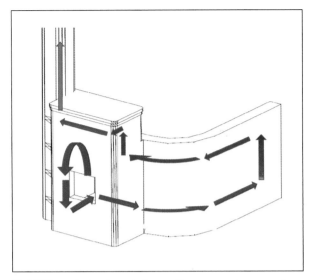

FIGURE 8.8. A simple and elegant flue-gas pattern completes the design.

at the table; they snap green beans there; they read the mail there, too. To them, the solution was natural: Have the masonry heater located where a table and chairs would have to be anyway.

From that decision come repeated sketches and drawings to produce ideas—springboards for more ideas and choices—until a finished shape is in place. For some people, this will not take long at all. Others struggle to find the shapes they like. This is the easy part. Once a shape is in place, the hardest part ensues: Finding the right colors and textures mated to the best performance options. People are amazed at how hard it is to select colors for such a permanent addition to the home. It takes some talent and careful observation to discern what the best colors will be for individuals. Then, if the people involved have varying opinions about colors, they will have to reconcile differences to get a final result. It can be a painstaking process and involves noticing what colors the owners choose for other important items in their lives.

From Concept to Reality

The last part of the design process is solely in the hands of the masonry heater professional. The chosen design has to be translated from drawing board to a functional heater, using all the considerations outlined earlier.

Often this will involve some tweaking of the outer design as well as accommodating the various flues. If the process has been done carefully, however, the changes are relatively minor in the scope of the project.

In this sample, the 13,500 cm² (2,093 in²) firebox will fit into a small container with a glass door facing the living room of the home. For purposes of the following descriptions, this glass door represents the "front" of the heater; "left" and "right" or "forward" and "backward" assume that you're facing the "front" of the masonry heater. The exhaust will take a journey of approximately 24 feet through the flues. The course begins with a left and downward flow, followed by an abrupt movement backward to enter the base of the dinette seat supports. From there, the flow follows the seats, just above floor level, all the way to the point farthest from the firebox. Then the flue gases go slightly up and then come forward to follow the seats again all the way back around the radius to the chimney area. Then the path is up into the area above the firebox and then exiting into the chimney itself. It's a simple, elegant design. Figure 8.8 shows the exhaust-flow pattern.

The Construction of a Custom-Designed Heater

Up to this point, a theoretical simple house has been used as a model to aid in understanding the general design process—including the heating needs of the house through to a completed heater design.

Now, for a thorough understanding of the construction process, it is time to segue into reality with an actual project. Not every project starts with just a floor plan and infinite possibilities as portrayed through chapter 7 and up to here. A homeowner may want to set aside meeting specific heating requirements to achieve other aims, like a specific size, style, or appearance of the heater itself. This is the case with the project shown on the following pages.

The parameters of this project were indeed determined not by the size of the space and its heating

FIGURE 8.9. This was the starting point for the masonry heater project. The heater must fit in the space defined by the existing stonework and must not "overpower" the room. Photo by Peggy Brown.

FIGURE 8.10. The final design. The owner, however, rejected the use of white stucco in favor of soapstone for the bench supports.

needs, but by the desires of the homeowners. Rather than wanting a specific heating capacity, the homeowners wanted the masonry heater to occupy a certain amount of space and no more. I was given a maximum height, a maximum width, and a maximum depth to work within. The owners did not want this heater to be "too big for the room," which is approximately 15 by 20 feet. This living room opens via an archway into a large kitchen, via a doorway into the dining room, and another door leads to the foyer.

Originally, the owners heated part of the house with a little metal woodstove, as seen in figure 8.9. The clients (initially) did not want to entirely give up the stone base or the stone wall behind. These stone structures, then, were the length, width, and height limitations. The footprint is approximately 5 feet wide, 4 feet deep, and 4 feet tall. The homeowners requested that the masonry heater never be higher than the existing stone mantel. Similarly, they liked the "clipped" corners of the stone base and requested that this shape be incorporated into the new masonry heater. Further, they also wished that the flue exit location be unchanged from what existed for the metal woodstove. And finally,

the homeowners required symmetry in appearance; no asymmetrical designs would be considered. My job became meeting their design wishes and putting it into a package that would provide as much heat as possible.

As described earlier, the starting point for the design of the whole heater is the container: What will it look like? All the inner life will then conform to the shape created. After some time and surprisingly few revisions, an appearance was in place. A drawing was provided to the homeowners and was accepted. Figure 8.10 is the design they approved.

The project outlined was a small heater with wraparound heated benches. The body of the heater would be all soapstone with all horizontal surfaces in black granite. A few granite vertical trim pieces and soot doors would provide some additional character. A little "cupola" on top keeps the heater from looking like just a big box. Originally, the vertical bench supports, shown in figure 8.10 in white, were to be stucco. The homeowners later decided to have these done in soapstone as well.

With a design firmly in place, the on-site construction was started as soon as all the necessary materials became available. The first order of business normally

FIGURE 8.11. A close-up of the air-intake control handle, which will be carefully set into the soapstone veneer. The knob pulls out about 1 inch to open.

FIGURE 8.12. The project under way. Visible is a 6-inch-diameter air-supply duct at left middle. The cable attached to the stone wall is the control to open and close the gasketed air-intake damper. The working surface is cement board over Foamglas insulation to minimize heat transfer to the floor below.

is building a foundation for the heater (this subject is covered in detail in chapter 9). In general, the support structure is designed to fully support a slab of concrete on which the heater is built. That slab generally follows the shape of the footprint of the masonry heater, together with any extended hearths or additional masonry trim that may be desired. For this project, the support was already in place as there was a concrete block structure under the floor already. The homeowners were unsure of its original purpose, though it looked like the foundation for a fireplace. Floor joists were doubled and extra joists added to carry the weight of the heater.

This heater is to have outside air fed to it through a 6-inch-diameter duct, similar to the galvanized ductwork used for conventional furnace installations. Though I don't generally find outside air to be necessary (see chapter 9), local building officials often do. Sometimes a homeowner will request it as well, despite my recommendations.

The air supply was installed between floor joists in the basement leading to the outside, where it is screened to keep animals out. Inline of that duct is a pivoting air-supply damper with a rubber-gasketed seal to guarantee no intake of cold air when the masonry heater is not in use. The ductwork elbows up into and near the center of the masonry heater location. The air-supply damper is operated with a cable that has been carefully bolted to the wall behind the masonry heater. The operating knob is situated in a relatively out-of-sight location near the floor and toward the back of the bench, as seen in figure 8.11.

There is a wood-framed floor directly under the heater, and I had severe height restrictions as outlined earlier. So the old stone stove base was removed. This provided the vertical space needed to install a layer of noncombustible insulation covered by cement board. These materials will protect the wood floor from the heat of the masonry heater for its lifetime (see figure 8.12).

The building of the masonry heater's inner life is entirely dependent on the construction of the container for the inner life. Just as you would not pour out water first, then look for a container in which to put it, the skin—often called veneer—of the masonry heater is what holds the core in place. This is the case with any masonry heater built with the integrated "no-air gap" method in which the inner life is bonded directly to the outer facing material for superior heat conductance. Many other cores are built with insulation or an air gap, and it is then possible to build the core first and build a skin second, because the two are

FIGURE 8.13. The first course of soapstone is custom-shaped to fit the existing stone wall. The stone wall is a veneer on a wood-framed wall and should be insulated from the inner life of the heater. Visible is the circular cleanout opening for access to the heated bench and the heater's first flue—a down flue from the firebox.

FIGURE 8.14. Skamolex insulation creates the back wall "veneer" of this heater, limiting heat transfer to the combustible wall behind the stone. The insulation board is set in clay mortar.

essentially independent of each other. Our project uses the former approach. (The bonding of the inner life to the structural veneer is best seen in figures 8.20, 8.21, and 8.38.)

Therefore, the first step of actual heater construction is to permanently build in place the outer structural veneer wall to a height that will allow the construction of inner-life components against it. How high to build the exterior before work commences on the inner life will vary from job to job and from one material and design to the next.

The first course on this project encloses all the flues occupying the heated benches as well as the support for the firebox and main body of the heater. The entire first course is seen in figures 8.13–8.24. The

firebox-support structure also forms a pathway for combustion air coming from outdoors to the firebox of the heater. Since the inner life occupies space below where the rest of the veneer will be built, it was not possible to build more of the exterior until the inner-life components were in place. In a different design, 2 or 3 feet of the "container" might be built before the inner life is added.

Since the owners wanted to retain the stone on the wall, the soapstone pieces were carefully shaped to fit snugly to the uneven stone wall, as seen in figure 8.13. Soot doors (cleanouts) are strategically located to provide access to all flue passages. One of these cleanouts is detailed in figures 8.15 and 8.16. In addition, because the existing stone is built against a wood-framed (combustible) wall, the heater will, from start to finish, have structural insulation board and an air space between it and the stone wall, as seen in figure 8.14. The soapstone elements are wired to one another and to the insulation board; then the bench flue runs and the rest of the inner life are constructed.

Whether the outer facing is soapstone, *kacheln,* or stucco-coated bricks, this general procedure is the same. The facing pieces are fully mortared together with an appropriate material such as a clay mortar for tiles and bricks. The soapstone in this project was mortared together with a calcium-alumina mortar. After the

FIGURE 8.15. The inner life is begun with a layer of 1½-inch refractory plates. The little square is a cleanout access cut into the plate. Behind the square is the circular opening in the soapstone seen in figure 8.16. The square cleanout piece has a shaped wire handle, seen bent against the inside here.

FIGURE 8.17. All the plates and bricks of the inner life are set in clay mortar. Pieces are connected with rigid, spring-steel, U-shaped clips, serving as tendons holding everything together. Heat will make the pieces expand and want to push one another apart. The clips assure that they remain in their original position as they cool. Mechanically joined pieces can never fall out of place even after years of expansion and contraction.

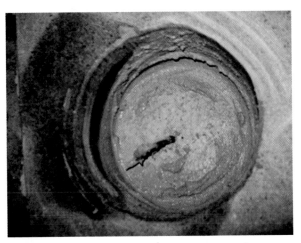

FIGURE 8.16. A view of the same cleanout seen in figure 8.15, this time through the soapstone opening as you would see it after the heater is done (minus the eventual soot door).

FIGURE 8.18. Here the *rumpfs* of structural heater tiles (*kacheln*) from a different project have been filled with large pieces of refractory plates and clay mortar prior to setting the inner life. Filling this way adds mass and continues the uninterrupted means of heat conduction from the inner life outward. The unfilled *rumpf* of these same tiles can be seen in figure 6.41.

mortar has adequately solidified, the bricks, tiles, or stones are mechanically fastened to one another side-to-side and top-to-bottom (see figures 8.17 and 8.28). These mechanical fastenings are the "tendons" that will allow the heater to move and expand with increased heat, yet will force it always back to its original location as it cools. With soapstone, stucco, or brick heaters, the work on the core proceeds as soon as the outer skin has been mechanically reinforced. With *kacheln,* an extra

step is needed—the *rumpf* (as seen in figure 6.41) on the back of the tile would be filled with bricks and clay *before* the tiles are pinned together and the inner life is built. (See figure 8.18.)

The inner life is built entirely with high-quality refractory materials (firebricks and similar resources; a collection of bricks can be seen in figure 8.19). A

FIGURE 8.19. A partial pallet of heater materials. Standing on top is the soapstone and all the refractories used to build this chapter's project. From left to right: 2⅜-inch soapstone; 1¼-inch refractory plate; 1½-inch refractory plate; 2½-inch refractory plate; 2½-inch firebrick; and 2-inch firebrick. The thinner plates are 12 inches square while the 2½-inch plate is 12 by 24 inches.

FIGURE 8.20. The base course of soapstone is in place, as is the first course of the inner life. This first course outlines the heated bench and flues 3 through 9 of the heater—approximately 12 linear feet of flues. The exhaust will travel from the upper left of the picture counterclockwise to the upper right through this bench.

FIGURE 8.21. The support structure for the rest of the heater is built inside the container. The innermost rectangle roughly outlines the firebox floor to be built above it. The L-shaped pieces begin to outline the air-supply slot to the firebox. Notice that all plates lining the bench flues are "backed up" by additional bricks or plates. Inexpensive tile was used to line the floor of the flues. Everything was set in clay mortar and pinned together (though some pieces are not yet pinned in this and the following figure).

FIGURE 8.22. A perspective view of the base course of the inner life. The two parallel plates behind the support structure mark the beginning of the two vertical flues that are located behind the firebox.

masonry heater is meant to last lifetimes, so you should not scrimp on quality for these pieces that will constantly cycle between hot and warm for, potentially, a lifetime or more. In this project, all the inner refractory components subjected to exhaust are made for high-heat use, rather than the common firebrick often found in brickyards.

Common firebricks are used only in low-stress areas away from exhaust. These materials were purchased at refractory supply houses or firms specializing in refractory construction. Figures 8.20–8.23 show the "filling" of this short container with the inner life.

FIGURE 8.23. Two layers of plates over the base course further outline the inner life and form a structure on which to build the rest. The bench flues are being capped with Skamolex to reduce the temperature of the bench slabs. Note the skew cuts on the first layer of horizontal plates. The skew supports the Skamolex while providing a surface that is partially canti-levered over the bench flues to catch both the granite bench stones and the soapstone veneer of the rest of the heater.

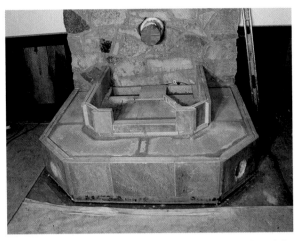

FIGURE 8.24. The entire set of bench flues is capped, and the first course of main-body soapstone is built. The shorter piece at front center is the base of the door opening. The soapstone overhangs the pieces on which it rests, forming a notch for inserting the granite, which was not yet available as this stage was reached.

Notice that the size of the refractory elements used to line the flues changes as the flue proceeds. For example, in figure 8.21, the refractory plates bonded to the soapstone on the left are 1½ inches thick while the ones on the far right are 1¼ inches thick. As mentioned earlier, a carefully calculated heater will take into consideration changes in pressure and temperature as exhaust gases make their way through the system. Since all the refractory elements have roughly the same heat-transfer properties, and one of the goals of good heater design is to have exterior surface temperatures as uniform as possible, thinner materials are used as you work farther along the flue length. This is, of course, somewhat limited by what materials are available in the North American market. In Europe, where there is a many-centuries-old masonry heater tradition, many more shapes and sizes of refractory components are available to those who build masonry heaters.

The inner refractory bricks are bonded to the inside face of the veneer material with clay, then, like the facing itself, are mechanically fastened together. The inner life lines the whole skin of the heater, but work on the core always stops before it is as high as the outer veneer. This is because the next layer or course of the veneer will have to be mechanically joined to the course below; this cannot be done if construction of the inner life has proceeded too far (see figure 8.28).

Since the benches are only one course tall, the inner-life construction proceeds to the top of the bench course and firebox-floor level. Normally, the bench slabs would be installed at this point, but a delay in their production meant the construction proceeded without them. A notch at the base of the first short course of soapstone will accommodate the granite slabs when they become available (see figure 8.24). Completed, the heated benches of this little heater have approximately 11 linear feet of horizontal flues. The whole heater, when done, will have more than 20 feet of internal flues and is designed to consume a maximum of only 28 pounds of wood per firing.

Next, it is time for the soapstone skin outside the firebox to be constructed, as seen step-by-step in figures 8.25–8.27. Once again, the soapstone is installed first and reinforced as before with metal fastenings. In this little heater, the upper part of the heater mainly

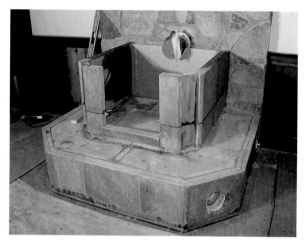

FIGURE 8.25. Following the rule that the container is built first, the next course of soapstone is erected. Note the continuing back wall of insulation board.

FIGURE 8.26. A view into the container. The cleaner plates forming a square in the middle are dry-set firebox floor elements. The floor will be two layers that are both set dry. These removable pieces allow access to clean the air-supply area that will, over the course of a year, accumulate some ash. The two rear flues are well defined here.

FIGURE 8.27. A large air gap between the container of soapstone and the firebox walls (or flue walls) permits convective in addition to radiant heating of the exterior. A small air gap of ¼ to ½ inch would, instead, serve as insulation against heat transfer.

houses the firebox and just a couple of flues above and behind it. Figure 8.27 shows a significant air gap (about 2 inches) between the side walls of the firebox and the soapstone veneer.

Unlike the small (½ inch or less) air gap mentioned earlier in regard to many manufactured cores, this gap is about 2 inches. This space is large enough to become a source of convection heat to help warm the outer soapstone. Air is heated by the firebox materials

and rises, then cools as it exchanges its heat with the much cooler soapstone. Simultaneously, the hot firebox components will send radiant heat directly to the soapstone. While most of the heater construction has no air gap and outer materials are heated by conduction, in this region the soapstone is heated by convection and radiation. The departure from the rule of having no air gap at all is trumped here by the need to keep the firebox at its optimum size. On the other hand, making the firebox walls very thick so that they did, indeed,

FIGURE 8.28. The backside (inner-life side) of the soapstone, showing metal clips binding the stone together both horizontally and vertically.

FIGURE 8.30. The insulation board is cut around the stainless-steel flue. In this project, an uninsulated metal 8-inch flue was relined with an insulated 6-inch flue.

FIGURE 8.29. The start of the "outburn" from the firebox, which is the exit from the firebox into the first vertical flue. The skew cuts direct the exhaust of the fire to the flue that is snugly built into the back left corner of the heater.

FIGURE 8.31. A notch at the corner of the outburn will accept the lining of the first flue, yet to be placed. The notch guarantees that the refractory lining can never fall out of place.

contact the outer soapstone would create too much mass for good, responsive heat transfer.

Once the upper container of soapstone and insulation board is completed, the firebox itself and the flues behind it are constructed. In the back of the firebox (combustion chamber) you can see, in figure 8.29, the "outburn" or exit from the firebox leading to the first flue—a downward passage connecting to the already-constructed bench flue runs. Also in evidence in figures 8.32 and 8.36, is the gas slot, which is a small but direct connection of the combustion chamber to the chimney connector. The gas slot assures that there can never be an accumulation of carbon monoxide in the heater should someone shut down the air supply before the fire is completely finished burning. The gas slot, like most other aspects of the heater, is sized according to the amount of fuel to be used in the heater.

The firebox ceiling consists of two layers of material, as seen in figures 8.35 and 8.37. First to go on is a sheet of "hot face" insulation—noncombustible insulation material that can be exposed directly to

FIGURE 8.32. The completed firebox. Visible just inside the door opening is the air-intake slot that later will have a cover/ deflector built over it to keep out ash and coals. In the middle back of the picture is the little gas slot—a direct connection to the flue to guarantee no collection of flammable gases. The outburn is complete, and the door opening is being lined with refractory to protect the soapstone from direct heat from flames. Note that all inner and outer firebox slabs are pinned together to create a fully integrated assembly that will stay together under expansion and contraction.

FIGURE 8.34. A full-plan view of the completed firebox, two rear vertical flues, the outburn, the gas slot, and flue exit. Note the 2-inch air space on either side of the firebox. This large space provides enough volume that a convective heat transfer will take place between the hot firebox walls and the soapstone veneer.

FIGURE 8.35. The firebox and first flue are covered with "hot face" Skamolex insulation. Insulating the ceiling of the firebox ensures that high combustion temperatures are maintained for maximum combustion efficiency and, therefore, clean emissions.

FIGURE 8.33. A view of the updraft vertical channel coming from the heated bench. Note the corners of the mitered refractory plates visible just under the opening of the steel flue. Again, mitered joints assure that the parts of the flue cannot fall inward during expansion and contraction. Pins or clips are unnecessary where such a mechanical preventive measure is taken.

fire. The application of insulation here is designed to maximize firebox temperatures. Since high combustion temperatures are the key to clean combustion, this is the one place within a masonry heater that really benefits from this material. The insulation here will guarantee rapid increase in firebox temperatures at start-up and consistently high temperatures

FIGURE 8.36. A view through the firebox door opening. Visible are the insulation board, the gas slot and flue behind, and the outburn to the left. Note how the soapstone at the door opening is fully protected from intensely hot fires by refractory plates that create an opening slightly smaller than the soapstone opening.

FIGURE 8.38. The entire inner life, whenever possible, is built directly against the exterior "container" of soapstone, assuring ideal heat transfer.

FIGURE 8.37. Thick 2½-by-12-by-24-inch refractory slabs cover the insulation board and will create the surface on which the upper flues are built. These slabs do not rest on the insulation board, which is set dry (without mortar). The slabs span the insulation and rest on the other firebrick pieces pinned together on either side of the insulation board.

FIGURE 8.39. Note pins holding soapstone to soapstone, insulation board to soapstone, and a (difficult-to-see) mitered corner—all precautions to keep the inner life and the container operating together like one living being.

throughout the combustion cycle. Once the insulation board is in place, a solid refractory cap, 2½ inches thick, is installed above it.

Figures 8.30–8.40 show the details of the inner life as it progresses alongside the firebox, which is shown fully capped off in figure 8.40. Figure 8.37 also shows the last major course of soapstone in place. The smaller "cupola" shown in the original design (figure 8.10) contains no active flues and is only decorative. At this point all that is left is to complete the inner life above the firebox. The soapstone skin is once again lined with refractory plates set in clay mortar and pinned together as seen in figure 8.43.

FIGURE 8.40. The completed cap over firebox and flues. Clay joints throughout. Note another notch at middle right to capture a plate from that vertical flue.

FIGURE 8.42. Another skew cut aids the final exhaust trip to the chimney connector. The chimney connector has been carefully insulated to seal tightly.

FIGURE 8.41. The right rear corner (vertical flue). More insulation board protects the stone-covered combustible wall behind. A sawn notch will capture another plate. Note also the skew cut on the lower right of the picture to aid the flow of exhaust into the upper flues.

FIGURE 8.43. The container has been lined with more refractory plates pinned together and clay mortared directly to the soapstone. Visible pencil markings indicate centers of flue and locations of remaining linings.

The remaining few flues are assembled on top of the solid cap, as seen in figures 8.45–8.48. They form the final connection to the chimney connector. You can see the way some pieces are cut with a skew or angle to benefit the flow of gases around corners on their way to the heater exit.

The last flue passages are capped with solid refractory. The final exterior caps of granite and soapstone

will be bonded to this layer of clay parged refractory that is shown in figures 8.49 and 8.50. The clay serves as extra bonding and a seal against exhaust leakage over the heater's lifetime. Once again, there is no insulation or air space (air gap) separating exterior stone from interior components whenever possible so that ideal heat transfer occurs. Air spaces, when they must occur for specific reasons (as they did on either side

FIGURE 8.44. A view of the heater in progress. The soapstone "container" is complete here. All of the inner life is within what is shown here. The cleanout openings will have custom-made granite covers, and the skewed corners are prepared for thick granite inlays. Granite bench slabs will slide partially under the first course of soapstone.

FIGURE 8.45. The last flues are in place. The exhaust comes up the back right (after exiting the bench flues). The gases travel clockwise to get to the flue exit. The diagonally placed plate in the upper left was necessary to maintain appropriate flue gas speed by maintaining a smaller flue cross section.

FIGURE 8.46. A detail view shows the final pieces mortared and pinned together. More difficult to see is the half-lapped joint in the upper right locking pieces together mechanically.

FIGURE 8.47. Another view of the updraft flue showing insulation board, half-lapped joint (lower left), and skew cut.

of the firebox in this heater), are made large enough for convective heat transfer. Here at the top, the inner life can again be integral with the skin. This allows the top to be yet another radiating surface of this masonry heater.

Since this particular heater is short and the top is easy to reach, the final, topmost cap of granite on the cupola will be removable to access the cleanout doors cut into the top of the refractory slabs as well as to access the cleaning of the chimney connector. The top cleanout doors mortared in place with clay but not parged can be seen in figure 8.50. They have a ring of steel as a handle for removal and replacement when the inside of the heater is eventually cleaned.

With inner construction complete, the door is

FIGURE 8.48. An exhaust-gas view of the final trip to the chimney connector. In total, this little heater that is not even 4 feet tall contains more than 19 feet, 6 inches of linear flues.

FIGURE 8.50. Once all the caps are installed, the entire "lid" is parged with clay mortar reinforced with fiberglass mesh. The mesh is again coated with clay to make a solid clay seal at the top of the masonry heater. The mesh is a reinforcement to add strength to the assembly. Two cleanout doors are set in place with clay mortar but left free of clay over their tops for future access.

FIGURE 8.49. The inner life is capped with 1¼-inch refractory slabs. The middle slab is fully supported from below, but the others are not. The skew cuts will provide structural support as needed. At top is a cleanout access. Again, skew cuts will guarantee that the cleanout "door" can never fall into the heater. Gravity and clay mortar will guarantee, as well, a gas-tight seal.

FIGURE 8.51. A door is installed, and the heater is ready for granite benches, trim, caps, accents, and final cleanup.

installed as seen in figure 8.51, and custom-made soot doors are fabricated and put in place. When, at last, the granite became available, the benches and the other horizontal surfaces were laid in a bed of clay mortar.

The construction site is cleaned and the customers move back into the living space. This masonry heater, as shown in figures 8.52 and 8.53, is finished and ready for generations of warmth.

FIGURE 8.52 (right). The completed soapstone masonry heater. Note the granite benches, cleanout doors, inlays, and caps. The topmost cap is set without mortar to provide lifetime access to the cleanouts on top of the heater.

FIGURE 8.53. The heater in its final setting. When this photo was taken, the heater had been in regular use for slightly more than a week. Just prior to lighting a small fire for photos, the heater was checked for temperature. The bench sides, bench tops, and vertical sides of the main body of the heater were uniformly about 135°F; the left rear (where the exhaust first exits the firebox) was higher by about 25°. All the top horizontal pieces, both soapstone and granite, were uniformly at about 110°. These measurements were taken about three hours after the morning fire, which consumed just 28 pounds of fuel.

Premanufactured Masonry Heaters and Core Kits

In his autobiography *My Life and Work,* Henry Ford wrote, "I will build a car for the great multitude. It will be large enough for the family, but small enough for the individual to run and care for. It will be constructed of the best materials, by the best men to be hired, after the simplest designs that modern engineering can devise. But it will be low in price that no man making a good salary will be unable to own one—and enjoy with his family the blessing of hours of pleasure. . . . "[1] His idea was to produce a mode of transportation that could suitably be used by both individuals and families—a single solution to everyone's transportation needs at a price everyone could afford.

It would seem that those in North America who are producing manufactured cores for masonry heaters may have a similar dream. By producing a single design of masonry heater, there are no complex calculations to do once the first is designed. The heater is big enough for fairly large spaces yet not too big for many smaller ones. If the producer of the core is also the builder, he becomes adept and highly efficient at building the same heater time and again. The complexities are diminished as the same "problems" are encountered every time the same heater is built, to the point that every problem is foreseeable and, thus, no longer a problem. It's a single solution to the heating needs of many people.

Likewise, an accomplished core designer with much construction experience can write a manual alerting first-time builders to all the potential difficulties and providing step-by-step instructions. With step-by-step instructions and problems pre-solved, virtually anyone with a modicum of masonry experience can build the Model T of masonry heaters—a one-size-fits-all heat-storage fireplace. Henry Ford also said, "Any customer can have a car painted any colour that he wants so long as it is black."[2] Currently in the North American market, the revised quote might read, "Any customer can have any kind of masonry heater he wants as long as it is of Finnish design." Currently the Finnish design predominates in the premanufactured core and heater market.

The Finnish design, often called the Finnish contra-flow, is basically a downdraft fireplace. This means that, like a traditional American fireplace, the exhaust initially leaves the firebox and goes through a throat. In a conventional fireplace, the smoke then encounters a larger cavity at the smoke shelf before it continues upward to exit out the chimney. In a Finnish contra-flow, what might have been the smoke shelf area is often called the secondary combustion chamber and, in some versions, doubles as a bakeoven. The Finnish design does not allow the smoke to then escape up the chimney. Instead, it must first take a downward path (a downdraft) along both sides of the combustion chamber, to about floor level, before it enters a chimney and actually exits the system, as seen in figure 8.54. Thus, this design is basically a simple modification of a conventional fireplace, incorporating downdrafts on either side of the firebox.

Hot air rises. The Finnish design seeks to capitalize on this fact by introducing a downward path that hot air does not want to take. The idea is to trap hotter gases in the upper part of the heater while cooler gases will more easily be carried by draft out of the system. As the gases move through the channels, their heat is taken up by the walls of the downdraft flues so that the exhaust is significantly cooled by the time it reaches the chimney. The whole mass becomes an effective, warm radiant fireplace.

FIGURE 8.54. In a Finnish contraflow design, the exhaust travels up through a throat into a secondary combustion chamber then flows downward, typically on both sides of the heater. Then the smoke exits to a chimney connector at the base. In this cutaway photo, only one side can be seen. Photo courtesy of Tulikivi Corporation.

The Finnish contraflow concept holds an attraction for many for the simple fact that it seems to jibe with American sensibilities about what a fireplace should be. It tends to have a door centered on the mass and an upright appearance. It is often outfitted with the largest door possible, coinciding with many people's desire to have a large, cavernous firebox. Many masons veneer the predesigned core with common brick or with various kinds of natural stone you might see on traditional fireplaces. Often the heater is also outfitted with a mantel above the door. All these recognizable features make this kind of masonry heater attractive in the North American market.

Finnish Contraflow Kits

Owing to its popularity, it is no surprise that several manufacturers of cores of this design exist. Following are three well-established producers of such cores. There are others as well. Some core producers did not wish to be mentioned in this text; other individuals or companies make their cores mainly for their own use.

The Albie-Core

Albie Barden, coauthor of *Finnish Fireplaces: Heart of the Home,* is often credited with bringing the Finnish contraflow heater design to the North American market decades ago. For many years, he facilitated workshops building such heaters strictly with firebricks, clay, refractory mortar, and common mortar. As he moved firmly into the masonry heater business, Mr. Barden developed a simple but elegant core kit that permits the construction of the inner life of a Finnish contraflow heater with a minimum of brick cutting and a minimum of time. Albie found the name *Albie-Core* a memorable and humorous play on the name of a well-recognized tuna variety.

The Albie-Core features several elements cast out of refractory concrete, as seen in figure 8.55. Mainly, Mr. Barden sought to cast pieces that otherwise involve a great deal of time at a brick saw due to many angles and special shapes. Notable are the firebox-floor elements that are designed to slope toward a central grate—aiding the consolidation of embers and coals into a pile over the primary air supply for rapid, clean combustion as the firing process concludes. This core design also features a set of dry-set, removable/replaceable throat elements above the firebox (see figure 8.56). Once again, these angled elements replace laborious angle cuts and mortared bricks. And since so many people interested in this design also like the idea of the bakeoven, the core kit includes arched elements for an oven ceiling as well as a lintel over an arch-top oven door.

The basic version of this core kit creates a ready-to-veneer inner life that is 27 inches square. The kit intentionally does not include precast heat-exchange channels for several reasons, including the fact that veneer bricks are available in many sizes. By building the flues on site, you can accommodate precisely whatever size bricks have been chosen for the exterior. This kit is available or capable of being modified to make a see-through firebox unit, a double-downdraft "supersized" Albie-Core (4½ inches deeper and much wider), a corner unit, and (of course) both—with or without a bakeoven.

The Albie-Core instructions call for using standard firebrick for the flues on either side of the central core, providing significant mass for heat storage in

FIGURE 8.55. The Albie-Core completed (left) and its component cast pieces in gray. Illustration courtesy of Maine Wood Heat Company.

FIGURE 8.56. This view reveals the sloping firebox-floor pieces. In the foreground are two trapezoid-shaped elements of the Albie-Core that support the large, sloped dry-set throat pieces yet to come. Photo courtesy of Maine Wood Heat Company.

this design. These heat-exchange channels are separated from the central core by an expansion gap filled with mineral wool insulation. The instructions further delineate a full mineral wool separation of the finished inner life and flue assembly from the final outside veneer materials.

The Temp-Cast

The Temp-Cast is notably different from the preceding core kit. Though it, too, produces a Finnish contraflow design, this core package is made entirely of cast refractory concrete pieces. No firebricks are necessary, and the company markets this kit as one that can be built by anyone—even those with no previous masonry experience. The Temp-Cast core consists of just thirty-seven large blocks of precisely cast pieces that mate to one another with a tongue-and-groove arrangement (see figure 8.57). With a good understanding of the instructions, even a first-time builder can assemble the entire inner life in just a matter of hours, not days.

The way the individual pieces are keyed to one another controls movement of pieces as the inner life expands and contracts with heating and cooling. The company also states that these keys assure that there is no leakage of exhaust gases from one part of the system to another; such "short circuits" could be unsafe or simply make an inefficient unit. The individual tongues and grooves also serve to make assembly nearly foolproof.

The Temp-Cast basic design produces a completed core that is 22½ inches deep, 36 inches wide (including cast flue elements), and 77 inches tall. Like other contraflow kits, there are available additional features such as a see-through firebox, a corner model, and a version with a bakeoven. A finished Temp-Cast heater is shown in figure 8.58.

FIGURE 8.57. A cutaway view of the Temp-Cast heater shows the large tongue-and-groove blocks of cast refractory components in light gray. Illustration courtesy of Temp-Cast Enviroheat.

FIGURE 8.58. A completed Temp-Cast masonry heater. Photo courtesy of Temp-Cast Enviroheat.

The Crossfire

The Crossfire is another Finnish contraflow design with different proportions. The company touts its models as having the largest firebox door in the industry. Like the Temp-Cast, the Crossfire is factory made of large, interlocking blocks. This, the simplest core offered, has just twenty-six pieces ready to be assembled in just hours—even by inexperienced builders. An easy-to-follow manual and the fact that the core can only go together one way make installation almost impossible to mess up. Still, I would recommend an experienced mason for any core project. One mistake is literally set in stone.

Like all the kits mentioned thus far, the Crossfire is built first and separated from the exterior veneer with an expansion gap created by wrapping the entire inner life with cardboard prior to finish work (as seen previously in figure 8.2). The cardboard eventually disintegrates, leaving a small air gap around the whole heater core.

Like most contraflow kits, the Crossfire offers options such as a bakeoven and see-through firebox. It also offers three different sizes for heating different living spaces. Each core has the same footprint dimensions of 16 inches by 46 inches. The smallest model is only 56 inches tall while the medium is 76 inches tall and the large, a full 8 feet. By far, among manufactured core kits, the Crossfire is the widest and simultaneously the shallowest. The extra width is what makes the very large door possible.

The combination of the wide, large door and the overall wide appearance of the fully assembled and veneered core makes this kit heater look the most like a traditional American open fireplace, while, of course, functioning as a masonry heater, with a company-stated heating efficiency of 78 percent.

Other Cores and Solutions

Although Finnish contraflow designs seem to dominate the manufactured-core field in North America as of this writing, there are other options as well. These range from core kits developed from other European traditions to complete manufactured masonry heaters, and even some that come very close to duplicating the custom-design process outlined earlier. The following does not purport to be a comprehensive list of all possible manufacturers' products that may be available in the United States and Canada. However, it is representative of some of the greatest volume of heaters sold in North America outside the Finnish contraflow kits already outlined. Here you will also find some newer innovations.

The Biofire

Of all the kit-type heaters, the Biofire is the one that perhaps most closely resembles a truly custom-designed masonry heater. Rather than one set modular core design, the Biofire is constructed using modular pieces that can be rearranged in an infinite number of ways to produce very differently sized and shaped masonry heaters. Figure 8.60 shows a cutaway view

FIGURE 8.59. A Crossfire masonry heater just after completion. Notice how narrow it is. No other standard kit makes a heater this narrow. Photo courtesy of Crossfire Fireplaces.

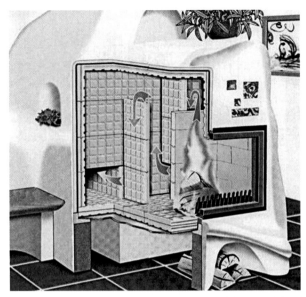

FIGURE 8.60. An internal view reveals some of the inner life of a stucco Biofire. This same heater in operation is in figure 4.18. Image courtesy of Biofire, Inc.

FIGURE 8.61. Biofire creates a wooden model of each project to number and show the placement of each piece in the inner life.

of a Biofire design, illustrating the exhaust flow. As with the Envirotech Radiant Fireplace (later in this section) and the Temp-Cast, these modular pieces have tongue-and-groove joints to assure proper alignment and structural integrity.

As with a true custom design, many important factors are taken into consideration to produce a Biofire. The company aims to design each new heater specifically for a given home or living space. Biofire's engineers consider what kind, size, and height the chimney is or will be for the project before creating a design. Biofire also wants to know the geographic elevation of the building site. All this information is used to calculate the eventual speed of the gases traveling through the system as well as flue and firebox sizes.

To augment this design process and to aid the builder (who must be specially trained by the company), a wooden model is made showing the entire construction and how each piece will be assembled into the unit. As with some of the other core kits that have interlocking pieces that can go into the project only one way, the wooden model seeks to guarantee that each piece of a Biofire puzzle will be installed correctly to achieve the aims of the careful design and engineering. The model

FIGURE 8.62. A Biofire in stucco with just a few tile accents. Photo courtesy of Biofire, Inc.

is small, as seen in figure 8.61, but each flue is shown and each piece defining a flue is numbered.

No other modular system in North America considers chimney height, type, and size as well as home elevation in its design. As discussed earlier in this chapter, these considerations are crucial to forming the best heater possible.

Biofire masonry heaters are principally finished with either stucco or high-quality heater tiles from Austria. The company offers a wide variety of colors and shapes of *kacheln* as well as a broad selection of superb doors (see figure 8.62). The exterior tiles, the core modules themselves, and the doors are imported from Europe where the selection of masonry heater materials is much more developed and complete than in North America.

The Double-Bell Heater

The double-bell heater design is based not on the use of flues, as has been outlined earlier in this chapter, but on what is called the system of free gas movement. The general idea of these designs is that gases, like water, will fill any volume ("bell" or chamber) completely and will naturally stratify by temperature. The hottest gases will naturally push their way to the top of the chamber. The coolest gases will naturally be displaced to the lowest part of the chamber. It is called "free gas movement" because no external force is required to drive this stratification; the stratification happens freely in the presence of gravity.

Chimney draft, the driving force in all other masonry heater designs, has only one purpose in the system of free gas movement: Chimney draft pulls the cooled by-products of combustion out of the system. The final chimney connection always occurs in a location low in a given volume so that the exhaust is always cooler than what remains in the heater. While a draft-powered system moves all the gases, hottest and coolest mixed together, through the whole system, the double-bell system naturally assures that the coolest gases always remain separate from the hottest gases. Only the coolest gases at the bottom of any given bell (volume or chamber) are able to move to an exit such as a chimney

or an entrance into another chamber. Because of this separation, and the inherent fact that only the coolest gases move on to the chimney, proponents of the double-bell system believe it is superior in overall efficiency and heat retention.

The name *double-bell* stems from the fact that most typical residential installations of this kind of heater

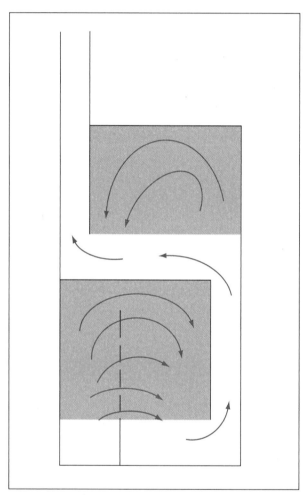

FIGURE 8.63. An upper compartment (bell) and a lower compartment each collect hot gases. Since gases naturally stratify by temperature, the coolest gases fall to the bottom and eventually move on toward the chimney. Image by Igor Kuznetsov.

FIGURE 8.64. This heater, built using the system of free gas movement, is a good example of the versatility of this system. The benches and all the other shapes are defined by containers for naturally stratifying hot gases. Designed and built by Stovemaster; photo courtesy of Alex Chernov.

have two chambers or "bells." In reality, a heater based on the system of free gas movement could have any number of chambers. There are heaters with only one "bell" and others with many "bells." The number of chambers is determined by the plan of the entire heater concept, rather than any set core design. The drawing in figure 8.63 shows the basic concept of the double-bell heater.

As you can imagine, given the fact that combustion gases will fully occupy a volume of any shape or size, the system of free gas movement offers unending design possibilities. Unusual shapes and layouts are possible with this method. Heated benches, compartments, ovens, stovetops, and more are potential features and will be very functional. The natural temperature stratification of hotter and cooler gases within any provided space assures evenly heated surfaces regardless of the configuration.

The system of free gas movement has most notably been popularized in Russia by Igor Kuznetsov, who is said to be responsible for several thousand such heaters in his country. The double-bell concept has arrived in North America, though very few are properly educated on designing such heaters. Alex Chernov has studied under Mr. Kuznetsov and has years of experience building heaters with this method of design. Figure 8.64 is one example of such a heater, and several others are pictured in this book, including figures 1.1, 3.9, 3.10, 5.8, 6.19, and 11.2.

Envirotech Radiant Fireplace

The Envirotech Radiant Fireplace is a modular core kit created more in line with the German masonry heater tradition. Unlike the Finnish contraflow, which just has two downdraft channels on either side of the firebox, the Envirotech Radiant Fireplace core has five updraft and four downdraft flues in its basic design as seen in the cutaway view in figure 8.65. Its manufacturer touts this heater as "the cleanest burning (lowest emissions) of any masonry heater yet tested in North America by an EPA certified laboratory" with total emissions of 0.8 g/kg of fuel burned. It meets strict regulatory requirements in the states of Washington

FIGURE 8.65. A cutaway view of the Envirotech Radiant Fireplace reveals its intricate workings. Image courtesy of Envirotech Masonry Heaters.

and Colorado—requirements that some other masonry heaters have not met.

The Envirotech Radiant Fireplace inner life is, like the Temp-Cast outlined earlier, made entirely of cast refractory concrete components as seen in figure 8.66. Every piece is numbered/labeled for quick assembly per the manufacturer's instructions. All the separate blocks are mated to one another with a tongue-and-groove system that assures structural integrity and proper assembly and fit. A builder familiar with this product can assemble this modular core kit in less than one day.

FIGURE 8.66. A completed Envirotech Radiant Fireplace core kit. The entire inner life is cast blocks of refractory concrete. Project by Masonry Heater Store; photo by Wendell Short.

FIGURE 8.67. The Envirotech Radiant Fireplace "Classic" veneered in brick. Photo by Wendell Short.

The Envirotech Radiant Fireplace "Classic" (see figure 8.67) is the standard-sized heater and, when faced with a 4-inch veneer like common brick, results in a heater that is 2 feet, 8 inches deep and 5 feet, 8 inches long. It is also available in a smaller "Compact" version that is only 4 feet, 8 inches long. As with other heaters, this system offers a see-through and bake-oven option as well. When veneered, it makes a heater approximately 8 feet tall.

As with other core kits, the Envirotech Radiant Fireplace core kit is assembled first. It is then wrapped in corrugated cardboard, as was seen in figure 8.2, to form an expansion gap between core and veneer. The inner life of this design is then enclosed by the veneer of the owner/builder's choice. As this book goes to press, the company is getting ready to offer premade veneers of either colored concrete or granite.

The Helios

Debuting in 2010 is a new modular masonry heater called the Helios. The originator and manufacturer, New England Hearth and Soapstone, introduced this tested wood-burning appliance as one that can be retrofitted into an existing house (or built into a new house) in a matter of a few days by trained technicians. It is built on eight leveling legs to accommodate imperfect site conditions often present in older homes. The Helios's introduction at the 2010 HPBA Expo won it a finalist placing in the organization's annual Vesta Awards.

The heater itself is modern-looking rectangular cube measuring 40½ inches wide, 35½ inches deep, and 73 inches tall. The Helios comes with many outside veneer options supplied. The standard outer finish is a stucco finish, applied over fireclay plates and mesh. As mentioned in chapter 6, stucco offers many texture and

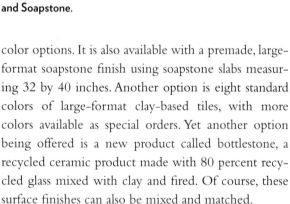

FIGURE 8.68. The Helios is the newest modular heater available in North America. Photo courtesy of New England Hearth and Soapstone.

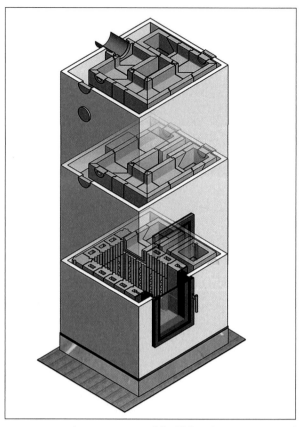

FIGURE 8.69. A cutaway view of the Helios. Image courtesy of New England Hearth and Soapstone.

color options. It is also available with a premade, large-format soapstone finish using soapstone slabs measuring 32 by 40 inches. Another option is eight standard colors of large-format clay-based tiles, with more colors available as special orders. Yet another option being offered is a new product called bottlestone, a recycled ceramic product made with 80 percent recycled glass mixed with clay and fired. Of course, these surface finishes can also be mixed and matched.

The Helios was designed to use the "no-air-gap" method of construction and was designed with careful calculation of the flues. The heater is connected to an appropriately sized chimney, which is determined by using a chart supplied with the product that relates available chimney height to the site's geographic elevation. In this way, the Helios manufacturer combines many of the custom design factors described in this

text in a modular heater. A cutaway view of the Helios is in figure 8.69.

This masonry heater weighs a little under 4,000 pounds with most of the veneer options and outputs approximately 13,000 BTUs per hour. Limited emissions testing so far on its performance shows the lowest particulate emissions of any masonry heater yet tested in North America, at 0.384g/kg of fuel. The manufacturer credits much of the clean performance to the air-delivery method used. About 50 percent of the air washes the double-pane door glass, and the other half is delivered through the firebox walls. (You can see a similar firebox with air supply in figure 11.6.)

Tulikivi Soapstone Fireplaces and Bakeovens
The Finnish company Tulikivi is responsible for a significant percentage of all masonry heaters sold in the

FIGURE 8.70. Tulikivi is known to produce high-quality, uniformly finished soapstone masonry heaters. This stove has some incredible details like the carved lizards, a custom brass-and-iron door, and a tapered upper body above the deeply shaped mantel. Notice how the stones surrounding the door are like radians of the circle. Photo courtesy of Tulikivi Corporation.

FIGURE 8.71. Ceramic-lined Tulikivi fireboxes will burn hotter and cleaner than the all-soapstone version. Photo courtesy of Tulikivi Corporation.

North American market today. Tulikivi creates masonry heaters that are entirely soapstone inside and out. The firebox and inner life are made of soapstone, creating an immense mass of heat-storage capability. As you may surmise, this Finnish company mainly produces a contraflow masonry heater, with few exceptions. Some alter the Finnish downdraft design by incorporating one or more "up" flues so that a chimney can connect to the top of the heater.

The Tulikivi Corporation manufactures a very finely produced, expertly crafted product with extremely tight tolerances on the fit of all stone components. Doors and other hardware are very high quality, as is the uniformity of stone finish. The soapstone is always high quality and superbly and uniformly finished.

In recent years, Tulikivi has developed improved air-supply and firebox designs, called the "whirlbox," for hotter and more complete combustion. By lining the otherwise-soapstone firebox with a ceramic liner, as seen in figure 8.71, which also serves as part of the air-delivery system, combustion temperatures are higher than the more classic design with the all-soapstone firebox. As we saw in chapter 6, soapstone transfers heat quickly compared with other masonry and, when used in a firebox, can even transfer too much heat from the fire, lowering combustion temperatures. Changing to the newer firebox design not only

improves performance but also introduces an easily replaceable system in the part of the heater that gets the most stress—the firebox.

While the custom-design process outlined earlier produces a heater for a specific home or living space, Tulikivi Corporation produces literally dozens of standard models, suggests minimum flue requirements, and promotes their heaters for heating specific *size ranges* of spaces. Their slant is to offer many options for a given space in a ready-to-deliver and -install package. The manufacturing facility in Finland cuts all the pieces so that builders in North America need only unpack the crates and begin building. Most Tulikivi heaters can be built on site in just a few days. In a sense, Tulikivi models are about as close as you can get to a masonry heater equivalent of a metal woodstove: It is taken to a home, built by factory-authorized technicians, has a chimney attached, and is ready to use. Tulikivi does also offer complete custom heater designs, but usually the best economy is accomplished by modifying existing standard models.

The Inner Life Lives On

A masonry heater can be almost anything the owner would like. The inner life is what makes it all function and produce its wonderful heat. It must be carefully designed to achieve the best results, maximum efficiency, and cleanliness of burn. Everything from the elevation of the building site to the size and height of the chimney influence how the heater will perform and how the core should be designed. The firebox size must relate to the amount of heat you want to produce (quantity of fuel); that one fact will influence all other aspects of the heater.

For those without the skills to properly design a heater, numerous core kits are available in the North American market. These manufactured heater cores take the head-scratching out of building a masonry heater and offer simple construction, predictable results, reasonable prices, and, invariably, happy customers. Though most kits offer somewhat limited shape options, the fact that a masonry heater can be veneered with any masonry material means there is a masonry heater solution in North America for everyone.

Without the inner life, a masonry heater has no life at all. When fed good fuel, a masonry heater puffs out its chest and, like a hardworking laborer, produces volumes of heat. As it cools, it relaxes and exhales, shrinking back to its original size. Good core design lets the heater breathe like this for decades: Working, relaxing, working, relaxing. The heater is a living being in the heart of the house, providing real warmth to the human beings fortunate enough to live and breathe with it.

FIGURE 9.1. A Tulikivi boulder heater is the focal point in the center of this home. Note the broad raised hearth with natural, free-form edge. The backside of this heater is shown in figure 11.11. Photo courtesy of WarmStone Fireplaces and Designs.

CHAPTER NINE

Codes, Clearances, Footers, and Foundations

Few people have heard of the Tower of Suurhusen. It was built in the Middle Ages in Suurhusen, East Frisia, Germany, as an addition to the town church. The tower stands nearly 90 feet tall. According to the church's Web site,[1] the church has served many important functions over its multicentury existence, including (of course) its religious functions, as a safe haven during wars and severe storms, and even as a Latin school run by Dutchmen in the sixteenth century. Like many old buildings, it has had its share of repairs over the many years. No one, however, has attempted to correct the lean that puts this tower off center, at the top, by nearly 8 feet. It holds the Guinness world record as the most tilted tower in the world. It leans at an angle of more than 5 degrees, thus exceeding the lean of the more famous Tower of Pisa by more than a degree.

Apparently, the church and accompanying tower were built on marshy ground. The massive masonry structures aboveground were laid on a foundation of oak planks. The presumed story is that the oak planks were sufficient while the ground remained wet and the wood remained soaked. Then, when the ground was drained in the nineteenth century, the wet wood simply rotted and the tower began sinking into the soft mush below. The leaning of the tower was first noticed and documented in 1885. Since then, remedial action has been taken to prevent its total collapse, and the building has been used as recently as the mid-1980s.

The moral of the story seems to be, "Do not support your massive masonry structure on oak planks in marshy ground, then subsequently drain the land." Okay, maybe that's a little facetious, but it is certainly the case that a heavy masonry structure like a masonry heater, which could easily weigh several tons, needs a dependable foundation that can be expected to last as long as the heater itself. The leaning tower example also

introduces the role of codes. Building codes throughout North America have as their primary purpose to aid in building safe structures—ones that are not going to lean or otherwise become a potential hazard. Code and clearance issues will be addressed in the latter part of this chapter.

Masonry construction, by itself, is the most durable way to build a structure, since, unlike wood, it is not readily biodegradable. When masonry is protected completely from weather and, particularly, water, it has a near-endless longevity. A masonry heater is destined for a very long life. It's wise to support it with complementary techniques.

Support Your Local Masonry Heater

There are a few basic choices as to the type of foundation or support structure to put under a masonry heater. All of them work, have been used, and will last if designed properly. What is best in a given project generally depends on the zoning of the area and the exact type of heater to be installed. It is possible to support some masonry heaters with wood framing, with steel framing, or with masonry construction. All have certain advantages and disadvantages, depending on the situation. One way or the other, all support methods (foundations) ultimately transfer the weight of the masonry heater to the earth itself, spreading the load over a large area via footers.

Footers

A footer, as the name suggests, is the actual thing that contacts the earth. Like human feet, a footer's purpose is to provide adequate stability and to absorb and spread the weight of everything on top of it over the ground such that the leaning tower described previously cannot happen. Usually, in modern construction, the footers of buildings or any other permanent structure are made of reinforced concrete—concrete with reinforcing fibers or steel rods embedded permanently in the mix. The principal idea of footers is to have enough surface area contacting the ground in proportion to the amount of total weight being borne that the structure will always be stable and *not* sink into the ground—ever.

In the case of human beings, the weight and pressures (from walking, running, or jumping) can be several thousand pounds per square inch (psi). If all that pressure was terminated in the anklebones, a joint having a cross-sectional area of perhaps 6 or 7 square inches, a person would sink into even some very hard ground. A grown man, however, may have a foot that is truly close to a foot long and averaging 3 to 4 inches in width. This means the pressures are spread over an area of about 36 square inches—five times the area of the ankle itself. In this way, 3,000 pounds of pressure, created from a grown man jumping, is dispersed with an average pressure of just over 80 pounds per square inch. Since most soils can readily support such weight without substantially deforming, the man can jump up and down on the ground and leave little or no footprint. Of course, most of us are aware that the same pressure applied on loose, sandy soil would have a different, highly visible result.

Such is the case with the structural footers of homes and masonry heaters. The footer must be designed to spread out that weight so that the whole assembly—footer, foundation, and masonry heater—will never be unstable. Throughout the North American continent, soil types vary considerably. Even in one locality, differences can be substantial. In my area of Ohio, soil that resembles beach sand (which it apparently once was thousands of years ago) is found just 20 miles from hard clay soil and 20 miles in another direction from very loamy soil. Every soil type has a different capacity to absorb weight. A footer designed for one area may not be good enough for another. For this reason, local building codes, code officials, or, more reliably, a structural engineer or architect should be consulted if there is any doubt as to how to design a footer for a specific soil condition.

Now that I've dispensed with such warnings and alarms, you should be aware that, for the most part, masonry heaters, though very dense, still exert relatively small amounts of pressure. For example, a 7-foot-tall heater—with relatively narrow dimensions of 4 feet by 3 feet—has a total footprint of 12 square feet. Twelve square feet is 1,728 square inches. If the heater is made with a lot of very dense materials, like soapstone, for example, it could weigh close to 8,000 pounds. If it were sitting on a footer exactly the size of its footprint, 12 square feet, it would exert a pressure of about 4 pounds, 10 ounces per square inch. Most of us can visualize that most soils on which a home might be built will readily handle 5 psi without deforming or failing—without allowing the masonry heater to become a leaning tower of heat.

This is a simplification, for sure, since no consideration was given to, perhaps, a tall masonry chimney as well as the foundation itself on which the heater may sit. All of these add weight and pressure. It should be clear, though, that the overall pressures are not immense. And a masonry heater that has a larger footprint will have even smaller total pressure. To put this in perspective, consider a 250-pound man standing on one foot. If his foot has an area of 35 square inches, as proposed above, he exerts about 7 psi—more psi than our 4-by-3-by-7 masonry heater—on the earth!

Though local building officials can overrule a written guideline, in general, footer thickness is 12 inches. Of course, it should always be below frost level and poured on undisturbed or mechanically compacted soil. In addition, the footer usually is specified to be *larger* than whatever mass may be resting on it; often the footer must be larger by at least 6 inches, on every side, than the foundation. The mix of concrete from which a footer is poured is also sometimes dictated by code or specified by an engineer or architect. Frequently, a 3,000 psi mix is used. In addition, reinforcement should be added to the formwork. Reinforcing steel bars (rebar) or reinforcing fibers in the mix serve to prevent concrete from failing. It is said that the one certain thing about concrete is that it will crack. Reinforcement assures that even if the concrete does crack, it will not come apart thanks to the mechanical connections created by the reinforcement. Additional requirements may be necessary in areas considered seismic zones. There is no substitute here for doing research on local requirements and methods; this is the true basis of an heirloom, many-lifetime appliance.

Foundations

While the footer is like the human foot, ultimately absorbing all the shocks or weight from everything above it, the foundation or support structure under a masonry heater is like the human legs. The foundation, the legs of the construction, carries the load of the masonry heater above and transfers it down to the footer.

It is, of course, possible to have no foundation at all and just a footer. Such would be the case with a house that has a poured concrete slab and no crawl space or basement. Here the middleman has been cut out of the equation because the load of the heater rests directly on the footer, often poured contiguously with the slab itself.

Most homes, however, have either a crawl space or a basement below the main living areas. Since the main living area is almost always the prime place for a masonry heater, it will need a foundation.

Masonry Foundations

There is no equal to the strength, permanence, and economy of a simple masonry foundation under a masonry heater. This point cannot be repeated enough: Every masonry heater is a unique, potentially heirloom installation that will outlive the original owners and their children alike. The masonry foundation completes a package of nearly indestructible quality and endurance. A masonry foundation cannot burn, will not deteriorate from weather since it is within the home, will not be eaten by bugs, far exceeds strength requirements for a masonry heater, and rarely requires substantial engineering—as the other options may—to assure proper load tolerance. Its permanence matches

that of the masonry heater. They are meant for each other.

Masonry, in this case, refers to either poured concrete or a concrete block structure underneath the masonry heater. Obviously, brick and stone could also be used, but rarely are for this utilitarian purpose because they add unnecessary expense, unless the basement decor will require such a look anyway. Masonry materials are extremely inexpensive for this application, especially when factored over the expected lifetime of the appliance. Good masons can build a typical support for a masonry heater in very short order. In brief, the *only* two downsides I can think to attribute to masonry foundations is that they take up space and are not pretty. Even the space issue, however, can be addressed in creative ways, as shall be seen.

One of the best features of the all-masonry foundation structure is that it entirely liberates the whole masonry heater construction from the wood-framed structure of the house. In zoned areas with strict adherence to building and fire codes such as those of the International Residential Code and the National Fire Protection Association, there will be no other acceptable support structure for a wood-burning masonry heater. Every aspect of such an installation has to be separated by uninsulated air spaces that guarantee no heat can accumulate and transfer to wooden framing members of the house. This assures that the wood-burning heater can never be the cause of a fire in a house, except by utter negligence of the user.

Builders will often look at a masonry heater foundation as another support they can use. To them, it may seem a convenient structure on which to rest a major wooden beam or part of the floor system. Strictly followed fire code will not allow this use; it should only be done with the blessings of the local code official or an architect.

Masonry Foundation Anatomy

It is easy to picture the foundation and footer of a construction as a leg and foot supporting everything above. A more accurate comparison, however, is seen by looking at the way a typical house is built, because a

FIGURE 9.2 (left). Concrete is poured into the formed cavity for a foundation capping slab. Notice steel rebar tied together on 6-inch centers. The protruding insulation-wrapped wood in the foreground is to form a passageway through the poured slab for dumping ash into the foundation cavity below. | **FIGURE 9.3 (right).** The concrete pour is complete. Photos by Julie Cline.

masonry heater and its foundation are a microcosm of that more extensive construction. The house itself has its own footer. On that footer rests a foundation wall. On that foundation wall rests a wood-framed platform. Finally, on that platform—the first-floor deck as it is called—the rest of the house is constructed, including exterior walls, interior walls, additional floor levels, and the roof.

The masonry heater assembly is constructed in the same way. A footer is poured and foundation walls constructed upon it. At the top of the foundation a capping slab—literally a slab that caps the top of the foundation—is poured. The capping slab is the "deck" on which the rest of the masonry heater is built. Usually, the capping slab is larger than the foundation structure itself and cantilevers over its edges on one or more sides. Often this is for purposes of extended

hearths or additional sitting benches. However, a slab also may be cantilevered purposely to minimize how much space is taken up in the basement by the foundation. For example, if the heater itself is to be 6 feet long but a 6-foot-long foundation in the basement would impede mechanical systems or other use of the space, a 4-foot-6-inch-long foundation may be built with the capping slab cantilevered the extra 18 inches (see figure 9.4).

Sometimes the first thing on the "deck" created by the capping slab is a structural insulated base that prevents heat from the masonry heater wicking into the foundation structure and, by conduction, to the earth. A number of materials can be used for this purpose, including Skamolex, Foamglas, and insulated firebricks. Note that sometimes this insulation layer is omitted because other provisions are taken to prevent

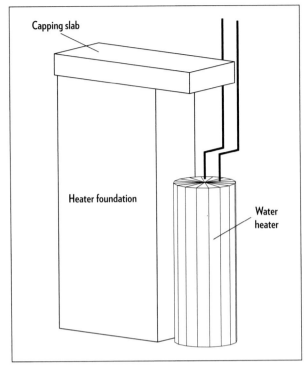

FIGURE 9.4. A cantilevered slab can bridge over obstructions below or simply can be made to support an extended hearth. Either way, it reduces the total footprint size of the foundation.

FIGURE 9.5. Foamglas, the charcoal-colored material, was laid on the foundation capping slab. Cement board was then bonded to the Foamglas. Photo by Julie Cline.

loss of heat into the slab. For example, a heater might be built on legs; or it may have been designed to have insulation internally do the same job.

On top of the structural insulation is often a cement board product or simply a base course or "subfloor" of bricks. This "subfloor" is often at the same level or just slightly below the wooden subfloor of the home, though at times it will be higher. From that point begins the actual construction of the masonry heater.

A Utilitarian Foundation

As described, the masonry heater foundation is very much a foundation within the foundation of the house. Just as the foundation of a house may create a usable space commonly called a basement, the foundation of a masonry heater likewise creates a potentially usable space. How that space is used depends on the desires of the homeowner and, possibly, on the design of the masonry heater.

Ash Collection One very common use of this little foundation cavity is for ash collection. Even old traditional fireplaces were often fitted with an ash door in the floor of the firebox that allowed the homeowner to sweep ashes down into the foundation cavity. This can sometimes be done with a masonry heater as well, depending on its design. In the basement, the foundation itself must have a cleanout door so that, ultimately, ashes can be removed at the basement level. This helps prevent the spillage of ashes in the main living area. A masonry heater foundation may have enough space for

FIGURE 9.6. An ash dump from the firebox delivers ash to the foundation cavity. An 8-by-8-inch cleanout door in the foundation allows access for ash removal in the basement. Photo by Julie Cline.

several seasons of ash collection (though most owners clean out the ash at least annually).

Ash Collection Plus! Basements sometimes have a door to the outside. The "walk-out" basement is particularly popular with homes built on hillsides. Well, the foundation for the masonry heater can be a "walk-in" foundation. If the masonry heater complex that it is supporting is large enough, it may be feasible to install a door opening into this cavity and use it for storage or some other purpose. It is still possible to mount a metal ash collection box or canister to the "ceiling" of this little room, so that you can enjoy the convenience of a small closet in the basement while still being able to remove ashes there.

The Walk-Through and More Though the basement of a house usually has as many (exterior) walls as the house itself, a masonry heater foundation doesn't necessarily have to be an enclosed foundation. What *is* necessary is that the foundation provide adequate support for the capping slab and the masonry heater itself. Sometimes this can be achieved with a U-shaped foundation, two parallel foundation walls, or maybe one foundation

wall and a couple of columns (see figures 9.7–9.9).

These ideas can come in particularly handy depending on the situation. For example, some people finish a basement to be a completely self-sufficient apartment. Perhaps in the middle of this apartment is a hallway. But wait, in the middle of the main floor of the house is supposed to be a masonry heater! Solution? A walk-through foundation can become a part of that hallway at the same time it fulfills its structural function.

A U-shaped foundation could be transformed into an entertainment center for a finished basement recreation area, a reflective wall for a downstairs conventional metal stove in an infrequently used workshop, or as a wood-storage container perhaps right next to a wood waiter (described in chapter 6). It can also simply be a space divider. Anytime the plan is to actually use the basement, whether it is as a work area, play or living area, or some combination, it is usually possible to come up with ideas as to how to make the masonry heater foundation an asset and not just a space occupier.

In all cases, alternative foundation designs should be reviewed by a structural engineer to be certain they will withstand the weight of the mass above and the test of time. Every heater and situation is different and

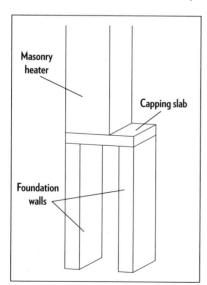
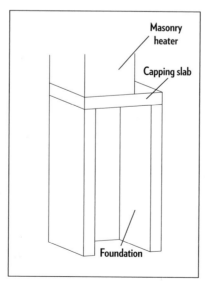
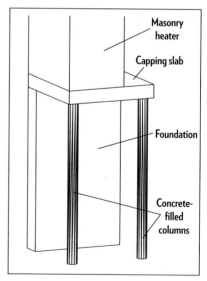

FIGURE 9.7. (left) A masonry heater sits on a capping slab bridging two parallel foundation walls, making a walk-through foundation. | **FIGURE 9.8.** (center) A heater on a slab bridging a U-shaped foundation structure. The cavity created can be used for storage, shelves, an entertainment center, or the like in the basement. | **FIGURE 9.9.** (right) A masonry heater on a slab supported by one foundation wall and two concrete-filled steel columns.

may call for different concrete thicknesses, different amounts of steel reinforcement, and so on. It's worth having a professional review the details.

A masonry foundation can be built in a variety of ways and yet provides ultimate strength and longevity—like the masonry heater itself. In new construction, it is easily the best choice for supporting a masonry heater. Yet masonry heaters of many shapes, sizes, and weights have been constructed on alternative support structures or foundations and probably will be in the future. Wood- and steel-framed structures are here to stay, so it is worth looking at how they are done as well.

Wood-Framed Foundation

Most masons will cringe at the thought of supporting a masonry structure like a masonry heater on some type of wood framing. It certainly can be argued that wood does not have the guaranteed life expectancy that the masonry has, so why would you want to jeopardize the one for the other? For example, a house fire normally would not necessarily destroy a masonry heater, but it certainly could destroy a wooden foundation and thus topple a masonry heater. Wood is also subject to rot and decay if not treated.

The flip side of this argument, however, is that, again, the masonry heater is entirely *inside* the protective confines of the home. The support structure will not be exposed to weather elements such as water that will rot it. And while wood is combustible, it is worth asking the question, "If the house burns to the ground, of what value is the masonry heater anyway?" In other words, assuming the house is maintained in good condition and used as designed, it is likely that a wood support structure or foundation for a masonry heater is feasible and can endure.

In general, there are a couple of ways in which wood framing might be used to support a masonry heater. The first is to simply use the wood framing that otherwise supports the main living level floor and modify it to support the masonry heater. This method would likely be chosen in order to avoid taking up space directly under the masonry heater with a foundation. The other method would be to build a structure

LOCAL REQUIREMENTS

Some jurisdictions and building departments strictly follow International Residential Code and national fire safety codes and regulations, which specifically require any masonry solid-fuel-burning appliance to be built only on a masonry foundation. Consult local authorities before considering alternatives. Ideas suggested here should be thoroughly reviewed by the architect or engineer on the job and/or all applicable building-code officials. The appearance of these nonmasonry solutions in this book in no way constitutes a recommendation for their use in any particular project. Some Underwriter's Laboratories (UL) listed manufactured brands of masonry heaters have been tested and approved to be built on combustible floor structures. Those masonry heaters without similar credentials may have to be supported on a masonry foundation.

directly under the masonry heater itself, through the basement or crawl space, to a footer below.

Using Common Floor Framing

Most wood-framed floors in houses are not engineered to support a heavy item with a small footprint like a masonry heater. Sure, they may support a grand piano, but that is still less than a ton, while masonry heaters generally are a ton or more. The truth is, a common wood-framed floor system might support a ton of weight. What it will do, however, is show a lot of deflection. In other words, a masonry heater would bend the floor-framing members—showing that it is massively stressing the wood. (Consider that a conventional wood-framed floor is designed to carry loads of about 65 pounds per square foot. A small masonry heater that weighs 2,000 pounds and covers 6 square feet of floor exerts 333 pounds per square foot. There is no reconciliation here, only the option to redesign.) Under these conditions, the floor would be bouncy and not all that far from physical failure. A normally framed floor needs modification to its design and construction if it is to support such unusual weights.

Since every home design is different and every floor span is different, it is impractical in this text to attempt detailed analysis of every possible situation. Suffice it to say that a relatively conventional wooden floor system will have to incorporate either more floor joists (spaced closer together than normal), larger framing members (in the vertical dimension; for example, 2 by 12s instead of 2 by 10s), or some combination of these. In addition, today's builder and architect has additional special wood products available such as laminated wood beams, truss-shaped joists, and so on that can be used for special loading situations like this. The best advice is to have an engineer or architect properly design for such a special circumstance.

Using a Wooden Substructure

While the first option depends on designing wood-framing members that are running horizontally (floor joists) to support a heavy load, the idea of a wooden structure directly under the masonry heater mass does not. Instead, it makes use of wood's considerable compressive strength. Wood standing on end, as in the vertical wood framing members in typical house construction, is very suitable to carrying heavy loads. Even softwoods like pine can take more than 5,000 pounds per square inch of pressure without crushing. This is precisely why the conventionally framed house works so well: tremendous floor loads are evenly distributed over numerous vertical studs that transfer all the loads to the foundation and footer below.

The simplest application of this principle is achieved by mimicking the wall structure of the house. Once the footprint size of the masonry heater is known, a plan can be drawn for a "room" made of stud walls the size of the heater. For compact heaters, this might be more like a closet. For large complexes, it could indeed be a small room. This "room" could be built under the floor joists of the main floor, which have been, perhaps, doubled or tripled as per an engineer's instructions (see figure 9.10). Alternatively, the little room walls can be used to support a concrete slab on which the heater

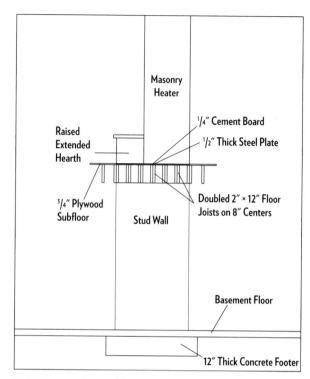

FIGURE 9.10. A possible support-structure scenario utilizing stud walls and doubled joists on narrow centers.

will be built. If so, the wood members should be separated from the slab with a moisture barrier. Either way, this arrangement provides an enclosed space in the basement level that can have a doorway and become useful as storage, an entertainment center, or a children's hideout.

A more open configuration of wooden support would make use of heavy timber columns and beams performing the same function as the stud walls described above (see figure 9.11). In this case, the wood framing may be permanently exposed. Though it obviously occupies space in the basement, the fact that you can see past all the framing members means it leaves an appearance of openness that cannot be achieved by building a small room there. This is also a more likely and simple option for a crawl space where it is obvious there is no value to a small "room." As always, check with an architect or engineer to ascertain the appropriate dimension for the timbers used in this solution.

An important note for any situation in which a masonry heater will be built on a wood floor is that

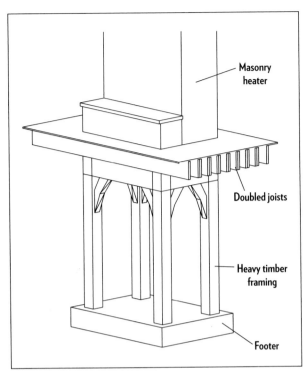

FIGURE 9.11. A masonry heater with heavy timber supports under doubled floor joists. The heater rests on a thick steel plate, cement board, and structural insulation. The structural insulation protects the wooden floor from heat.

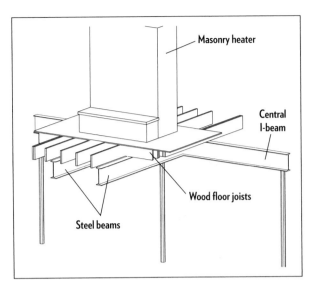

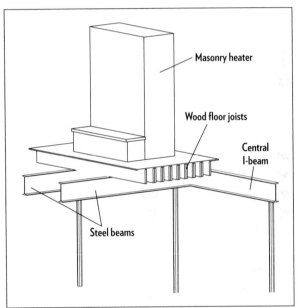

FIGURE 9.12 (top). The home's central I-beam supports two additional steel beams that carry the load of the heater. Instead of the doubled wooden floor joists shown, the steel beams could be spanned by reinforced concrete. | **FIGURE 9.13 (bottom).** Parallel steel beams joined to the home's central I-beam. Doubled joists rest on the beams; some wooden members not shown for sake of clarity.

appropriate methods need to be used to separate the masonry heater, which may get quite warm near floor level, and the wooden floor. A structural insulation material—one that will not compress under the weight of the heater—*must* be used. Depending on the design of the heater itself, you may need to take additional precautions to guarantee that there is no fire hazard from hot masonry near wood structures. For more on clearance to combustible materials, see that section later in this chapter.

Steel Framing

Like its natural equivalent, wood, steel-framing solutions come in two general configurations. Either horizontal beams are used to carry the load of the masonry heater, or a vertical steel substructure is built under it. There are a couple of advantages to using steel rather than wood. First, steel is fireproof, rot-proof, and not a target of any insects. In this way, steel framing is more

forgiving of unexpected occurrences in the life span of a home. Should the basement or crawl space turn out to be damper than expected, for example, you needn't fear that the steel will rot, while untreated wood might. If there happened to be a fire localized near the heater,

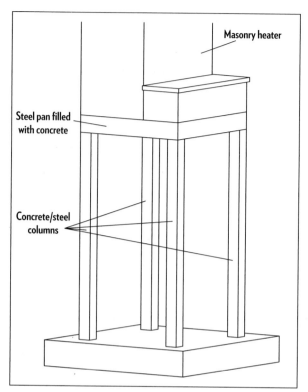

Masonry heater

Steel pan filled
with concrete

Concrete/steel
columns

FIGURE 9.14. Concrete-filled steel columns support a steel pan in which a concrete pad is poured. The heater is built on that reinforced pad. Notice 12-inch-thick (or thicker, per engineering) concrete footer under everything, including the basement floor.

the substructure of the heater is likely safe. Also, steel beams and columns are vastly stronger than wooden counterparts of the same size. In the case of a long free span and a heavy load, wooden beams may need to be quite large, particularly in the vertical dimension, compared with steel beams.

Using Steel Beams

Many homes built today are already designed with one or more steel beams, often supported by steel posts, running the length of the house and supporting the wooden floor joists above. A parallel beam alongside or a couple of perpendicular steel beams attached to that central one could create a framework on which to pour a concrete slab that would then hold the masonry heater. Likewise, a couple of parallel beams can support doubled or tripled wooden floor joists in the area of

the heater, providing enough support for the heavy weight (see figures 9.12 and 9.13).

Using a Steel Substructure

Like its wooden counterpart, a steel foundation could be made with steel studs and finished to be a room, or it could be simpler assemblies of beams and steel posts. Once again, this structure can support a slab on which the masonry heater rests, or it can directly support the wooden framing of the floor, as shown in figure 9.14.

Building Codes and Clearance to Combustible Framing

Safety is the principal concern of building codes. Some builders and homeowners dislike or are suspicious of the bureaucracy inherent in building-code regulations and enforcement. Nevertheless, the intent is to provide greater assurance that structures that are built will be safe for the inhabitants both now and long into the future. If you adopt the outlook that safety is the primary objective, you can effectively develop rapport with code officials. When they and their department know that a project is being approached with the intent of doing quality work and carefully considering safety, most code officials are happy to discuss details and help find solutions that may not appear in a written code book.

In regard to masonry heaters, the principal safety concerns will always be structural integrity and fire safety. If the heater is intended to be the sole source of heat for a home, heating output and efficiency will also be a consideration, because many codes require assurance that a heating system will maintain a temperature of at least 68°F throughout the winter season in the zoned area. This is the purpose of having a complete grasp of the information presented in chapters 7 and 8. Structural integrity mainly relates to sound construction practices of the foundation, the heater itself, and a masonry chimney (if equipped).

It is not the intent of this text to teach or describe correct structural masonry construction techniques.

Suffice it to say that a masonry heater project should be performed by someone fully aware of such proper masonry methods and willing to follow details generated by code officials or engineers involved in a project. In seismic zones, in particular, great care should be taken to follow appropriate seismic reinforcing requirements of the building code. For example, the International Residential Code, which includes masonry heaters and has been adopted at either the state or local level in forty-eight of the United States, dictates that a masonry heater must be anchored to the masonry foundation in Seismic Design Categories D_0, D_1, and D_2. In addition, if the masonry heater is more than three and a half times taller than its width, it must be seismically reinforced, as it must if it supports a masonry chimney. The chimney itself must be reinforced if it shares a facing wall of the masonry heater itself. Masons in these particular regions of the continent must know how to adequately perform these reinforcements.

There are additional code considerations regarding fire safety and clearance to combustible materials. As noted elsewhere, the masonry heater is unique in the solid-fuel-heating world with regard to the way it burns and the temperatures it achieves. Yet in every properly designed case, a masonry heater has outer surface temperatures under 230°F and usually operates at exterior temperatures much lower than even this. As mentioned in chapter 4, the flash point of wood is 572°F. In other words, this is the temperature to which wood must be brought in order for it to burst into flames. Although the normal average operating exterior temperature of a masonry heater is only about one-third of wood's flash point, that does not mean the heat from a masonry heater's surface can never result in a fire. When an object, like a masonry heater, is continuously outputting and there is some region in the heater from which that heat cannot dissipate, higher temperatures can develop to the danger point. This is the purpose of clearance guidelines.

Most clearance guidelines appear in the International Residential Code as referenced above. The text of the International Residential Code (IRC) references

WHAT IS A COMBUSTIBLE MATERIAL?

To people who work with the term *combustible material* on a daily basis, this seems like a silly question. The term is not always clear to the layman, however. The surest way to understand the word *combustible* is to take it as literally as possible. Very simply, if a product used for construction has, as one of its components, a material that will ignite, burn, smolder, smoke, or otherwise encourage or support a live flame, it is a combustible material. For example, many people think of drywall, a product that is mainly made from gypsum, as a noncombustible material. However, most commonly used gypsum-board materials have a paper facing. Therefore, this is an example of a combustible material that cannot be closer to a masonry heater than code allows.

the language of ASTM International's specification E1602, "Standard Guide for Construction of Solid Fuel Burning Masonry Heaters." It should be noted by homeowners and masons alike that this is a "standard guide" rather than an unbreakable set of rules. Throughout the text of this guide and the building code are terms such as "or as accepted by the authority having jurisdiction." The ASTM specification itself begins by stating that, "It is not restricted to a specific method of construction, nor does it provide all specific details of construction of masonry heaters." Further, it says, "Construction of masonry heaters is complex, and in order to ensure their safety and performance, construction shall be done by or under the supervision of a skilled and experienced masonry heater builder." Nowhere, of course, does it define this person called a "skilled and experienced masonry heater builder."

In other words, a "skilled and experienced masonry heater builder" can convince the "authority having jurisdiction" that he knows a better way than what is stated in the code or standard. Indeed, there *are* ways of doing things that are not mentioned in these codes that are legitimate ways of producing safe and, perhaps, even superior masonry heaters. At the same time, there may be "skilled and experienced masonry heater builders" who really don't have much experience with designing masonry heaters who can lead both homeowners *and* building officials astray. As always, *laissez l'acheteur prenne gardelet*—let the buyer beware!

Clearances at the Floor

Since most homes today are wood-framed and have their main floors constructed of a platform assembly consisting of wooden joists or beams, a subfloor of plywood or oriented strand board, and a finished floor of the customer's choice (more wood, carpet, or sheet goods), this discussion assumes a floor made of entirely combustible materials. Obviously, if the floor is made entirely of concrete and finished with ceramic tile, there is no combustibility issue.

The first critical intersection between the masonry heater assembly and the combustible materials of the home is where the foundation passes through the wooden platform of the floor system. As noted earlier, an all-masonry project, by both fire and building code, is completely separated from the wooden structure of the home. The IRC requires 2 inches of space between combustible framing and the masonry heater foundation. It is permitted that the wood-based subfloor or sheathing extend all the way to the structure. Presumably, the 2-inch air space provides enough air circulation to prevent the buildup of heat, while the sheathing is thin enough that it will not easily accumulate heat.

The next major concern at the floor level is the danger of live sparks, coals, or burning wood landing on the wooden floor and igniting a fire. One of the safety features of a masonry heater is that virtually all designs incorporate a solid metal or glass door. The heater is not operated with the door open, and there is no reason to open the door in the middle of a firing cycle. Therefore, the danger of logs rolling out or sparks jumping on the floor is very low, though not entirely nonexistent. Certainly there are times when an owner cannot resist rearranging burning logs or perhaps opens the door briefly just to throw a scrap of

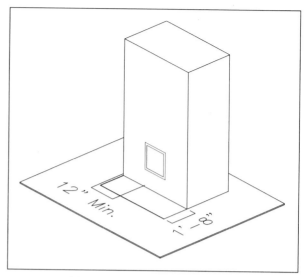

FIGURE 9.15. Minimum distances for hearth extensions.

wood on the vigorous fire. Anytime the door is opened the risk exists, though it is tempered by the fact that the user is there, paying attention to the fire.

Regardless, the building code seeks to further minimize the risks involved by establishing guidelines for the floor surface itself. In front of the door and extending a distance to either side of the door opening, the flooring material must be noncombustible materials. This space in front of the loading door is called the hearth extension. The "hearth" is generally defined as the slab on which the heater is built, occupying at least the same footprint as the heater. The hearth *extension* is the part that extends in front of the heater; it is assumed that the side with the loading door is the "front." A heater with two doors—a see-through model—for purposes of code has two "fronts" and should have two hearth extensions. This also holds true for a heater with a loading door on one side and a baking chamber on another side *if* the baking chamber can also be used as a combustion chamber.

More specifically, for masonry heaters that are designed to be operated with the doors closed (or which are not operated that way, but have large openings greater than 0.6 square meters in size), the hearth extension should be 20 inches deep and also extend 12 inches to either side of the door opening (see figure 9.15). A masonry heater that is designed to have an open firebox (unusual) that is less than 0.6m² in size should have a hearth extension at least 16 inches deep and at least 8 inches to either side of the door opening. Likewise, if the masonry heater incorporates a raised hearth or bench that is at least 8 inches high and is directly under the door opening, the extension depth need only be 16 inches.

In summary, the principal clearance and code concerns at the floor level with masonry heaters are two: the foundation of the heater should be separated from the combustible floor framing by a 2-inch space; and there should be an extended hearth of noncombustible material 20 inches in front of and 12 inches to either side of the masonry heater door opening.

Clearances at the Main Body of the Masonry Heater

By definition, masonry heaters are to be designed so that the surface temperature of the exterior masonry does not exceed 230°F under normal operating conditions. This design parameter does not, however, apply to the loading door of the heater. Considering that the firebox, enclosed partially by the metal and/or glass door, contains a fire that may achieve temperatures of 1,500° to 2,000°, it can be expected that the door itself gets very hot and that temperatures radiating from the door opening area will be very high. There are, then, requirements for clearances to combustible materials for most of the heater and distinct requirements for the loading door/firebox area of the heater.

Clearances from Loading Doors

The code restrictions for clearances directly in front of the doors stem from two concerns: fire safety and practicality. Since the loading doors need to be accessed on at least a daily basis during the heating season, it is impractical to have permanent obstructions right in front of the doors. The guide requires that a space of 4 feet always be maintained in the area directly in front of the doors. This amount of space makes carrying wood to the firebox possible. A person has enough room under these conditions to stand or kneel, open the doors, and put wood into the firebox.

From the safety standpoint, the 4-foot distance is

likewise legitimate. The glass and metal temperatures in the middle of a very hot fire can exceed 600°F—the equivalent of the body of an all-metal wood-burning stove. Obviously, many people operate such stoves without hazard. Safety codes like this, however, are not just for this eventuality, but also for the fact that someone could abuse the masonry heater. Someone who didn't properly understand the way a masonry heater is operated may continually stoke the firebox with more fuel, and the heat radiating from metal and glass surfaces could skyrocket to temperatures that could ignite combustible materials nearby. For this reason no provisions are given in the International Residential Code guidelines for, in any case, decreasing this 4-foot clearance requirement in front of the doors.

Clearances from the door to combustible materials in other directions also have a 4-foot requirement. However, there are provisions for reducing that distance "if the combustible material is protected by an engineered protection system acceptable to the authority having jurisdiction." In other words, the doors of the masonry heater may be closer than 4 feet to a combustible wall to the side of the doors, for example, if the wall is protected in a fashion that satisfies the safety requirements of the local code official. Such protection could come in the form of a site-constructed heat shield designed or approved by an architect, engineer, the builder of the masonry heater, or the building officials themselves.

Clearances from the Other Vertical Sides of the Heater

The remainder of the body of a masonry heater never gets nearly as hot as the doors and glass. Nevertheless, the 2006 version of the International Residential Code requires that clearances meet the requirements of the National Fire Protection Association guidelines known as NFPA 211, Section 8–7. This is a general code for solid-fuel-burning appliances and makes (as of 2006) no distinction for the particular qualities of masonry heaters.

Masonry heaters, then, per the IRC, must be installed 36 inches from combustible materials except when the overall wall thickness of the masonry heater is at least 8 inches thick of solid masonry and the total thickness of the heat-exchange walls is at least 5 inches of solid masonry. The 8-inch specification applies mainly to the thickness of the materials that make up the firebox of the masonry heater. If the firebox itself is made with bricks or refractory slabs that are 4 inches thick and the exterior surface of the heater is made with materials that are 4 inches thick, then the heater is considered to have 8-inch-thick walls. Likewise, if the facing material is 2½ inches thick and so is the material used to make the heat-exchange channels, then the heat-exchange channels will have 5 inches of solid masonry. If these conditions are met, combustible materials may be placed as close as 4 inches from the body of the heater.

Always bear in mind, however, that in almost all cases, the local building-code officials have the last say in any code application. There are those who will look at what is being built and say, "Sorry, the wall is only 7 inches thick. I'm afraid you'll have to keep that thing 36 inches from any combustibles." Then there are code officials who will consult with the masonry heater designer and/or builder. A well-educated heater mason or designer will know how to build a heater that is safe around combustible materials even if the various wall thicknesses do not meet the written criteria. If such a builder can convey his designs and show that his intentions and plans will be quite safe, the local officials will usually be very cooperative. Likewise—and the IRC mentions this—if a particular masonry heater has been tested or UL-listed with reduced clearances, the code officials must accept such certifications as long as the heater is installed according to the listed directions.

In addition, some people may want to use a masonry heater as *part* of a wall such that it completely closes one room from another—a through-the-wall design such as was mentioned in chapter 6. In this case, you want no separation between wall and heater. This can be done, but not usually in conjunction with a wall made with combustible materials. For example, if you'd like the front face of a heater to be completely flush with the face of the wall (so that it appears to be part of

the wall), at least the first 4 inches of that wall coming off the heater corners must be made completely with noncombustible materials with a thickness not to exceed 4 inches. If the wall is to come off a side of the heater and more than 8 inches from a corner of the heater, it needs to be at least 8 inches of noncombustible material and no more than 4 inches thick.

Clearances to Ceilings and Beams

Although it seems counterintuitive, the top surface of most tall masonry heaters is often one of the coolest spots on the whole heater. Most would assume that—since they hold the idea that "heat rises"—the top is one of the hottest parts. The reason that the top may not be all that hot is that most masonry heaters are designed to have warm, radiant, vertical sides. The designer achieves this by directing hot exhaust through the various flues just within the facade walls of the heater. When the top of the heater is relatively close to the ceiling, it's often not considered advantageous to have it be particularly warm. Many masonry heaters, then, have insulation just under the finishing material that assures the top of the heater is cooler than the sides. (Many custom designs *do* use the top as another hot, radiating surface—as was the case with the little soapstone heater in the construction sequence of chapter 8. The decision in this regard is based on desired total heat output and practicality.)

Regardless of which method is most common, the International Residential Code includes the top of the heater as a part of the main body of the masonry heater and dictates the 36-inch clearance to combustibles for that top surface as well. Obviously, with common 8-foot-high ceilings, this would require that no masonry heater over 5 feet tall could be installed. However, as in the previous section relating to the main walls of a masonry heater, it is recognized that if there is at least 5 inches of solid masonry separating the heat-exchange channels (flues) from the exterior, the clearance distance to combustible ceiling materials can be reduced to 8 inches.

This 8-inch distance is actually measured from the ceiling (or beam or whatever material is closest) to

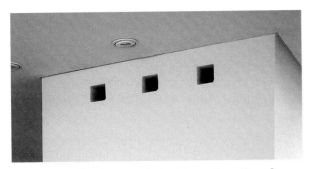

FIGURE 9.16. This heater is built tight to the ceiling. Square openings near the ceiling provide ventilation of the space. Without such provisions, heat accumulates around combustible framing members of the ceiling. Designed and built by Stovemaster; photo courtesy of Alex Chernov.

the top surface of whatever slabs (called capping slabs) are used to "cap" the top of the heat-exchange channels. Some common heater constructions will have a few inches of noncombustible insulation, like mineral wool, on top of the capping slab, an air space, then the final heater-top covering or slabs. Therefore, based on these code restrictions, it is possible to have the actual top of the heater just a few inches from the ceiling.

As mentioned previously, rules and codes can be manipulated as long as the authority having jurisdiction can understand and be confident that safe conditions are present. It is even possible to have the masonry heater built tightly to the ceiling. This is accomplished by the appropriate use of insulating materials and, also, by venting the cavity above the capping slab of the heater so that no hot air is ever trapped against the ceiling. Venting is often accomplished by leaving out bricks (or whatever veneer material is used) to a size matching a decorative grating material; see the example in figure 9.16. By having at least one open vent on opposite sides of a heater, for example, free air flow is encouraged, minimizing the amount of hot air that can accumulate.

Chimney Clearances to Combustible Materials

Code authorities make no distinction between a chimney for a masonry heater and a chimney for any other wood-burning stove or fireplace. The fact that masonry heaters burn cleanly and produce no creosote

if properly fueled *and* the fact that the exhaust from a masonry heater entering a chimney is at temperatures too low to ignite anything makes no difference in the fire and safety rules applied to chimneys that service masonry heaters. As in many codes, the rules applied to space between chimneys and combustible materials are geared toward worst-case scenarios: *if* creosote *were* to accumulate and *if* the chimney *does* get sparks or flame in it, *then* there might be a chimney fire; therefore, there are restrictions on how close combustible materials can be to a chimney. These rules are outlined in the following two sections.

Masonry heaters are connected to one of two general categories of chimneys. Either they are connected to metal, manufactured chimney sections or they are connected to a masonry chimney. Since the two types of chimney operate and perform in completely different ways, there are likewise completely different rules for each family of flues.

Manufactured Chimneys

Factory-manufactured chimneys, according to the International Residential Code, should be installed as per manufacturer's directions. Most such chimney systems have been tested to one or another Underwriter's Laboratories listing standards. Such testing is specific to the way the chimney is made with whatever component parts it has. When it has achieved the appropriate listing, it has done so with all the component parts assembled as directed by the manufacturer. The only way these systems, then, are warranted by the manufacturer (and accepted by code or building officials) is when they have been properly assembled on site according to those same directions. These directions will specify appropriate clearances to combustible materials given the proper installation.

Masonry Chimneys

Like the masonry heater itself, a masonry chimney (which is often built right next to or as part of a masonry heater) is to have a proper masonry support structure with the same clearances and other parameters as the support structure of the masonry heater.

The rules governing clearances through the rest of the house, however, are unique to the chimney and covered separately by the International Residential Code or, usually, any other state or municipally accepted building code. Since the IRC is the only code structure including masonry heaters, IRC masonry chimney clearance guidelines are covered here.

Once again, you should be aware that seismic areas will require additional reinforcement of masonry chimneys. There are specific anchorage and reinforcement guidelines in Seismic Design Categories D_0, D_1, and D_2 but there are not for Seismic Design Categories A, B, and C. These details are particularly important for a tall, massive structure like a masonry chimney.

Indoor masonry chimneys, as is always recommended for a wood-burning appliance, are expected to be kept 2 inches from combustible materials throughout their height. The assumption here is that this is a masonry chimney with a clay flue liner inside it. Likewise, code will dictate that the chimney itself will have a masonry wall thickness of (nominally) 4 inches. Clay-lined masonry chimneys are the most common, though there are other manufactured options that, like metal flues, generally will require following manufacturer's directions for proper clearances and installations.

As a clay-lined masonry chimney passes through, for example, a second-floor level, it will likewise need to maintain a 2-inch distance from the combustible materials. It is generally not permitted to support wood framing members and other structural aspects of the house with the chimney unless it has been specifically designed for that purpose. Note, however, that wood sheathing—like the plywood subfloor at the second floor—is permitted to abut the masonry as long as it remains at least 6 inches from the *inside* of the nearest clay flue liner. This same rule applies to wooden trim around the chimney.

The actual air space created by separating a chimney from a ceiling or floor structure is always to be fireblocked. Fireblocking is material installed within or to cover the space so as to prevent fire from having easy passage from one floor or level to the next. In the event of a fire, an open air cavity is an invitation for the fire to rapidly spread from one floor to the next. Fireblocking seeks to minimize that risk. The IRC does not dictate exactly what material is used but only says that these spaces "shall be fireblocked with noncombustible material." Such material might be metal, cement board, or a noncombustible insulation material such as mineral wool or ceramic wool. It is wise to consult the authority having jurisdiction to clarify which of these is considered acceptable. This same fireblocking strategy must be used at every floor or ceiling penetration.

Additional Code Requirements of Note

Though the whole IRC cannot be explained in this chapter, it is useful to look at issues pertinent to most masonry heater installations. For example, though the required clearances from combustible materials have been covered, not yet discussed is a very common question: How high above the roof must the chimney go? Frequently, if you were to ask ten masons the same question, you just might receive ten different answers. The IRC makes it plain and clear.

Exterior Chimney Height

A chimney must be 2 feet taller than any part of the building that is within 10 feet of it. At the same time, the chimney must be no less than 3 feet taller than the highest part of the roof through which it penetrates. If, say, a dormer, or other part of the house is within 10 feet of the chimney and happens to be taller than that chimney, then the chimney must be built to be at least 2 feet taller than that dormer. Likewise, if the ridge of the roof, for example, is within 10 feet of the chimney, the chimney must be built at least 2 feet taller than the ridge. And, finally, if the chimney happens to pass through the roof far from the ridge (more than 10 feet), the chimney still must be at least 2 feet taller than the tallest part of the roof plane that is 10 feet away. See figures 9.17 and 9.18.

As you can imagine, with a steep-pitched roof, this could mean that the chimney above the roof can be quite tall—and maybe spindly looking—if it does not penetrate the plane of the roof near the ridge. This is

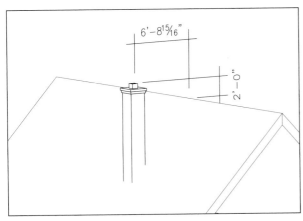

FIGURE 9.17. This chimney is within 10 feet of the ridge and so must be at least 2 feet higher than the ridge.

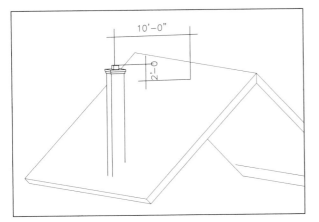

FIGURE 9.18. A chimney low on the roof must be 2 feet higher than the highest point on the roof plane within 10 feet. Notice how tall and spindly the chimney can become.

FIGURE 9.19. Three cleanouts are visible on the lower part of this beautiful brick heater; one is on either side of the ash box door, and one is at the base of the chimney on the left. Photo courtesy of Maine Wood Heat Company.

yet another reason to strive for positioning a masonry heater close to the middle of the house. The chimney will pass through the roof close to the ridge and be an attractive architectural piece, rather than an out-of-place skyscraping structure.

Cleanout Accesses

Chimneys also need to be cleaned from time to time. Building codes recognize this need, and the IRC dictates that every masonry chimney shall have a cleanout door or port within 6 inches of the base of every flue in the chimney. The masonry heater itself should also be designed with suitable cleanout accesses.

While building codes do not specify locations for these cleanouts on the masonry heater, ASTM E1602, the "Standard Guide for Construction of Solid Fuel Burning Masonry Heaters," says, "If the design limits natural access, install cleanout openings or a means for cleaning all chimney flues and heat exchange areas." This is rather unspecific language. Suffice it to say that a person designing and building a masonry heater must carefully consider how every internal flue might be accessed for inspection and cleaning. You'd hate to think of a masonry heater one day becoming inoperable because ash accumulated somewhere that can't be cleaned!

Outside Combustion Air

The wording of the International Residential Code in regard to requirements for providing combustion air from outside the building for masonry heaters is vague at best. The IRC language addresses outside air for "factory-built or masonry fireplaces in this chapter [of the code]." It does not mention masonry heaters. Masonry heaters are listed within the same IRC chapter with masonry fireplaces and factory-built fireplaces but are clearly recognized as a category different from masonry fireplaces. You're led to believe by the code language, therefore, that outside air requirements do not exist, at least in the IRC, for masonry heaters.

The bottom line on this topic is that the authority having jurisdiction in whatever municipality or location at which the heater is being built can dictate whether outside combustion air is a necessity. I have seen no compelling evidence suggesting that outside air is either necessary or beneficial to the operation or safety of a masonry heater.

Outside combustion air, though sounding like a highly technical term, often simply means manufacturing a leak in the house. Many times these "systems" are simply air-vented from outside to an outlet close to the air-intake area of the masonry heater. As discussed in chapter 7, the heating requirements for a house are partially calculated based on how "tight" the house is—how much hot air is lost by infiltration. For all practical purposes, vents bringing outside air into the house to feed a masonry heater are just holes in the house envelope, intentionally making the house leakier.

There are houses that are so carefully constructed and so "tight" that they do not even provide enough air infiltration for basic human life support. Such homes require mechanical devices to refresh the air—typically air-to-air heat exchangers. I think that such a design is counterproductive. A house, after all, is meant to be a place in which people live, rejuvenate, and recharge. Building a home that, by itself, cannot sustain that basic function is faulty, not successful. It is a sign that the way we heat buildings normally is not sustainable and based on abundant, free, or renewable energy, but on fuels and conditions that must be metered and tightly controlled.

Masonry heaters use a fraction of the air that an open conventional fireplace would use. Still, a masonry heater may use a roomful of air in a firing. A typical living room volume might be about 2,000 cubic feet. So the masonry heater uses 2,000 cubic feet of air in a two-hour combustion session. (You may recall that the sample house from chapter 7 had a total volume of 10,000 cubic feet.) Well, how much air enters a home when an exterior door is opened for someone to go outside? How much air does each person need each day?

Most adults will need slightly less than 400 cubic feet of air each day. A family of four adults would thus require no more than 1,600 cubic feet of fresh air each day. Together, four people and a large masonry heater (if fired twice per day) would need 5,600 cubic feet of total air each day. The sample house had an air-change rate of about 0.5 air changes per hour (ACH). It is clear that the 10,000-cubic-foot home gets nearly enough air naturally every hour for the fresh-air requirements for all the inhabitants and the masonry heater *even if no one ever opens a door to go outside!* Who would want to add an intentional air leak (outside combustion air) to such a scenario?

A tightly built house may need an interlocked system to compensate for excessive depressurization. For example, a tight home with several bathroom exhausts, a powerful range hood exhaust, and perhaps a powered water heater exhaust could become severely depressurized if all or many of those fans are running simultaneously. This could reverse the draft in an otherwise properly designed and situated masonry heater. A mechanically interlocked system here would compensate with an intake of air to prevent depressurization. This is intelligent use of metered and controlled incoming air triggered by the use of exhaust fans to address a true, specific, potential problem instead of simply making an extra hole in the house for more air to enter.

One more point about outside air for masonry heaters is that, obviously, masonry heaters are used in cold weather. Their operation depends on high combustion temperatures. This good operation is augmented by using warm, indoor air. Deliberately feeding cold, outside winter air into the firebox of a masonry heater serves to decrease combustion temperatures—undermining many aspects of the function of the heater like clean combustion and maximum heat storage. If general outdoor combustion air is a questionable idea, feeding cold air directly to the fire of a masonry heater is something much worse.

Unfortunately, the best solution, if outside air is required by the building inspector or the homeowner, is to direct outside air specifically to the firebox and not just into the room. This can be done using a tightly closing, rubber-gasketed damper as outlined in the construction project in chapter 8. In this way, cold air is never introduced into the living space itself, just to the fire. These gasketed air supplies are also available with a computerized mechanism that senses the demand for air at the fire and automatically operates the air intake according to the needs of clean combustion. With the high-tech air control, the user need only load the fuel and light the fire. The computer monitors air needs for near-perfect combustion conditions and automatically closes the air supply when demand for air drops low enough. Whether with a manual or automatic control, making sure an outside air supply is closed as soon as it is no longer necessary (see chapter 11) will maximize the performance under these conditions.

Code Finale

The entire building-code structure is daunting, complex, and often not understood even by competent builders, let alone the common homeowner. Although it isn't possible—or even worthwhile—to quote and explain every possible aspect present in codes relating to masonry heaters, this chapter has outlined many important parts of safety and fire issues that most code or building officials will want to know are done "right."

Building codes are for safety. When you keep in mind the safety of yourself, your children, and future possible inhabitants of a house, it becomes easier to please the building inspector. It is always important to remember that many building codes are unspecific and that special circumstances or building methods often are not specifically addressed in the written documentation. Though masonry heaters, as a category, now appear in the codes of many jurisdictions, each unique, one-of-a-kind heater has its own special attributes and is located in one specific room in one specific house. There is no substitute for carefully considering how a masonry heater is meant to perform in a specific setting and approaching the "authority having jurisdiction" with well-reasoned ways of handling any safety concerns that might exist.

A STEP BACK IN TIME

According to Rita Short, "The best pumpkin pie we have made was made in the masonry heater's bakeoven." She pauses a moment and adds, "It had a perfect crust and was even baked without foil on the crust." Now, if that isn't a reason to add a bakeoven feature to a masonry heater, what reason could there be? Of course, not everyone likes to bake; or, at least they think they don't until they taste pizza or bread or cookies out of a real stone or brick oven. Suddenly they develop a desire to mix, knead, roll, proof, and bake.

Rita and Wendell Short live with their two children outside the little town of Archbold, in northwest Ohio. Archbold is known for its quaintness and for its historic attraction, Sauder Village—a farmstead where you can go to see how life was lived in the 1800s. Sauder Village is named for Erie Sauder, a woodworker who started a (then) little company called Sauder Woodworking, now a leading producer of ready-to-assemble furniture in the United States. Wendell Short is director of new product development at Sauder Woodworking.

In some respects, it seems like stepping back in time to visit the Shorts' homestead in the country. On the hill is a big old barn. Chickens run around the yard and under the pear trees just in front of the house. The house itself, though just completed ten years ago, looks old as well, at least in design. If you look close, you see the home boasts high-efficiency windows and cement board siding and many other quality features to guarantee durability and longevity. When you step into the front porch, you find hundred-year-old barn timbers supporting the roof of the four-season room. Open one more door into the main house and the first thing in view is a massive brick masonry heater with an arch-top door and wide, inviting, raised brick hearth. When Wendell and Rita had the heater built, they ordered recycled bricks and wanted it to "look like it had been there a hundred years." That's just the way it looks.

The look is perfect for the home, half of which is a warm and inviting timber-frame made with recycled Douglas fir timbers. Over the large timber floor joists is a ceiling (which doubles as the upstairs floor) of pine barn siding painted a luscious dark green. The pinkish orange oiled wood goes well with the old red bricks of the heater. The other half of the house is actually an 1800s log home that the Shorts relocated from another part of the property and added onto to create their unique residence.

The decision to have a masonry heater started for them when they were perusing home-building magazines and spotted an advertisement for a masonry heater. Wendell explains, "The thing that sold us on the concept was the efficient combustion with very clean emissions—thus

FIGURE 9.20. This heater was built to look like it has been used for a hundred years. Photo by Wendell Short.

keeping the chimney clean and eliminating the risk of chimney fires. We had a chimney fire in an older home with a woodstove insert in an old fireplace. It was not a good experience other than we got to meet the fire department and a couple neighbors." The couple had just moved into the neighborhood a few months earlier; the chimney fire was not exactly the housewarming they had anticipated.

And so it is that many masonry heater owners appreciate their investment for its security benefits. The Shorts had very little experience with wood heating other than the mishap with the stove insert. Their previous homes had forced-air or conventional radiators. Rita relates, "We found, from our prior homes, that we liked the warmth of radiant heat, but wanted something more efficient and that worked without electricity. It is great to not have to worry when the power goes out on a cold, wintry night!" Chalk up another point for security.

It's not just security that they enjoy, however. Nor just the pumpkin pies that come from the oven. Rita, who homeschools her two boys, relates that the hill on which their barn sits is also an attraction in the winter for kids and their sleds. "The neighbor's children like to come and sled down our barn hill. Afterward they come in to play and we line the heater with snow-covered snow bibs,

coats, scarves, mittens, and boots. By the time they are ready to go home their clothes and boots are warm and dry." So is it an oven, a fireplace, a heater, or a clothes dryer? Apparently, it's all of the above.

Both agree that, though hauling, splitting, and stacking wood is strenuous work, it has the other-side-of-the-coin benefit of just plain getting them out of the house and getting some fresh air and exercise. Wendell comments, "This is a great way to work off the stress of long hours in the office during the week." It's clear that both of them can see a silver lining in every cloud. The rest of the story of using wood in a masonry heater, however, is that "We use a lot less wood than others we know who have a regular fireplace or a woodstove." Imagine splitting, hauling, and stacking eight cords of wood instead of the four or so that Wendell and Rita go through!

The Shorts never did install a backup heating system. They depend entirely on the masonry heater. They comment that this limits their ability to travel in the wintertime, but they admit that was their decision and that it is not for everyone. But like the settlers of northwest Ohio in the 1800s, Wendell and Rita have made themselves 100 percent responsible for having heat in the house. In their own way, they are pioneers, too.

PART FOUR

Living with a Piece of the Sun

Well, it's done! The careful design was executed in the perfect location. Materials were selected and purchased. Codes were consulted. The inner life was designed and put in place. The masonry heater was built. Now what?

If you randomly asked people on the street how to drive and care for a car, they could probably give detailed instructions on how to do everything from inserting the key in the ignition, to replacing windshield wipers, to changing the oil every few thousand miles. If these same folks were asked how to operate and maintain a masonry heater, however, they would likely ask, "A what?" Masonry heaters are not yet common enough in North America that people know how to use them to best advantage and with the least effort.

Easily the single most important factor in good operation of a masonry heater is the right fuel. Chapter 10 covers in significant detail how to obtain wood, how to store it, and how much of it to set aside. Chapter 11 is a guide to using a typical masonry heater, including cookstoves and heaters with baking ovens. This includes information about breaking in a newly constructed heater, and the simple task of burning daily charges of fuel. The final chapter explains how to maintain a masonry heater.

Living with a masonry heater is the easiest part of the whole range of topics covered in this book. The work, the planning and designing, the locating, the selecting of materials, shapes, and options are the head-scratching, time-consuming part of getting to the point of first use. Owners-to-be sometimes will spend weeks or months selecting the colors for a masonry heater. But living with one is primarily a simple act of enjoying fire and warmth with family and friends. None of the enjoyment, however, is possible without fuel.

FIGURE 10.1. A stucco heater centrally located in the home. The loading door at lower left is at waist level for easy loading without bending over. Niches, shelves, and curved elements add visual interest and a place to set decorations. Photo courtesy of Biofire, Inc.

CHAPTER TEN

Fuel to Burn

Real energy is free. It is free for those who plan, prepare, and are aware. Each day, 412 BTU/hr per square foot (1.36 kW/m²) of energy reaches the earth from the sun. In chapter 7, our hypothetical house required 13,600 BTU/hr for heating purposes. The sun, therefore, freely sends to earth enough energy, in a 33-square-foot area, to heat that home. In other words, there is enough power reaching the earth from the sun every hour on an area the size of a sheet of plywood to heat a well-insulated, 1,000-square-foot home in northern Ohio for one hour. Despite this well-documented fact, we live in a society that calls a natural-gas-burning furnace a modern technological wonder. As a society, we have not yet advanced enough to know that real energy is free.

The gas furnace requires you to be connected via pipelines, trucks, refineries, and wells at vast expense for construction, maintenance, and continued exploration. All these costly dependencies appear in a monthly bill for services and product. If a pipeline breaks, there is no fuel. If a well goes dry, there is no fuel. If the electric lines break, the furnace won't work. If a fuse breaks in the home, the furnace won't work. Myriad other technologically "advanced" parts break, wear out, and fail. All this expense, dependency, and risk revolve around the most technological solutions developed in the modern world for heating homes. While human dependency lingers, the sun continues to send its free energy to the earth, just begging us to use it.

Of course, solar energy itself remains likewise elusive and undependable. It is likely that if you could always depend on the sun to shine in a clear sky every day throughout every winter, by now *everyone* would have some kind of solar-powered home. That is obviously not the case. (In fact, even in southern climates where the sun *does* dependably shine virtually every day, solar energy is still used much less than it could be.) In the cold northern areas of North America, winter sunshine can be very fleeting. Days of glorious, clear skies are sometimes followed by many days or even weeks when you'd think cloud cover is permanent. As great as pure sunshine can be, it is not the final solution until a good way is found to store that abundant energy for a rainy (or snowy) day.

Whenever I go out to my woodshed, I marvel that nature not only sends all the free energy to the earth, but also provides the free batteries for its snowy-day storage. Each air-dried pound of wood stores 6,400 BTUs of solar energy. A single oak log contains over 30,000 BTUs. Holding a 5-pound oak log is like holding 60 square feet of sunshine in hand (because that one log, when burned efficiently, will release about 1,000 BTUs per hour through an efficient masonry heater). Thus freed from concern over the presence or not of the sun, an owner of a masonry heater enjoys the sun's radiant heat even on those innumerable, cloudy days of winter.

It would be naive, however, to pretend there is no dependence at all. Even when food is acquired, cooked, and placed on a table in front of you, you still need to lift a fork and knife, cut the food, and put it in your mouth. You need energy to keep the house warm and so must accumulate the batteries of heat just as others accumulate the dollars to pay for gas or fuel oil. The dependence now, however, is on yourself. Who is more dependable than yourself? As free as the energy may be, you still need to go out and gather it, prepare it, and house it so that it is ready for wintertime use.

How Much Wood?

Chapter 7 discussed how to calculate the heat needed in a given house or room being heated by a masonry heater. The results developed as a total number of

BTUs per hour needed in any particular living space. This total, however, was a total for the coldest day of the heating season for a given location in a home with specific construction attributes. This single figure, though crucial for determining what size masonry heater to build, does little to explain how much heat the home needs through the whole heating season.

Especially in the northern parts of the United States and into Canada, the heating season will easily last seven months or more. That coldest day, which often occurs in January, is months away from both the beginning and end of the heating season. If you've taken the time to discover how much heat you need on the coldest day and developed the design for a masonry heater, it stands to reason that one of the next questions to answer will be how much firewood you need for the entire heating season. In fact, it's a good idea to begin accumulating heating fuel as soon as you know the house will be heated with wood. That way it will have maximum time to season properly before you use it in the newly constructed masonry heater.

The best way to get a good estimate of the total amount of fuel you'll need is to refer to a chart of the total heating degree days for the town or municipality closest to the house. A heating degree day is the number of degrees that a day's average temperature is below the temperature at which buildings need to be heated. Usually, it is assumed that you begin heating anytime the outdoor temperature is below 65°F. For example, if a geographic location averages 35° on December 1, then its heating degree days (HDD) for December 1 are 30. If that area averages 35° for the whole month (thirty-one days), then the total HDD for December are 930. Total heating degree days for a whole season are found for many areas in appendix D.

Continuing the sample project begun in chapter 7, the total firewood needs for the 1,000-square-foot home in Cleveland can be estimated as follows: first, it was estimated that the total heat loss (THL) of this house is 269.26 BTU/hr-°F. Multiplying this number by 24 gives the THL for a whole day (per °F) instead of per hour. (Note that this calculation is not taking into account possible solar gain, heat gain from living inhabitants and appliances, and so forth. The purpose here is to have a good minimum estimate of how much firewood is likely to be needed. It is never a bad idea to overestimate in this regard, for it's much better to have more wood than not enough as the heating season progresses.)

The calculation is:

$$24 \text{ hr} \times 269.26 \text{ BTU/hr-°F or } 6{,}462.24 \text{ BTU/day-°F}$$

Consulting appendix D, we find that the total heating degree days for Cleveland is 5,717 in the whole heating season. By simply multiplying the THL by the total HDD, a number representing total season BTUs is obtained. In this case

$$6{,}462.24 \text{ BTU/day-°F} \times 5{,}717 \text{ °F-day} = 36{,}944{,}626 \text{ BTU}$$

If 1 pound of air-dried wood contains 6,400 BTUs, this house will need

$$36{,}944{,}626 \text{ BTU} \div 6{,}400 \text{ BTU/lb} = 5{,}773 \text{ pounds}$$
$$\text{of wood for one year}$$

Table 10.1 indicates that every cord of air-dried silver maple firewood weighs 2,970 pounds. Simply dividing the total pounds needed by the weight of a cord provides the total estimated number of cords needed.

$$5{,}773 \text{ lbs} \div 2{,}970 \text{ lb/cord} = 1.94 \text{ cords of silver maple.}$$

In this case, you'd be wise to have 2 cords of maple on hand for the heating season. If you are planning to stockpile oak, a denser firewood, less total cordage of wood will do the same job. A cord of white oak weighs 3,863 pounds. The heating for this house will likely require

$$5{,}773 \div 3{,}863 = 1.5 \text{ cords of white oak}$$

Although these calculations purport to determine how much wood is needed for a given living space, remember that the numbers—especially the heating degree days—are based on *historical averages*. Both history

Table 10.1. Approximate weight per standard cord (80 cubic feet of solid wood content) of various woods (green and air-dried to 20-percent moisture content) and potential heat of air-dried wood.

	Pounds green*	Pounds air-dried**	Million BTU available***
Ash	3,940	3,370	23.6
Basswood	3,360	2,100	14.7
Box Elder	3,500	2,500	17.5
Cottonwood	3,920	2,304	16.1
Elm (American)	4,293	2,868	20.1
Elm (red)	4,480	3,056	21.4
Hackberry	4,000	3,080	21.6
Hickory (shagbark)	4,980	4,160	29.1
Locust (black)	4,640	4,010	28.1
Maple (silver)	3,783	2,970	20.8
Maple (sugar)	4,386	3,577	25.0
Oak (red)	4,988	3,609	25.3
Oak (white)	4,942	3,863	27.0
Osage orange	5,480	4,380	30.7
Pine (shortleaf)	4,120	2,713	19.0
Red Cedar	3,260	2,700	18.9
Sycamore	4,160	2,956	20.7
Walnut (black)	4,640	3,120	21.8

*Approximate weight of standard cord (occupying 128 cubic feet of space and containing 80 cubic feet of solid wood), for the first two columns of figures. **To 20% moisture content ***Potential available heat from standard cord with 100% unit efficiency. Heat at 20% moisture content. Reprinted from "Wood Fuel for Heating" by John P. Slusher, School of Natural Resources, University of Missouri-Columbia, 1995 (1985).

and averages are, by nature, *not* indicative of what may happen in a given year. Additionally, the HDD figure, in the United States, is commonly based on a presumed indoor air temperature of 65°F. If the home or living space will be kept warmer than that, the actual amount of fuel used may increase. When you are solely responsible for accumulating heating fuel, it is always better to plan for the unexpected and have extra on hand. Any extra, if stored properly, is never wasted and can be the safety net for the next heating season.

Acquiring Firewood

Knowing how much wood you need each year is just a start. The task is to get that amount of wood in storage long before you need it. There is no joy in having a beautiful masonry heater installed but no fuel, or only inadequately seasoned fuel with which to warm it. It's like salivating for a porterhouse steak, then having the waitress tell you the restaurant just cooked its last one for the guy across the room. Being responsible for your own fuel supply is very different from the dependency-induced coma of just setting the thermostat to "auto" when the weather turns cool. You must think ahead. As long as you do that, the task itself isn't too hard for anyone to handle. Everyone from petite ladies to husky men can secure a season's firewood using today's modern conveniences like chain saws and pickup trucks, though you need not own either to effectively and inexpensively heat with wood.

Own the Land

There is no better guarantee of having free fuel than having wooded property. Those who are planning and are aware of the possibilities can, indeed, have firewood free for the taking. While geologists must speculate, test, and eventually drill in the hope of finding adequate supplies of gas and oil, an owner of real property only needs to look to see both the forest and the trees. The property owner with eyes knows in an instant if there is fuel on the land. A wooded property of just 10 acres can keep you supplied with wood on a sustainable, lifelong basis. An acre of wooded property will grow about one-third of a cord of wood per year. If well managed, 10 acres will adequately yield between 3 and 4 cords of wood each season.

Using our sample home, we determined that about 2 cords of maple would be an adequate supply of wood for this house. In this case, a 6-acre wooded lot brimming with maple trees will supply you with a lifetime

FIGURE 10.2. Although only the soapstone heater in the middle of the picture retains heat, the use of soapstone slabs for seats and soapstone tile pieces for accents creates the image of a much larger heater. Notice the soapstone tile clock and soapstone goblets at top center. The wing benches have wooden doors to open to access firewood or other stored items. **Photo courtesy of Tulikivi Corporation.**

of solar batteries. Woods that have never been managed at all may contain several years' worth of dead trees or stands that desperately need thinning. A 10-acre, previously unmanaged parcel could have as much as 6 cords of wood that can be removed without affecting the ability of that woodlot to produce a third of a cord of wood per acre each year. In this way, the person who only needs 2 cords per year could secure a three-year supply just by thinning and cleaning out the woods the first time. By the time this owner has consumed his first 6 cords, the 10-acre woods will have already grown another 10 or more cords of wood.

Even those with smaller parcels of wooded land can supplement heating with the wood thereon. A single acre, well wooded, will annually drop branches and twigs that are useful for fire starting, prewarming a masonry heater, or even firing small masonry heaters and cookstoves for much of the season. Likewise, neighbors who do not burn wood may be thrilled to have someone take fallen branches, twigs, and even unwanted trees off their land. Of course, plenty of masonry heater owners will have smaller lots with only a few trees. They will not be fuel self-sufficient.

Another way to "own the land," however, is to

become aware of publicly owned forest in the vicinity. Tax dollars pay to maintain and support these public forests, so why not make use of the land of which you're part owner? Varying from state to state or province to province, many public forests do allow limited removal of wood for fuel. Sometimes there will be a license requirement. Think of this as being the equivalent of a hunting license, except that instead of hunting animals, it is trees that you're stalking. Just like the hunting equivalent, such an arrangement frequently will allow only a certain amount of wood to be removed per permit holder.

You need not fret if these "own the land" options don't work in a particular area, however. There are still many other ways to find and acquire wood for a masonry heater.

Landscape and Tree Services

In many ways, local and regional landscape and tree-service businesses are better than owning your own woodlot. Within a city, in particular, those hired to remove trees from homesites are sometimes desperate to find places to dump all the wood. Although it is not true in all cases, some of these businesses do not have the necessary space and infrastructure for keeping the cut wood, splitting it, and storing it while it is advertised to sell. Such operations will be happy to know of places they can take the wood and dump it, and they will do it at no charge to the recipient. What's more, they often will cut most of the larger parts of the trunk into short, common firebox lengths of 16 to 20 inches.

Likewise, if such a company is seen in a neighborhood working at tree removal, it is always worthwhile to stop and talk to the foreman about the possibility of getting the wood. Especially if the trip is short, they may be quite happy to know of a place to take it. In addition, many of these services will mulch even large branches of 3 to 4 inches in diameter. Such timber is perfect fuel for most masonry heaters. It's possible the tree service will gladly skip handling all that extra wood and just send it along with the primary logs upon request.

The downside of this option is that, already, more and more people are burning wood and are making the same arrangements. There may actually be a waiting list of people who want to get wood from a tree service. In this case, the likelihood of getting this free fuel may be small. The service may begin delivering only to those who are on the list *and* who are within close proximity to the place from which the tree is removed. The best hedge against this is to make sure friends, relatives, and acquaintances know that, if they don't want the wood from a tree they are having removed, you do. Usually, people who hire a service to cut a tree can request that it be taken to a specific place. After all, it's their tree! The owner of the tree can make sure that specific place is your house.

Finally, some landscape and tree-service companies will actually sell what they call "limb wood." Because very few woodstove owners have an interest in small logs and limbs, these services, if they do not mulch all these pieces, will sometimes sell a pickup truck load of perfectly good masonry heater fuel at a very low cost.

Sawmills and Cabinetmakers

One of the absolute best values in firewood for masonry heaters is the sawmill slabs at local sawmills. Small, regional sawmills often process hardwoods for local and regional industries like window, door, and cabinetmaking companies. Every time a sawmill processes a raw log, one of the first operations is to "slab" it. This means that the naturally round log is sawn on four sides to make the log square. In one operation, this process removes bark, wane, and sapwood—all the "undesirable" parts of an otherwise valuable length of wood. Since these slabs are useless to the mill for making boards that may become flooring, window, door, or cabinet lumber, the mill will often bundle large quantities with banding and set them aside as junk wood for sale.

Of course, this "junk" wood burns just as well as any other firewood in a masonry heater. Nonetheless, those who own metal woodstoves and conventional fireplaces are generally not attracted to these slabs because they are thin boards rather than thick logs.

FIGURE 10.3. This tile-and-stucco heater has handmade and hand-painted tiles. Both the seat and the mass behind the tiled firebox are for heat storage. *Kachelofen* **designed, built, and photographed by Ernst Kiesling, Canadian Kachelofen.**

In any appliance in which the goal is to keep a fire always burning, such thin pieces of scrap are not a top choice. Their loss is the masonry heater owner's gain. I have purchased huge bundles of these sawmill slabs—roughly the equivalent of a cord of wood—for as little as $15! Some mills will even deliver these bundles at a nominal cost if more than a couple are purchased.

These bundles of slabs are sometimes 8, 10, or 12 feet long and 4 or 5 feet in diameter. Frequently they are held together by metal strapping. This makes preparing the wood for storage very easy. You saw through the bundle of wood while it is still together, making the pieces whatever length you like. Some slabs might be quite wide—10 or 12 inches—and can be easily split once if desired. Otherwise, these thin slabs will dry relatively quickly if properly stacked and stored, and make excellent masonry heater fuel.

In a similar fashion, companies that actually make final wood products like cabinets, doors, windows, or furniture will often have a scrap pile of rejected wood and various cutoffs or ripped lengths. For example, a furniture maker may need boards that are exactly 4 inches wide. They may order lumber that is 10 inches wide (or more) so that the wood can be ripped into two boards at the desired 4 inches. The remaining "rippings," of just 1 or 2 inches, may be completely useless and relegated to the scrap pile. Very often these scrap piles are available for the taking for anyone who inquires first.

Pallet and Construction Scraps

One of the simplest ways to get free wood is to find a local business that receives shipments on wooden pallets or in wooden crates. Pallets and crates are easy to break, pry, or cut apart and usually offer dry wood that is ready to burn. A local establishment that has no use for (or an expense related to) such pallets is often looking for ways to get rid of the excess material and may even save them specifically for someone who offers to come on a regular basis and take them away. Even places that normally recycle or reuse crates and pallets will have some that are damaged and not worth their time to repair.

I once supplied my whole heating needs for an entire season using wood scrounged in this way. A local steel plant, on a daily basis, was discarding hundreds of 8-foot-long 2-by-4s that had been used as shipping material for its products. The plant's personnel hauled all these perfectly good (for firewood) pieces of wood to the dumpster whence I retrieved them by the dozen. In very short order I had accumulated several cords of wood. The only preparation this wood needed was to be cut to length. Only very rarely did I find nails or other fasteners in it.

It should be clear that only solid-wood crating should be viewed as potential firewood. Plywood, particleboard, and oriented strand board containers should not be used for firewood because the various glues and additives in the adhesives used in these products can be highly toxic when burned. Also avoid pressure-treated wood, which likewise contains harmful chemicals. Most pallets, however, are made with simple, sawn wood. Some will even be oak or other hardwoods.

FIGURE 10.4. A floor-to-ceiling and window-to-window stone masonry heater. Tight joints on the stonework are a hallmark of good craftsmanship. Photo courtesy of Empire Masonry Heaters, Inc.

Likewise, construction scraps are perfectly suitable for fueling a masonry heater. Most lumber used today in home construction is dimensional softwood lumber such as 2-by-4s, 2-by-6s, and the like. On the other hand, you can also stumble upon scraps from hardwood flooring and trim to add to the hardwood collection of firewood. As in pallets and crating, you should avoid plywood, laminated beams, and other manufactured wood products that will have a preponderance of adhesives. Also be very conscious of the hazard that nails present when gathering these scraps.

Both construction scraps and pallets or crating are excellent fuels for masonry heaters because the lumber is generally small-dimensioned and dry. Such wood is perfect for the hot, relatively fast fire in properly designed and operated heaters. Owners of metal wood-stoves and regular open fireplaces are not so interested in these options, normally, because this small wood is not long lasting in a fire and can therefore add to the nuisance of constant reloading of fuel. Again, the efficient, fast-burning masonry heater offers an advantage when it comes to getting this discarded firewood.

There are some additional cautions, and, perhaps, disadvantages to such material. One is that pallets, in particular, are loaded with nails or staples (which are often present, as noted, in construction scraps as well). Very industrious people may go to the trouble of completely dismantling pallets and removing all nails in the process. Those who wish to salvage their firewood without using power tools may find this worthwhile. Those who want to make the job quick, however, will simply saw the pallets apart with either a chain saw or an electric circular saw.

In the latter cases, all the nails will go through the combustion process of the masonry heater and end up in the ashes. This is no problem if the ashes are going to be eventually bagged and discarded. (Caution! Hot ashes should *always* be cooled in a metal container before being bagged for disposal via garbage pickup.) However, if you wish to use the ashes in the garden, or spread them on an icy driveway, you'll have to remove the nails either by screening or with a magnet. Otherwise, they will be a constant safety hazard.

The other caveat with construction and crating materials is to watch out for chemically treated wood. Most pallet-making operations are meant to be low-budget. After all, the makers of pallets and crating know that their product is going to be used, perhaps reused, eventually will break, and then will be discarded. There is no incentive in this business to use specially treated wood in most cases, though it's not impossible to find pallets made from treated wood. For example, pallets that are used for international shipping are required to meet International Plant Protection Convention (IPPC) rules that aim to protect against the movement of invasive insect or plant species from one international region to another. Some of these pallets are therefore treated specially; any such treatment is marked on the pallet itself.

One way these pallets are treated is with heat. The pallet itself or the materials used to make it are subjected to temperatures high enough to kill any insects, insect eggs, or seeds from invasive plant species. If a crating material is so heat-treated, it will be stamped with an IPPC label with an HT designation. If the IPPC label contains the MB designation, on the other hand, it has been treated with methyl bromide, a pesticide of relatively high toxicity.

Methyl bromide is a gas used as a fumigant, not as a penetrating liquid. As such it dissipates quickly and substantially and is thought to pose no toxic risk via the materials so treated. In fact, methyl bromide occurs naturally; the oceans of the world are the major source of this gas. However, people considering burning pallets treated this way should be aware of its existence and use. Crating treated with this chemical has no distinguishing colors or markings other than the IPPC label. If it is locally made and just looks like clean wood, it probably is. However, there is no substitute for

FIGURE 10.5. A large soapstone heater sits well centered between a dining and living room. The stone-wrapped chimney rises near the ridge of the cathedral ceiling. The heater features rock-faced soapstone "bricks," wraparound mantel and benches, and a green serpentine arch over the door. Photo courtesy of Tulikivi Corporation.

investigation if you have any reason to believe wood has been chemically contaminated.

Other lumber that is chemically treated, as in construction scraps, usually bears an obvious unnatural color such as the greenish tint of what is commonly referred to as "treated lumber." This type of lumber may contain a host of chemicals that also should not be burned. The distinctive appearance of this wood when discarded at a building site is hard to miss, so wood scroungers should simply avoid it.

The Old-Fashioned Way: Buy It

There are many people who simply will not be inclined to do the work of securing their own firewood. Time constraints, physical restrictions, family commitments, and dozens of other reasons exist for a person to choose the "easy" way out—just buy the fuel.

The landscape and tree-service contractors mentioned earlier in this chapter, if they have the space and personnel, will often sell firewood they've retrieved from their services. Likewise, there are entrepreneurs who already have a connection in one way or another with such services and regularly cut, split, and make available wood for sale. Of course, there are also those who own a lot of land or have permits to access public lands for acquiring firewood. In general, in any area of North America in which there are trees, there is likely to be someone who will sell firewood. Likely, you can look in the phone book or local newspaper and find someone selling wood.

One of the attractive aspects of buying wood is that many entrepreneurs truly run a full-service firewood business. They will (in particular with regular, return customers) ask how small to split the wood, ask what lengths of wood are desired, deliver it, and even stack it in the location of your choice. In areas with a lot of wood and a lot of firewood businesses, prices for these services can be very attractive and competitive. Considering that, at least at the time of this writing, firewood prices still average $150 to $200 per cord (or less) in most parts of the United States, even masonry heater owners receiving these deluxe full services will still be paying a fraction of the cost of most fossil fuel

options for heating a living space or home. Our sample home in Cleveland, for example, would at these prices only need $300 to $400 worth of oak firewood for a whole heating season.

Those who are going to buy all the firewood they need should, indeed, seek out suppliers who will provide firewood cut properly for the particular masonry heater(s) to be fired with it. Don't be shy about requesting the appropriate fuel. There is little point in purchasing firewood that you need to cut or split again once it is delivered (unless, of course, there is substantial savings in doing so). This is, again, one of the beautiful aspects of wood as fuel. It can be custom-cut to whatever size is perfect for the firebox of the heater being used.

Finally, there are some people who feel that firewood is just a messy fuel and that is reason enough to not use a masonry heater. A clean and easily managed solution is purchasing manufactured firewood. Some lumber, flooring, and other companies now use collected sawdust and compress it under heat and pressure to make blocks of "hardwood" fuel suitable for masonry heaters. The fuel is neatly packaged and stacked on pallets for storage in a garage or barn. Because it is densely compacted, it takes less (in volume) of these blocks to do the same heating as regular cordwood. Some manufacturers claim that one pallet (approximately 4 feet square) is the equivalent of 1 cord of firewood. This option offers a fuel solution that is orderly, clean, and free from moisture, rot, and bugs for those who just don't want to deal with cordwood. You can find some sources for this type of fuel in appendix A.

Firewood Species for Masonry Heaters

All wood-burning fireplaces, stoves, and furnaces require quality fuel to provide quality heat. One of the great advantages of a masonry heater is that it isn't as picky as other stoves when it comes to fuel. I encourage the use of any wood species in my heaters. On the other hand, many stove manufacturers and retailers will be quick to inform customers that there are specific species of wood that will give the best performance from a wood-burning device. Because of this trend, many people now believe that more heat is produced from woods like oak, maple, and cherry than from any other type of wood. In particular, it is believed that softwoods like pine and fir have very little heat value.

It's true that pine, fir, hemlock, and cedars are not the best fuels for a conventional woodstove, but not because they are poor fuels. In fact, a measured pound of dry pine will have virtually the identical energy content as a measured pound of oak. Pine, larch, cedar, fir, hemlock, and all other softwoods are on par with any hardwood when it comes to heat content on a per-pound basis. Conventional metal woodstoves and fireplaces, in order to supply constant heat, need a constant supply of wood during all hours of every day. Softwoods like pine burn quickly, so if a fire needs to be burning all day and it is being fueled with pine, you'll have to add fuel much more frequently than you would to an appliance fueled with longer-burning hardwood species.

Softwoods also contain a lot of resinous sap. Conventional stoves burn wood in an oxygen-starved environment, and those resins often don't completely burn under such conditions. Indeed, such an environment results in incomplete combustion of any wood. Resinous softwoods contribute greatly to the accumulation of unburned residue (creosote) inside a stove and chimney. To put it plainly, softwoods draw attention to the deficiencies of the woodstove itself. An appliance that burns wood correctly can burn any dry wood without creating a creosote-accumulation problem.

Masonry heaters burn wood correctly. Correctly burning wood simply means the firing process is given enough air for complete combustion. In addition, the masonry heater firebox design facilitates high temperatures—the other requisite of complete combustion. Masonry heaters burn everything combustible in wood. Pitch, sap, and other oils in softwoods are just more fuel for a masonry heater. The masonry heater does not need constant stoking to heat a living space all day, so it doesn't matter if pine or some other wood burns quickly. The heat still accumulates in the heater and is later released into the home.

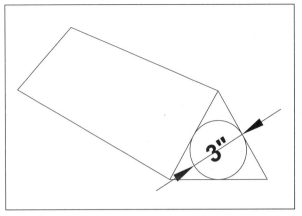

FIGURE 10.6. A good rule of thumb for judging if a piece of split wood is the proper size is to see if a 3-inch-diameter circle will fit inside the triangular cross section. If a larger circle would fit, that piece may be worth splitting once more.

The appropriate, quality fuel for a masonry heater is simply any dry cordwood split to 3 or 4 inches in diameter, or limbs and branches of the right length and smaller than 3 or 4 inches in diameter. When contemplating split wood that might have a triangular cross section, think about whether a 3-inch-diameter circle would touch the three sides of that triangle. If it wouldn't, you may need to split the piece of wood once more (see figure 10.6). My personal rule of thumb is that if I'm unsure if it is small enough, I split it again. The species of wood just does not matter. The more important consideration for firewood is its seasoning.

Firewood Seasoning

If there is one part of this book that must be read by every person who burns wood, it is this one. Nearly 100 percent of all new masonry heater owners who think their investment may have been a poor one have tried to operate their high-performance masonry heater using low-octane fuel; in other words, they used wood that was not properly seasoned and contained a lot of water. Almost every "problem" that customers have with a masonry heater has little to do with the design or construction of the heater and mostly has to do with not having seasoned wood. The comparison to gasoline is very apropos. If the fuel tank of a car accumulates even a relatively small amount of water, the engine will sputter, hesitate, and perhaps not even run. In short, the car will not perform as designed. The same can be said of a masonry heater.

Water does not burn. This statement is so ridiculously obvious, yet every year tons of wood is fed to all manner of wood-burning devices when it is freshly cut, or nearly so. Using wet wood is the equivalent of burning well-dried wood but spraying water on the fire at frequent intervals. It is difficult to get heat out of a wood fire if it is continuously doused with water.

Trees, like all plants, contain vast amounts of water. Many have heard the statement that human beings are 95 percent water. Well, trees are thought to be about 50 percent water. At harvest, freshly felled hardwoods hold approximately 60 percent of their dry weight in water. Softwoods can contain more than 120 percent of their dry weight in water. I hope the case has been made: Wood contains a lot of water that will not burn.

To make wood suitable for any wood-burning appliance, it must be seasoned. The word *seasoned* derives specifically from the idea that cut and split wood must dry over many seasons before it will be suitable fuel. The question becomes, "How many seasons and under what conditions?" Or, more simply, "How is firewood dried?"

Wood Moisture

There are two types of moisture in wood. There is "free" moisture and there is chemically bound moisture. As the term implies, free moisture is simply water within the various capillaries of the wood. Like water spilled on the floor, free moisture in a log simply needs to evaporate—most conveniently by making its way by capillary action to the ends of the log where it will meet the open air, which whisks it away.

Chemically bound moisture, on the other hand, is part of the structure of the wood itself. This moisture, again as the name implies, is *bound* to the molecules of the other constituents of the material. The drying process for water so enslaved is more time consuming.

The water must first, of course, be liberated—freed—so that it, too, can make the trip out of the log and into the air. A visitor to the county jail can simply walk down the hall and out the door into the bright sunshine. A prisoner, bound to his cell by bars and a court sentence, requires more time and additional mechanisms before he will be able to walk out the door to freedom. In other words, it takes more energy and time to remove chemically bound moisture.

Water Liberation

The two mechanisms most advantageous for drying wood—freeing all moisture and letting it evaporate—are air movement and warm temperatures. Air movement alone will not necessarily dry wood quickly, and neither will warm temperatures alone. For example, wet wood exposed to wind on a freezing-cold day will dry much slower than the same wood exposed to wind on a warm day. And wood exposed to hot temperatures when there is little air movement will not dry as fast as wood exposed to high temperatures and wind. Both warm temperatures and good air movement are necessary for rapid wood drying.

This should help to explain why it takes many seasons for wood to dry. Depending on the geographic location, every season is different, and only a relatively small fraction of a given calendar year of seasons provides the ideal conditions for drying wood. Some locations will have very humid, nearly windless summers, which slow the drying time. Others, especially more northern climates, where masonry heaters are much more prevalent, have very short summers and long, cold winters. There are no places in North America where ideal wood-drying conditions persist throughout the year. This is why it is necessary to have most wood dry for close to two years—eight seasons—before it will be ready as fuel.

The key to good firewood seasoning is good cover *and* good ventilation over a two-year period. Out in the country you will sometimes see wood stacked on the ground between trees out in the open. This makes for great ventilation, but not good cover. A stack of wood that is not covered on top will continue to be

FIGURE 10.7. A combination tile-and-stucco masonry heater occupies one whole wall of this room. Organic, curved shapes and multiple layers provide maximum surface area for heat radiation. Note the wood storage on the left and plentiful seating on the wooden bench. Photo courtesy of Biofire, Inc.

wet and will frequently grow mosses, molds, and even mushrooms. Rain and melting snow penetrate into the center of the stack and keep it continually moist. This does not produce good fuel for any fireplace. In fact, storing wood for two years under these conditions will likely produce firewood that is spongy and nearly impossible to burn.

Likewise, some people will store wood in a closed garage or shed. This is excellent cover, but poor ventilation. The wood is always protected from precipitation, yet there is little opportunity for the excess moisture to escape the confines of the enclosure. Once again the result is often improperly seasoned firewood. Wood

stored in a closed shed or garage will take much longer to dry.

Additionally, storing green (freshly cut) wood indoors can invite other unattractive problems. It is truly incredible how much moisture is present in new wood. In an indoor, warm environment, like an attached heated garage, the humidity level can increase dramatically in a short period of time. Having nowhere else to go (if the building is not ventilated), the moisture can condense on walls, windows, cars, and anything else present. This can lead to oxidation of metals and mold and mildew growth on wood, drywall, and other surfaces. In short order many things can be thus ruined. To make matters worse, the high moisture environment attracts every manner of insect; insects will thrive in the wood, the walls, and throughout the area. Eventually, these bugs are brought into the home with the firewood. This is how the idea was formed that wood burning involves a lot of mess and bugs; spongy, insect-infested wood is always wood that has not been properly stored.

Proper Wood Storage

There are many ways of stacking and storing wood. Some are permanent constructions and some are built from the firewood itself. There is no "right" firewood-seasoning venue other than following the rules of allowing air circulation and exposure to warmth when possible. Here are several viable ways of storing sun batteries in a backyard.

The Low-Cost Way

Proper wood storage can be very simple and without expense. A good starter wood-storage method begins with obtaining some good pallets from a local business that may be happy to have them hauled away. These are situated one-after-the-other in a row on the ground as a "floor." Since a cord of wood is 4 feet wide and 8 feet long by 4 feet high (4' × 4' × 8') and a typical pallet is close to 4 feet square, every two pallets can represent a cord of wood if stacked 4 feet high with firewood. It's also a good idea to put some bricks or concrete blocks under the corners and center of each pallet to elevate both pallet and wood off the ground. This way, the pallets will not rot or sink into the earth. The pallets themselves, owing to their method of construction, will permit air circulation underneath all the wood that is stacked on them, further aiding the drying process.

The wood is then stacked crisscross- or log-cabin-style, leaving a little space between the pieces (see figure 10.8). Presumably, if you have a single cord of wood, you'll use just two pallets; for 2 cords, four pallets are used, and so on. It's generally easiest to work from one

FIGURE 10.8. Firewood stacked in a crisscross or log-cabin style. One row is turned perpendicular to the next, making a stable stack.

end, stacking roughly a third of a pallet at a time so that it is never necessary to reach over a tall stack of wood to fill out a pallet. The log-cabin style of stacking makes each stack on a pallet stable, if you take care that it is not leaning substantially one way or another. In this way, no additional construction is necessary to secure and hold the wood in place. As the last of the wood is placed, you can look over the whole stack and add the last amount of wood strategically to make sure all the stacks are the same height.

Those who are detail-oriented may want to attempt to make one whole edge of the resulting rectangular solid of stacked wood higher than the opposite end. This will aid in draining water off the mass of wood once a cover has been placed. Simple covers for wood stacked in this manner can be plastic tarps over plywood or old pieces of corrugated metal roofing. Anything that will shed water can be used as a "roof" over the wood. The point is to cover the entire top of the stacks of wood but leave all the sides open. The 4-foot-tall stacks of wood will get wet on the sides from driving rains, but such water will not penetrate the stacks deeply enough to be a concern. The "roof" can be held in place with bricks or other heavy materials, or it can be strapped down with rope or bungee cords. Otherwise, strong winds will blow it off the wood pile.

The *Holzmiete*

The German word *holzmiete* translates literally as "wood clamp." Although the word *clamp* in English usually makes us think of a device for squeezing two things or surfaces tightly together, what "wood clamp" really means in this case is a structure for holding wood. So the German *holzmiete* is simply a wood holder. More specifically, it is a traditional way of storing a lot of wood in a relatively small space and in a manner in which it will still dry effectively in a two-year period. The structure is essentially a short silo of wood as opposed to the rectangular block described in the previous section. It can be fun and challenging to build and is easiest to do with several people working on it together.

The first consideration when building a *holzmiete* is knowing how much wood you have. A good, stable *holzmiete* should be at least 2 to 3 yards in diameter to be stable and well constructed. Such a structure, if built 3 yards tall, which is not uncommon, will hold close to 4 cords of wood. Thus a structure like this will hold a lot of wood in a relatively small area.

Throughout the following instructions, plan to continuously set aside in a separate pile any large pieces of bark or pieces of firewood with bark still adhering. You'll use them at the very end of the construction:

Find a flat, well-drained area that will accommodate the *holzmiete* size desired. Begin by nailing a stake or peg in the center of the location and using a length of string equal to the radius of the *holzmiete*. Use the string as a guide to make a ring of wood to that desired size, laying wood pieces end-to-end all the way around the circle. Preferably, this ring of logs is made with pieces of small-diameter wood, perhaps 3 inches. Then you can remove the string and stake, as they will no longer be needed.

Next, place pieces of wood perpendicular to and on top of the first ring so that they create a circle of logs leaning lengthwise in toward the center of the circle. (In other words, a marble laid on the high side of one of these logs should roll down the log toward the center of the circle.) Only one end of these pieces should be on top of the initial ring. The other end rests on the ground. (Note that this structure could also be built on a foundation of pallets.)

From here, you begin merely placing more wood on top of this leaning ring. Care must be taken to fit pieces together well enough that they do not become unstable, yet remain loose enough that there is some room for air circulation. It will not be long before you'll have to fill in the space inside this big circle lest pieces slide off their neighbors into the center.

The center area is filled by placing logs vertically against one another and against the outer ring of wood. This part of the construction is where help is most needed: One person stands inside the ring placing wood, while one or more stand outside feeding in the wood. Some builders of *holzmiete* are not so fussy and just toss wood into the center area and let it fall where it may.

The construction method continues until the outer ring is built and the insides are filled. As it becomes clear that the firewood supply for construction is dwindling, it is time to begin transitioning toward completion. To do this, the construction of the outer ring ceases and wood gets piled up in the center so that it is taller than the height of the outside "wall." Some effort should be made to make a uniform slope, so that it looks like the conical roof of a yurt.

The very top layers of this "roof" will be made with the saved pieces of wood with bark still attached, as well as with loose bark by itself, forming a natural shake roof to shed water from the construction. Start at the "eave" of the *holzmiete,* just as when roofing a house. Bark and wood are overlapped both around the perimeter and eave to the ridge. Envision the path of a stream of water and attempt to assure that said stream will always make it from the ridge of the cone all the way to the "eave" without penetrating the center mass of firewood. In this way a water-impervious structure

FIGURE 10.9. The *holzmiete* is a creative way to store and season firewood. Photo courtesy of www.holzmiete.de.

is completed entirely with the firewood itself (see figure 10.9).

Of course, it is also possible to cover the top with tarps, plywood, metal roofing, or any other water-shedding material. The original and traditional method uses only the bark and bark-covered wood as protection. The idea is to maintain air space that will allow moisture to be wicked out of the *holzmiete*. Theoretically, the outer ring of wood will naturally give up its moisture to the outside air. The inner wood, standing vertically, will presumably foster vertical movement of air through its mass, helping it to dry. Tarps or other impermeable roofs will inhibit this action, though metal roofing or wooden boards would still allow such air movement.

The resulting structure looks like a wooden hut or yurt and houses a great quantity of wood in a small space. The "walls" often slope slightly in toward the center as a result of the way firewood was sloped from the very beginning. Some people, however, build the walls vertically.

For those with a couple of years' supply of wood, several such structures can be built one next to the other. There have been claims made that the *holzmiete* will

dry wood faster than more conventional methods—like stacking the wood on pallets—but even Germans who use the *holzmiete* say that you should store wood like this for about two years before using it.

The Permanent Woodshed

For a total firewood connoisseur, consider a firewood shed with a permanent, wide, overhanging roof, and an elevated, ventilated floor. Walls can be nonexistent or mostly open to again allow the drying breezes to pass. This type of shelter can be well worth the effort to build because the covers over less permanent wood storage can become an obstacle when they become snow-covered or when strong winds blow. If the stack of wood itself is what supports the protective weather cover, then as firewood is used, the support for the roof becomes uneven or unstable. The result can be snow-covered wood at the time of year when dry wood is needed most. Investing in a building devoted specifically to firewood creates a lifetime of simplified wood storage.

There are many possible structures that can be used or converted to use for this purpose. A simple large shed with a footprint of about 12 feet by 16 feet and having an 8-foot ceiling height can house 8 cords of wood and still have a walkway/air corridor down the middle. By keeping soffits and over-hangs uncovered, or making walls with wooden slats rather than complete siding, good air circulation is achieved. Once again, pallets on the floor promote air circulation under the stacked wood, promoting the best drying conditions. Some rural masonry heater owners use retired corn cribs and airy barns to store and season their firewood.

One simple design promoted by the Washington State University Department of Ecology is shown in figures 10.11 and 10.12. This simple structure can be built in a weekend, yet will provide many years of abundant protection for firewood. The best strategy to use in conjunction with this design is to make sure the large opening is facing away from the prevailing winds, and, once again, use pallets or some treated wooden members on the floor to elevate the wood off the ground.

FIGURE 10.10. A well-built, roofed wood shelter. This shelter has solid sides on all but one side, other shelters use latticework so more wood is exposed to the drying effects of the wind.

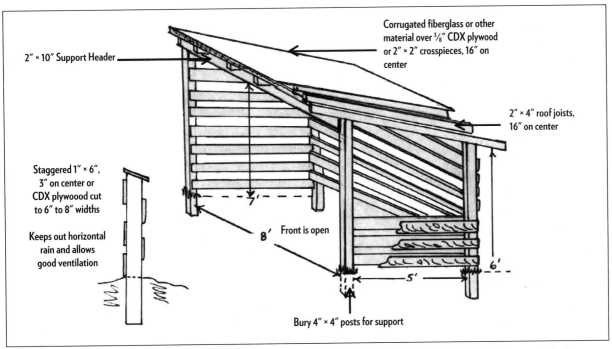

2" × 10" Support Header

Corrugated fiberglass or other material over ⅜" CDX plywood or 2" × 2" crosspieces, 16" on center

2" × 4" roof joists, 16" on center

Staggered 1" × 6", 3" on center or CDX plywoood cut to 6" to 8" widths

Keeps out horizontal rain and allows good ventilation

7'

8'

Front is open

6'

5'

Bury 4" × 4" posts for support

FIGURE 10.11. A simple, easy-to-build wood-storage shelter. Design by Washington State University Department of Ecology.

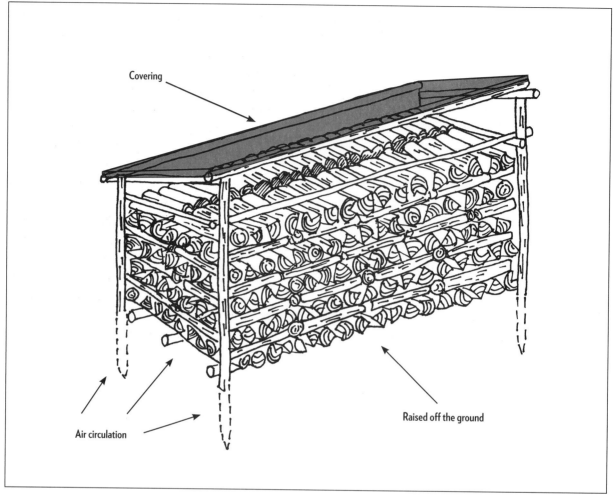

Covering

Air circulation

Raised off the ground

FIGURE 10.12. Note that wood is supported off the ground to keep it as dry as possible. Design by Washington State University Department of Ecology.

Sparks of Insight

There is no substitute for properly dried wood for a masonry heater. I cannot stress enough that this is the single most important aspect of properly operating a heater. The best way to make sure plenty of dry wood is available is to begin by securing at least a two-year supply from the outset and planning always to maintain that cushion of extra wood. It is common, however, for owners to encounter times when they run out of wood for a variety of reasons. If the masonry heater is the sole source of heat for a living space, this is a huge dilemma. Somehow, quality

wood must be obtained in short order. This may be harder than it seems.

Be cautious about simply opening the phone book or responding to ads to find "seasoned" firewood. Remember that the word *seasoned* means the wood has been cut and stored for, it is hoped, more than one season (say, summer and fall). The word *seasoned* in no way assures anyone that the wood has been stored properly under cover for more than a year. To some dealers, seasoned can mean the wood was cut and thrown in a pile for a few months. The wood at the inside base of that pile can literally be sitting in puddles of water for the duration of that "seasoning." The vendor may be entirely honest in his statements that he is selling "seasoned" wood, based on his understanding of the term, but that does not guarantee that the wood is dry at all.

Ask at least the following questions:

- How long has the wood been stored?
- Has the wood been stacked neatly for drying?
- Has the wood been covered during the whole seasoning period?
- How small has the wood been split?
- What length are the wood pieces? (Will they fit my firebox?)

By asking these five simple questions, you can determine immediately how well prepared this wood really is. If it has been stored for less than a year, uncovered, in a random pile and many logs have been split only in half, you can safely assume the wood won't be ready for use in a masonry heater for as long as two years. If you need wood immediately, find another source. There is no magic solution to this quest.

Finally, a last tip that is good for all wood burning is that properly seasoned wood will be at its absolute best if you bring it into your home at least a few hours before you actually burn it. Residual surface moisture on the wood, from humid weather conditions, will evaporate in that period of time within the drier confines of the home. In addition, the wood will be warmed to room temperature, thus jump-starting the heating process of the actual fire. No energy will be consumed in the firebox to warm the wood by, perhaps, 70°F. This last detail makes good wood superb and promises a warm masonry heater with which to snuggle on those terribly cold winter nights.

THE JOHN HENRY OF MASONRY HEATERS

Lindsay and Kathy Graham live, as Lindsay puts it, "in God's country," on a narrow farm lane in northwest Ohio. Lindsay, a jack-of-all-trades, builds custom furniture using great slabs of wood with live edges or with book-matched pairs. He also raises grass-fed beef cattle and free-range chickens when he's not helping people with alternative healing techniques. Kathy is a registered nurse and runs a kidney dialysis unit at a local medical center. Their home is a recycled barn with all the beams and joists exposed, wide plank floors, barn siding for walls, and stucco here and there. Right next to the stairway, close to the kitchen, sits a massive limestone masonry heater with heated benches on the front and one side, a baking oven, and a large glass double door.

Kathy and Lindsay have lived with their masonry heater for about seven years now, but they are not new to heating with wood. Prior to installing the masonry heater, their home was heated with a wood-fired boiler. Lindsay remembers that what he did like about that boiler was that it wasn't picky about wood size; he could "chuck just about any piece of a tree into that thing." They also occasionally used an antique wood-fired cast-iron stove, though that was mainly a novelty item. (It did save their behinds one Thanksgiving when the electric range died and they needed a way to cook the turkey!)

Lindsay likes the masonry heater, though, because

FIGURE 10.13. Lindsay Graham and his son Zach veneered this heater with local limestone and sandstone. It's now the primary heat source for the Graham household. This heater is also pictured in figure 6.35.

it provides what no other heating system does. "Its big advantage is that it is a concentrated source of heat. It's a place that I can go and sit against after going out in the cold to do chores," says Lindsay. He first heard of masonry heaters in the late 1980s, but he didn't really understand what they did until I demonstrated the one in my house. He was impressed by the fact that it was giving off so much heat though it had no fire in it. He also liked the fact that it was an "electricity-proof" way to heat. While his wood-fired boiler needed electricity to pump water through the house, the masonry heater is completely self-sufficient and off the grid.

Lindsay chuckles in a way that makes anyone laugh, and he does so when he describes the laborious wood-processing procedure he went through for the first few years of masonry heater ownership. "It's what you might call 'recreational wood-moving,'" he says with a smile. "I'd split it and stack it in the yard under metal roofing. Then, after it had sat for months like that, I'd move it again into the permanently roofed woodshed. Then, of course, from there, I'd move it a third time into the house to burn it. A guy has to be nuts!"

For all his work, he found that the wood was still not dry, even after a year of enduring his process. Now he splits it and stacks it once outside under sheet-metal coverings.

What is making the real difference in drying, he says, is that he no longer stacks 4-foot-wide piles. He makes all his stacks narrower so that they get maximum exposure to the drying effects of wind. In his older method, the wood that was stuck in the middle of a 4-foot-wide stack just never dried right.

"Another thing," Lindsay adds. "People think those hydraulic wood splitters are a time saver. I know for a fact that they aren't. I can split my wood by hand with a maul much faster than that machine can. By the time you wait for the hydraulic splitter to reset its stroke from one pass, I've already split a couple more pieces." He owned a splitter for several years and found that storing it, moving it around, and using it were more of a problem than it was worth. So he sold it "for $50 more than I paid for it," he laughs.

"People need to know that a masonry heater is a commitment," Lindsay adds. This John Henry of the twenty-first century is not deterred by the effort required. He already has wood split at least a year in advance and works on it a little at a time all through the cooler seasons. Much of the fuel comes from 3 acres of his wooded land. He and Kathy appreciate knowing that they are not dependent on anyone for energy and they always have a warm spot in the house no matter what it does outside.

FIGURE 11.1. A brick heater, oven, and cookstove combination in the heart of the home. The cooker has its own metal oven while the masonry heater has a black oven. In this photo flames from the fire in the main firebox can be seen in the oven. Notice the granite oven shelf and backsplash on the heater side to protect the brick from cooktop splatters. Photo courtesy of Maine Wood Heat Company.

CHAPTER ELEVEN

Using a Masonry Heater, Bakeoven, and Cookstove

For people who've never lived with a masonry heater but have only heard great things about them, there is a great deal of excitement about this particular part of a new house or room addition. Sometimes the heater mason is treated like a king (to the dismay of other workers on the site) because he is bringing something so unique, so revolutionary, and so special into the mix. He or she gets wined and dined, treated with kid gloves, and spoken to with something near reverence. This does not happen all the time. For some homeowners, however, the masonry heater is the crown jewel of the home, and they can't wait to see it built.

Once it is built, the anticipation hits an all-time high. The homeowner was part of the design process. Maybe the house plans were altered or adjusted to make the masonry heater fill a space in just the right way. Maybe some amenities of the proposed house were eliminated to accommodate the masonry heater. The owner has heard about the pleasure of radiant heat but not yet experienced it fully. In truth, the convoluted flue path of the heater still amazes, and maybe even concerns the homeowner. *Will it actually work? Will the smoke actually make it to the chimney instead of coming into the house? What will this heater really feel like? Is it really as good as we've heard?* Many a new masonry heater owner has said, "I can't wait for cold weather so I can finally use this thing!"

Using a Masonry Heater

Eventually, the weather does turn colder and the opportunity presents itself. So here it is, something that isn't quite a fireplace and isn't quite a woodstove. How in the world does it work? How does the wood get loaded? How do you start the fire? How do you know how much air it needs? The questions can be numerous and each one answered, like the Hydra's decapitation, spawns two more in its place. Fortunately, a masonry heater is quite easy to use. Homeowners quickly find that a masonry heater is really the lazy man's way to heat with wood.

The Break-In Period

Perhaps the most critical point in the long life of a masonry heater is its infancy. Like a newborn baby, it is wet behind the ears in the most literal way. A freshly completed masonry heater may actually contain gallons of water in all its mass. The mason may have soaked firebricks to improve mortar bonding as he proceeded. Clay mortars hold an immense amount of water, and even common mortar, if used on the exterior, contains a great deal of moisture. When a masonry heater is new, it is wet.

All of this moisture *must* be carefully driven out of the masonry heater. Wood ignites at 572°F, more than twice the boiling point of water. Dry wood burning in the firebox of a masonry heater will rapidly escalate in temperature, reaching six or more times the boiling point of water. If any significant amount of water remains in the mass of the masonry when temperatures rapidly climb, it will be turned to steam. Water molecules, when heated rapidly, start moving violently and take up more and more space as the moisture turns from liquid to gas. Needing more and more space, the hot water molecules will create space where there was none. In other words, moisture trapped in masonry, then heated to steam, will crack the masonry as easily as I can break a toothpick. The sound is a sickening *pop,* or perhaps a *thud* that reminds you of hearing, in the distance, the screech of tires, then a quick crash when two cars hit each other. Without even seeing it, you know that damage has been done.

TWO DAMPERS?

One proud new owner found that he did not have draft despite otherwise perfect conditions. When it became obvious that *something* had to be wrong with the chimney, but he could see nothing by looking into it from above, he decided to lower a brick down the flue to verify that it was clear. It was not! He discovered that the mason who had built the chimney had left the chimney damper closed during his chimney work. Apparently he was a little careless with mortar, which fell down the flue and landed on the damper. The damper—in this case a guillotine-like plate of steel—operated by simply pushing it in to close it across the opening or pulling it out to open the flue (see figure 7.12). Enough mortar accumulated on the damper and splashed up on the flue tiles that when it cured, it became a thin "damper" of mortar. The owner could open the metal damper, and the mortar "damper" stayed in place just above it. Fortunately, this capable homeowner was able to use that brick-on-a-rope as a battering ram to knock the mortar out of the flue. After that, he had good draft.

The first step to drying the heater is simply to let it rest. All openings, doors, or accesses should be left open. This includes loading doors, bakeoven doors, soot (cleanout) doors or plugs, air-supply dampers or controls, chimney dampers, and ash box doors. If it would help to expose the inside of the heater to circulating air, it should be opened. Not all masonry heaters have all of the items listed. Some will just have a loading door, air inlet, and a few cleanout openings. The point is to provide every means for moisture to passively wick out of the masonry. Preferably, this resting period lasts two or three weeks. If it was a professional heater mason who installed the heater, you should carefully follow whatever instructions he or she provided, though it's hard to go wrong with the gentle approach outlined here.

This desiccation period can be augmented by the use of small electric heaters or even lights. The tiny, 1,500-watt electric room heaters work well, either the passive radiant type or the kind with blowers. High-intensity work lights or even the common "trouble" lights can be positioned shining on or into flues and fireboxes. Any low-level source of heat like this will effectively evaporate a lot of moisture from the heater, though by no means is this a requirement.

After the resting period of two to three weeks (or as per the builder's directions), the next step is to begin having small fires in the heater. It is easy to get impatient at this point. After all, the heater *looks* good, and it *looks* dry. The temptation can be great to fill the firebox with an armload of firewood and finally get down to business. You must summon your last reserves of forbearance, however, because it only takes a little bit of water to do a whole lot of damage. A vast amount of water has been dissipated by the resting period and electric heaters, if used. Chances are good to excellent, however, that some pockets of moisture remain. They will be driven out by these undersized fires.

Draft Check

Before you light a match, it's wise to verify that there is actually chimney draft suitable to carry the exhaust up the chimney. There is no joy in lighting the first fire in a masonry heater only to have it puff smoke back out the door! Even if the chimney is tall, it's properly placed centrally in the house, and all the other "chimney rules" are followed, there may be unexpected conditions. See the sidebar for an example of such a surprise.

Initially, you check for draft with a match or lighter. Open the chimney damper (if equipped) and the air-supply vent, air-supply door, or slides. A lit match or lighter flame held close to the air inlet should noticeably get pulled into or toward the heater. This is

FIGURE 11.2. Dry-stacked stone contrasts with vertical lines in a heater featuring heated seating and a bakeoven. Heater designed and built by Stovemaster; photo courtesy of Alex Chernov.

FIGURE 11.3. Notice how the flame of the candle is pulled horizontally into the heater—a sure sign of good positive draft. It's wise to do this test before lighting a large load of wood.

what you want; it means there is positive draft. If the flame does not get pulled toward the heater, there is extremely weak or nonexistent draft. If, instead, the flame is pushed *out* away from the heater, there is a backdraft, and successfully starting a fire will be almost impossible.

In the first of these possibilities, draft exists, and it is definitely okay to proceed with a fire. In the second case, there apparently is no draft, but there is good likelihood that draft can be established. The heater (and probably the chimney, too) is, after all, still cold and wet inside—conditions not conducive to encouraging stack effect. In heaters equipped with a gas slot or a bypass damper, it's likely that draft will be easily established. A bypass damper is a mechanical control that circumvents the long flue path of the masonry heater and directs exhaust immediately to the chimney. A good way to proceed is to burn five or six crumpled pieces of newspaper in the firebox with chimney and bypass dampers (if so equipped) and air intakes open, and the fuel-loading door closed. The paper should burn briskly with tall flames. After this burn, perform the match flame test immediately; it should now show the requisite draft. Repeat if necessary until it is clear there is chimney draft.

In heaters without a gas slot or bypass, one strategy is to remove the soot cleanout plug or door at the base of the chimney and burn the crumpled newspaper there. Again, if the chimney is equipped with a damper of some kind, it must be in the open position. Alternatively, you can use a hair dryer to prime the chimney in lieu of the newspapers. Some homeowners use a propane torch for this purpose. Repeat this procedure as necessary to assure there is draft. Always check using the simple flame test rather than assuming draft is established.

If the initial flame test showed the flame being pushed away from the heater, there is a significant downdraft condition. Except under very peculiar weather conditions (some of these might include an outdoor temperature that's quite close to the indoor temperature, rain, or high humidity), this only happens if the "chimney rules" weren't all followed. Depending on how severe the backdraft really is, you may still be able to reverse it—especially if the reversal is minimal. First, check that no bathroom or kitchen exhaust fans are running. It is a good idea to then try a heater, blow dryer, or hot light to warm the chimney or firebox and establish a draft. Lighting even a tiny fire of newspapers when there is reversed draft is just asking for smoke in the house.

If the initial flame test drove the little flame strongly horizontally away from the heater—particularly if it did so in harmony with a strong wind outside—you have virtually no hope of establishing draft. This is likely a harbinger of future draft problems as well, and again, it's almost always related to having a chimney that is shorter than the tallest heated part of the house or a chimney that is entirely or mostly outside the house. It is possible the backdraft is caused by various exhaust devices in the house if a number of them are running during this test, so it's always worth checking those before throwing in the towel. Barring that, if a backdraft is quite strong, it's a good idea to consult a professional heater mason or chimney specialist at once.

Small Break-In Fires

Once you're certain that the masonry heater has adequate draft, it's time to proceed with small break-in

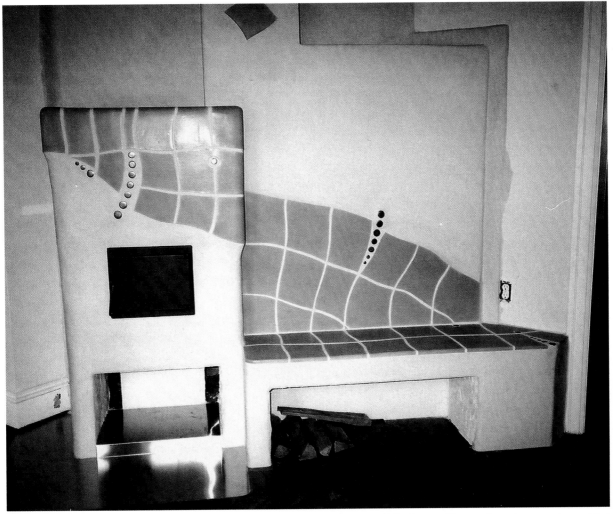

FIGURE 11.4. Handmade tiles and stucco cover the mass and firebox elements of this heater. Plenty of wood storage is provided under both the firebox and the unheated bench. Designed, built, and photographed by Ernst Kiesling, Canadian Kachelofen.

fires. A small fire mainly consists of several crumpled pieces of newspaper combined with kindling and small pieces of wood (1 to 3 inches in diameter) totaling approximately one-tenth (by weight) of the full load recommended by the builder or manufacturer. For example, if the designer of the masonry heater says a full load is 35 pounds of wood, then use no more than about 3 to 4 pounds of total kindling and dry wood. It will be best to use just kindling for these small fires since the duration of the burn will be quite short and temperatures may not rise high enough to completely consume anything approaching the size of regular cordwood. And, yes, the fact that these measurements

are given in pounds *does* mean that you should weigh the wood on a scale—at least until you can accurately estimate without one.

A good rule of thumb is to plan on having about ten small fires before fully loading the heater. Each subsequent small fire is slightly larger than the one that preceded it. Plan to increase the weight of wood used by about 5 and no more than 10 percent (of the full load weight) each time. For example, the heater that takes 35 pounds of wood will use about 3 pounds of wood the first time, about 5 pounds the next time, 7 the next, and so on. By the tenth fire, the total weight will be a significant percentage of the maximum suggested load of wood. As the fires grow in quantity of wood (by weight) and duration, the size of the pieces used can be increased as well. Once you're using more than 10 pounds of wood, it is reasonable to include more regular cordwood and less kindling and scraps.

An important part of this slow break-in period is to leave the air-supply inlet (and the chimney damper, if so equipped) open continuously even after the fire is out. The idea is to slowly warm the mass and make use of continuous draft conditions to carry moisture out of the system. If you closed the heater after every one of these fires, the moisture liberated by warmth would remain in the heater, defeating the purpose of this process. An open air supply and open chimney ensures that excess moisture is carried up and out of the system.

Also, these small fires should have a resting time of at least eight hours; preferably there should be twelve hours between them. Fires spaced too close to each other in time will result in heating the mass too quickly. Providing half a day of rest between fires allows the heat of the fire and the continuous draft to slowly warm every part of the inner life of the heater. This timing tends to work well with most people's schedules anyway. Light a small fire in the morning before you go off to work and another in the evening after work.

Finally, it is wise to briefly look over the heater's exterior and firebox prior to each little fire. If there is evidence of a lot of moisture or condensation at any time—especially *inside* the heater—it is best to miss a fire and let the heater rest another eight or more hours. This is a good opportunity to substitute the gentle heat of an electric heater or lamp to evaporate that excess water, yet still introduce some heat into the process. When water is visible, there is no reason to risk turning water to steam and forfeiting all the progress to that point. Like the tortoise racing the hare, slow and steady wins the race.

New owners may open their loading door to look inside and see a white, crystalline "growth" on the surface of the firebox. Some take one look at this fuzzy white stuff and think there is mold growing on the firebricks. Indeed, it does look, at first glance, like

FIGURE 11.5. It may look like mold, but it's just a structure of minerals, called efflorescence, "growing" on the bricks as they dry. Photo courtesy of Charles Buell Inspections, Inc.

white mold, but it is more like a powder than a living growth. There is no need for alarm: the white material is simply efflorescence. This is a deposit of minerals on the surface of the bricks that occurs as they and the cement dry. It happens as the water, laden with salts, wicks to the surface and dries; the mineral salts are left on the surface of the bricks. Figure 11.5 is a close-up of crystalline mineral buildup on masonry. If the mason soaked the firebricks in water before setting them, there may have been salts in the soak water that then appear later as efflorescence. Other minerals may have been in the mortar or clay that was used. The appearance of the efflorescence is in no way a sign of poor installation or that proper mortar bonding did not occur. It is simply a benign deposit of mineral salts. No action needs to be taken, though the efflorescence can simply be wiped away.

Otherwise, by the time you've lit your tenth fire and are using a good percentage of the maximum load of wood, you will in all likelihood feel some heat on the exterior surface of the heater. This may be barely perceptible on some heaters; others might be noticeably warm. An easy check is to place a hand palm-down on a table or other furniture near the heater, then immediately move the same palm to the masonry heater. If you can detect more warmth on the heater, it's getting warm. If it's not, make a few more incrementally larger

UNDERFIRE/OVERFIRE AIR?

Underfire air and *overfire air* refer to the way combustion air is fed to the fire of a masonry heater in the firebox. Underfire air comes into the burning fuel from underneath, usually through a grate in the floor of the firebox. Overfire air feeds the fire from somewhere above the coal bed of the fire (above the firebox floor).

Overfire air can take many forms. In many cases, the air is brought into the firebox along the front (the side with the door) and may even wash over the door glass before being pulled into the combustion process. Other systems will have numerous outlets along all the walls of the firebox to provide air from virtually every part of the wall (see figure 11.6). The idea is always to send just enough air to the combustion process, and to do so in such a way that every part of the fire gets its share of oxygen. Repeated investigations have shown that overfire air supplies reliably result in cleaner, more complete combustion than underfire air.

FIGURE 11.6. A good example of a firebox with provision for air supplied to the fire at all levels. What look like columns of the letter *A* are holes every couple of inches up the height of the firebox walls. Also, the corrugated nature of the wall means that fuel falling against it will not restrict the air supply. Project by New England Hearth and Soapstone.

fires. When you've used the small break-in fires religiously and you feel some warmth, it's time to move on to a full-scale fire.

A Real Fire at Last

When a masonry heater has been gently warmed day after day until it's finally warm, it is also dry. A properly designed and constructed masonry heater is supposed to evenly warm the vertical surfaces of the heater. If these surfaces are only mildly warm, the interior is much warmer. Just as the human body has a core temperature of 98.6°F while outer skin temperatures are 10° to 15° cooler, the masonry heater will always be warmer inside than out. If the outside of the heater has gotten dry enough to feel warm, the inner life has likewise dried sufficiently. At last, it is time for a real fire.

By the time you reach this stage, you're quite accustomed to the procedure for operating the heater. Air supply, dampers, doors, and so on have been used

repeatedly. Kindling or fire starters and firewood have been weighed, placed, and lit. The procedure for a full-sized fire is really no different than with all the break-in fires except that now the quantity of actual cordwood is at its maximum.

There are some people who literally have no experience with building fires. What must be emphasized with a masonry heater is that, in order to achieve high combustion temperatures, there must be some space between pieces of wood. The idea is to make sure each burning piece of firewood can get enough air for vigorous burning. Those with little experience may be inclined to simply place pieces of wood randomly one atop the next and side by side with no air space at all. You can get away with this with a really hot heater, but it isn't a good idea for one that's barely warm.

The first step before any fire is laid is to verify that the chimney damper (if equipped) is open, as is any air supply. Note that some contraflow heater designs

FIGURE 11.7. A firewood load built in the "crib" style. Notice that paper is on top for starting a "top-down" fire.

in particular may have two different air-supply locations. If the heater is equipped with a metal grate in the firebox floor, there is a good chance it was designed to have an air intake below the level of the firebox providing air that travels through the grate and under the fire. This is called underfire air. The same heater may have air intake at about the level of the firebox floor through air slides in the door itself.

Most other heaters will have only one air intake. This may be located at firebox level, but it actually feeds air to the fire at or slightly above firebox-floor level—though some advanced designs feed the air to the fire through passages in the firebox walls. Combustion air supplied to the fire at or above firebox level is called overfire air. Again, overfire air intake may be through slides or an opening at the bottom of the loading door, or possibly through a computer-controlled vent designed to precisely gauge the correct amount of air the fire needs throughout the burn. Unless the builder, designer, or manufacturer specified otherwise, simply opening the air-vent slides should be all that is necessary. Once these settings are made, it is time to load the fuel.

The Basic Crib Fire

As with break-in fires, you should use a scale to weigh the quantity of wood to be placed in the masonry heater. The easiest way to do this is to weigh yourself on a bathroom scale without and with an armload of wood. The difference between the two weights is the weight of the firewood. It is wise to make note of how many pieces of cordwood you need to have the right amount of wood. For example, if the masonry heater requires 35 pounds of wood and ten pieces of wood weigh 35 pounds, you can simply gather ten pieces of wood every time a full load is to be burned (assuming that, overall, the firewood is uniformly split). Using the scale several times at first is a good idea to verify that the firewood is, indeed, uniform.

The most basic way to start an effective, hot fire in a masonry heater is to crumple half a dozen sheets of newspaper on the floor of the firebox. On the paper, place very dry kindling wood—pieces no larger than your little finger. Avoid scrimping on the kindling. Half a dozen pieces of kindling may not be enough. Use kindling such that you can't quite hold all the pieces in one hand. A few more than that can't hurt, either. This is all fuel that will heat the living space! One of the big reasons people grow to dislike wood burning is the idea that it is hard to start fires. Using plenty of good, dry kindling together with good, dry cordwood makes it very simple. It's also okay to forgo the newspaper and kindling in favor of manufactured fire starters.

On top of the kindling—or just in front of the kindling—close to the loading door, place a single piece of cordwood parallel to the front of the heater. Then place a row of cordwood pieces side by side perpendicular to and on top of the single piece in the front. There should be some space—just ½ inch is fine—between pieces. On top of that row, set another row perpendicular to the first with similar spacing. Continue this method row by row until you've loaded the entire quantity of fuel. This way of loading wood can be called "crib style," and is shown in figure 11.7.

With the wood loaded, it's often a good idea to check one more time that air supply and chimney damper (if equipped) are ready for operation. Once everything is appropriately set, light a match and ignite newspaper or fire starter. Shut the door and start enjoying a brisk, wonderful fire.

The Top-Down Crib

The construction of a "top-down" crib is primarily the same as the basic crib. The paper and kindling (or fire starter) are not placed at the base of the crib; they will be going near the top. Instead of starting with a single piece of cordwood parallel to the front of the firebox, lay a complete first row of wood at the base and then follow the same construction method as the basic crib until you've loaded all the primary wood. Then, on top of the last row of firewood, insert the kindling and paper atop the crib you've so far constructed. In this case, larger, finger-sized pieces of kindling go on top of the main fuel load, followed by small kindling pieces, then newspaper (and, perhaps, a little more kindling).

It is vital in this type of fire building to use plenty of kindling. Otherwise you may meet with aggravation when the kindling is consumed but does not ignite the main firewood load, and you have to repeat the process. Most people, again, are not interested in wood burning when it becomes difficult to start fires. With good, dry firewood, this should not happen, but it can. For this reason it's also perfectly acceptable to put some cordwood above the kindling load—particularly some smaller, very dry pieces.

The reason that this top-down method is useful and beneficial is that it alters the physics of the fire itself as it progresses from ignition to conflagration. In the basic crib fire, the initial fire progresses relatively rapidly through the entire load of wood. However, the beginning of this process creates more smoke as all the unburned wood robs heat from the fledgling fire. Temperatures haven't yet risen enough for clean combustion, so that smoke contains waste fuel that departs the system. In other words, it is not until all the wood is in flames that combustion temperature rises quickly to a clean burning level.

As the top-down fire burns, its not-yet-fully-consumed coals are the starter for the wood below. When that lower wood begins burning, its intense combustion will fully consume those coals, which in a bottom-up fire may not happen quite as well. Also, as the wood in the lower part of the crib gets heated to near ignition and begins releasing volatile gases (the smoke contains a lot of unburned hydrocarbons), that smoke is forced to rise up through the already-superheated flames above it, where those gases can be consumed rather than leave the system unburned as smoke. In this way, the top-down fire burns cleaner as it methodically moves *down* the stack of wood, igniting one layer at a time—the smoke generated being devoured by the hot combustion above it and coals being completely consumed as well.

If the builder or manufacturer of the masonry heater has given specific instruction as to how to fire the appliance, and those instructions do *not* include a top-down way of burning, it is worth finding out why. There may be good reason; perhaps the specific way the heater is designed to get air to the fire makes the top-down approach unnecessary or irrelevant. Otherwise, it is a good approach to firing a masonry heater or any other wood-burning fireplace or stove.

The Tepee Fire

Another way of building an effective fire is what is known as the tepee fire. As the name implies, the firewood is simply stood on end in the firebox in the manner of the framework of the Native American mobile home. Typically, you lean the first few pieces of wood against the back or side wall of the firebox. Add pieces leaning against the first few. Leave a space, like a tepee door, at the base of the structure. In this "door" you insert the paper and kindling or the fire starter. (Alternatively, you can place the paper and kindling first and build the tepee around them.)

The tepee fire is another clean-burning method that produces relatively little smoke. It develops heat fast as all the flames funnel together toward the top of the construction, producing a good deal of heat and burning the ingredients of the smoke. Some will find it more difficult to use the recommended full charge of wood in a tepee style since, to create stability, the cordwood pieces tend to have more space between them at the base, where they sit on the firebox floor. Some owners have found the quick development of heat from the tepee fire is an aid to establishing strong draft under poor pressure conditions.

Enjoying a Fire

No instructions are necessary for enjoying a fire. This is one of the most pleasant aspects of operating a masonry heater. Once the fire is going, the loading door is closed and the fire viewing begins. There's no need to poke or prod the fire, add more wood, change draft settings (for most heaters), or in any other way tinker with the fire. One of the greatest things about masonry heaters is that the fire is easy to start and, once it is going, it just goes and goes and goes.

An experienced owner can go to the woodshed for fuel, bring it in the house, load the wood, and start the fire in a matter of about ten minutes. If the wood is already in the house, the time can be less than five minutes. That five-minute investment will generally reward you with twelve or perhaps twenty-four hours of warmth from the heater along with about two hours of fire-viewing enjoyment. The most difficult part of the task is pulling the cork on a bottle of wine or popping the cap on a beer—maybe brewing a cup of tea or coffee. It is a good idea to at least check on the fire occasionally, just in case something unusual does happen. Since most people want to watch the fire anyway, this is no big commitment.

The fire of a masonry heater is different from most fires you've seen in a fireplace or woodstove. Most metal woodstoves are designed to operate with the fire severely damped. This means the fire primarily burns with the oxygen present in the wood itself plus a small amount from outside the firebox. The result is a lazy, slowly moving fire. On the other hand, open fireplaces (with no doors or simple, ungasketed glass doors) burn with so much excess oxygen that they are much cooler than a fire in a masonry heater. The masonry heater fire is more robust and powerful.

Some homeowners, upon their first experience with such a large, vigorous fire, are actually frightened! It is a remarkable sight to see 40 pounds of dry wood all blazing vigorously. The flames will be bright yellow—perhaps even white as the fire burns at its maximum efficiency and temperature. New users may need to check the air and damper (if equipped) settings to make sure the fire is burning optimally. The fire should always be vigorous, but certainly not out of control. An out-of-control vigorous fire may have various characteristics: It may puff loudly like a locomotive engine, or it may swirl in an uncontrolled fashion in the firebox—first coming toward the door glass, then moving away.

The large, energetic flames should move uniformly in the direction of the exit from the firebox, which may either be up, to one side, or to the back. Ideally, it is a long column of flame rather than a seemingly disorganized burn. If it's huffing and puffing or doing other strange things, it could be that it is actually getting too much air too quickly—or maybe not enough air, depending on the design of the heater. Sometimes this can be caused by wind conditions outside the house. Experiment with carefully adjusting the air supply and/or the chimney damper setting to see if you can bring the fire into a more controlled burn. In those heaters that supply both underfire and overfire air, one or the other may need more adjustment. The fire should never be severely dampened such that the flames adopt the slow-moving, lazy look that typifies a metal woodstove fire. Such a burn is inefficient; it wastes wood and produces less heat for storage in the mass of the heater.

Note that heaters carefully designed according to geographic location, chimney height and size, and heat output rarely experience these temperamental conditions because they were custom-made for the house. With flues, firebox size, air supply, and mass all specifically designed for a particular project, it is rare to encounter an uncontrolled burn—though, again, strange weather conditions could create one. Usually it is premanufactured heaters or heater cores that produce unexpected results during changing environmental conditions— these fires will need more human intervention.

The fact that the fire may, indeed, roar is not necessarily a sign that it is out of control. A hot fire needs adequate air and, again, 40 or more pounds of wood blazing all at once will produce a definitely audible roar or hum along with the more familiar crackles

FIGURE 11.8. A fire in a masonry heater is much more vigorous than that in an open fireplace or metal woodstove. This heater is also featured at the opening of part 4 and in figure 5.3.

and pops. On the other hand, with heaters that are equipped with a chimney barely meeting the chimney rules, the great roar may be much more subdued. It should still burn vigorously, but the flames may not be quite so long. Likewise, custom-calculated heaters will burn vigorously, but usually not as briskly as others.

In summary, the fire should be strong and bright. If at any time there is a question about whether it is really burning correctly, the builder or manufacturer of the heater should be willing to consult and, if possible, make an on-site call to help assess performance. Most owners quickly grow accustomed to the energy of the fire and simply become entranced while watching the flames. You get used to the air-control settings for a given amount of fuel and will automatically set them in the appropriate range. Such is the state of being in control of your own heating. You quickly learn new skills that before long become second nature.

The Shutdown Procedure

Eventually, of course, the fire burns to the point at which there are no flames. Given the large amount of fuel consumed, there is a relatively large accumulation of red-hot coals on the firebox floor. Depending on the type of masonry heater, the shutdown procedure may vary. For many heaters, it is customary at this stage to do the only "poking" that is ever done in a masonry heater. (And some heaters may not require even this intervention. Consult with the builder or manufacturer if you have any doubt.)

At this point, the air supply for underfire air should be temporarily closed. In fact, any air supply can be closed. Then the loading door should be carefully opened just a crack and held there for a count of ten. This action permits the fire to adjust to getting air from the door rather than from below. If there is still air coming through a grate below the fire, and the door is opened quickly, that action can draw exhaust gases out of the door into the room. Closing that air supply and opening the door carefully assures that the remaining coals want to draw air *in* through the door instead. The ten-second count is usually adequate, after which the door can be opened.

With the door open, the coals can be raked into a consolidated pile that will encourage their rapid final combustion. (Certainly they could be left to die without such stirring. Opening the door to stir the coals introduces room-temperature air en masse to the firebox and whole system of flues, which may be counterproductive. Consult the designer or builder of your heater for recommendations in this regard.) The point of raking the coals together is that each coal contributes heat to the others and the last remnants are completely consumed more quickly. You can also use the rake or poker to break larger coals down to the size of most others so that, again, all of them will uniformly be diminished in this last stage of the burn.

When this raking is done, close the loading door and open the underfire air (if equipped). If the masonry heater has no underfire air, then you should open whatever principal air supply it does have. In those heaters that have both underfire and overfire air intakes, only the underfire air should be open at this stage as it directs air pointedly through the coal bed. The idea here is to quickly consume the coals, drawing every last ounce of heat energy out of the remaining coals for storage in the mass. The action of raking the coals together, closing the door, and opening the air supply usually results in the coals bursting once again into a short-lived but robust fire. This time, instead of bright yellow flames, you're likely to see pale blue flames that last only for a few minutes. The blue is the combustion of carbon monoxide—produced from the incomplete combustion that occurs as the fire temperature decreases. The coals after this point will be greatly reduced in size and once again will turn deep red.

Once there is no more sign of flame, you can close the heater's chimney damper (if equipped). Most of the dangerous carbon monoxide has now been consumed or dissipated. Additionally, most dampers for masonry heaters only have 95 percent closure so that if there are any remaining gases, they can still escape up the chimney. A while later, the coals will turn mainly black and the final air supplies can be closed. The fire is finished.

For those heaters without dampers, but equipped with tight-fitting, gasketed doors, this entire process

FIGURE 11.9. Tulikivi Corporation often suggests back-to-back firings in heaters like this. Notice how soapstone goes well with other stone and the tile floor. This heater features a panorama (multisided) door, large, rock-faced "bricks" that are carefully mitered at the corners, and sandblasted carvings in the stone centered above the firebox. Photo courtesy of Tulikivi Corporation.

is usually different: you merely wait until there are no more flames; at this point you can close the air supply. There will be no more flames and no draft up the chimney. The remaining hot coals will contribute additional heat to the mass, and no excess room air is introduced into the hot inner life.

A Note About Back-to-Back Firings

Some masonry heater builders or manufacturers will provide for or even encourage a back-to-back firing method. By this it is meant that you could have the equivalent of two full-sized fires one after the other—perhaps all in one evening. The idea of the back-to-back method is that you charge the masonry heater with enough heat energy to last a longer period of time—usually twenty-four hours. Not all heaters are designed for a back-to-back burn, so it is best not to do so without consulting your builder or manufacturer. The key elements here are the abilities of the heater to both withstand the extra-high temperatures that will result from two consecutive fires and the ability of the heater to store so much heat energy in such a short period of time. There is no point in burning an immediate second fire if most of that heat cannot be stored (because the heater is "fully charged") and is just sent up the chimney.

In general, the procedure to follow is that when the first load of wood has burned to a coal bed, instead of opening the door to rake the coals you fill the firebox with a second load of wood. The door is closed, the

FIGURE 11.10. This is a masonry heater and bakeoven and cookstove—from nineteenth-century Germany! Photo courtesy of Vintage Elements, Greenwood, South Carolina.

wood quickly bursts into flames, and the firing process essentially begins all over again.

For those heaters in which succession firings are encouraged (or at least provided as an option), the point to emphasize is that every masonry heater is designed to burn a certain amount of fuel every twenty-four-hour period. Instructions for back-to-back firing are *not* license by the builder or manufacturer to burn twice as much fuel! If the heater is designed to consume 40 pounds of wood each day, then the back-to-back firing should not use more than 40 pounds of wood—perhaps 20 pounds in two loads.

Back-to-back fires can be useful and convenient. If

you know that you'll be especially busy the next day, or if you're going out of town for a twenty-four-hour period (or more), then you may want to charge the mass with as much heat as possible all at once. If you'll have no opportunity to fire the heater again before twenty-four hours is over, this can be a way to keep heat in the space.

The other side of this issue is that you'll always get more even heating of the space from a masonry heater that is fired on a shorter interval. Firing a day's worth of fuel all at once charges the mass with a tremendous amount of heat energy. Most of that heat will be released from the mass in the first twelve to sixteen hours after the burn. Although the heater will indeed still be releasing a lot of heat after twenty-four hours, it will be considerably less than what was released in the first twelve hours. In this manner, a greater temperature gradient will occur in the living space between the first twelve hours and the last few hours of the twenty-four-hour period. If you wish to use this method on a daily basis, it is probably best to have the "double burn" in the morning. This way, you enjoy maximum heat in the living space during the active time of the day; the reduced output occurs when the family is tucked warmly in bed. (Of course, this may mean the heater isn't at high output when the family gathers for breakfast, but that may not be an issue for many people.)

For heaters generally designed for maximum output with two firings per day, there is a very small difference in temperatures over the course of the day when those two fires occur about twelve hours apart. The masonry heater stays more uniform in temperature overall and, thus, so does the living space. Two fires spaced equally apart in time also keep the inner life of the heater more stable in temperature. The components aren't subjected to quite as much thermal shock since the inner bricks are regularly at a higher temperature each time a fire is built. For these reasons, I recommend that the back-to-back firing method only be used in unusual circumstances and, again, *only* if the heater is designed to be used this way.

Using a Bakeoven

Many masonry heaters in the United States have built-in baking ovens. A bakeoven in a masonry heater is an accessory or option and is not usually the principal reason for the heater's existence. The masonry heater is meant to heat living space first. Cooking food is a secondary purpose. There are those who build masonry baking ovens that are *not* masonry heaters. Certainly anyone who wants both a masonry heater for heating the space and a wood-fired bakeoven specifically for baking should consult with the heater mason, who may also be versed in bakeoven construction, to create a complex that includes all the desired elements. In this section, I'll discuss using the bakeoven accessory of a masonry heater.

In most cases, the baking chamber of a masonry heater is substantially smaller than its main firebox chamber. One of the hallmarks of a baking chamber, in particular, is that its ceiling is quite low, whereas that is rarely a description of the firebox. The low ceiling gives many people the impression that the oven is small and has limited use. In this modern age, people are accustomed to the cavernous oven chamber of the typical fossil-fuel-fired or electric oven. In such an oven, you can put several trays of food at once on the various racks. Obviously, you won't have several racks of food in an oven that is, perhaps, less than 12 inches tall at its highest point.

As with every other aspect of a masonry heater, the low ceiling of a bakeoven is entirely functional in nature and relates to the superior baking qualities of a heat-retaining baking chamber. While a conventional gas or electric oven cooks food entirely with hot air generated by the burning fuel or hot element, a brick or stone oven cooks food using all the available types of heat: the hot oven surfaces do heat the air within the oven in a manner similar to a conventional oven. Also, however, every surface of the oven chamber—walls, floor, and ceiling—is a hot *radiator,* sending direct radiant heat at the food. Food is often cooked directly on the brick or stone oven floor, exposing it to direct conducted heat as well. No other type of oven will cook food with all three methods at once the way this oven will.

The low ceiling is specifically meant to aid in evenly exposing the food to the finest high-intensity radiant heat and keeps the whole oven chamber at a very even air temperature. A higher ceiling would reduce the radiant effect and introduce temperature stratification in the oven chamber. Some masonry heater bakeovens will also have an arched ceiling. Again, this is a functional element that makes the oven ceiling simulate a parabolic reflector that constantly directs its heat at a specific point—the food on the center of the floor of the oven. Although you sacrifice the quantity of food

FIGURE 11.11. The shape of the door is often a hint as to the general size of the oven option in a masonry heater. This is the backside of the Tulikivi "boulder" heater shown in figure 9.1. The door is roughly 16 inches wide by 10 inches tall. The oven is only a little larger than this. Photo courtesy of WarmStone Fireplaces and Designs.

that can be put into a brick oven when compared with a modern conventional oven, the substantial gain in taste and quality of the cooked food is well worth the trade-off to most owners.

It's important to note that the bakeoven accessory of most masonry heaters is only usable during the heating season and principally during the coldest part of the season when the heater is always at higher levels of output. Although such an oven can be used in some ways in the early fall and late spring—as a warming oven, for example—generally it is not hot enough for serious baking until the heater itself is fired regularly with a significant quantity of wood. Obviously, the overall number of days the oven can be enjoyed each year is directly related to the number of days that the heater needs to be fired. Some ovens, as described in the next section, may be usable over a slightly longer period each year just because of the way they are fired. For most temperate zones of the United States, this still means the oven will be fully functional six months of the year or more. More northern areas of the United States and most of Canada will have about two-thirds of the year in which to bake.

A Black and White Issue

There are three types of baking ovens that are installed as accessory items in masonry heaters. Good arguments exist for or against all of them, and you'll have to decide which is best for your situation. There are white ovens, black ovens, and hybrid versions that can serve as either a white or black oven.

Black Ovens

A black oven is simply an oven that actually "sees" the fire and smoke within its confines. It's called a "black" oven for the simple fact that, like any firebox, black soot will sometimes accumulate within it. The soot doesn't generally survive long in a properly fired masonry heater, so the name is somewhat of a misnomer, but it conveys the fact that smoke, flames, and sometimes the fuel itself are present in the oven in order to warm it to baking temperatures.

A black oven on some masonry heaters is *the* primary firebox (see figure 11.12), but this is the exception rather than the rule. Most black ovens are chambers that are somewhere downstream from the actual masonry heater firebox. Many Finnish contraflow designs incorporate this feature by placing the baking oven where the upper chamber of the inner life is located. Since a secondary burning chamber is typical in this traditional design, turning it into a useful bakeoven is a common occurrence.

In the case of these Finnish designs, the flames and exhaust of the fire often enter the oven through a narrow throat somewhere in the floor of the bakeoven—often in the center. In other designs, the exhaust path may enter the oven from a side or the back and leave either through another side or out the oven ceiling. In the Finnish contraflow, the exit is usually in the oven ceiling.

Some owners object to the "hole" in the oven floor created by the throat, and others think they can just cover the throat with a baking stone—permanently! This will not work, because the throat "hole" is essential to the flow of exhaust and flames in the masonry heater. However, when there is no longer any fire in the masonry heater, an oven stone can be set in to make a complete oven floor for baking purposes. An owner

FIGURE 11.12. The baking chamber in this masonry heater is the primary firebox for warming the whole mass. A cookstove is added to the side of the bakeoven, turning this into a complete cooking complex. Photo courtesy of Tulikivi Corporation.

who decides to do this *must* remember to remove that stone before starting another fire in the firebox or be rewarded with smoke filling the house instead of going up the chimney. Otherwise, pans can be used that span the opening or, in the case of bread, loaves can be set on the oven floor next to the throat.

Another objection raised about black ovens is the ash itself. Since the fire and exhaust travel through the oven at every firing, ash will accumulate on the floor of the oven on a regular basis. In a wood-fired oven used specifically for baking, the baker normally swabs the oven floor with an oven mop before baking. This not only cleans the oven floor but also introduces *additional* moisture into the oven, which complements the baking process. Masonry heater owners would do well to imitate this behavior. For those heaters with an

open throat in the oven floor, the bulk of the ash can be swept out of the oven down that throat to the firebox below. In other designs, a special ash dump may have been provided. If not, anything but a dusting of ash will have to be scooped out before swabbing the oven floor.

Despite the level of maintenance required, the black oven has peculiar advantages: because it is directly exposed to the fire and exhaust, it generally heats quickly and achieves very high temperatures. Also, the waiting time for use of the newly introduced heat is generally pretty short. Once the fire in the masonry heater is out, usually a wait is required to allow the oven temperatures to stabilize. Immediately after the fire, some parts of the oven may be dramatically hotter than others. A waiting period of approximately an

FIGURE 11.13. Between the baking loaves of bread is the throat of this Finnish masonry heater. Project by Maren Cooke and Ken Matesz; photo by Maren Cooke.

hour allows those temperatures to become more even throughout the oven. Yet those temperatures are very high and will provide, in the hours following, the full range of baking options. You can start with pizzas or unleavened crackers with high temperatures of 600°F or more and proceed through the day with breads at 450°, pies or cookies or cake at 350°, and stews, soups, or porridge at lower temperatures.

Although some black oven chambers can serve as the place to load and burn fuel, this usually is not done since the oven is directly exposed to the flue gases anyway. For information about burning fires directly in a bakeoven chamber, see the "White/Black Hybrids" section.

White Ovens

The term *white oven* stems from the fact that it is clean or "white"; fuel, smoke, or flames never see the inside of the baking chamber. A white oven is warmed from the outside in. In most installations, the masonry heater flues are designed to, in some way, surround or contact the sides, top, and bottom of the oven. The oven floor or sides may actually be structural walls of some of these flues, or the oven may be a "box" set into or among the flues. Either way, the oven is always free of soot and ash. It is an oven more comparable in operation to a

conventional oven in that the heat source is outside the oven.

Like a conventional oven, a white oven in a masonry heater is usable anytime since there is no fire or smoke in it. However, like a black oven, it is usually only at even and predictable temperatures during the period *after* a fire has been burned rather than during a fire. You could put food in a white oven while the masonry heater is being fired, but be aware that the temperatures in the oven will likely be rising throughout that time. As with a black oven, particular sides of the oven may get warmer during the fire or immediately after the fire goes out. Letting the oven rest for a period of time allows the temperatures to stabilize for more predictable baking results.

Though a white oven option is always clean, it may have its own drawbacks depending entirely on the design, knowledge, and skill of the builder. It should be emphasized that the primary purpose of a masonry heater is to heat living space, not to cook food. Good heater design should *first* accomplish this goal while the baking chamber performance should be a secondary object. If cooking is your principal goal, it is not a masonry heater that you necessarily want. Two of the potential weaknesses of a white oven are lower achievable temperatures and shorter total baking time.

The farther along the flue path the oven is from the primary firebox, the less hot the oven will get. An oven exposed to flue gases directly coming out of the firebox will get much warmer than one that does not encounter exhaust until it has traveled many feet. Some of the heat of the fire will have been absorbed in the preceding flues and will not be able to charge the oven. Likewise, some ovens may have one surface—the floor, for example—exposed to the hottest part of the fire, like an oven directly above the firebox. Yet if the walls and ceiling of such an oven do not "see" any exhaust until several feet of flue have been traveled, the oven still may not get as hot as you'd expect.

Often the desired location of the oven, the design of the heater and flues, and the demands of creating the best *heater* possible may necessitate the creation of a less perfect oven. Trade-offs may be necessary depending

FIGURE 11.15. A white/black hybrid oven can be used either as a combustion chamber or as a white oven. In the center back of the oven is an ash dump door. In the upper back is a damper to open the oven to the flues of the heater when used as a combustion chamber.

FIGURE 11.14. A white oven in a heater under construction. The opening in the back is a cleanout access to flues beyond. Photo by Julie Cline.

on what is most important to you. If you want the oven to face the kitchen, yet that side of the masonry heater is far from the firebox, you'll make a sacrifice in oven performance, while locating the oven closer to the hottest part of fire may make it less convenient to the kitchen.

The white oven also may not offer as much time for baking because it depends entirely on the time delay of heat traveling *through* the masonry materials to get to the inner oven environment. This delay is unlike the black oven, which is incredibly hot immediately after the fire dies. The length of the delay will depend on the thickness of the materials as well as their characteristics (see chapter 6). With thinner materials, the oven may get hot quite fast, but it will also cool quicker, while with thicker materials it will take longer for the oven to get warm and the thickness may result in lower overall temperatures once the heat does transfer.

White/Black Hybrids

An oven that is usable as both a white oven and a black oven is more versatile than either one by itself.

However, not every heater design can accommodate such a hybrid. The white/black hybrid is designed differently than a typical black oven. It is its own firebox and it never sees fire, flame, or smoke unless you intentionally build a fire in it. Thus it is usually warmed by the fire of the primary firebox of the masonry heater. Its versatility stems from the fact that in warmer weather, when you may not want to fire the masonry heater hot enough to fully charge a white oven, the oven itself can be fired specifically for baking. You can see the inside of such a hybrid oven in figure 11.15.

A white/black oven usually has a door or damper of some kind connecting it to the flue path of the masonry heater. This connection needs to be opened in order to use the oven as a firebox, and such a use generally precludes the simultaneous use of the main masonry heater firebox. On the other hand, some clever designs provide separate flue paths for the masonry heater and the bakeoven so they can be used at the same time. The masonry heater and oven in this case are essentially separate appliances melded together. Depending on the total configuration, the bakeoven part may or may not be considered a masonry heater. It may simply have a flue exit that feeds directly into a chimney rather than additional flues to warm the masonry mass.

Firing and Regulating a Black (or White/Black) Bakeoven

Overall, the method of firing a black bakeoven is similar to firing the masonry heater itself. However, as noted earlier, the bakeoven does not have the volume of the main firebox of a masonry heater. It is unlikely that you can load a full complement of firewood in a bakeoven all at once. In most cases, the bakeoven is an accessory for baking, not a firebox designed to charge the whole masonry heater mass with heat. The bakeoven is fired, therefore, in a somewhat more intermittent manner to achieve the desired baking temperatures.

If you're planning a day of baking in a black oven, it is a good idea to start a day in advance. In a solely white oven, the warmth and use of the oven are

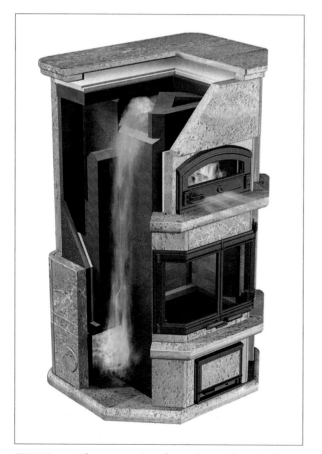

FIGURE 11.16. A cutaway view shows the smoke path from a black oven in a Finnish contraflow design. The exhaust goes briefly up, then down both sides before exiting into a chimney connector. Illustration courtesy of Tulikivi Corporation.

entirely controlled by burning wood in the masonry heater firebox. The white oven temperatures are entirely restricted by how much fuel can be used in the masonry heater. With a white/black option, you can fire the masonry heater the evening before baking day to get the oven to some increased temperature. Then, early on baking day, fire the bakeoven itself to achieve the temperatures at which you'd like to start. Since the bakeoven is prewarmed from the previous evening, the process does not take long.

Like the masonry heater firebox, the black/white oven will have an air intake—often as part of the door—which must be opened. As mentioned earlier, there is likely a door or damper that must be opened before loading and burning wood in the oven as well. Likewise, of course, the chimney damper (if equipped) must be open.

In the bakeoven firebox, it is a good idea to use smaller-diameter wood than you generally do in the masonry heater's primary firebox. Since the volume is smaller, the total quantity of wood used all at once is less. Smaller pieces—perhaps 2 to 3 inches in diameter—will more readily achieve the high temperatures needed for clean combustion in this limited-space environment. There is no room for a tepee fire in the bakeoven, so the wood should be loaded in a crib fashion as described previously. In general, top-down or bottom-up is irrelevant in this compressed environment. Start the fire burning with newspaper and kindling or fire starter material.

Some masonry heater bakeovens will be equipped with a long-stem thermometer that reaches into the stones or bricks of the oven chamber (see figure 11.17). If so equipped, you can monitor the temperature as it rises during firing. You may need to reload the oven with fuel one or more times to achieve the desired temperatures. (As with the masonry heater itself, if the builder or manufacturer provided information about the maximum amount of wood to be burned, this limit should not be exceeded in the oven either.) Unlike a conventional oven thermometer, this embedded thermometer is measuring the temperature *inside the mass* of the structure rather than the air temperature in the oven. A temperature of 350°F in the mass is *not* the same as a 350° air temperature in a conventional oven. It is likely that if the inner mass is 350°, the temperature within the oven chamber is higher during a fire or just after a fire has been burned. (It is not possible to insert a normal oven thermometer in the baking chamber while the fire is burning. Many a thermometer has been destroyed by being forgotten in the baking chamber when a black oven was fired!)

Learning to bake in a masonry heater bakeoven is a matter of developing new skills and awareness. You may have no experience with driving a car with a standard transmission. Yet driving that car isn't all that different from driving one with an automatic transmission. A few new skills have to be mastered, and before long they become second nature. A person who loves to bake will find that most baking skills readily transfer to using a wood-fired oven, but it may take a little time and a few errors. It does not take long for experienced cooks to master the peculiarities of a wood-fired oven. Like learning to drive a stick shift, it just takes a little time and attention.

When the desired temperature is nearly reached—it is within, say, 25°F—no more wood should be added to the fire. You can check the target temperature using the built-in thermometer, a point-and-shoot infrared thermometer (see appendix A), or by experiential methods such as throwing cornmeal on the hearth to see how quickly it browns or blackens. Eventually, ardent bakers become intimately familiar with how much wood produces what baking range of temperatures. You can always insert a standard oven thermometer after the fire is out. Still, a brick or stone oven at a given temperature generally performs like a *hotter* standard oven because it cooks with radiant, convection, and conduction heat simultaneously. There is no escaping the need to relearn the art of baking in a heat-retaining oven.

Cooking pizza and other flatbreads on the oven floor is often done with red hot coals still in the oven chamber, pushed to the edges to make room for the food. For most other foods, the coals are removed first before baking. Some, but not all, masonry heater black ovens will have some kind of hatch or other means to

FIGURE 11.17. A long-stemmed thermometer registers the temperature of the masonry above the oven. This one reads in degrees Celsius.

push coals out of the oven chamber—usually to fall into either an ash pan or into the masonry heater firebox, where they will finally extinguish. In the latter case, be mindful of having some air supply to those rejected coals as well as a route for the escape of the remaining exhaust. This is usually accomplished by resetting the bakeoven damper to the place that is required when the masonry heater is operated normally. In an oven without a hatch to dump coals, you may need to shovel coals out—putting them into a metal container and removing them from the house. The latter is good reason to specify with the masonry heater builder that a coal hatch must be supplied.

The next step after removing coals is to let the oven rest for a while to allow the temperatures to stabilize. For a period of time after the coals are first removed, the oven may still rise in temperature slightly before settling. After a half to one hour, the oven should be ready for baking. If it's still too hot for your recipe, all you can do is wait while the bakeoven slowly cools to the target temperature. Again, experience will make this kind of wait less likely in the future.

A well-constructed white/black oven fired as outlined here will provide many hours of cooking time with temperatures starting quite high for pizzas or bread and eventually cooling to a steady heat just

FIGURE 11.18. A well-designed masonry cookstove adds tremendous versatility to heating with wood. This model has both a functional cooktop and a bakeoven that can be fired separately. Photo courtesy of Tulikivi Corporation.

right for cooking stews or soups. When it finally cools to boiling temperature, the bakeoven is just right for cooking porridge overnight for a wonderful hot cereal in the morning. There really are very few things that cannot be cooked in a masonry heater's bakeoven once you've taken some time to observe and experiment with it.

The Masonry Cookstove

A masonry cookstove is usually a separately standing, peculiar masonry heater that happens to have a cast-iron cooktop. Although a cooktop can be integral to a larger masonry heater, this is not often the case. And while a masonry cookstove is a masonry heater having flues within its mass for transferring heat for retention and later radiation, it also acts in some ways like a metal woodstove. Most masonry cookstoves are designed to have the flames and exhaust of the fire contact the metal top first, providing heat to "burners" on which you can then cook food or heat water.

This metal cooktop, then, becomes a quite hot radiating surface. Yet because of the internal flue design, the masonry will store significant amounts of heat for later use. In this way, the masonry cookstove is a versatile appliance. It can produce exceptionally quick heat almost immediately to the living area along with stored heat for longer-term heating. It does this while also frying eggs, boiling water, and simmering soup! Some cookers, as cookstoves are frequently called, also incorporate either a white or a black oven (see figure 11.18). The cooker then becomes an amazing device that can be used to cook any dish a family may want while contributing to the heating requirements of the house as well.

FIGURE 11.19. A better view of the cookstove in the heater seen in figure 11.1. The oven even has a glass door. Photo courtesy of Maine Wood Heat Company.

Firing a Cookstove

All the same break-in procedures used for a new masonry heater apply equally to a new cookstove. Like the black bakeoven, a masonry cookstove is best operated using smaller pieces of wood. The firebox for a cooker is even smaller than that of an oven and does not readily accept large pieces of cordwood. Firewood pieces 1 to 2 inches in diameter are excellent for this purpose. Because of its small firebox size, which may be as narrow as about 7 inches, the cookstove will need to be fired in a more continuous fashion than a true masonry heater, especially if the cooktop is to be used for an extended time, to both heat the cooktop and charge the mass with heat. Again, like its larger and heavier counterparts (full-sized masonry heaters), it should not be fired with more total firewood than is recommended by the builder or manufacturer.

The first step to firing is to open the chimney damper (if equipped) and to make sure the cookstove has adequate draft. It's also a good idea to remove excess ash from the firebox and to make sure the ash pan (if equipped) is not full. Depending on the design, the cookstove may have a specific air-supply vent, slides for air in the door(s), or it may be fed by cracking open the firebox or ash box door itself. The air supply should be opened before lighting the fire. Load the firebox with kindling, newspaper, and one or two pieces of the main fuel load. Then light the fire and monitor it regularly, because you'll need to add more fuel at fairly regular intervals until the maximum weight of fuel has been consumed. Usually, no more than about 5 pounds of wood can be burned at one time in the small firebox of a cookstove.

As in any masonry heater, the fire should burn briskly and with little smoke. Dry, small pieces of firewood should burn with bright yellow or even white

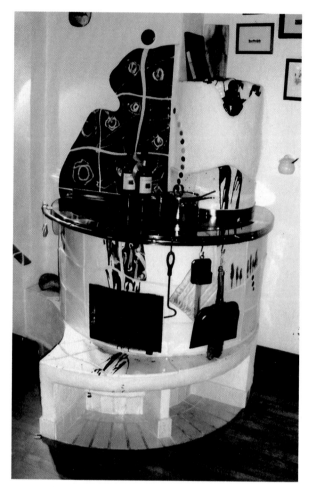

FIGURE 11.20. A unique and functional cookstove and heater in handmade tiles. It isn't often that we see a round cookstove. *Kachelofen* designed, built, and photographed by Ernst Kiesling, Canadian Kachelofen.

flames and produce quick heat to the metal cooktop. Adjust the air intake to guarantee plenty of air to the fire. Cookstoves, like all masonry heaters, are not meant to be operated in a dampened fashion, starving the fuel of oxygen. Depending on the size and species of wood used, you'll need to feed the fire again every half hour or so until you're done using the cooktop or you've used the recommended weight of fuel.

At this point, you can let the fuel load burn to coals. When there is no more flame, even with a light stirring, close the chimney damper (if equipped). When the coals are all consumed and turn black, indicating no more fire, close the air supply as well.

Using the Cooktop

The cast-iron cooktop of a masonry cookstove is usually coated with a protective oil to prevent rusting during storage and shipment. The oil is harmless and will burn off when the appliance is fired. It may, however, produce an acrid odor. If one is available, use an exhaust vent when you fire the cooktop the first time. Otherwise, it is advisable to break in the cooktop during weather in which you can open a window or door to release this. Otherwise, the first use of a cookstove is the equivalent of the first use of most masonry heaters.

Like the bakeoven accessory of a masonry heater, a masonry cookstove requires some basic retraining of cooking habits. Unlike a modern range, it is not possible to simply set a burner at "high" or "low." The stovetop locations closest to the firebox will always be the hottest and are ideal for boiling water and other tasks that require the highest temperatures. The "burners" or hobs, as they are called, farthest from the firebox will be more suitable for the medium and lower temperatures needed for simmering. A teakettle or pan of water can be an effective gauge of the temperature at first, but with experience you'll get a feel for the correct time to use the various stove positions based on the quantity of fuel used and the time that has passed. Cooking has always been an art, and wood-fired cooking raises that art form to a new level.

You'll get the best use of a wood-fired cookstove by using cast-iron cookware, though this is not a requirement. Like the cooktop itself, cast-iron cookware stores more heat than thinner steel or aluminum pans and will help to moderate temperature fluctuations as a fire burns through its cycle of ignition, full combustion, and coal stages. This moderation of temperatures can be augmented further by always keeping a large pot of water on the stovetop. Thin steel pans will have their place, and the accomplished cook will have an innate sense about when to use which pans for which purposes. As with the masonry heater bakeoven, there is no substitute for experimentation and experience, which will serve to hone the skills of every cook. It is best not to fire the stove continuously without actually heating something on the top. The cast iron top, subjected to the intense heat with nothing to moderate it, can be structurally damaged.

The metal cooktop can be easily cleaned with typical kitchen dishwashing soap and water. Stubborn spills or rust stains can be dressed with fine steel wool as well. Though this isn't necessary, it is best that you coat the cast-iron top lightly with vegetable oil when you won't be using it for a long period of time to prevent rusting. As with the original coating, this will harmlessly burn off the metal when you use the cookstove again.

Conclusion

A masonry heater is very easy to use, and learning to heat with a masonry heater, use its bakeoven, and cook on a cookstove is rewarding and quick. It was not that long ago that everyone heated and cooked with wood. Many who have grown up with modern appliances are, at first, overwhelmed by what must be done to heat and cook with wood using heat-storage technologies. Once the skills are learned, however, they become second nature. What's more, the process isn't time consuming considering all the rewards of gentle, healthy, radiant heat and the unique flavors of food cooked in a wood-fired, heat-retaining oven.

Masonry heaters, black bakeovens, and cookstoves all operate on the same basic principles. Each needs to be gently brought up to temperature when newly constructed or after a long period of disuse. Once warmed and used regularly, a masonry heater firebox is always warm and conducive to quick fire starting. The chimney must be clear and open, air supplies must be open, and the firebox and/or ash pans must be free from excess ash. Kindling, newspaper, and main

FIGURE 11.21. An all-tile heater, oven, and cookstove designed, built, and photographed by Ernst Kiesling, Canadian Kachelofen.

fuel charges are loaded in quantities recommended by the designer, builder, or manufacturer. Once the fire is lit, you can sit back and enjoy until it naturally extinguishes itself. As long as the fire burns briskly and brightly, there is nothing more you need to do. A few minutes of fire building results in many hours of radiant heat. A masonry heater could be called the lazy man's way to heat with wood since it requires no poking or prodding, continual addition of fuel, or other constant attention.

FIGURE 12.1. A massive five-sided stone masonry heater occupies the corner of this central space. The giant chimney hugs the corner all the way to the tall cathedral ceiling. Photo courtesy of Temp-Cast Enviroheat.

CHAPTER TWELVE

Masonry Heater Maintenance

I grew up in a brick ranch house. My parents raised me with a good work ethic. My father, while I was a youngster, almost never hired anyone to fix anything. He repaired cars, dishwashers, dryers, furnaces, and refrigerators. Everything he fixed, he cleaned thoroughly so it looked like new again when he was done. My mother cleaned the whole house religiously every Thursday. The kitchen was always spotless. She never went to bed with a dirty dish in the sink. Outside, my mother was usually the one to paint the overhangs, paint the front door, and wash the windows. My brother and I helped with these tasks. I was often the "gopher" for Dad. I would "gopher" the screwdriver, then "gopher" the wrench, and "gopher" the paint.

When I think back to all the home maintenance and repair projects my parents and I got into, all the cleaning, all the scrubbing, all the meticulous care of every aspect, I cannot recall one single time that anything was ever done to maintain the brick facade of the house in the twenty or so years I lived there. I never saw it washed, scrubbed, or repaired. They still live in that same house. After forty years, that brick on the house still looks like new. That's what it's like to maintain masonry.

Of course, a masonry heater is different from just a brick wall. On the other hand, my parents' brick walls have been exposed to driving rains, wind, freezing temperatures, heat waves, sunshine, and every other manner of weather since the house was constructed in the 1950s. Masonry veneers inside the house have the easy life, in comparison. But the masonry heater, as a whole, is a workhorse that toils six or eight months of the year, then gets a summer break. When it goes on break, it behooves you to pamper it some—give it a spa treatment if you will—so that it will be well rested and rejuvenated when the weather again turns cold.

After-Season Maintenance

When it is clear that the masonry heater will not be used for heating until the next heating season arrives, there are simple maintenance tasks that are best done right away to keep the heater in the best condition. Throughout the heating season, time devoted each day to retrieving firewood and loading it into the heater was minimal. About ten minutes—fifteen minutes tops—is required to start a fire and subsequently shut down the heater. The year-end tasks aren't much more demanding.

General Ash Removal

It's a good idea to remove *all* accumulated ash from the firebox, ash pan, or other ash collection area, and a black bakeoven. Ashes are hygroscopic, meaning they readily absorb moisture. Since moisture is the number one thing not desired in a masonry heater, it's a good idea to remove all the ashes. Ash mixed with moisture becomes lye—a corrosive alkaline substance that is the basis of lye soap. Wet ashes can burn the skin, and lye itself has been observed corroding even glass. This is why it should be removed as completely as possible.

The firebox can initially be scooped with a fireplace shovel or a gardening trowel, as can the other areas. Some masonry heaters will have ash dumps that direct ashes down into the foundation cavity. Others will have removable metal boxes to collect and remove most of the ash (see figures 12.2 and 12.3). Once the vast majority of the ashes have been removed with a shovel or a box, use a shop vacuum fitted with a quality dust bag to remove the remainder. It is also possible to buy, through a hearth retailer, special vacuums designed specifically for cleaning ashes. See appendix A for more on ash vacuums.

FIGURE 12.2. If equipped, the ash box door is usually right below the firebox.

FIGURE 12.3. An ash box ready to be emptied.

The ash and dust remaining from burning wood in a masonry heater can be fine enough to slip right through conventional dust bags on regular sweepers. You can end up using the vacuum as a blower, spreading fine dust all over the living area, unless you use the right vacuum and bags. If you're in doubt about how well a vacuum will contain the ash, take it outside and use it to vacuum ash out of a container in which most of the ash was collected. If the vacuum sucks the ash

in and does not spew dust out its blower ports, it will probably be all right. Otherwise it will be better to obtain better bags, get a different vacuum, or just sweep out the heater by hand as thoroughly as possible.

If the heater was built so that ash could be dumped regularly down into a foundation cavity, spring is also a good time to empty this. There should be a cleanout door easily accessible in the basement or crawl space. Usually this is a hatch about 8 inches square, as was seen in figure 9.6, though bigger (and smaller) ones are sometimes used. Like the heater itself, this can be primarily emptied with a shovel, then vacuumed clean.

Chimney Cleaning

Those who own and those who build masonry heaters will give varied answers as to how often to have the chimney inspected and cleaned. Two of the most frequently asked questions about masonry heaters and their operation are how much creosote collects in the chimney and how is it removed. Chapter 4 addressed creosote in more detail, but a properly constructed, well-designed, and properly fired masonry heater will not develop creosote in the chimney lining. If an appliance does not develop creosote, there really is nothing to clean from the chimney, though some fly ash may accumulate at its base.

It is best to err on the side of caution, however, with a new heater. Novice operators may not have properly fired the masonry heater. There is a chance that green or wet wood was used. Some people have burned things not recommended as fuel in a masonry heater. Perhaps the masonry heater, if part of a remodeling job, was connected to a chimney that was already lined with creosote. These possibilities are good enough reason to have the chimney of a new masonry heater checked after the first season of use. If there are undesirable deposits on the inside of the chimney, it is a message to the homeowner that something is not right; the most likely culprit is wood that was not sufficiently dry.

A professional chimney sweep should be able to determine, based on this first inspection, how often the chimney really will need cleaning. One who finds a chimney that still looks like it's new with just a small accumulation of fly ash at the base may suggest that the chimney need not be inspected every year. You can do a simple check as well by opening a nearby cleanout and using a mirror positioned to look up the chimney. In daylight, you should be able to see if the walls of the chimney look smooth and clean or rough with a coating on them. A properly operating chimney will have the former appearance year after year. My masonry heater chimney has been used for fifteen years with no accumulation in it.

Ash Removal Through Soot Plugs/Doors/Cleanouts

If the chimney sweep does brush the chimney (from up on the roof), the debris will fall to the base. There should be a cleanout access to get to the area below the chimney. Often it is accessed through one of the soot plugs or doors in the side of either the heater or the chimney itself (see figure 12.4). The heater itself should have a number of cleanout openings and accompanying soot doors at all the crucial locations. Usually, at every place that the internal flues change direction, there are soot plugs. If a chimney sweep is on site to clean the chimney, there's a possibility he or she is also knowledgeable enough to clean the flues of the heater through the various cleanout accesses.

The designer or builder of the masonry heater should be able to give suggestions as to how often you must open these doors or remove the soot plugs to clean. Some will say this needs to be done annually, while others feel that several years can pass. There is no "right" answer to this except what is recommended by the maker of the masonry heater and what you learn by use and experience.

As with the chimney itself, if you check inside the heater's cleanout openings and find a lot of ash after one year, it may be a message that the heater does need this service annually. If inspection after three years finds almost no ash accumulation, then it is clear that several years can pass without cleaning through the soot plugs. Generally, the more accurately and painstakingly a masonry heater was designed, the less often the chimney will need to be cleaned, simply because the heater burns the wood more completely. Bear in mind that

FIGURE 12.4. Soot plugs are removed annually to access the flues of the masonry heater. The access hole is usually large enough for a shop vacuum hose.

FIGURE 12.5. Some of the cleanout (soot) doors available. Both of the black doors are held into their frames by gravity. The soapstone plug fits by friction of the fiberglass rope inside a sawn-out circle. See figures 2.1 and 7.16 for square tile cleanout covers that are held in by clay mortar.

a change in the species of wood you're burning can influence ash buildup as well.

The actual cleaning through the soot doors is simple and not very time consuming. On many heaters, the soot doors are metal and held in place by gravity locking either a pin or casting behind a manufactured catch. Others are plugs that fit snugly into a hole and are held in place by the friction of a band of fiberglass rope or tape against the inside of the hole. Yet others are held in place by a clay-based mortar. Some will have the metal door on the outside but an inner plug held in place with a clay mortar. Some will have both the inner and outer doors held in place with clay. In the case of soot doors held by clay mortar, you may wish to have the heater mason return to reinstall the plug after cleaning (or have the mason do the actual service).

Once the soot door is removed, you can look inside the opening or feel inside with a hand to see to what depth the ash has accumulated. The builder or designer of the heater may have provided basic instructions or drawings showing the cleanouts and what areas you should be able to reach and clean through those cleanouts. If there is a lot of ash and the access is large enough, it is possible to use a small shovel or trowel to remove the bulk of the ash. Otherwise, use a good vacuum with a dust bag (and only if the heater has been unused long enough that nothing is warm anymore!) to reach all the accessible areas.

Once again, a small mirror is a handy device to look inside the various soot doors to verify that cleaning has been thorough. Some hardware stores carry mirrors with a universal joint on a long rod so that you can adjust the mirror, insert it into such a cavity, and see in various directions. Not being equipped with one of these is no liability. At the very least, insert the vacuum hose into the cleanout and move it in all directions to get as much debris as possible.

Cleaning through the soot doors with a vacuum should only take an hour or less for most masonry heaters. If you plan to do this, it's wise to wear old work clothes and lay a tarp, blanket, sheet, or even newspapers under the area of the cleanouts to catch any ash that may escape. If the builder or designer of the masonry heater supplied a "map" of the flues, it will be easy to know which directions to send a vacuum hose. This simple investment of time at the end of a heating season assures maximum performance of the heater in the fall.

Door Glass Cleaning

There are many different types of doors available for masonry heaters, and some stay cleaner than others. For example, some have double glazing—two panes of ceramic glass separated by air space. This arrangement means the inner pane of glass gets hotter than a single pane would; it is much more likely to stay clean since soot that might get on it (like from a log falling against it) will burn off the glass because of the superior temperatures. Double-paned glass, by the way, also results in cleaner and hotter combustion overall since less heat is transferred and lost through the door glass. More heat is sent through the flues of the heater for long-term storage. In addition, many masonry heaters incorporate an air-wash system in which combustion air is directed across the inside of the door, keeping it mostly clean.

Even the best glass doors may need some cleaning on occasion, however. This is more likely true during the break-in or initial warming period at the beginning of the season. Since you don't use much wood during these times and the mass is not yet warm, soot can accumulate on just about everything in the heater, including the glass of the door. Once the heater is up to temperature, this should not occur if you're using the proper amount of dry wood at each firing, unless, of course, a log does fall against the glass.

In general, there are three types of material that may need to be cleaned off masonry heater door glass: ash, soot, and hardened minerals. The first of these, simple fine ash, is very easily removed with just a wet paper towel or other soft damp cloth. If the glass is quite hot, it is best to wait for it to cool before wiping with something wet. However, the interior glass will almost always be warm to hot, so it makes sense to wipe the glass with hot water to avoid subjecting it to the thermal shock of cold water against hot glass. Ash will easily be removed and the glass should be dried, if needed, with a soft dry towel.

Black soot and light coatings of brown creosote (that can condense on glass if wet wood was burned) can both be cleaned from glass with a little more elbow grease, two wet cloths or towels, one dry cloth, and

FIGURE 12.6. The fine ash and small amount of soot accumulated on this door over a two-week period. An air wash keeps it mostly clean. The glass can be easily cleaned with a wet cloth dipped in ash.

some white ash from the firebox. As mentioned previously, ash mixed with water makes a harsh alkaline substance called lye, the basis for soap. A wet rag dipped in ash will effectively clean soot and light creosote off glass just as powdered cleanser is used on a kitchen countertop stain. It is best to wear rubber gloves for this cleaning operation, though this isn't absolutely necessary if you avoid the wet ash on the cloth and wash your hands immediately after cleaning.

The ash/lye "soap" will cut through the deposits quickly if you use a circular scrubbing motion. Once all the soot has been thereby loosened, use a second clean, damp cloth to rinse and a third dry towel to dry and polish the glass until it is perfectly clear again.

Mineral deposits are a little more difficult to remove and so are best addressed as soon as you notice them. These deposits can occur from burning wood that is too wet; the mineral-laden water condenses on the cooler glass and evaporates, leaving the minerals. It can also be partially a result of the very cleaning discussed above. Cleaning often using hard water on hot glass can aid in creating a buildup of minerals. One of the ways to recognize this problem is if the glass or some part of it just looks a little hazy, but when it is wiped with a wet cloth it looks perfectly clean. The glass then dries with the same hazy appearance.

You can find cleaners for this mineral buildup at fireplace and barbecue stores, but it is also possible to remove it with white vinegar and salt. Dip a barely damp cloth in straight vinegar, then into some common table salt. Scrub the problem area thoroughly until you've removed all the minerals. The salt, in this case, is mainly serving as an abrasive, and may or may not be necessary, depending on the severity of the buildup. If the mineral accumulation has gone on for a long time, this can be a time-consuming cleaning job; this is why it's best to clean it as soon as it is noticed. One owner waited years, thinking the mineral buildup was a permanent etching in the glass. It took more than an hour of scrubbing to restore clarity to the glass.

Fire viewing is a joy to most people. Keeping the glass of a masonry heater clean and clear is a simple task that can be accomplished in just a few minutes either every day or at least once per week. If it is not done as regular maintenance, it will take longer. Like any other home maintenance task, a little bit done regularly reaps the most reward for the least time spent.

Masonry Heater Bath

A structure of masonry materials is nearly indestructible in the home environment. It will, however, collect dust, cobwebs, and other normal household dirt and, like home furnishings, should be cleaned and regularly maintained for best appearance and enjoyment. As discussed in chapter 6, the choice of materials used for a heater should include consideration of the ease of maintenance. Though a weekly quick cleaning is recommended, a deeper cleaning should only be necessary once per year when the heater is not being used. The method of cleaning differs depending on the surface materials.

For those heaters with very smooth or semi-smooth surfaces like polished or honed stone, *kacheln* (tiles), or plain stucco, the surface can be dusted regularly with a feather duster or soft cloth. If a deeper cleaning is required, all these surfaces respond well to warm, soapy water. Typical dishwashing soap works very well for this purpose. Tiles in particular are virtually impossible to stain and will always look brand new if regularly

FIGURE 12.7. This symmetrical stucco heater features matching sitting areas for enjoying not only the fire but the ensuing heat as well. Cushions, niches, and compartments make the whole stove an interesting gathering point. Photo courtesy of Biofire, Inc.

wiped with a clean, damp cloth. Polished granite is about the same, though some granites can be stained permanently—not a good thing for a permanent installation like a masonry heater. Honed soapstone cannot be stained permanently. However, it will accept body oils that can accumulate on the surface, making the stone look darker. Again, warm soapy water will readily clean soapstone. You can also purchase cleaners made specifically for stone surfaces at a hardware store, home center, or stone countertop supplier.

Brick and natural (split) stone veneers are more of a challenge for regular maintenance. Sometimes a feather duster deposits more dirt on a brick surface than it removes! A more practical strategy for brick and rough stone is to brush the surface with a fairly coarse bristle brush, allowing the dirt to fall on the floor where it can be swept or vacuumed. It also works to use a vacuum with a brush attachment on such a rough surface. For deeper cleaning, the only real option is to wash the heater with lots of water and a brush. Obviously, this can only be done if the floor will not be harmed by water or some method is used to keep water off the floor.

In addition to the masonry surface, the metal parts like door frames or soot doors and ash box doors will need some infrequent cleaning. As with the entire heater, quickly wiping these parts each week when the ashes are removed or the door glass is cleaned is usually sufficient, and a once-per-year good cleaning with soapy water is recommended. These parts can be simply washed and rinsed and should be thoroughly dried to prevent rusting. If this maintenance is done right at the end of the heating season, it's also a good idea to lightly coat these surfaces with some vegetable oil. This is a particularly good idea for stovetops and for masonry heaters in homes that may be vacated for the whole summer season (like a vacation home). The vegetable oil prevents rust and will burn away when the heater is used again in the fall.

Masonry Heater Cracks

The constant expansion and contraction of a masonry heater from daily heating and subsequent slow cooling puts a lot of stress on the dense, hard masonry components. Bricks and stones just don't flex like a rubber band. Though great efforts are often made to accommodate such movement (as shown in chapter 8), it is always possible that any masonry piece could crack. The firebox in particular takes a real beating and is the most likely place for cracks to occur. But hairline cracks on the outside of a masonry heater are always a possibility, too.

Such cracks are not necessarily a sign of poor craftsmanship. In well-built heaters, in fact, the more likely reason for cracking is that there was already an internal weakness in the tile, brick, or stone that could not withstand the pressures of its environment. In the vast majority of cases, hairline cracks in the exterior are completely superficial to the veneer and

FIGURE 12.8. A brick masonry heater can be easily cleaned with the brush attachment on a vacuum cleaner. The brick and dark, oiled soapstone complement the rustic interior of this log home. Notice the small seat with wood storage below and an iron rack attached to the brick side for hanging fireplace implements. Photo courtesy of New England Hearth and Soapstone.

will not affect the operation and enjoyment of the masonry heater.

If cracks have developed internally in a masonry heater, it's best to arrange for its builder to assess the situation. In many cases, nothing needs to be done. If, however, the crack is something that is constantly growing, it may need attention sooner rather than later. Reconstruction of some or the entire firebox may be necessary in those that have large and growing cracks. An older heater that has deteriorating bricks may need similar attention. Generally, fireboxes should last decades without needing service if properly built and properly used.

If the heater has joints between stones or bricks on the veneer that keep opening larger, then closing as the heater is used and cooled, it may be that the heater was not built with mechanical connections and depends only on common mortar to bond elements together. One solution is to have a mason service these joints while the heater is still in use and hot as follows:

1. The joints are held at their largest with a wedge.
2. Old mortar is removed.
3. New mortar is tucked into the opened cracks.
4. The heater is allowed to cool completely.
5. The wedges are removed and any holes created by them patched.

For similar opening and closing joints between large stones of a bench or other horizontal surface, a working solution is to use a flexible silicone caulk in the joint so the joint can freely move. The caulk will move with the stone. If you can't find such a caulk of a color complementary to the stonework, sometimes you can carefully mix clear or colored caulk with dust from cutting the stone to make a caulk that pretty well matches.

Masonry heaters built in North America, if built by well-trained professionals, always have an inner life and an outer veneer. Small cracks in the outer veneer are not generally of concern, though it never hurts to check with the builder or another person familiar with masonry heaters. Likewise, most heaters will not develop any cracks at all on the exterior, but even the original builder or manufacturer is not likely to guarantee that none will ever occur. The best advice in this regard is to always hire the most reputable and best-trained masons for a masonry heater project for maximum durability and lifelong enjoyment.

Living with a Masonry Heater

A masonry heater is more like a piece of furniture than it is a fireplace or woodstove. (Some of my customers have said it's more like a living being.) You can always sit on or near it, even when it is at maximum output of heat. Because it is only fueled once or twice a day during the heating season, debris from firewood can be removed and the area kept clean throughout the day, in contrast with open fireplaces or metal woodstoves that need regular feeding. Since the firebox is always warm, fires are easily started and chimney draft is immediate. You get used to the cycle of heat output from the heater and can gauge how much fuel to use based on weather predictions.

By keeping an eye open for opportunities, you can often get free firewood from a variety of sources, and a typical family can secure a one-year supply of split firewood in dry storage in one weekend. Regular cleaning and maintenance take less than an hour per week. More thorough cleaning at the end of the season can usually be done in less than half a day. Heating with a masonry heater requires you to think ahead and plan and pay attention to the surroundings, the weather, and the future needs of the family. The physical effort required is minimal considering the return in enjoyment of fire viewing, gentle radiant heat, the use of a forever renewable fuel, and all the other advantages inherent in masonry heaters.

Living with a masonry heater is easy and delightful. There is no doubt that securing your own fuel and physically maintaining heat in a home takes some time and effort. But there is no other reliable way to heat living space with renewable fuel that demands so little attention and yet adds so much to the health, comfort, and well-being of the inhabitants at the same time it beautifies the interior of the home. Most significantly, a masonry heater guarantees that, with minimal effort, there is actually something in the house that is truly warm. It is not possible to snuggle up against the hot air coming out of the furnace registers of a house. It's crazy to think about snuggling against a warm floor. A metal woodstove is too hot to get near. But you can snuggle up against a lover—or a masonry heater.

FIGURE 12.9. An heirloom masonry heater will provide a lifetime of enjoyment. This soapstone custom "Lohi" model produced by Tulikivi has built-in shelves and seating. The partial dome shape and carved fish are always conversation pieces. Courtesy of WarmStone Fireplaces and Designs; photo courtesy of Impact Photography.

APPENDICES

Appendix A: Resources

Antique Masonry Heaters

Vintage Elements
European Flooring and Design
    Elements
216 Brookfield Drive
Greenwood, SC 29646
864-344-0529
www.vintageelements.com

Ash Vacuums

The Love-Less Ash Company
1285 East 650 South
Price, UT 84501
800-568-3949
435-637-5885
www.lovelessash.com

Compressed Sawdust Fuel

Eco-energy Fuel
PO Box 458
679 Johnson Lane
South Shore, KY 41175
606-932-3117
linda@eco-energyfuel.com
www.eco-energyfuel.com

Ecolog
1081, rue Industrielle C.P. 4
Mont-Joli, Quebec
Canada G5H 3K8
418-775-5370
866-549-9428
info@ecologcanada.com
www.ecologcanada.com

O'Hara Corporation
120 Tillson
Rockland, ME 04841
207-594-4444
info@gogreenwithoharas.com
www.gogreenwithoharas.com

Gasketed Air-Supply Dampers

Arzel Zoning Technology, Inc.
4801 Commerce Parkway
Cleveland, OH 44128
800-611-8312
216-831-6068
www.arzelzoning.com

New England Hearth and Soapstone,
    LLC
127 North Street
Goshen, CT 06756
860-491-3091
www.rodzander.com

Handheld Infrared Thermometers

Extech Instruments Corporation
285 Bear Hill Road
Waltham, MA 02451
781-890-7440, ext. 220
www.extech.com

Instrumart
PO Box 1073
8 Leroy Road
Williston, VT 05495
800-884-4967
802-863-0085
www.instrumart.com

Omega Engineering, Inc.
PO Box 4047
1 Omega Drive
Stamford, CT 06907
203-359-7700
www.omega.com

Raytek Corporation
800-866-5478
www.raytek.com

Masonry Heater Companies Featured (Chapter 8)

Albie-Core
Maine Wood Heat Company, Inc.
254 Father Rasle Road
Norridgewock, ME 04957
207-696-5442
info@mainewoodheat.com
www.mainewoodheat.com

Biofire, US
Biofire, Inc.
3220 Melbourne
Salt Lake City, UT 84106
801-486-0266
biofire@aol.com
www.biofireinc.com

Kuznetsov's Stoves
Igor Kuznetsov
www.stove.ru
Double-bell or system of free gas movement.

Stovemaster
20655 Shaws Creek Road
Caledon, Ontario
Canada L7K 1L7
519-938-9166
alex_stovemaster@yahoo.ca
www.stovemaster.com

Envirotech Radiant Fireplaces and
    Envirotech Masonry Heaters
By Empire Masonry Heaters
245 Reed Road
Scottsville, NY 14546
585-889-2002
jsteele@empiremasonryheaters.com
www.empiremasonryheaters.com

The Helios
New England Hearth and Soapstone, LLC
127 North Street
Goshen, CT 06756
860-491-3091
rod@rodzander.com
www.rodzander.com

Crossfire Fireplaces
249 Bridge Street West
PO Box 121
Campbellford, Ontario
Canada K0L 1L0
800-865-8784
sheaff@trytel.net
www.crossfirefireplaces.com

Temp-Cast Enviroheat
PO Box 94059
3409 Yonge Street
Toronto, Ontario
Canada M4N 3R1
800-561-8594
staywarm@tempcast.com
www.tempcast.com

Tulikivi
Tulikivi US, Inc.
c/o Drayer and Company PC
195 Riverbend Drive, Suite 3
Charlottesville, VA 22911
1-800-843-3473
www.tulikivi.com

Masonry Heater Organizations

Alliance of Masonry Heater and Oven Professionals, Inc.
www.masonryheaters.org

Masonry Heater Association of North America
www.mha-net.org

Masonry Heater Workshops and Education

Though many craftsmen offer workshops from time to time, the individuals or groups listed here have made a concerted effort over years to regularly host and advertise training. This list may not be exhaustive, but represents reputable sources of education and training. Also see "Masonry Heater Organizations," above.

Kachelofen Masonry Heater School of Canada (KMSC)
405 Langille's Lake Road
Blockhouse, Nova Scotia
Canada B0J 1E0
902-624-9583
www.kachelofenschool.com
Offers a comprehensive program in traditional kachelofen *and* grundofen *design, construction, and sales.*

Maine Wood Heat Company
254 Father Rasle Road
Norridgewock, ME 04957
207-696-5442
info@mainewoodheat.com
www.mainewoodheat.com
Maine Wood Heat Company has been advertising and hosting workshops for more than 30 years.

Related Industry Organizations

ASTM International
PO Box C700
100 Barr Harbor Drive
West Conshohocken, PA 19428
www.astm.org

Chimney Safety Institute of America (CSIA)
2155 Commercial Drive
Plainfield, IN 46168
317-837-5362
www.csia.org

Hearth Patio and Barbecue Association
1901 North Moore Street, Suite 600
Arlington, VA 22209
703-522-0086
www.hpba.org

International Code Council
500 New Jersey Avenue, NW, 6th Floor
Washington, DC 20001
888-ICC-SAFE (422-7233)
www.iccsafe.org

Kachelofenverband (The Austrian Stove Association)
Contact: Thomas Schiffert
Dassanowskyweg 8
1220 Wien
+43 1 25658850
Fax +43 1 256588520
office@kachelofenverband.at
www.kachelofenverband.at

National Fireplace Institute
1901 North Moore Street, Suite 600
Arlington, VA 22209
703-524-8030
www.nficertified.org

Woodwaiters

Butler's Buddy, Inc.
423 East 10th Street
Berwick, PA 18603
888-441-9810
570-759-0550
www.butlersbuddy.com

W. B. Fowler Industries, Inc.
4665 Nichol Road
Waterville, Quebec
Canada, J0B 3H0
800-290-8510
819-562-8510
www.woodwaiter.com
www.wbfowler.com

Appendix B: R-Values of Common Building Materials

Description	R - Value For Thickness Listed
BUILDING BOARD	
Gypsum or plaster board 0.375 in.	0.32
0.5 in.	0.45
0.625 in.	0.56
Plywood (Douglas Fir) 0.25 in.	0.31
0.375 in.	0.47
0.5 in.	0.63
0.625 in.	0.77
Plywood or wood panels 0.75 in.	0.93
Vegetable fiber board	
Sheathing regular density 0.5 in.	1.31
0.75 in.	2.04
Sheathing intermediate density 0.5 in.	1.08
Nail-base Sheathing 0.5 in.	1.08
Shingle backer 0.375 in.	0.97
0.3125 in.	0.79
Sound deadening board 0.5 in.	1.36
Tile and lay-in panels, plain or accoustic 0.5 in.	1.25
0.75 in.	1.87
Particle board underlayment 0.625 in.	0.79
Wood subfloor 0.75 in.	0.93
BUILDING MEMBRANE	
Vapor-permeable felt	0.06
Vapor-seal, 2 layers of mopped felt	1.19
Vapor-seal, plastic film	0
FINISH FLOORING MATERIALS	
Carpet and fibrous pad	2.08
Carpet and rubber pad	1.23
Cork tile	0.28
Terrazo	0.08
Tile - asphalt, linoleum, vinyl, rubber	0.05
Wood, hardwood finish 0.75 in.	0.68

Description	R - Value For Thickness Listed
INSULATING MATERIALS	
Blanket and Batt	
Mineral fiber, fibrous form processed from rock, slag, or glass (ie. fiberglass batts) 3.5 in.	12
5.5 in.	19
7.25 in.	25
10 in.	35
Board and Slabs	
Cellular glass 1 in.	2.8
Expanded polystyrene, extruded (smooth skin surface as, for example, Styrofoam) 1 in.	5
Expanded polystyrene, molded beads 1 in.	4
Cellular polyisocyanurate 1 in.	7.04
Acoustical Tile 0.5 in.	1.25
Loose Fill	
Cellulose (milled paper or wood pulp) 1 in.	3.13
Perlite, expanded 1 in.	2.7
Mineral fiber (rock, slag, or glass) 1 in.	3.5
Vermiculite 1 in.	2.13
Spray Applied	
Polyurethane foam 1 in.	3.6
Ureaformaldehyde foam 1 in.	4
Cellulose fiber 1 in.	2.8
Glass fiber 1 in.	2.9
ROOFING	
Asphalt roll roofing	0.15
Asphalt shingles	0.44
Wood shingles	0.94
MASONRY MATERIALS	
Brick	0.44
Concrete blocks 8 in.	1
12 in.	1.23
SIDING MATERIALS	
Beveled wood siding	1.02
Hardboard siding	0.34
Aluminum, steel or vinyl, over sheathing	
Hollow-backed	0.61
Insulating-board backed	1.8

Description	R - Value For Thickness Listed
WINDOWS	
Single Glass	0.92
With Storm	2
Double insulating glass (0.25 in. air space)	1.69
0.5 in. air space	2.04
0.5 in. air space with Low E coating	3.13
Addition for tight-fitting drapes or closed blinds	0.29
DOORS	
Wood (hollow-core, flush, 1.75 in.)	2.17
Solid Core 1.75 in.	3.03
Storm door (Wood, 50% glass)	1.25
Metal	1
Metal Insulated Door (2 in. with urethane)	15
WOODS	
Hardwoods	
Oak 1 in.	0.85
Birch 1 in.	0.84
Maple 1 in.	0.87
Ash 1 in.	0.91
Softwoods	
Southern Pine 1 in.	0.95
Douglas Fir-Larch 1 in.	1.03
Southern Cypress 1 in.	1.1
Hem-Fir, Spruce-Pine-Fir 1 in.	1.2
Cedars 1 in.	1.25
California Redwood 1 in.	1.27

Adapted and selected from American Society of Heating, Refrigerating, and Air-Conditioning Engineers, (ASHRAE), 1993 Handbook of Fundamentals and with permission from R. L. Martin and Associates, Inc., Windsor, CO

Appendix C: Elevation and Outside Design Temperatures for Various Cities

State and City	Latitude °	Latitude '	Elevation (feet)	Outside Winter Design Temperature (°F)
ALABAMA				
Anniston	33	4	599	5
Birmingham	33	3	610	10
Mobile	30	4	211	15
Montgomery	32	2	195	10
ARIZONA				
Flagstaff	35	1	6,973	-10
Phoenix	33	3	1,117	25
Tucson	33	1	2,584	25
Winslow	35	0	4,880	-10
Yuma	32	4	199	30
ARKANSAS				
Fort Smith	35	2	449	10
Little Rock	34	4	257	5
CALIFORNIA				
Bakersfield	35	2	495	25
Eureka	41	0	217	30
Fresno	36	5	326	25
Los Angeles	34	0	99	35
Oakland	37	4	3	30
Sacramento	38	3	17	30
San Diego	32	4	19	35
San Francisco	37	4	8	35
San Jose	37	2	70	25
COLORADO				
Denver	39	5	5,283	-10
Fort Collins	40	4	5,001	-30
Grand Junction	39	1	4,849	-15
Pueblo	38	2	4,639	-20
CONNECTICUT				
Bridgeport	41	1	7	0
Hartford	41	5	15	0

State and City	Latitude °	Latitude '	Elevation (feet)	Outside Winter Design Temperature (°F)
CONNECTICUT (continued)				
New Haven	41	2	6	0
Waterbury	41	3	605	-15
DELAWARE				
Wilmington	39	4	78	0
DISTRICT OF COLUMBIA				
Washington	38	5	14	0
FLORIDA				
Jacksonville	30	3	24	25
Key West	24	3	6	45
Miami	25	5	7	35
Pensacola	30	3	13	20
Tallahassee	30	2	58	25
Tampa	28	0	19	30
GEORGIA				
Atlanta	33	4	1,005	10
Augusta	33	2	143	10
Macon	32	4	356	15
Savannah	32	1	52	20
IDAHO				
Boise	43	3	2,842	-10
Lewiston	46	2	1,413	5
Pocatello	43	0	4,444	-5
Twin Falls	42	3	4,148	-10
ILLINOIS				
Chicago	41	5	594	-10
Danville	40	1	558	-5
Moline	41	3	582	-10
Peoria	40	4	652	-10
Springfield	39	5	587	-10
INDIANA				
Evansville	38	0	381	0

State and City	Latitude °	Latitude '	Elevation (feet)	Outside Winter Design Temperature (°F)
INDIANA (continued)				
Fort Wayne	41	0	791	-10
Indianapolis	39	4	793	-10
South Bend	41	4	773	-5
IOWA				
Cedar Rapids	41	5	863	-5
Des Moines	41	3	948	-15
Dubuque	42	2	1,065	-20
Fort Dodge	42	3	1,111	-20
Keokuk	40	2	526	-10
Sioux City	42	2	1,095	-20
Waterloo	42	3	868	-15
KANSAS				
Dodge City	37	5	2,594	-10
Salina	38	5	1,271	-15
Topeka	39	0	877	-10
Wichita	37	4	1,321	-10
KENTUCKY				
Lexington	38	0	979	0
Louisville	38	1	474	0
LOUISIANA				
Alexandria	31	2	92	20
New Orleans	30	0	3	20
Shreveport	32	3	252	20
MAINE				
Millinocket	45	4	405	-20
Portland	43	4	61	-5
Waterville	44	3	89	-15
MARYLAND				
Baltimore	39	1	146	0
Frederick	39	2	294	-5
Salisbury	38	2	52	10

State and City	Latitude °	Latitude '	Elevation (feet)	Outside Winter Design Temperature (°F)
MASSACHUSETTS				
Boston	42	2	15	0
Fall River	41	4	190	-10
Lowell	42	3	90	-15
New Bedford	41	4	70	0
Springfield	42	1	247	-10
Worcester	42	2	986	0
MICHIGAN				
Alpena	45	0	689	-10
Detroit	42	2	633	-10
Escanaba	45	4	594	-15
Flint	43	0	766	-10
Grand Rapids	42	5	681	-10
Kalamazoo	42	1	930	-5
Lansing	42	5	852	-10
Marquette	46	3	677	-10
Sault Ste. Marie	46	3	721	-20
MINNESOTA				
Alexandria	45	5	1,421	-25
Duluth	46	5	1,426	-25
Minneapolis	44	5	822	-20
St. Cloud	45	4	1,034	-25
St. Paul	44	5	822	-20
MISSISSIPPI				
Jackson	32	2	330	15
Meridian	32	2	294	10
Vicksburg	32	2	234	10
MISSOURI				
Columbia	39	0	778	-10
Kansas City	39	1	742	-10
St. Joseph	39	5	809	-10
St. Louis	38	5	535	0
Springfield	37	1	1,265	-10

State and City	Latitude °	Latitude '	Elevation (feet)	Outside Winter Design Temperature (°F)
MONTANA				
Billings	45	5	3,567	-25
Butte	46	0	5,526	-20
Great Falls	47	3	3,664	-20
Havre	48	3	2,488	-30
Helena	46	4	3,893	-20
Kalispell	48	2	2,965	-20
Miles City	46	3	2,629	-35
Missoula	46	5	3,200	-20
NEBRASKA				
Grand Island	41	0	1,841	-20
Lincoln	40	5	1,150	-10
Norfolk	42	0	1,532	-15
North Platte	41	1	2,779	-20
Omaha	41	2	978	-10
NEVADA				
Las Vegas	36	1	2,162	20
Reno	39	3	4,404	-5
Tonopah	38	0	5,426	5
Winnemucca	40	5	4,299	-15
NEW HAMPSHIRE				
Berlin	44	3	1,110	-25
Concord	43	1	339	-15
Keene	43	0	490	-20
NEW JERSEY				
Atlantic City	39	3	11	5
Newark	40	4	11	0
Trenton	40	1	144	0
NEW MEXICO				
Albuquerque	35	0	5,310	0
Roswell	33	2	3,643	-10
Santa Fe	35	4	7,045	0
NEW YORK				
Albany	42	5	277	-10

State and City	Latitude °	Latitude '	Elevation (feet)	Outside Winter Design Temperature (°F)
NEW YORK (continued)				
Binghamton	42	1	858	-10
Buffalo	43	0	705	-5
Cortland	42	4	1,129	-10
Glens Falls	43	2	321	-15
Ithaca	42	3	950	-15
Jamestown	42	1	1,390	-10
New York City	40	5	132	0
Oneonta	42	3	1,150	-15
Oswego	43	3	300	-10
Rochester	43	1	543	-5
Syracuse	43	1	424	-10
Watertown	44	0	497	-15
NORTH CAROLINA				
Asheville	35	3	2,170	0
Charlotte	35	1	735	10
Greensboro	36	1	897	10
Raleigh	35	5	433	10
Wilmington	34	2	30	15
NORTH DAKOTA				
Bismark	46	5	1,647	-30
Devils Lake	48	1	1,471	-30
Fargo	46	5	900	-25
Grand Forks	48	0	832	-25
Williston	48	1	1,877	-35
OHIO				
Akron	41	0	1,210	-5
Cincinnati	39	1	761	0
Cleveland	41	2	777	0
Columbus	40	0	812	-10
Dayton	39	5	997	0
Lima	40	4	860	-5
Sandusky	41	3	606	0

State and City	Latitude °	Latitude '	Elevation (feet)	Outside Winter Design Temperature (°F)
OKLAHOMA				
Ardmore	34	2	880	10
Bartlesville	36	5	715	-10
Oklahoma City	35	2	1,280	0
Tulsa	36	1	650	0
OREGON				
Baker City	44	5	3,368	-5
Eugene	44	1	364	-15
Pendleton	45	4	1,492	-15
Portland	45	4	21	10
PENNSYLVANIA				
Altoona	40	2	1,468	-5
Erie	42	1	732	-5
Harrisburg	40	1	335	0
New Castle	41	0	825	0
Philadelphia	39	5	7	0
Pittsburgh	40	3	1,137	0
Reading	40	2	226	0
Scranton	41	2	940	-5
Warren	41	5	1,280	-15
Williamsport	41	1	527	-5
RHODE ISLAND				
Providence	41	4	55	0
SOUTH CAROLINA				
Charleston	32	5	41	15
Columbia	34	0	217	10
Greenville	34	5	957	10
SOUTH DAKOTA				
Huron	44	3	1,282	-20
Rapid City	44	0	3,165	-20
Sioux Falls	43	4	1,420	-20
TENNESSEE				
Chattanooga	35	0	670	10
Knoxville	35	5	980	0

State and City	Latitude °	Latitude '	Elevation (feet)	Outside Winter Design Temperature (°F)
TENNESSEE (continued)				
Memphis	35	0	263	0
Nashville	36	1	577	0
TEXAS				
Abilene	32	3	1,759	15
Amarillo	35	1	3,607	-10
Austin	30	2	597	20
Brownsville	25	5	16	30
Corpus Christi	27	5	43	20
Dallas	32	5	481	0
Del Rio	29	2	1,072	15
El Paso	31	5	3,918	10
Fort Worth	32	5	544	10
Galveston	29	2	5	20
Houston	29	4	50	20
Palestine	31	5	580	15
Port Arthur	30	0	16	20
San Antonio	29	3	792	20
UTAH				
Logan	41	4	4,775	-15
Ogden	41	1	4,400	-10
Salt Lake City	40	5	4,220	-10
VERMONT				
Burlington	44	3	331	-10
Rutland	43	3	620	-20
VIRGINIA				
Lynchburg	37	2	947	5
Norfolk	36	5	26	15
Richmond	37	3	162	15
Roanoke	37	2	1,174	0
WASHINGTON				
Seattle	47	3	386	15
Spokane	47	4	2,357	-15
Tacoma	47	1	350	15

State and City	Latitude °	Latitude '	Elevation (feet)	Outside Winter Design Temperature (°F)
WASHINGTON (continued)				
Walla Walla	46	1	1,185	-10
Yakima	46	3	1,061	5
WEST VIRGINIA				
Charleston	38	2	939	0
Elkins	38	5	1,970	-10
Huntington	38	2	565	-5
Martinsburg	39	2	537	-5
Parkersburg	39	2	615	-10
Wheeling	40	1	659	-5
WISCONSIN				
Ashland	46	3	650	-20
Eau Claire	44	5	888	-20
Green Bay	44	3	683	-20
La Crosse	43	5	652	-25
Madison	43	1	858	-15
Milwaukee	43	0	672	-15
WYOMING				
Casper	42	5	5,319	-20
Cheyenne	41	1	6,126	-15
Lander	42	5	5,563	-18
Sheridan	44	5	3,942	-30

State and City	Latitude °	Latitude '	Elevation (feet)	Outside Winter Design Temperature (°F)
ALBERTA				
Edmonton	53	34	2,218	-33
BRITISH COLUMBIA				
Prince George	53	53	2,218	-32
Vancouver	49	11	0	11
MANITOBA				
Winnipeg	49	54	814	-29
NEWFOUNDLAND				
Gander	48	57	482	-3
NOVA SCOTIA				
Halifax	44	39	98	4
ONTARIO				
Kapuskasing	49	25	95	-30
Toronto	43	41	577	0
QUEBEC				
Montreal	45	28	98	-9
SASKATCHEWAN				
Regina	50	26	1,893	-34

Adapted and reprinted from the Cooling and Heating Manual, U. S. Department of Housing and Urban Development Office of Policy Development and Research.

Appendix D: Heating Degree Days of Various Cities

State	Station	Avg. Winter Temp[d]	July	Aug.	Sept.	Oct.	Nov.	Dec.	Jan.	Feb.	Mar.	Apr.	May	June	Yearly Total
Ala.	Birmingham .... A	54.2	0	0	6	93	363	555	592	462	363	108	9	0	2551
	Huntsville .... A	51.3	0	0	12	127	426	663	694	557	434	138	19	0	3070
	Mobile................................ A	59.9	0	0	0	22	213	357	415	300	211	42	0	0	1560
	Montgomery .... A	55.4	0	0	0	68	330	527	543	417	316	90	0	0	2291
Alaska	Anchorage .... A	23.0	245	291	516	930	1284	1572	1631	1316	1293	879	592	315	10864
	Fairbanks .... A	6.7	171	332	642	1203	1833	2254	2359	1901	1739	1068	555	222	14279
	Juneau................................. A	32.1	301	338	483	725	921	1135	1237	1070	1073	810	601	381	9075
	Nome .... A	13.1	481	496	693	1094	1455	1820	1879	1666	1770	1314	930	573	14171
Ariz.	Flagstaff .... A	35.6	46	68	201	558	867	1073	1169	991	911	651	437	180	7152
	Phoenix............................... A	58.5	0	0	0	22	234	415	474	328	217	75	0	0	1765
	Tucson .... A	58.1	0	0	0	25	231	406	471	344	242	75	6	0	1800
	Winslow .... A	43.0	0	0	6	245	711	1008	1054	770	601	291	96	0	4782
	Yuma .... A	64.2	0	0	0	0	108	264	307	190	90	15	0	0	974
Ark.	Fort Smith .... A	50.3	0	0	12	127	450	704	781	596	456	144	22	0	3292
	Little Rock .... A	50.5	0	0	9	127	465	716	756	577	434	126	9	0	3219
	Texarkana............................ A	54.2	0	0	0	78	345	561	626	468	350	105	0	0	2533
Calif.	Bakersfield .... A	55.4	0	0	0	37	282	502	546	364	267	105	19	0	2122
	Bishop................................. A	46.0	0	0	48	260	576	797	874	680	555	306	143	36	4275
	Blue Canyon......................... A	42.2	28	37	108	347	594	781	896	795	806	597	412	195	5596
	Burbank .... A	58.6	0	0	6	43	177	301	366	277	239	138	81	18	1646
	Eureka C	49.9	270	257	258	329	414	499	546	470	505	438	372	285	4643
	Fresno .... A	53.3	0	0	0	84	354	577	605	426	335	162	62	6	2611
	Long Beach .... A	57.8	0	0	9	47	171	316	397	311	264	171	93	24	1803
	Los Angeles .... A	57.4	28	28	42	78	180	291	372	302	288	219	158	81	2061
	Los Angeles C	60.3	0	0	6	31	132	229	310	230	202	123	68	18	1349
	Mt. Shasta C	41.2	25	34	123	406	696	902	983	784	738	525	347	159	5722
	Oakland .... A	53.5	53	50	45	127	309	481	527	400	353	255	180	90	2870
	Red Bluff .... A	53.8	0	0	0	53	318	555	605	428	341	168	47	0	2515
	Sacramento.......................... A	53.9	0	0	0	56	321	546	583	414	332	178	72	0	2502
	Sacramento.......................... C	54.4	0	0	0	62	312	533	561	392	310	173	76	0	2419
	Sandberg............................. C	46.8	0	0	30	202	480	691	778	661	620	426	264	57	4209
	San Diego............................ A	59.5	9	0	21	43	135	236	298	235	214	135	90	42	1458
	San Francisco....................... A	53.4	81	78	60	143	306	462	508	395	363	279	214	126	3015
	San Francisco....................... C	55.1	192	174	102	118	231	388	443	336	319	279	239	180	3001
	Santa Maria .... A	54.3	99	93	96	146	270	391	459	370	363	282	233	165	2967
Colo.	Alamosa .... A	29.7	65	99	279	639	1065	1420	1476	1162	1020	696	440	168	8529
	Colorado Springs .... A	37.3	9	25	132	456	825	1032	1128	938	893	582	319	84	6423
	Denver .... A	37.6	6	9	117	428	819	1035	1132	938	887	558	288	66	6283
	Denver C	40.8	0	0	90	366	714	905	1004	851	800	492	254	48	5524
	Grand Junction .... A	39.3	0	0	30	313	786	1113	1209	907	729	387	146	21	5641
	Pueblo................................. A	40.4	0	0	54	326	750	986	1085	871	772	429	174	15	5462
Conn.	Bridgeport .... A	39.9	0	0	66	307	615	986	1079	966	853	510	208	27	5617
	Hartford .... A	37.3	0	12	117	394	714	1101	1190	1042	908	519	205	33	6235
	New Haven .... A	39.0	0	12	87	347	648	1011	1097	991	871	543	245	45	5897
Del.	Wilmington.......................... A	42.5	0	0	51	270	588	927	980	874	735	387	112	6	4930
D.C.	Washington .... A	45.7	0	0	33	217	519	834	871	762	626	288	74	0	4224
Fla.	Apalachicola......................... C	61.2	0	0	0	16	153	319	347	260	180	33	0	0	1308
	Daytona Beach...................... A	64.5	0	0	0	0	75	211	248	190	140	15	0	0	879
	Fort Myers .... A	68.6	0	0	0	0	24	109	146	101	62	0	0	0	442
	Jacksonville .... A	61.9	0	0	0	12	144	310	332	246	174	21	0	0	1239
	Key West .... A	73.1	0	0	0	0	0	28	40	31	9	0	0	0	108
	Lakeland.............................. C	66.7	0	0	0	0	57	164	195	146	99	0	0	0	661
	Miami .... A	71.1	0	0	0	0	0	65	74	56	19	0	0	0	214

[a] Data for United States cities from a publication of the United States Weather Bureau, *Monthly Normals of Temperature, Precipitation and Heating Degree Days,* 1962, are for the period 1931 to 1960 inclusive. These data also include information from the 1963 revisions to this publication, where available.

[b] Data for airport stations, A, and city stations, C, are both given where available.

[c] Data for Canadian cities were computed by the Climatology Division, Department of Transport from normal monthly mean temperatures, and the monthly values of heating degree days data were obtained using the National Research Council computer and a method devised by H. C. S. Thom of the United States Weather Bureau. The heating degree days are based on the period from 1931 to 1960.

[d] For period October to April, inclusive.

State	Station	Avg. Winter Temp[d]	July	Aug.	Sept.	Oct.	Nov.	Dec.	Jan.	Feb.	Mar.	Apr.	May	June	Yearly Total
Fla. (Cont'd)	Miami Beach C	72.5	0	0	0	0	0	40	56	36	9	0	0	0	141
	Orlando.................... A	65.7	0	0	0	0	72	198	220	165	105	6	0	0	766
	Pensacola .... A	60.4	0	0	0	19	195	353	400	277	183	36	0	0	1463
	Tallahassee .... A	60.1	0	0	0	28	198	360	375	286	202	36	0	0	1485
	Tampa..................... A	66.4	0	0	0	0	60	171	202	148	102	0	0	0	683
	West Palm Beach ..... A	68.4	0	0	0	0	6	65	87	64	31	0	0	0	253
Ga.	Athens .... A	51.8	0	0	12	115	405	632	642	529	431	141	22	0	2929
	Atlanta .... A	51.7	0	0	18	124	417	648	636	518	428	147	25	0	2961
	Augusta .... A	54.5	0	0	0	78	333	552	549	445	350	90	0	0	2397
	Columbus .... A	54.8	0	0	0	87	333	543	552	434	338	96	0	0	2383
	Macon .... A	56.2	0	0	0	71	297	502	505	403	295	63	0	0	2136
	Rome .... A	49.9	0	0	24	161	474	701	710	577	468	177	34	0	3326
	Savannah .... A	57.8	0	0	0	47	246	437	437	353	254	45	0	0	1819
	Thomasville C	60.0	0	0	0	25	198	366	394	305	208	33	0	0	1529
Hawaii	Lihue....................... A	72.7	0	0	0	0	0	0	0	0	0	0	0	0	0
	Honolulu.................. A	74.2	0	0	0	0	0	0	0	0	0	0	0	0	0
	Hilo........................ A	71.9	0	0	0	0	0	0	0	0	0	0	0	0	0
Idaho	Boise .... A	39.7	0	0	132	415	792	1017	1113	854	722	438	245	81	5809
	Lewiston .... A	41.0	0	0	123	403	756	933	1063	815	694	426	239	90	5542
	Pocatello.................. A	34.8	0	0	172	493	900	1166	1324	1058	905	555	319	141	7033
Ill.	Cairo....................... C	47.9	0	0	36	164	513	791	856	680	539	195	47	0	3821
	Chicago (O'Hare)..... A	35.8	0	12	117	381	807	1166	1265	1086	939	534	260	72	6639
	Chicago (Midway) .... A	37.5	0	0	81	326	753	1113	1209	1044	890	480	211	48	6155
	Chicago C	38.9	0	0	66	279	705	1051	1150	1000	868	489	226	48	5882
	Moline .... A	36.4	0	9	99	335	774	1181	1314	1100	918	450	189	39	6408
	Peoria .... A	38.1	0	6	87	326	759	1113	1218	1025	849	426	183	33	6025
	Rockford.................. A	34.8	6	9	114	400	837	1221	1333	1137	961	516	236	60	6830
	Springfield............... A	40.6	0	0	72	291	696	1023	1135	935	769	354	136	18	5429
Ind.	Evansville .... A	45.0	0	0	66	220	606	896	955	767	620	237	68	0	4435
	Fort Wayne .... A	37.3	0	9	105	378	783	1135	1178	1028	890	471	189	39	6205
	Indianapolis .... A	39.6	0	0	90	316	723	1051	1113	949	809	432	177	39	5699
	South Bend.............. A	36.6	0	6	111	372	777	1125	1221	1070	933	525	239	60	6439
Iowa	Burlington .... A	37.6	0	0	93	322	768	1135	1259	1042	859	426	177	33	6114
	Des Moines .... A	35.5	0	6	96	363	828	1225	1370	1137	915	438	180	30	6588
	Dubuque.................. A	32.7	12	31	156	450	906	1287	1420	1204	1026	546	260	78	7376
	Sioux City................ A	34.0	0	9	108	369	867	1240	1435	1198	989	483	214	39	6951
	Waterloo .... A	32.6	12	19	138	428	909	1296	1460	1221	1023	531	229	54	7320
Kans.	Concordia .... A	40.4	0	0	57	276	705	1023	1163	935	781	372	149	18	5479
	Dodge City .... A	42.5	0	0	33	251	666	939	1051	840	719	354	124	9	4986
	Goodland .... A	37.8	0	6	81	381	810	1073	1166	955	884	507	236	42	6141
	Topeka .... A	41.7	0	0	57	270	672	980	1122	893	722	330	124	12	5182
	Wichita .... A	44.2	0	0	33	229	618	905	1023	804	645	270	87	6	4620
Ky.	Covington .... A	41.4	0	0	75	291	669	983	1035	893	756	390	149	24	5265
	Lexington .... A	43.8	0	0	54	239	609	902	946	818	685	325	105	0	4683
	Louisville .... A	44.0	0	0	54	248	609	890	930	818	682	315	105	9	4660
La.	Alexandria .... A	57.5	0	0	0	56	273	431	471	361	260	69	0	0	1921
	Baton Rouge .... A	59.8	0	0	0	31	216	369	409	294	208	33	0	0	1560
	Lake Charles .... A	60.5	0	0	0	19	210	341	381	274	195	39	0	0	1459
	New Orleans............ A	61.0	0	0	0	19	192	322	363	258	192	39	0	0	1385
	New Orleans............ C	61.8	0	0	0	12	165	291	344	241	177	24	0	0	1254
	Shreveport............... A	56.2	0	0	0	47	297	477	552	426	304	81	0	0	2184
Me.	Caribou .... A	24.4	78	115	336	682	1044	1535	1690	1470	1308	858	468	183	9767
	Portland .... A	33.0	12	53	195	508	807	1215	1339	1182	1042	675	372	111	7511
Md.	Baltimore .... A	43.7	0	0	48	264	585	905	936	820	679	327	90	0	4654
	Baltimore C	46.2	0	0	27	189	486	806	859	762	629	288	65	0	4111
	Frederick .... A	42.0	0	0	66	307	624	955	995	876	741	384	127	12	5087
Mass.	Boston..................... A	40.0	0	9	60	316	603	983	1088	972	846	513	208	36	5634
	Nantucket .... A	40.2	12	22	93	332	573	896	992	941	896	621	384	129	5891
	Pittsfield .... A	32.6	25	59	219	524	831	1231	1339	1196	1063	660	326	105	7578
	Worcester .... A	34.7	6	34	147	450	774	1172	1271	1123	998	612	304	78	6969

State	Station	Avg. Winter Temp[d]	July	Aug.	Sept.	Oct.	Nov.	Dec.	Jan.	Feb.	Mar.	Apr.	May	June	Yearly Total
Mich.	Alpena .... A	29.7	68	105	273	580	912	1268	1404	1299	1218	777	446	156	8506
	Detroit (City)...................... A	37.2	0	0	87	360	738	1088	1181	1058	936	522	220	42	6232
	Detroit (Wayne)................... A	37.1	0	0	96	353	738	1088	1194	1061	933	534	239	57	6293
	Detroit (Willow Run) .... A	37.2	0	0	90	357	750	1104	1190	1053	921	519	229	45	6258
	Escanaba................................ C	29.6	59	87	243	539	924	1293	1445	1296	1203	777	456	159	8481
	Flint..................................... A	33.1	16	40	159	465	843	1212	1330	1198	1066	639	319	90	7377
	Grand Rapids........................ A	34.9	9	28	135	434	804	1147	1259	1134	1011	579	279	75	6894
	Lansing................................. A	34.8	6	22	138	431	813	1163	1262	1142	1011	579	273	69	6909
	Marquette............................. C	30.2	59	81	240	527	936	1268	1411	1268	1187	771	468	177	8393
	Muskegon.............................. A	36.0	12	28	120	400	762	1088	1209	1100	995	594	310	78	6696
	Sault Ste. Marie .... A	27.7	96	105	279	580	951	1367	1525	1380	1277	810	477	201	9048
Minn.	Duluth................................... A	23.4	71	109	330	632	1131	1581	1745	1518	1355	840	490	198	10000
	Minneapolis.......................... A	28.3	22	31	189	505	1014	1454	1631	1380	1166	621	288	81	8382
	Rochester.............................. A	28.8	25	34	186	474	1005	1438	1593	1366	1150	630	301	93	8295
Miss.	Jackson .... A	55.7	0	0	0	65	315	502	546	414	310	87	0	0	2239
	Meridian............................... A	55.4	0	0	0	81	339	518	543	417	310	81	0	0	2289
	Vicksburg C	56.9	0	0	0	53	279	462	512	384	282	69	0	0	2041
Mo.	Columbia .... A	42.3	0	0	54	251	651	967	1076	874	716	324	121	12	5046
	Kansas City .... A	43.9	0	0	39	220	612	905	1032	818	682	294	109	0	4711
	St. Joseph .... A	40.3	0	6	60	285	708	1039	1172	949	769	348	133	15	5484
	St. Louis............................... A	43.1	0	0	60	251	627	936	1026	848	704	312	121	15	4900
	St. Louis............................... C	44.8	0	0	36	202	576	884	977	801	651	270	87	0	4484
	Springfield............................ A	44.5	0	0	45	223	600	877	973	781	660	291	105	6	4900
Mont.	Billings .... A	34.5	6	15	186	487	897	1135	1296	1100	970	570	285	102	7049
	Glasgow................................ A	26.4	31	47	270	608	1104	1466	1711	1439	1187	648	335	150	8996
	Great Falls .... A	32.8	28	53	258	543	921	1169	1349	1154	1063	642	384	186	7750
	Havre................................... A	28.1	28	53	306	595	1065	1367	1584	1364	1181	657	338	162	8700
	Havre................................... C	29.8	19	37	252	539	1014	1321	1528	1305	1116	612	304	135	8182
	Helena.................................. A	31.1	31	59	294	601	1002	1265	1438	1170	1042	651	381	195	8129
	Kalispell .... A	31.4	50	99	321	654	1020	1240	1401	1134	1029	639	397	207	8191
	Miles City .... A	31.2	6	6	174	502	972	1296	1504	1252	1057	579	276	99	7723
	Missoula............................... A	31.5	34	74	303	651	1035	1287	1420	1120	970	621	391	219	8125
Neb.	Grand Island .... A	36.0	0	6	108	381	834	1172	1314	1089	908	462	211	45	6530
	Lincoln C	38.8	0	6	75	301	726	1066	1237	1016	834	402	171	30	5864
	Norfolk................................. A	34.0	9	0	111	397	873	1234	1414	1179	983	498	233	48	6979
	North Platte......................... A	35.5	0	6	123	440	885	1166	1271	1039	930	519	248	57	6684
	Omaha.................................. A	35.6	0	12	105	357	828	1175	1355	1126	939	465	208	42	6612
	Scottsbluff............................ A	35.9	0	0	138	459	876	1128	1231	1008	921	552	285	75	6673
	Valentine.............................. A	32.6	9	12	165	493	942	1237	1395	1176	1045	579	288	84	7425
Nev.	Elko .... A	34.0	9	34	225	561	924	1197	1314	1036	911	621	409	192	7433
	Ely .... A	33.1	28	43	234	592	939	1184	1308	1075	977	672	456	225	7733
	Las Vegas .... A	53.5	0	0	0	78	387	617	688	487	335	111	6	0	2709
	Reno .... A	39.3	43	87	204	490	801	1026	1073	823	729	510	357	189	6332
	Winnemucca.......................... A	36.7	0	34	210	536	876	1091	1172	916	837	573	363	153	6761
N.H.	Concord .... A	33.0	6	50	177	505	822	1240	1358	1184	1032	636	298	75	7383
	Mt. Washington Obsv..............	15.2	493	536	720	1057	1341	1742	1820	1663	1652	1260	930	603	13817
N.J.	Atlantic City .... A	43.2	0	0	39	251	549	880	936	848	741	420	133	15	4812
	Newark................................. A	42.8	0	0	30	248	573	921	983	876	729	381	118	0	4589
	Trenton................................ C	42.4	0	0	57	264	576	924	989	885	753	399	121	12	4980
N. M.	Albuquerque......................... A	45.0	0	0	12	229	642	868	930	703	595	288	81	0	4348
	Clayton................................ A	42.0	0	6	66	310	699	899	986	812	747	429	183	21	5158
	Raton................................... A	38.1	9	28	126	431	825	1048	1116	904	834	543	301	63	6228
	Roswell................................ A	47.5	0	0	18	202	573	806	840	641	481	201	31	0	3793
	Silver City .... A	48.0	0	0	6	183	525	729	791	605	518	261	87	0	3705
N.Y.	Albany .... A	34.6	0	19	138	440	777	1194	1311	1156	992	564	239	45	6875
	Albany C	37.2	0	9	102	375	699	1104	1218	1072	908	498	186	30	6201
	Binghamton .... A	33.9	22	65	201	471	810	1184	1277	1154	1045	645	313	99	7286
	Binghamton C	36.6	0	28	141	406	732	1107	1190	1081	949	543	229	45	6451
	Buffalo .... A	34.5	19	37	141	440	777	1156	1256	1145	1039	645	329	78	7062
	New York (Cent. Park)........ C	42.8	0	0	30	233	540	902	986	885	760	408	118	9	4871
	New York (La Guardia) ...... A	43.1	0	0	27	223	528	887	973	879	750	414	124	6	4811

State	Station	Avg. Winter Temp[d]	July	Aug.	Sept.	Oct.	Nov.	Dec.	Jan.	Feb.	Mar.	Apr.	May	June	Yearly Total
	New York (Kennedy) .... A	41.4	0	0	36	248	564	933	1029	935	815	480	167	12	5219
	Rochester .... A	35.4	9	31	126	415	747	1125	1234	1123	1014	597	279	48	6748
	Schenectady C	35.4	0	22	123	422	756	1159	1283	1131	970	543	211	30	6650
	Syracuse .... A	35.2	6	28	132	415	744	1153	1271	1140	1004	570	248	45	6756
N. C.	Asheville C	46.7	0	0	48	245	555	775	784	683	592	273	87	0	4042
	Cape Hatteras	53.3	0	0	0	78	273	521	580	518	440	177	25	0	2612
	Charlotte........................... A	50.4	0	0	6	124	438	691	691	582	481	156	22	0	3191
	Greensboro....................... A	47.5	0	0	33	192	513	778	784	672	552	234	47	0	3805
	Raleigh .... A	49.4	0	0	21	164	450	716	725	616	487	180	34	0	3393
	Wilmington....................... A	54.6	0	0	0	74	291	521	546	462	357	96	0	0	2347
	Winston-Salem.................. A	48.4	0	0	21	171	483	747	753	652	524	207	37	0	3595
N. D.	Bismarck............................ A	26.6	34	28	222	577	1083	1463	1708	1442	1203	645	329	117	8851
	Devils Lake C	22.4	40	53	273	642	1191	1634	1872	1579	1345	753	381	138	9901
	Fargo................................. A	24.8	28	37	219	574	1107	1569	1789	1520	1262	690	332	99	9226
	Williston........................... A	25.2	31	43	261	601	1122	1513	1758	1473	1262	681	357	141	9243
Ohio	Akron-Canton.................... A	38.1	0	9	96	381	726	1070	1138	1016	871	489	202	39	6037
	Cincinnati C	45.1	0	0	39	208	558	862	915	790	642	294	96	6	4410
	Cleveland .... A	37.2	9	25	105	384	738	1088	1159	1047	918	552	260	66	6351
	Columbus .... A	39.7	0	6	84	347	714	1039	1088	949	809	426	171	27	5660
	Columbus C	41.5	0	0	57	285	651	977	1032	902	760	396	136	15	5211
	Dayton .... A	39.8	0	6	78	310	696	1045	1097	955	809	429	167	30	5622
	Mansfield .... A	36.9	9	22	114	397	768	1110	1169	1042	924	543	245	60	6403
	Sandusky C	39.1	0	6	66	313	684	1032	1107	991	868	495	198	36	5796
	Toledo............................... A	36.4	0	16	117	406	792	1138	1200	1056	924	543	242	60	6494
	Youngstown .... A	36.8	6	19	120	412	771	1104	1169	1047	921	540	248	60	6417
Okla.	Oklahoma City.................... A	48.3	0	0	15	164	498	766	868	664	527	189	34	0	3725
	Tulsa................................. A	47.7	0	0	18	158	522	787	893	683	539	213	47	0	3860
Ore.	Astoria .... A	45.6	146	130	210	375	561	679	753	622	636	480	363	231	5186
	Burns C	35.9	12	37	210	515	867	1113	1246	988	856	570	366	177	6957
	Eugene .... A	45.6	34	34	129	366	585	719	803	627	589	426	279	135	4726
	Meacham .... A	34.2	84	124	288	580	918	1091	1209	1005	983	726	527	339	7874
	Medford .... A	43.2	0	0	78	372	678	871	918	697	642	432	242	78	5008
	Pendleton .... A	42.6	0	0	111	350	711	884	1017	773	617	396	205	63	5127
	Portland .... A	45.6	25	28	114	335	597	735	825	644	586	396	245	105	4635
	Portland C	47.4	12	16	75	267	534	679	769	594	536	351	198	78	4109
	Roseburg........................... A	46.3	22	16	105	329	567	713	766	608	570	405	267	123	4491
	Salem .... A	45.4	37	31	111	338	594	729	822	647	611	417	273	144	4754
Pa.	Allentown .... A	38.9	0	0	90	353	693	1045	1116	1002	849	471	167	24	5810
	Erie .... A	36.8	0	25	102	391	714	1063	1169	1081	973	585	288	60	6451
	Harrisburg .... A	41.2	0	0	63	298	648	992	1045	907	766	396	124	12	5251
	Philadelphia .... A	41.8	0	0	60	297	620	965	1016	889	747	392	118	40	5144
	Philadelphia C	44.5	0	0	30	205	513	856	924	823	691	351	93	0	4486
	Pittsburgh .... A	38.4	0	9	105	375	726	1063	1119	1002	874	480	195	39	5987
	Pittsburgh C	42.2	0	0	60	291	615	930	983	885	763	390	124	12	5053
	Reading.............................. C	42.4	0	0	54	257	597	939	1001	885	735	372	105	0	4945
	Scranton .... A	37.2	0	19	132	434	762	1104	1156	1028	893	498	195	33	6254
	Williamsport...................... A	38.5	0	9	111	375	717	1073	1122	1002	856	468	177	24	5934
R. I.	Block Island .... A	40.1	0	16	78	307	594	902	1020	955	877	612	344	99	5804
	Providence .... A	38.8	0	16	96	372	660	1023	1110	988	868	534	236	51	5954
S. C.	Charleston .... A	56.4	0	0	0	59	282	471	487	389	291	54	0	0	2033
	Charleston C	57.9	0	0	0	34	210	425	443	367	273	42	0	0	1794
	Columbia .... A	54.0	0	0	0	84	345	577	570	470	357	81	0	0	2484
	Florence............................ A	54.5	0	0	0	78	315	552	552	459	347	84	0	0	2387
	Greenville-Spartanburg .... A	51.6	0	0	6	121	399	651	660	546	446	132	19	0	2980
S. D.	Huron .... A	28.8	9	12	165	508	1014	1432	1628	1355	1125	600	288	87	8223
	Rapid City .... A	33.4	22	12	165	481	897	1172	1333	1145	1051	615	326	126	7345
	Sioux Falls .... A	30.6	19	25	168	462	972	1361	1544	1285	1082	573	270	78	7839
Tenn.	Bristol............................... A	46.2	0	0	51	236	573	828	828	700	598	261	68	0	4143
	Chattanooga .... A	50.3	0	0	18	143	468	698	722	577	453	150	25	0	3254
	Knoxville .... A	49.2	0	0	30	171	489	725	732	613	493	198	43	0	3494
	Memphis .... A	50.5	0	0	18	130	447	698	729	585	456	147	22	0	3232

State or Prov.	Station	Avg. Winter Temp[d]	July	Aug.	Sept.	Oct.	Nov.	Dec.	Jan.	Feb.	Mar.	Apr.	May	June	Yearly Total
	Memphis C	51.6	0	0	12	102	396	648	710	568	434	129	16	0	3015
	Nashville .... A	48.9	0	0	30	158	495	732	778	644	512	189	40	0	3578
	Oak Ridge C	47.7	0	0	39	192	531	772	778	669	552	228	56	0	3817
Tex.	Abilene .... A	53.9	0	0	0	99	366	586	642	470	347	114	0	0	2624
	Amarillo .... A	47.0	0	0	18	205	570	797	877	664	546	252	56	0	3985
	Austin .... A	59.1	0	0	0	31	225	388	468	325	223	51	0	0	1711
	Brownsville .... A	67.7	0	0	0	0	66	149	205	106	74	0	0	0	600
	Corpus Christi ...... A	64.6	0	0	0	0	120	220	291	174	109	0	0	0	914
	Dallas .... A	55.3	0	0	0	62	321	524	601	440	319	90	6	0	2363
	El Paso .... A	52.9	0	0	0	84	414	648	685	445	319	105	0	0	2700
	Fort Worth........... A	55.1	0	0	0	65	324	536	614	448	319	99	0	0	2405
	Galveston .... A	62.2	0	0	0	6	147	276	360	263	189	33	0	0	1274
	Galveston C	62.0	0	0	0	0	138	270	350	258	189	30	0	0	1235
	Houston .... A	61.0	0	0	0	6	183	307	384	288	192	36	0	0	1396
	Houston C	62.0	0	0	0	0	165	288	363	258	174	30	0	0	1278
	Laredo .... A	66.0	0	0	0	0	105	217	267	134	74	0	0	0	797
	Lubbock .... A	48.8	0	0	18	174	513	744	800	613	484	201	31	0	3578
	Midland .... A	53.8	0	0	0	87	381	592	651	468	322	90	0	0	2591
	Port Arthur .... A	60.5	0	0	0	22	207	329	384	274	192	39	0	0	1447
	San Angelo .... A	56.0	0	0	0	68	318	536	567	412	288	66	0	0	2255
	San Antonio .... A	60.1	0	0	0	31	204	363	428	286	195	39	0	0	1546
	Victoria................ A	62.7	0	0	0	6	150	270	344	230	152	21	0	0	1173
	Waco .... A	57.2	0	0	0	43	270	456	536	389	270	66	0	0	2030
	Wichita Falls .... A	53.0	0	0	0	99	381	632	698	518	378	120	6	0	2832
Utah	Milford .... A	36.5	0	0	99	443	867	1141	1252	988	822	519	279	87	6497
	Salt Lake City ...... A	38.4	0	0	81	419	849	1082	1172	910	763	459	233	84	6052
	Wendover .... A	39.1	0	0	48	372	822	1091	1178	902	729	408	177	51	5778
Vt.	Burlington .... A	29.4	28	65	207	539	891	1349	1513	1333	1187	714	353	90	8269
Va.	Cape Henry C	50.0	0	0	0	112	360	645	694	633	536	246	53	0	3279
	Lynchburg .... A	46.0	0	0	51	223	540	822	849	731	605	267	78	0	4166
	Norfolk .... A	49.2	0	0	0	136	408	698	738	655	533	216	37	0	3421
	Richmond.............. A	47.3	0	0	36	214	495	784	815	703	546	219	53	0	3865
	Roanoke .... A	46.1	0	0	51	229	549	825	834	722	614	261	65	0	4150
Wash.	Olympia .... A	44.2	68	71	198	422	636	753	834	675	645	450	307	177	5236
	Seattle-Tacoma...... A	44.2	56	62	162	391	633	750	828	678	657	474	295	159	5145
	Seattle C	46.9	50	47	129	329	543	657	738	599	577	396	242	117	4424
	Spokane .... A	36.5	9	25	168	493	879	1082	1231	980	834	531	288	135	6655
	Walla Walla C	43.8	0	0	87	310	681	843	986	745	589	342	177	45	4805
	Yakima .... A	39.1	0	12	144	450	828	1039	1163	868	713	435	220	69	5941
W. Va.	Charleston .... A	44.8	0	0	63	254	591	865	880	770	648	300	96	9	4476
	Elkins .... A	40.1	9	25	135	400	729	992	1008	896	791	444	198	48	5675
	Huntington .... A	45.0	0	0	63	257	585	856	880	764	636	294	99	12	4446
	Parkersburg C	43.5	0	0	60	264	606	905	942	826	691	339	115	6	4754
Wisc.	Green Bay .... A	30.3	28	50	174	484	924	1333	1494	1313	1141	654	335	99	8029
	La Crosse .... A	31.5	12	19	153	437	924	1339	1504	1277	1070	540	245	69	7589
	Madison .... A	30.9	25	40	174	474	930	1330	1473	1274	1113	618	310	102	7863
	Milwaukee .... A	32.6	43	47	174	471	876	1252	1376	1193	1054	642	372	135	7635
Wyo.	Casper.................. A	33.4	6	16	192	524	942	1169	1290	1084	1020	657	381	129	7410
	Cheyenne .... A	34.2	28	37	219	543	909	1085	1212	1042	1026	702	428	150	7381
	Lander .... A	31.4	6	19	204	555	1020	1299	1417	1145	1017	654	381	153	7870
	Sheridan .... A	32.5	25	31	219	539	948	1200	1355	1154	1051	642	366	150	7680
Alta.	Banff C	—	220	295	498	797	1185	1485	1624	1364	1237	855	589	402	10551
	Calgary .... A	—	109	186	402	719	1110	1389	1575	1379	1268	798	477	291	9703
	Edmonton .... A	—	74	180	411	738	1215	1603	1810	1520	1330	765	400	222	10268
	Lethbridge .... A	—	56	112	318	611	1011	1277	1497	1291	1159	696	403	213	8644
B. C.	Kamloops .... A	—	22	40	189	546	894	1138	1314	1057	818	462	217	102	6799
	Prince George* ...... A	—	236	251	444	747	1110	1420	1612	1319	1122	747	468	279	9755
	Prince Rupert........ C	—	273	248	339	539	708	868	936	808	812	648	493	357	7029
	Vancouver*............ A	—	81	87	219	456	657	787	862	723	676	501	310	156	5515
	Victoria*............... A	—	136	140	225	462	663	775	840	718	691	504	341	204	5699
	Victoria................ C	—	172	184	243	426	607	723	805	668	660	487	354	250	5579

State or Prov.	Station	Avg. Winter Temp^d	July	Aug.	Sept.	Oct.	Nov.	Dec.	Jan.	Feb.	Mar.	Apr.	May	June	Yearly Total
Man.	Brandon* .... A	—	47	90	357	747	1290	1792	2034	1737	1476	837	431	198	11036
	Churchill............................ A	—	360	375	681	1082	1620	2248	2558	2277	2130	1569	1153	675	16728
	The Pas.............................. C	—	59	127	429	831	1440	1981	2232	1853	1624	969	508	228	12281
	Winnipeg .... A	—	38	71	322	683	1251	1757	2008	1719	1465	813	405	147	10679
N. B.	Fredericton* .... A	—	78	68	234	592	915	1392	1541	1379	1172	753	406	141	8671
	Moncton C	—	62	105	276	611	891	1342	1482	1336	1194	789	468	171	8727
	St. John C	—	109	102	246	527	807	1194	1370	1229	1097	756	490	249	8219
Nfld.	Argentia .... A	—	260	167	294	564	750	1001	1159	1085	1091	879	707	483	8440
	Corner Brook C	—	102	133	324	642	873	1194	1358	1283	1212	885	639	333	8978
	Gander .... A	—	121	152	330	670	909	1231	1370	1266	1243	939	657	366	9254
	Goose* .... A	—	130	205	444	843	1227	1745	1947	1689	1494	1074	741	348	11887
	St. John's* .... A	—	186	180	342	651	831	1113	1262	1170	1187	927	710	432	8991
N. W. T.	Aklavik C	—	273	459	807	1414	2064	2530	2632	2336	2282	1674	1063	483	18017
	Fort Norman C	—	164	341	666	1234	1959	2474	2592	2209	2058	1386	732	294	16109
	Resolution Island................ C	—	843	831	900	1113	1311	1724	2021	1850	1817	1488	1181	942	16021
N. S.	Halifax C	—	58	51	180	457	710	1074	1213	1122	1030	742	487	237	7361
	Sydney .... A	—	62	71	219	518	765	1113	1262	1206	1150	840	567	276	8049
	Yarmouth .... A	—	102	115	225	471	696	1029	1156	1065	1004	726	493	258	7340
Ont.	Cochrane C	—	96	180	405	760	1233	1776	1978	1701	1528	963	570	222	11412
	Fort William .... A	—	90	133	366	694	1140	1597	1792	1557	1380	876	543	237	10405
	Kapuskasing....................... C	—	74	171	405	756	1245	1807	2037	1735	1562	978	580	222	11572
	Kitchener C	—	16	59	177	505	855	1234	1342	1226	1101	663	322	66	7566
	London .... A	—	12	43	159	477	837	1206	1305	1198	1066	648	332	66	7349
	North Bay C	—	37	90	267	608	990	1507	1680	1463	1277	780	400	120	9219
	Ottawa C	—	25	81	222	567	936	1469	1624	1441	1231	708	341	90	8735
	Toronto............................. C	—	7	18	151	439	760	1111	1233	1119	1013	616	298	62	6827
P.E.I.	Charlottetown...................... C	—	40	53	198	518	804	1215	1380	1274	1169	813	496	204	8164
	Summerside C	—	47	84	216	546	840	1246	1438	1291	1206	841	518	216	8488
Que.	Arvida............................... C	—	102	136	327	682	1074	1659	1879	1619	1407	891	521	231	10528
	Montreal*........................... A	—	9	43	165	521	882	1392	1566	1381	1175	684	316	69	8203
	Montreal C	—	16	28	165	496	864	1355	1510	1328	1138	657	288	54	7899
	Quebec* .... A	—	56	84	273	636	996	1516	1665	1477	1296	819	428	126	9372
	Quebec C	—	40	68	243	592	972	1473	1612	1418	1228	780	400	111	8937
Sasks	Prince Albert .... A	—	81	136	414	797	1368	1872	2108	1763	1559	867	446	219	11630
	Regina............................... A	—	78	93	360	741	1284	1711	1965	1687	1473	804	409	201	10806
	Saskatoon C	—	56	87	372	750	1302	1758	2006	1689	1463	798	403	186	10870
Y. T.	Dawson.............................. C	—	164	326	645	1197	1875	2415	2561	2150	1838	1068	570	258	15067
	Mayo Landing C	—	208	366	648	1135	1794	2325	2427	1992	1665	1020	580	294	14454

*The data for these normals were from the full ten-year period 1951–1960, adjusted to the standard normal period 1931–1960.

ENDNOTES

Introduction: What Is a Masonry Heater?

1. ASTM International, E1602-03: Standard Guide for Construction of Solid Fuel Burning Masonry Heaters, 2003.

1. The Hearth Is the Reason for the House

1. Christopher Alexander, et al., *A Pattern Language* (New York: Oxford University Press, 1977), p. 839.
2. HPBA Press Release, "New Data Show Increasing Consumer Demand for Fireplaces, Stoves, Inserts and Other Hearth Products," March 7, 2006.

2. A Brief History of Fire and Hot Rocks in North America

1. Johanna Spyri, *Heidi* (New York: Julian Messner, 1945), p. 229.
2. Olive Beaupré Miller, editor, *Over the Hill of My Book House* (Lake Bluff, IL: Book House for Children, 1965), pp. 163, 165.
3. Kate Seredy, *The Good Master* (New York: Viking Press, 1935), p. 36.
4. Miller, *Over the Hill*, p. 163.
5. Charles Neider, editor, *The Complete Essays of Mark Twain* (Cambridge, MA: Da Capo Press, 1991), pp. 103–4, 658–60.
6. Peter Clegg, *New Low-Cost Sources of Energy for the Home* (Charlotte, VT: Garden Way Publishing, 1975).
7. Heikki Hyytiainen and Albert Barden III, *Finnish Fireplaces: Heart of the Home* (Hanko, Finland: Building Book Limited, 1988), p. 7.
8. "Russian Fireplace: Demonstrations and Workshop," New Mexico Energy Institute, University of New Mexico, Albuquerque, 1981.

3. Thermal Comfort: The Vertical Radiant Advantage

1. John Siegenthaler, *Radiant Architecture: A Basic Course in Radiant Panel Heating Systems for Architects and Builders* (Loveland, CO: Teal International Corporation, 2002), p. 3.
2. Ibid.
3. Benedict Frederick Raber and Francis Williams Hutchinson, *Panel Heating and Cooling Analysis* (New York: John Wiley and Sons, 1947), p. 10.

4. Benefits of Masonry Heaters

1. Ziehe, Helmut, interview by Debra Lynn Dadd (October 2005). The article stemming from this interview is titled "About Bau-biologie" by Debra Lynn Dadd and can be found at www.debralynndadd.com.
2. Institute for Bau-biologie and Ecology (2008). http://buildingbiology.net/terms.php (accessed April 1, 2010).
3. Anton Schneider, *Correspondence Course Baubiologie*, translated by Helmut Ziehe (Clearwater, FL: International Institute for Baubiologie and Ecology, Inc. 1988), p. 31.
4. Robert O. Becker, *The Body Electric: Electromagnetism and the Foundation of Life* (New York: William Morrow, 1985), p. 284.
5. US Congress, Office of Technology Assessment, *Biological Effects of Power Frequency Electric & Magnetic Fields.* Background Paper, OTA-BP-E-53. (Washington, DC: US Government Printing Office, May 1989).
6. John R. Hall Jr., "Home Fires Involving Heating Equipment," National Fire Protection Association, January 2010, p. i.
7. Ibid., p. ix.

7. Heating Requirements of the House

1. You can find more information about solar gain in books such as Edward Mazria's *The Passive Solar Energy Book* as well as James Kachadorian's *The Passive Solar House.* Complete information is in the bibliography.

8. The Inner Life—Cores and Flues

1. Henry Ford, *My Life and Work* (Garden City, NY: Doubleday, 1922), p. 73.
2. Ibid., p. 72.

9. Codes, Clearances, Footers, and Foundations

1. www.kirche-suurhusen.de/turm/kirche.htm, (accessed November 15, 2009).

BIBLIOGRAPHY

Alexander, Christopher, et al. *A Pattern Language.* New York: Oxford University Press, 1977.

American Heritage Dictionary. n.d.

Anyanwu, Eber C. "The Validity of the Environmental Neurotoxic Effects of Toxigenic Molds and Mycotoxins." *Internet Journal of Toxicology* 5, no. 2 (2008).

ASHRAE Handbook Fundamentals. Atlanta: American Society of Heating, Refrigerating and Air-Conditioning Engineers, Inc., 2005.

Becker, Robert O. *The Body Electric: Electromagnetism and the Foundation of Life.* New York: William Morrow, 1985.

Blundell, Stephen J., and Katherine M. Blundell. *Concepts in Thermal Physics.* New York: Oxford University Press, 2006.

Clarke, J. A., P. P. Yaneske, and A. A. Pinney. *The Harmonisation of Thermal Properties of Building Materials.* Research Report. Watford, England: Building Research Establishment, 1990.

Craighhill, Jamie. "Proper Wood Storage/Woodshed Design." Washington State Department of Ecology (January 1992). www.ecy.wa.gov/biblio/91062.html, last accessed July 2009.

Egan, M. David. *Concepts in Thermal Comfort.* Englewood Cliffs, NJ: Prentice-Hall, 1975.

Environmental Protection Agency. *Indoor Air Facts No. 4—Sick Building Syndrome.* Research and Development. Washington, DC: US EPA, 1991.

———. *Inventory of US Greenhouse Gas Emissions and Sinks.* Washington, DC: US EPA, 2007.

———. *State Bioenergy Primer.* Washington, DC: US EPA, 2009.

Etzel, Ruth Ann "Indoor and Outdoor Air Pollution: Tobacco Smoke, Moulds and Diseases in Infants and Children." *International Journal of Hygiene and Environmental Health* 210, no. 5 (2007): 611–616.

Fanger, Poul Ole *Thermal Comfort: Analysis and Applications in Environmental Engineering.* New York: McGraw-Hill, 1972.

Ford, Henry, in collaboration with Samuel Crowther. *My Life and Work.* Garden City, NY: Doubleday, Page, 1922.

Ghaddar, Nesreen, Mohamad Salam, and Kamel Ghali. *Steady Thermal Comfort by Radiant Heat Transfer: The Impact of the Heater Position.* Beirut: Taylor and Francis Group, LLC, 2006.

Gulland, John. *The Fireplace in the House as a System.* Ontario: Gulland Associates, 1997.

Hageman, Jack M. *Contractor's Guide to the Building Code: Based on the 2006 IBC and IRC.* Carlsbad, CA: Craftsman Book Company, 2008.

Hyytiainen, Heikki, and Albert Barden III. *Finnish Fireplaces: Heart of the Home.* Hanko, Finland: Building Book Limited, 1988.

The Illusionist. Directed by Neil Burger. 2006.

International Programme on Chemical Safety. "IPCS Results List" (2009). http://inchemsearch.ccohs.ca/inchem/jsp/search/search.jsp?inchemcasreg=1&Coll=inchemall&serverSpec=charlie.ccohs.ca%3A9900&QueryText1=&QueryText2=methyl+bromide&Search.x=22&Search.y=12, last accessed August 2009.

"International Residential Code." International Code Council (ICC), 2006.

Jarvis, Bruce B., and J. David Miller. "Mycotoxins as Harmful Indoor Air Contaminants." *Applied Microbiology and Biotechnology* 66, no. 4 (2005): 367–372.

Jones, Nicola. "Feel the Force." *New Scientist* 6 (April 2002): 8.

Kachadorian, James. *The Passive Solar House: Using Solar Design to Heat and Cool Your Home.* White River Junction, VT: Chelsea Green Publishing, 1997.

Lyle, David. *The Book of Masonry Stoves.* Andover, MA: Brick House Publishing, 1984.

Mazria, Edward. *The Passive Solar Energy Book.* Emmaus, PA: Rodale Press, 1979.

Miller, Olive Beaupré, editor. *Over the Hills of My Book House.* Lake Bluff, IL: Book House for Children, 1920.

Mother Earth News editors. "My Mother's House: Part VII." *Mother Earth News* (September–October 1982).

Neider, Charles, editor. *The Complete Essays of Mark Twain.* Cambridge, MA: Da Capo Press, 1991.

"New Data Show Increasing Consumer Demand for Fireplaces, Stoves, Inserts and Other Hearth Products." *HPBA Press Release* 7 (March 2006).

Österreichisches Normungsinstitut. *One off Kachelgrundöfen/Putzgrundöfen (tiled/mortared stoves) - Calculation method.* Ref. No. prEN 15544:2006: E. Vienna: Österreichisches Normungsinstitut, 2006.

Parsons, Kenneth C. *Human Thermal Environments: The Effects of Hot, Moderate, and Cold Environments on Human Health, Comfort and Performance. The Principles and the Practice.* New York: Taylor and Francis, 1993.

Raber, Benedict Frederick, and Francis Williams Hutchinson. *Panel Heating and Cooling Analysis.* New York: John Wiley and Sons, 1947.

Ruedisili, Lon C., and Morris W. Firebaugh. *Perspectives on Energy.* New York: Oxford University Press, 1982.

Schneider, Anton, translated by Helmut Ziehe. *Bau-biologie Correspondence Course.* Clearwater, FL: International Institute for Bau-Biologie and Ecology, Inc., 1987.

Seredy, Kate. *The Good Master.* New York: Viking Press, 1935.

Siegenthaler, John, *Radiant Architecture: A Basic Course in Radiant Panel Heating Systems for Architects and Builders.* Loveland, CO: Teal International Corporation, 2002.

The Sound of Music. Directed by Robert Wise. 1965.

Spyri, Johanna. *Heidi.* New York: Dell Publishing, 1990.

"Standard Guide for Construction of Solid Fuel Burning Masonry Heaters." *ASTM E 1602-3.* West Conshohocken, PA: ASTM International, 2003.

Steiner, Rudolf. *Toward Social Renewal: Basic Issues of the Social Question.* London: Rudolf Steiner Press, 1977 (1923).

Thayer, Robert E. *Biopsychology of Mood and Arousal.* New York: Oxford University Press, 1989.

US Congress, Office of Technology Assessment. *Biological Effects of Power Frequency Electric and Magnetic Fields.* Background Paper, OTA-BP-E-53. Washington, DC: US Government Printing Office, 1989.

"Washington State Building Code." *WAC 51-50-31200 Section 31.204.2.* 2006.

Webster's New World Dicitonary. n.d.

www.epa.gov/region1/eco/energy/re_biomass.html, last accessed March 2010.

Zemansky, Mark W. *Heat and Thermodynamics.* New York: McGraw-Hill, 1951.

ACKNOWLEDGMENTS

I love this book. How could I not? It was a mere twinkle in my eye about six years ago. Four years ago I started getting really serious about it, writing notes and disconnected pages; two years ago I wrote a coherent chapter. I handed it to Judy Ludwig, a friend, fellow homeschooler, experienced editor, and masonry heater owner. She was excited but delightfully unforgiving and asked me to cut things that I knew couldn't possibly be cut from the text. That chapter was rewritten, revised, and reexamined more times than I care to admit. It was that chapter, molded under her guidance, that was sent to Chelsea Green as one of two sample chapters that, together with my formal proposal, landed the book contract. Judy had little time for my book when I wrote the other eleven chapters. Yet I often felt she was looking over my shoulder. As I typed each chapter, I could hear her saying, "Cut; then cut again!" For this, Judy Ludwig gets special recognition and admiration.

In Connecticut lives one of the most talented, knowledgeable, and devoted heater masons around. When it comes to masonry heaters, Rod Zander means business, and he knows no compromise to giving his best to a project. He expects the same from those who work with him. Rod and Elisabeth Zander invited me into their lives and home briefly as I was writing the last couple chapters. I had the honor of helping to build the *kachelofen* that appears as figure 2.1. Rod and Elisabeth Zander proved to be the most generous and helpful pair I encountered in this authorship odyssey. The little soapstone heater showcased in chapter 8, as well as much of the knowledge imparted there, would not exist without Rod's tutelage and generous manner. It was Rod who awakened me to the endless possibilities inherent in masonry heaters.

Yet before Rod or Judy or the seed of an idea for a book there was Albie Barden. Like so many others, I've attended Albie Barden masonry heater workshops and profited from his kindness and three-plus decades of experience in the heater world. I thank Albie for his deep commitment to matters of the heart and the hearth, and for writing a splendid foreword.

Tom Stroud generously gave of his hard-earned knowledge to show me and others the old German way to design heaters. I thank Tom for hours on the phone and a thorough review before the book was printed. Timothy Seaton, Cheryl Barden, Joe Parris, and Jerry Frisch and many unnamed others have all helped me in one way or another to get me where I am today. I thank Stan Sackett for his love of soapstone and his faith in me over the last nine years or so.

I thank Ron Pihl, John LaGamba, Ernst Kiesling, Edith Kiesling, Albie Barden, Scott Barden, Amy Clark, Heinz Flurer, Timothy Seaton, Jonathon Steele, Wendell Short, Erich Gundlach, Tom Tuer, Mady Salyer, and Rod Zander for putting up with my frequent and persistent requests for photographs for this book. Jeremy Johnson and Tulikivi provided immediate support and loads of fine pictures. Stefan Hartung, Matt Fowler at W.B. Fowler Industries, Tim Motz at the Toledo Museum of Art, and Stuart Davies were immediately responsive, and their photo contributions invaluable. Thanks also to Jon Sheaff at Crossfire Fireplaces. Special mention goes to Alex Chernov at Stovemaster, who not only sent wonderful photos, but took the time to learn details of what this book was really about before participating. The picture-fetching prize goes to Liz Antonelli at Yari Film Group, who secured a photo of one of the *kachelofens* from the movie The Illusionist in record-breaking time. I thank Julie Cline, Barbara Felton, Lindsay and Kathy Graham, Peggy and Ben Brown, David and Keri van Wingerden, and Jim and Diane Schoen for either sending photos or letting me invade their homes and escape with images. Particular recognition goes to Julie Rust for letting me rearrange her living room for photos on Christmas Eve while she busily, and single-handedly, prepared her son for a Christmas pageant because her husband, John, was working yet more long hours at the hospital. Maren Leyla Cooke not only took fantastic photos of her beautiful sandstone heater creation, but also took the time to write her own testimonial. (Sorry, the cover doesn't have your heater—or the girls! I tried!) This book could never have happened without the many people who have entrusted me with their projects. The pictures provided make this book very special; I am deeply indebted for all the help and cooperation with images.

Those who know me think of me as a man of few words, a pretty quiet guy. But if I'm handed a pen (or laptop), I can write and write and write. I would not be published today, however, if not for the wisdom and guidance of Elizabeth Lyon, a fellow native of northwest Ohio, whose book gave me the tools and last shove I needed to make it happen. Blessings to Ms. Lyon.

Of course, the whole staff at Chelsea Green has been fantastic. I especially appreciate the efforts of Cannon Labrie who, like Judy Ludwig before him, artfully blended praise for the book with the knowledge of what's superfluous. Thanks to Joni, Makenna, and Pati.

I will never forget Marc Ross, Professor Emeritus in the physics department at the University of Michigan. In his college office, crammed with books about thermodynamics and efficiency, Marc patiently spent a morning discussing second-law efficiency, combustion, and heat pumps with me as if I were his academic equal. Thank you, Marc.

Finally, I give my warmest and deepest appreciation, admiration, and love to my wife, Nancy, who told me to treat writing this book like a full-time job (which it was anyway). Over and over she told me she wanted the book done before Christmas 2009 so it wouldn't tarnish our holidays. Yet she sorted, read, and edited right beside me as we prepared to send the manuscript on December 30. I am humbled, eternally grateful, and truly blessed with her love, devotion, and confidence in me.

INDEX

About the Author

KEN MATESZ first learned about masonry heaters in the early 1980s, built his first one in the early 1990s, and opened the Masonry Heater Store, LLC, after the turn of the new century. Matesz's first solo heater project in 1994, a Finnish-style heater in his own home, gave his family heating-energy independence. Now, with his new book, *Masonry Heaters*, he hopes to show many others how they can achieve the same freedom and a better standard of living using this simple but elegant way of heating. He lives with his family in Swanton, Ohio.

About the Foreword Author

ALBIE BARDEN is the founder of Maine Wood Heat Company. He has been designing and building masonry heaters for more than thirty years.

JA

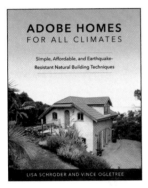

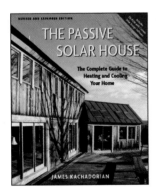

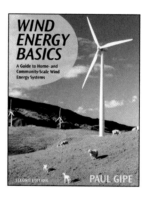